ISBN 0-15-317836-1

8 9 10 032 2004

Harcourt Language

SENIOR AUTHORS
Roger C. Farr ♦ Dorothy S. Strickland

AUTHORS
Helen Brown ♦ Karen S. Kutiper ♦ Hallie Kay Yopp

SENIOR CONSULTANT
Asa G. Hilliard III

CONSULTANT
Diane L. Lowe

Harcourt

Orlando   Boston   Dallas   Chicago   San Diego

Visit *The Learning Site!*
www.harcourtschool.com

Contents

Unit 1

Arts/Creativity

Grammar: Sentences
Writing: Expressive Writing   22

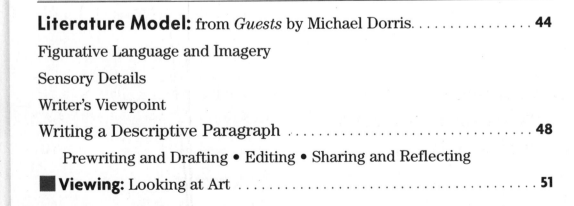

2

Unit 2

Social Studies

Grammar: More About Nouns and Verbs
Writing: Informative Writing: Explanation 92

Unit 3

Science

Grammar: More About Verbs
Writing: Persuasive Writing
164

6

Unit 4

Health

Grammar: Pronouns, Adjectives, and Adverbs
Writing: Informative Writing: Classification

CHAPTER 22   Adjectives and Adverbs

CHAPTER 23   More About Adjectives and Adverbs

CHAPTER 24   Writing Workshop: Comparison/Contrast Essay

Unit 5

Social Studies

Grammar: Phrases and Clauses
Writing: Research Report   308

Unit 6

Arts/Creativity

Grammar: Usage and Mechanics
Writing: Expressive Writing

Handbook

At a Glance

16

Listening and Speaking

We all learn to speak a language without thinking about how it works. For example, children who grow up speaking English learn to say *the gray cat* instead of *the cat gray* before they learn about adjectives and nouns. Later, we study grammar, the rules and patterns our language follows. Understanding grammar helps us to talk about language and writing and to communicate effectively.

The Building Blocks of Language

Words in English can be grouped into eight parts of speech. These are the building blocks of language.

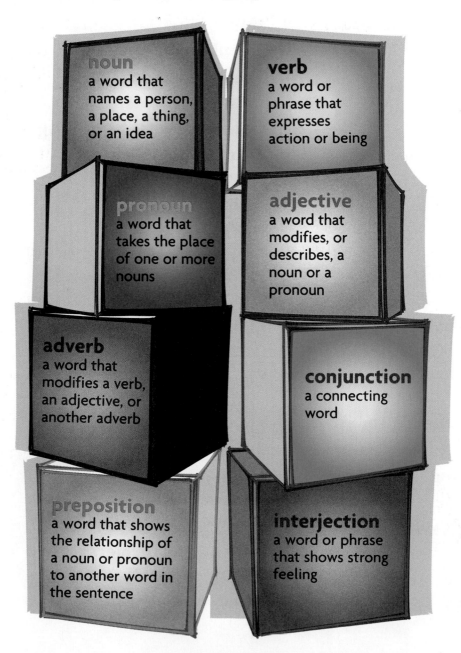

noun
a word that names a person, a place, a thing, or an idea

verb
a word or phrase that expresses action or being

pronoun
a word that takes the place of one or more nouns

adjective
a word that modifies, or describes, a noun or a pronoun

adverb
a word that modifies a verb, an adjective, or another adverb

conjunction
a connecting word

preposition
a word that shows the relationship of a noun or pronoun to another word in the sentence

interjection
a word or phrase that shows strong feeling

Writing: Understanding the Writing Process

When you look at a published piece of writing, you do not see the process the writer used to create it. What you see in print might not be much like the first plan for the book or story. The author might have rewritten the work many times.

The writing process is often divided into five stages. Most writers go back and forth through these stages. There is no one correct way to write.

Prewriting

In this stage, you plan what you are going to write. You choose a topic, identify your audience and purpose, brainstorm ideas, and organize information.

Drafting

In this stage, you express your ideas in sentences and paragraphs. Follow your prewriting plan to write a first version of your composition.

Revising

This stage is the first part of editing your writing. You may work by yourself or with a partner or a group. Reread your writing to see if it accomplishes its purpose. Make changes that will improve your composition.

Proofreading

In this stage, you finish editing by polishing your work. Check for errors in grammar, spelling, capitalization, and punctuation. Make a final copy of your composition.

Publishing

Finally, you choose a way to present your work to an audience. You may want to add illustrations, make a video, or combine your work with that of others. You may publish your work orally or in writing.

Using Writing Strategies

A **strategy** is a plan for doing something well. Using strategies can help you become a better writer. Read the list of strategies below. You will learn about these and other strategies in this book. As you write, look back at this list to remind yourself of the **strategies good writers use**.

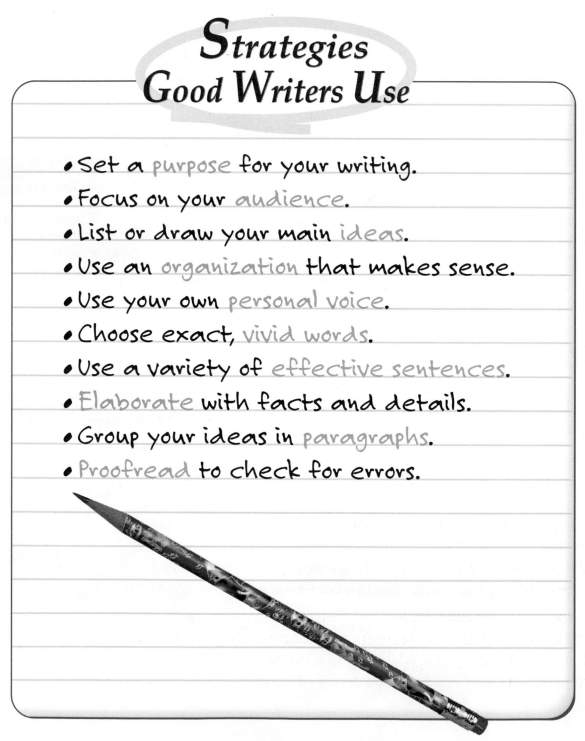

Strategies Good Writers Use

- Set a purpose for your writing.
- Focus on your audience.
- List or draw your main ideas.
- Use an organization that makes sense.
- Use your own personal voice.
- Choose exact, vivid words.
- Use a variety of effective sentences.
- Elaborate with facts and details.
- Group your ideas in paragraphs.
- Proofread to check for errors.

Keeping a Writer's Journal

Many writers keep journals of ideas for writing. A journal is a place to practice and to record ideas. It is not a place to keep final work, but a place to reflect and write freely, keep notes, and experiment with words.

You can keep your own writer's journal. Choose a notebook with lined paper in a size that is comfortable for you to handle. Decorate the cover if you wish. Then start filling the pages with your notes and ideas.

Vocabulary Power

In addition to writing in your journal, you may also want to keep a "word bank" of different kinds of words to use in your writing. Look for the Vocabulary Power word in every chapter. You can also add other colorful adjectives, strong verbs, and interesting nouns.

Keeping a Portfolio

A portfolio is a collection of work, such as writings and pictures. It is sometimes used as a showcase for a person's work.

Student writers often keep two types of portfolios. **Working portfolios** include pieces on which you are working. They may also include short practice pieces. **Show portfolios** include pieces that you are finished with and want to show to others. You choose the pieces you want to move from your working portfolio into your show portfolio.

You can use either kind of portfolio in writing conferences with your teacher. In a conference, talk about your work. Tell what you are doing and what you like doing. Look at the progress you have made, and set goals for yourself as a writer.

Unit 1

Grammar Sentences

Writing Expressive Writing

Day 3

Today our train crossed the border into British Columbia. We had breakfast in the dining car and watched the sun come up over mountains.

Sentences

A **sentence** is a group of words that expresses a complete thought. A sentence names someone or something and tells what that person or thing is or does.

The naming part of a sentence is called the **subject**, and the telling part is called the **predicate**. The two parts together make up a complete thought. A sentence always begins with a capital letter and ends with an end mark.

Example:

Naming Part (Subject)	Telling Part (Predicate)
My friend Mark	makes furniture by hand.

A group of words may not always form a sentence. If the group of words does not name who or what and tell what a person or thing is or does, it is not a sentence. Groups of words that are not sentences are called **fragments**.

Not a sentence: A person with skilled hands.
(What does this person do?)

Sentence: A person with skilled hands makes useful things.

Guided Practice

A. **Identify whether each group of words is a sentence or not a sentence.**

Example: Much prettier than the other kind. *not a sentence*

1. My family visited many cities this summer.
2. Spent hours in gift shops.
3. Works of art by people in the city.
4. Quilting is a traditional handicraft.
5. Some people make books and furniture by hand.
6. Other people make baskets.
7. Picture frames, tables, and many other things.
8. Handmade rugs are always nice.
9. Even lamps can be made by hand.
10. Beautiful handmade wall hangings.

Vocabulary Power

hand·i·craft
[han′di·kraft′] *n.* Skill in working with the hands. A trade, occupation, or art requiring such skill.

Independent Practice

Remember that a sentence always begins with a capital letter and ends with an end mark.

B. If the group of words is a sentence, write it. Put one line under the subject and two lines under the predicate. If the group of words is not a sentence, write *not a sentence.*

Examples: This pot is very old. This pot is very old.

Thousands of years ago by hand. *not a sentence*

11. Pots were once made by hand.
12. Out of natural materials.
13. Some beautiful jewelry is still made from shells.
14. Jewelry makers sometimes use special tools.
15. Needles, sewing machines, or knives.
16. Make things by hand.
17. Handicrafts are hobbies for some people.
18. Themselves as artists.
19. Make all kinds of things for everyday use.
20. Sell and take pride in their work.

C. Write each sentence and begin it with a capital letter. If a group of words is not a sentence, write *not a sentence.*

Example: the store sells many handmade items.
The store sells many handmade items.

21. ancient peoples made carvings from wood.
22. everything from clothes to houses.
23. the only way, for thousands of years.
24. machines changed people's lives.
25. handmade items were no longer in demand.

Writing Connection

Writer's Journal: Reflection Recall a time when you made something by hand or when a family member or friend taught you to make or do something. In your journal, write a few sentences that describe the memory. Begin every sentence with a capital letter. Make sure each sentence expresses a complete thought.

Declarative Sentence:

Embroidery is a way of sewing pictures on cloth.

Interrogative Sentence:

Who taught you to sew?

Imperative Sentence:

Try sewing this new stitch.

Exclamatory Sentence:

What a beautiful piece of embroidery that is!

Four Types of Sentences

A declarative sentence makes a statement. An **interrogative sentence** asks a question. An **imperative sentence** gives a command or makes a request. An **exclamatory sentence** expresses strong feeling or surprise.

End marks provide clues about what kind of sentence is being used. Look at the examples on the left. Notice the use of periods, question marks, and exclamation points.

An exclamatory sentence often begins with the word *what* or *how*. In sentences that begin this way, the subject and verb are sometimes omitted. (*What a beautiful piece of embroidery!*)

In imperative sentences, the word *you* is understood as the subject.

Example:
  Close the door, please. = (You) close the door, please.

Guided Practice

A. **Identify each sentence as declarative, interrogative, imperative, or exclamatory.**

Example: I finished a sampler last weekend. *declarative*

  1. A sampler starts with a piece of cloth.
  2. Then someone sews different stitches onto it.
  3. Why do people make samplers?
  4. Young people made samplers to learn to sew.
  5. Kids showed their sewing skills by making samplers.
  6. Look at this old sampler.
  7. What tiny stitches the person used!
  8. When was this sampler made?
  9. Please look for a date on it.
  10. How hard the artist must have worked!

Independent Practice

B. Write whether each sentence is declarative, interrogative, imperative, or exclamatory. If the group of words is not a sentence, write *not a sentence*.

Example: What do you think of this sampler? *interrogative*

11. What kinds of cloth did people use?
12. Some samplers were stitched on wool.
13. Did people ever use cotton?
14. This sampler was stitched on cotton.
15. Please show it to me.
16. How bright the colors are!
17. What did they sew on their samplers?
18. Some young girls stitched numerals.
19. Look at the lettering on this sampler.
20. Good practice for a young sewing student.
21. The birds on this sampler.
22. Tiny pictures were sewn on some samplers.
23. Sometimes a girl stitched her name, too.
24. Did they ever add the dates?
25. Read this girl's name and the date.
26. How very old this sampler is!
27. There were samplers in the 1500s.
28. Would you show me that page?
29. What kinds of samplers are on display?
30. They prefer ones with embroidered pictures.

Remember

that there are four types of sentences—declarative (a statement), interrogative (a question), imperative (a command or a request), and exclamatory (an expression of strong feeling or surprise).

Writing Connection

Technology: Choosing a Font Think of a kind of party you would like to have, and write an invitation. Use at least three kinds of sentences to make your invitation interesting. Input your invitation into a computer, and experiment with different fonts. Choose the font and size you like. Then use computer art to decorate your invitation.

USAGE AND MECHANICS

Punctuating Sentences

Use a period at the end of a declarative sentence or an imperative sentence. Use a question mark at the end of an interrogative sentence. Use an exclamation point at the end of an exclamatory sentence.

Examples:

Incorrect	Correct	Sentence Type
These paintings are colorful?	These paintings are colorful.	declarative
Are they painted by famous people!	Are they painted by famous people?	interrogative
Look at the price of this painting?	Look at the price of this painting.	imperative
How expensive it is.	How expensive it is!	exclamatory

Guided Practice

A. Tell what punctuation mark should end each sentence. Then identify whether the sentence is declarative, interrogative, imperative, or exclamatory.

Example: No, it was not *period, declarative*

1. What is folk art
2. What a beautiful quilt
3. Some folk artists are painters
4. Do all folk artists paint
5. Look for examples in books about folk art
6. Some folk artists are sculptors
7. Folk artists love what they do
8. What a great hobby
9. Please study this painting with me
10. How pretty the scene is

Independent Practice

B. Write each sentence, adding the correct end punctuation. Then write whether each sentence is declarative, interrogative, imperative, or exclamatory.

> **Example:** Were these things made by folk artists
> *Were these things made by folk artists?* interrogative

11. What else do folk artists create
12. Some folk artists work in crafts
13. Many artists create things such as rugs and furniture
14. What else do they make
15. Look at these quilts
16. Old store signs are types of folk art
17. How can signs be art
18. Many people could not read before 1870
19. Stores used pictures on signs to sell products
20. What bright colors the sign painters used

C. Write each sentence, adding the correct end punctuation. If a group of words is not a sentence, add words to make it a complete sentence.

> **Example:** Art on signs around town.
> Possible response:
> *Have you seen art on signs around town?*

21. Please show me the folk painting
22. A picture of a loaf of bread
23. Would a shoemaker's sign be in the shape of a boot
24. How strange to have signs with no words
25. More about the pictures on signs

Writing Connection

Real-Life Writing: Thank-You Note Imagine that someone has given you something that he or she made, such as a painting, a piece of embroidery, or a wood carving. Write a note or letter in which you thank the person for the gift. Try to use one of each type of sentence (declarative, interrogative, imperative, exclamatory). Exchange letters with a partner to check for capitalization and end punctuation.

Extra Practice

A. **Write whether each group of words is a sentence or not a sentence.** *pages 24–25*

Example: Folk art from around the world. *not a sentence*

1. Folk artists often carved wood.
2. Lions, tigers, horses, and other animals for merry-go-rounds.
3. Other artists carved toys for children.
4. They also carved decoys for hunters.
5. Wooden figures of ducks and geese.
6. Attracted wild birds, of course.
7. Weather vanes are examples of folk art.
8. Are weather vanes.
9. Information about changes in the weather.
10. Farmers and sailors read the wind's direction from weather vanes.

B. **Write whether each sentence is declarative, interrogative, imperative, or exclamatory.** *pages 26–27*

Example: Tell me more about folk artists. *imperative*

11. Did folk artists think of themselves as artists?
12. They probably did not think of their work as art.
13. Please explain what you mean.
14. They probably thought of their works as crafts.
15. Who were some American folk artists?
16. The names of most folk artists have been forgotten.
17. How sad that is!
18. Some folk artists wrote their names on their works.
19. Have you ever heard of an artist named Grandma Moses?
20. What wonderful paintings she created!

Remember

that a sentence is a group of words that expresses a complete thought. Sentences may be declarative (statements), interrogative (questions), imperative (commands or requests), or exclamatory (expressions of strong feeling).

For more activities with sentences, visit *The Learning Site:*

www.harcourtschool.com

C. Write each sentence. Add the correct end punctuation.

pages 28–29

Example: Where did you get that painting
Where did you get that painting?

21. When was most folk art created
22. Many pieces were made between 1780 and 1860
23. Many people had lost interest in handmade items by 1875
24. Why did people prefer machines
25. Machines could make more goods in less time
26. Did machines make as many mistakes as people did
27. Machines made fewer mistakes
28. What a great change that was
29. Most people ignored folk art until the 1900s
30. How could they make that mistake
31. What can we learn from folk art
32. We can see how people lived in a different time
33. Some paintings show activities that people have forgotten
34. How could a cow be the subject for a work of art
35. What a beautiful example of folk art

Remember

to use a **period** at the end of a declarative sentence or an imperative sentence. Use a **question mark** at the end of an interrogative sentence. Use an **exclamation point** at the end of an exclamatory sentence.

Writing Connection

Art With a partner, find a painting by Grandma Moses in a book or on the Internet. Write your own paragraph describing the painting. (You might want to refer to A Viewing Vocabulary on page 33.) Make sure that all your sentences are complete and have the correct end punctuation. Then exchange papers with your partner. Compare what each of you said about the same painting.

DID YOU KNOW?
In the 1880s, artist Wilhelm Schimmel used his folk art as money. He traveled through Pennsylvania, trading his animal figures for meals. Today his figures are extremely valuable.

Chapter Review

Read each sentence. Look at the underlined words in each one. There may be a mistake in punctuation or capitalization. If you find a mistake, choose the answer that is the best way to write the underlined section of the sentence. If there is no mistake, choose *Correct as is*.

STANDARDIZED TEST PREP

TIP Remember that any group of words can be capitalized and punctuated like a sentence. If the group of words does not express a complete thought, though, it is not a sentence.

1 What have we <u>learned about folk art?</u>
  A learned about folk art.
  B learned about folk art!
  C learned? About folk art.
  D Correct as is

2 <u>grandma Moses painted on boards.</u>
  F grandma Moses painted on boards!
  G Grandma Moses painted on boards.
  H Grandma Moses painted on boards?
  J Correct as is

3 In the early part of her <u>life, she embroidered pictures!</u>
  A life. She embroidered pictures.
  B life, she embroidered pictures.
  C life, she embroidered pictures?
  D Correct as is

4 She did not start painting <u>until she was in her seventies</u>
  F until she was in her seventies?
  G Until she was in her seventies!
  H until she was in her seventies.
  J Correct as is

5 <u>How people praised her work.</u>
  A How people praised her work!
  B how people praised her work?
  C How people praised her work?
  D Correct as is

6 Most of her paintings were about <u>her life in the late 1800s.</u>
  F her life in the late 1800s!
  G her life in the late 1800s?
  H Her life in the late 1800s.
  J Correct as is

For additional test preparation, visit *The Learning Site:*

A Viewing Vocabulary

Writers, illustrators, and artists use their work to tell stories or to communicate ideas and feelings. Writers use words and sentences. Artists and illustrators use art and design. Here are some of the terms used to describe pictures and illustrations.

background [bak′ground′]: The part of a work of art that appears to be in the distance and far from the viewer.

center of interest [sen′tər ov in′tər·ist]: The most important part of a work of art. All other parts should center around, provide background for, or draw attention to this part.

composition [kom•pə·zish′ən]: The arrangement of elements or details in a work of art.

contrast [kon′trast]: A difference revealed when two things are compared (for example, light and shadow).

emphasis [em′fə•sis]: The drawing of attention to an important area or object in a work of art.

foreground [fôr′ground′]: The part of a work of art that appears to be in the front or closest to the viewer.

symbols [sim′bəlz]: Things that stand for other things. For example, a dove often is a symbol of peace.

symmetry, symmetrical [sim′ə·trē, si·met′ri·kəl]: Having balance, so that each feature on one half of a figure or object has a matching feature on the other half.

YOUR TURN

DISCUSSION Look at the cover illustration of this book. Discuss the following questions with a group of classmates. Be prepared to share your answers with the class.

1. What do you see in the foreground?
2. Identify the center of interest.
3. What appears in the background?
4. Think about the composition of the illustration. How do you know what is the most important part of the artwork?
5. Is the illustration symmetrical? Why or why not?

TIP Spend a few minutes looking at a drawing or painting. Then think about how you could use some of these words to tell about the picture.

Complete and Simple Subjects

The **complete subject** includes all the words that name *who or what* the sentence is about. The **simple subject** is the main word or words in the complete subject.

Complete Subject	Predicate
The empty glass	fell onto the floor.
Pieces of glass	scattered everywhere.

Simple Subject
The empty <u>glass</u> fell onto the floor.
<u>Pieces</u> of glass scattered everywhere.

Sometimes the simple subject and the complete subject in a sentence are the same.

<u>Pieces</u> scattered everywhere.

The subject usually comes at the beginning of a declarative sentence. Notice where it comes in these questions.

Did **the glass** fall?

Where are **the pieces**?

Guided Practice

A. Identify the complete and simple subject in each sentence.

Example: Large machines weave cloth in factories.
Large machines, machines

1. Some cloth has colorful designs woven into it.
2. Tapestries often show scenes from history.
3. Students in our class saw a tapestry at the museum.
4. Did your class take a field trip to the museum?
5. Several groups of students take a field trip each year.

Independent Practice

B. Write the complete subject in each sentence.

Example: Each person in our country uses about 200 glass
containers every year. *Each person in our country*

6. Milky-colored glass is used to make lightbulbs.
7. Some kinds of glass do not break.
8. Other kinds of glass can be heated to very high
   temperatures.
9. Most windows are made of plain, flat glass.
10. Windshields for cars are made of clear glass with
    plastic in it.

C. Write each sentence. Underline the complete subject.
Circle the simple subject.

Example: A bolt of lightning can melt sand.
A (bolt) of lightning can melt sand.

11. Ancient people found glass near volcanoes.
12. People first made glass containers around 1500 B.C.
13. Some early glass containers were made in ancient
    Egypt.
14. Glass was hard to make at first.
15. The earliest glass objects were used as decorations.
16. Blown glass was shaped by air.
17. Glassmakers in England added lead to glass.
18. Glass in windows is called plate glass.
19. When were stained-glass windows popular?
20. These colorful windows were used in the Middle Ages.

Remember

that the simple subject is the main word or words in the complete subject. The simple subject and the complete subject can be the same.

Writing Connection

Writer's Journal: Expanding Sentences Find
a picture or an example of an art object, such as a
glass vase or a piece of pottery. Write several sentences describing the object. Then see if you can
expand the sentences by adding descriptive words or phrases to
make longer complete subjects.

Nouns in Subjects

A noun is a word that names a person, a place, a thing, or an idea. The simple subject of a sentence is usually a noun.

You know that the subject of a sentence names the person or thing the sentence is about. A noun in the complete or simple subject names a person, place, thing, or idea. Simple subjects are usually nouns.

Kinds of Subjects	
Person	Our **librarian** showed us a book about weaving.
Place	**New York City** has a large public library.
Thing	Craft and hobby **books** are popular.
Idea	**Creativity** helps people do things in new ways.

A complete subject may include more than one noun.

Weaving with **threads** of different **colors** makes beautiful cloth.
The simple subject is Weaving.

Guided Practice

A. **Identify the noun or nouns in the complete subject of each sentence. Tell which noun is the simple subject.**

Example: Strips of material are woven into fabric.
Strips, material; strips—simple subject

1. Paintings in ancient Egypt show weavers.
2. Weavers in China used thread made of silk.
3. Many groups of people used cotton.
4. Some craftspeople wove pictures into their cloth.
5. An inventor in England developed the first machine to weave cloth.
6. Machines in cloth factories produced cloth quickly.
7. Many people weave without using machines.
8. Some artists weave strips of colored paper.
9. People in art classes might weave yarn into wire sculptures.
10. A loom made of cardboard is handy for weaving.

Independent Practice

B. The nouns in each sentence are underlined. Choose and write the noun that is the simple subject.

Example: <u>Weavers</u> in <u>mills</u> use <u>threads</u> to make <u>cloth</u>. *Weavers*

11. Are the <u>rugs</u> on our <u>floors</u> woven?
12. <u>Threads</u> from natural <u>fibers</u> make excellent <u>cloth</u>.
13. <u>People</u> learned to weave <u>thousands</u> of <u>years</u> ago.
14. <u>Products</u> such as <u>screens</u> are also made by <u>weaving</u>.
15. Many <u>people</u> in the <u>world</u> design <u>fabrics</u> as a <u>hobby</u>.
16. <u>Weavers</u> put <u>threads</u> on a <u>frame</u> called a <u>loom</u>.
17. The <u>fabrics</u> from a <u>loom</u> have two <u>sets</u> of <u>threads</u>.
18. One <u>set</u> of <u>threads</u> on the <u>loom</u> is called the <u>warp</u>.
19. The <u>weaver</u> draws another <u>set</u> of <u>threads</u> over and under the <u>warp</u>.
20. These <u>threads</u> are called the <u>weft</u>.

C. Write each sentence. Underline each noun. Circle the noun that is the simple subject.

Example: Baskets were made in countries all over the world.
Ⓑⓐⓢⓚⓔⓣⓢ *(Baskets)* were made in <u>countries</u> all over the <u>world</u>.

21. Ancient people made baskets for food.
22. Baskets are often made with grasses.
23. Makers of baskets use tools such as knives.
24. Weavers use similar skills and materials.
25. People create baskets in many different ways.
26. Weaving is the simplest method.
27. Another method is braiding.
28. Artists use materials of different colors to make designs.
29. American Indians used baskets to store food.
30. Baskets were sometimes decorated with beads.

> **Remember** that words that name people, places, things, or ideas are **nouns**. **Simple subjects** are usually nouns.

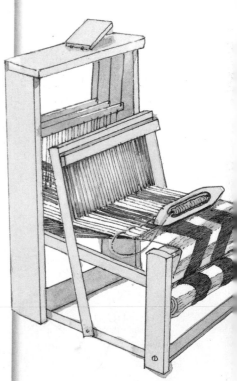

Writing Connection

Art Design an object that you could use at home, such as a piece of pottery, a basket, or a weaving. Draw a picture of your design. Write a description of the object, and tell how you would use it. Then exchange papers with a partner, and identify any nouns used as simple subjects in your partner's sentences.

**Common
Conjunctions**

and	or

USAGE AND MECHANICS

Combining Sentences: Compound Subjects

A compound subject is two or more subjects that are joined by a conjunction.

You know that every sentence has a subject. Some sentences have two or more subjects that are joined by a conjunction. A conjunction is a joining word. Words such as *and* and *or* are conjunctions. If three or more subjects are joined by a conjunction in a compound subject, use commas to separate them.

Examples:
Articles, photographs, **and** advertisements are included in magazines.

Stories **or** poems appear in each issue.

Notice that a comma is not used before the conjunction if it joins only two nouns.

Two or more sentences with similar predicates can sometimes be combined. The subjects of the sentences are joined by a conjunction to form a compound subject.

Example:
Books can be made into movies. Plays can also be made into movies.

***Books* and *plays** can be made into movies.*

Guided Practice

A. **In each sentence, identify the complete subject and the conjunction that joins the nouns.**

Example: Books and magazines are made of separate pieces of paper. *Books and magazines*

1. Pages and covers are the main parts of books.
2. Illustrations and pictures are sometimes printed in color.
3. Extra pages or special pages can be added to a book.
4. Glue, paste, or tape holds special pages in a book.
5. Bookbinders and bookmakers use machines to insert the extra pages.

Independent Practice

B. Write each sentence. Underline the complete subject. Circle the conjunction.

Example: Paper and ink have not always been the materials used for writing.
Paper (and) ink have not always been the materials used for writing.

6. Tablets and scrolls were the first books.
7. Leather and cloth were used for the first covers.
8. Glue and thread held the pages together.
9. Words and pictures were engraved on the leather.
10. Maps and plants were topics of early picture books.

C. Combine each pair of sentences to form one sentence. Use a conjunction to make a compound subject. Write each combined sentence.

Example: Machines made printing faster and easier. Inventions made printing faster and easier.
Machines and inventions made printing faster and easier.

11. Bookstores make books available to many people. Libraries make books available to many people.
12. Computers provided information. The Internet provided information.
13. Movies are entertaining. Books are entertaining. Plays are entertaining.
14. Book lovers still prefer books. Book collectors still prefer books.
15. Children enjoy books with pictures. Adults also enjoy books with pictures.

Remember that the subjects in a **compound subject** are joined by a **conjunction**, usually *and* or *or*. Commas are used to separate three or more subjects.

Writing Connection

Writer's Craft: Sentence Variety Find a partner, and talk to him or her about your favorite crafts or hobbies. Take notes as you talk. Use your notes to write a paragraph that describes two of your favorite crafts or hobbies. You might begin with a sentence such as this: _____ *and* _____ *are my favorite hobbies.* Use at least one other sentence with a compound subject in your paragraph. Exchange paragraphs with your partner. Look for the compound subjects your partner used.

hh
gg
ff
ee
dd

Extra Practice

A. Write each sentence. Underline the complete subject. Circle the simple subject. *pages 34–35*

Example: Colorful beads are small, round objects used for decoration.
<u>Colorful</u>(beads) *are small, round objects used for decoration.*

1. Some ancient people valued beads.
2. A pea is often the same size as a bead.
3. Beads are made of clay, wood, shells, or seeds.
4. Artists shape the material first.
5. A bright light is helpful for working with beads.
6. A person must have very good eyesight to work with beads.
7. Artists use a needle and thread to attach beads to clothing.
8. Ancient cultures believed that beads could protect a person from harm.
9. Beads were important to some Native American tribes.
10. Early explorers took beads with them to the Americas.
11. Beads made from shells were used as gifts.
12. Clothing was often decorated with beads.
13. Glass beads brought by explorers were valuable in the Americas.
14. Colorful designs were created with the beads.
15. Beads today are usually worn as decoration.

B. Write each sentence. Underline each noun. Circle the noun that is the simple subject. *pages 36–37*

Example: My art teacher showed the class how to weave baskets from leaves.
My art (teacher) *showed the* <u>class</u> *how to weave* <u>baskets</u> *from* <u>leaves</u>.

16. My art teacher also showed the class how to weave a simple piece of fabric.
17. Expert weavers use thread made of silk.
18. One weaver in our town uses cotton or wool.
19. My cousin from Canada told us about the wall hangings in castles.
20. Our class saw an early loom at the museum.

21. The large machine wove the fabric quickly.
22. My class also visited an artist who weaves by hand.
23. The artist wove strips of colored paper into designs.
24. My best friend tried to weave with paper.
25. The students saw a loom made out of a box.

C. **Rewrite each pair of sentences as one sentence with a compound subject.** *pages 38–39*

Example: Printing presses run at high speeds. Paper mills run at high speeds.
Printing presses and paper mills run at high speeds.

26. Trees are used to make things. Other plants are also used to make things.
27. Paper is made from trees. Furniture is made from trees.
28. Books are made from paper. Newspapers are made from paper.
29. Trees are important for the oxygen in the environment. Other plants are also important for the oxygen in the environment.
30. Papers can be recycled. Bottles can be recycled. Newspapers can be recycled.

Remember

that the subjects in a compound subject are joined by a conjunction. If there are three or more subjects, use commas to separate them.

DID YOU KNOW?
The Crystal Palace was a gigantic glass building built for the Great Exhibition of 1851 in London, England. The building had 900,000 square feet of glass. It was destroyed in a fire in 1936.

Writing Connection

Writer's Craft: Sensory Words Choose a place that you enjoy. It may be outdoors or indoors. Think about how you experience the place with all your senses. Write a descriptive paragraph about it. Use nouns that name objects in the place as the subjects of your sentences. Make the nouns interesting by adding descriptive words that involve sight, hearing, touch, smell, and taste. Then find two sentences that you can combine to make a compound subject.

For more activities with subjects, visit *The Learning Site:*

www.harcourtschool.com

Chapter Review

For Numbers 1 and 2, find the conjunction that best completes the sentence.

1 Tapestries ____ woven wall hangings are the same thing.
  A and
  B but
  C or
  D so

2 Silk thread ____ wool thread was used to weave fancy designs.
  F and
  G but
  H or
  J so

For Numbers 3 through 6, find the simple subject of the sentence.

3 One old <u>tapestry</u> was made by <u>hand</u> in the
             A   **B**
  eleventh <u>century</u> in <u>Germany</u>.
           C   **D**

4 At <u>museums</u>, <u>visitors</u> can see <u>pieces</u> of old <u>tapestries</u>.
       F   **G**   **H**   **J**

5 <u>Museums</u> in many <u>countries</u> display <u>tapestries</u> for
    A   **B**   **C**
  <u>people</u> to see.
  D

6 In the <u>past</u>, <u>kings</u> had <u>tapestries</u> in their <u>castles</u>.
        F   **G**   **H**   **J**

For Numbers 7 and 8, find the compound subject that best completes the sentence.

7 ____ had a tradition of weaving.
  A Ancient Chinese, and Incas
  B Ancient Chinese and Incas,
  C Ancient Chinese and Incas
  D Ancient, Chinese and Incas

8 ____ also knew how to weave.
  F Ancient Greeks and Hebrews and Romans
  G Ancient Greeks, Hebrews, and Romans
  H Ancient Greeks Hebrews and Romans
  J Ancient Greeks, Hebrews and Romans

STANDARDIZED
TEST PREP

TIP For fill-in-the-blank questions, read each of the possible answers before choosing one. Choose the answer that makes the most sense.

For additional test preparation, visit *The Learning Site:*
www.harcourtschool.com

Figurative Language

Figurative language uses unusual comparisons to make writing more interesting. Compare the sentence on the left with the sentences on the right.

Literal	Figurative
He ran down the sidewalk.	He ran like a racehorse down the sidewalk.
	He ran down the ribbon of sidewalk.

See the difference? Two common figures of speech are **metaphors** and **similes**, which compare things that are unlike. There is an important difference between metaphors and similes. Similes compare things by using the words *like* or *as*. Metaphors compare things without using *like* or *as*. These examples show the difference.

Metaphors	Similes
The night was a dark cloak.	The cloud looked like cotton.
The moon was white marble.	The cheese felt like rubber.
A colorful quilt of leaves covered the lawn.	Her eyes were as dark as blackberries.

Using figurative language is a way of appealing to the senses with words. By comparing two things that are not alike, you help your reader imagine something in a new way. You also lead the reader to feel a certain way about what you are describing. For example, compare the effect of these two similes: *Her teeth were like pearls. Her teeth were like needles.* Figurative language is a powerful tool, especially in expressive writing.

YOUR TURN

NEW IDEAS Many similes have been used so often that they are no longer fresh. Some examples are *cold as ice, bright as the sun, red as a beet,* and *soft as silk.* Think of a common simile, and write a sentence using it. Then rewrite the sentence, using a new simile or metaphor of your own. Add a few more sentences to your description, or turn it into a poem.

TIP Keep a picture of the object you are describing in front of you as you write. Use the picture to help you think of interesting comparisons.

Writer's Craft

Personal Voice

DESCRIPTIONS To give a good **description** you need to tell what something looks like. Depending on what you are describing, you might also tell how it sounds, how it feels when you touch it, how it smells, how it tastes, or what something does.

Read the following passage from the novel *Guests* by Michael Dorris. In this passage, a Native American boy has climbed a tree and is describing the forest below him. Notice the kinds of details the author includes in this description.

LITERATURE MODEL

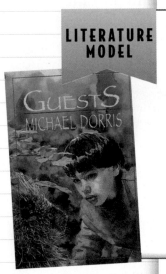

The forest, from above, was a different place. From where I lay, it was as though I floated on the surface of a clear pond—plants seemed to stretch toward me. Below me, paths snaked like grapevines in every direction, leading everywhere, anywhere. Bits of dust floated and glittered in the trees of light that filled the spaces between the trees of wood.

Hugging the bough with my arms, with my whole body, I joined in its stillness. I had fed at its table, I was at rest in its bed. I was the forest's welcomed guest.

Analyze THE Model

1. What does the boy see and hear in the forest?

2. What are some examples of figurative language that the writer uses?

3. How does the boy feel about the forest? How can you tell?

4. Do you think another writer would have described the forest in exactly the same way this writer did? Why or why not?

Vocabulary Power

per•spec•tive
[pər•spek′tiv] *n.* A way of seeing things in relation to one another; viewpoint.

Imagine that two different writers are describing the same thing. Why might they use different words and images? Each writer has a **personal voice**, or an individual way of expressing himself or herself. You have your own writing style that is not exactly like anyone else's.

Ways to Develop Personal Voice	Examples
Use figurative language and imagery. Common types of figurative language are **similes**, **metaphors**, and **personification**. Personification gives human qualities to an object. **Imagery** is vivid language that helps the reader form a mental picture.	**Personification:** The trees danced in the wind. (compares trees to dancers) **Imagery:** A frigid wind rattled the bare branches.
Include sensory details. **Sensory details** appeal to the five senses: sight, hearing, touch, smell, and taste. They help the reader share your experience.	**Sight** and **touch:** The rock lay heavily in my hand, a rough chunk of orange mottled with white.
Express your own viewpoint. Let your reader know how you feel about the subject. Remember that your viewpoint—your way of looking at something—is important.	Choose words and details that suggest emotions, such as happiness, fear, or fascination.

YOUR TURN

ANALYZE DESCRIPTIVE WRITING **With a small group of classmates, look back at stories, articles, or poems that you have read recently. Locate and share examples of descriptive writing. Then discuss how the author used his or her personal voice in each example.**

Answer these questions:

1. What person, place, thing, or event is the author describing?
2. How does this writer use figurative language and imagery?
3. What sensory details does the writer include?
4. What is the writer's perspective, or viewpoint? How is this viewpoint expressed?
5. How would you describe this writer's personal voice or writing style? Is it strong, lively, serious?

Figurative Language and Imagery

A. Think of an example of figurative language or imagery to complete each of the following sentences. Write the completed sentence on your paper.

1. Kelly said the giraffe looked like _____.
2. The child's laugh was _____.
3. Dry leaves _____ under her feet as she walked.
4. The skin of the peach felt as fuzzy as _____.
5. The room smelled like _____.
6. The sun was _____.
7. He crept across the yard like _____.
8. Her hands moved like _____.
9. The wind _____ like a _____.
10. The butterfly's wings were _____ blue.

Sensory Details

B. This chart shows sensory details that a writer might use to describe an apple. Draw a blank chart on your paper. Complete your chart with sensory details about a pickle. Try to list at least one word or phrase for each of the five senses.

sight	sound	touch	smell	taste
shiny red round	crunchy when you bite into it	smooth firm	fruity rich	crisp fresh tart

When you have finished your chart, share it in a small group. Compare the sensory details in group members' charts. What different feelings about pickles do the details show?

Writer's Viewpoint

C. Read each of the following descriptions. Then write a sentence that adds to the description and expresses the same viewpoint.

11. It was a beautiful spider.
12. The new town hall is an unattractive stone building.
13. The music of the violin had a sad, lonesome sound.
14. I couldn't wait to eat those strawberries.
15. Isn't the kangaroo a comical animal?

D. An author's personal voice and viewpoint are more important in some kinds of writing than in others. In a small group, discuss which writing form in each pair below shows an author's voice and viewpoint more.

16. poem   recipe
17. news article   short story
18. descriptive essay   how-to manual
19. friendly letter   textbook
20. play   encyclopedia article

Writing and Thinking

Writer's Journal

Write to Record Reflections When you speak, your family and friends probably recognize your voice. Do you think people recognize your personal voice or style when they read your writing? Why or why not? Write your ideas about your personal voice in your Writer's Journal.

Descriptive Paragraph

The author of *Guests* describes the forest as it looks to a Native American boy from the branch of a tree. Latisha lives in a city. She has never been to a forest, but she often visits the community vegetable garden on her street. Read the descriptive paragraph that Latisha wrote about the garden.

MODEL

writer's viewpoint —

simile —

sensory details —

imagery —

sensory details —

metaphor/writer's viewpoint —

> On my street there is a beautiful little garden where my neighbors grow vegetables. Mrs. Santiago has a tomato patch with tomatoes as round and red as the setting sun. Sometimes she slices a tomato right there in the garden and gives me a piece to eat, all juicy and warm on my tongue. Old Mr. Williams grows five different kinds of lettuce. I love to look at all the different shades of green, from pale and delicate to dark and hearty. Mrs. Finn lets me help her pull earthy-smelling orange carrots from the moist soil. Our neighborhood garden is a feast for the eyes and the nose as well as for the appetite.

Analyze THE Model

1. What is Latisha's purpose for writing?
2. How does Latisha use figurative language and imagery in her paragraph?
3. Do the sensory details that she includes help you understand what the garden is like? Explain your answer.
4. What is Latisha's perspective on the garden? How do you know?

WRITING PROMPT **Choose something from nature that you would like to describe. For example, you might choose a plant, an animal, a seashell, a mountain, or a kind of weather. Write a descriptive paragraph for classmates. Include figurative language, imagery, and sensory details to help your reader create a mental image. Be sure to express your viewpoint in your writing.**

STUDY THE PROMPT **Ask yourself these questions.**

1. What object from nature will you describe?

2. What writing form will you use?

3. What is your purpose for writing?

4. Who is your audience?

Prewriting and Drafting

Plan Your Paragraph Begin planning your paragraph by brainstorming descriptive words and phrases. Organize your ideas in a web like the one shown here. In the center, write the topic you have chosen. Then add words, phrases, and details to expand the web.

> **USING YOUR**
> # Handbook
> • Use the Writer's Thesaurus to find vivid words that appeal to the senses to help you describe your subject.

figurative language that helps describe the object

imagery that helps readers create a mental picture of the object

name of object

sensory details that tell how the object looks and maybe also how it sounds, feels, tastes, and smells

your viewpoint about the object

Editor's Marks

𝄒 delete text

∧ insert text

↷ move text

¶ new paragraph

≡ capitalize

/ lowercase

◯ correct spelling

Editing

Read over and evaluate the draft of your descriptive paragraph. Is there anything you would like to change? Can you add anything to create a more vivid picture for your reader? Use this checklist to help you revise your paragraph.

☑ **Does your writing create a clear, vivid picture for your readers?**

☑ **Can you add figurative language or imagery to your description?**

☑ **Have you included appropriate sensory details?**

☑ **Have you expressed your viewpoint clearly?**

☑ **Will your readers recognize your personal voice?**

Use this checklist as you proofread your paragraph.

☑ **I have used the correct capitalization and punctuation for my sentences.**

☑ **I have checked to see that every sentence has a subject.**

☑ **I have used compound subjects to combine sentences where possible.**

☑ **I have used a dictionary to check my spelling.**

Sharing and Reflecting

Writer's Journal

After you have made a final copy of your paragraph, share it in a group with several classmates. Tell what you like best about your classmates' descriptive paragraphs. Point out examples of figurative language, imagery, and sensory details that you especially like. Discuss each other's viewpoints and how they are expressed. Then write in your Writer's Journal about how you can improve your descriptive writing and continue to develop your own voice as a writer.

Looking at Art

Just as each writer has a personal voice, artists also have individual viewpoints and ways of expressing themselves. Each artist sees the world in a particular way. When you look at a painting, drawing, sculpture, or other work of art, you have the opportunity to see things as the artist sees them.

Study this illustration by Barton Stabler, titled *Computer Operator*.

YOUR TURN

With two or three classmates, discuss your impressions of *Computer Operator*. Follow these guidelines in your discussion:

- Describe the illustration in words. Use imagery and vivid details in your description.

- Identify and discuss the artist's viewpoint.

- Explain why and how *Computer Operator* can be called a metaphor.

After your discussion, look at some other artworks. Your school media specialist may be able to suggest resources that you can use. Notice each artist's individual style.

Complete and Simple Predicates

The complete predicate includes all the words that tell what the subject of the sentence is or does. The simple predicate is the main word or words in the complete predicate.

You know that every sentence must have a subject and a predicate. A complete predicate often gives more information about the simple predicate. Sometimes the simple predicate and the complete predicate are the same.

Examples:	
Complete Predicate	Natalie **worked on the sculpture**.
Simple Predicate	Natalie **worked** on the sculpture.
Complete Predicate	Her clay sculpture **is beautiful**.
Simple Predicate	Her clay sculpture **is** beautiful.

Guided Practice

A. **Identify the complete predicate and the simple predicate in each sentence.**

Examples: Juan spoke to the class about architecture.
spoke to the class about architecture, spoke

Architects design buildings for our cities.
design buildings for our cities, design

1. People cross the Brooklyn Bridge every day.
2. The bridge connects Manhattan and Long Island.
3. People traveled to Manhattan in boats long ago.
4. People use bridges now for city travel.
5. New Yorkers have pride in their many museums.
6. My friend and I visited one museum last week.
7. Statues, pottery, and vases lined the hallway.
8. The faces of the statues seemed real.
9. We looked with interest at the pottery.
10. All of the pottery had come from Mexico.

Independent Practice

B. Write whether the underlined word or words in each sentence are the complete predicate or the simple predicate.

Examples: *Skyscraper* <u>is</u> the word for a very tall building. *simple*

Elevators and metal frames <u>made tall buildings possible</u>. *complete*

11. Elevators <u>moved</u> people quickly and easily.
12. A steel frame <u>gives a skyscraper support</u>.
13. Tall skyscrapers <u>sway in the wind</u>.
14. The steel frame <u>keeps</u> the building upright.
15. The Eiffel Tower in Paris, France, <u>was once the world's tallest structure</u>.

C. Write each sentence. Draw a line between the complete subject and the complete predicate. Underline the simple predicate.

Example: The work of a sculptor interests me.
The work of a sculptor | <u>interests</u> me.

16. Some artists carve small statues of ivory and bone.
17. Others carve blocks of marble into statues.
18. Many sculptors mold clay into shapes.
19. Sometimes sculptors want color in their artwork.
20. Glaze adds color to a sculpture.

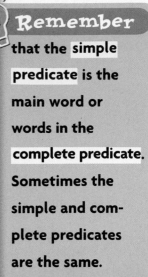
Remember

that the simple predicate is the main word or words in the complete predicate. Sometimes the simple and complete predicates are the same.

Writing Connection

Art What kinds of sculpture do you see in your community? For example, a local museum, a library, or another building may have a sculpture in front of it. Write five sentences about a local sculpture. (If you wish, imagine a sculpture that would fit in your community and then write about it.) When you finish, proofread your sentences. Make sure each one has a subject and a predicate.

Verbs in Predicates

Every predicate has a verb that tells what the subject is or does.

You know that every sentence must have a verb. The verb expresses action or being. The simple predicate in a sentence is always a verb. The verb may have more than one word.

Examples:

Michelangelo **was** an Italian sculptor in the 1500s.

He **carved** many marble statues.

Most people **admire** his work today.

We **have seen** pictures of his work.

Whether a word is a verb depends on the way it is used in a sentence. In which sentences below is *look* used as a verb?

Examples:

We **look** at the painting.

The face **looks** peaceful.

The face has a peaceful **look**.

In the first two sentences, *look* is a verb. It works with a subject to show action or being. In the third sentence, *look* is a noun. It names something that the face has.

Guided Practice

A. **Identify the verb in each sentence. Be ready to explain your answers.**

Examples: Michelangelo worked for four years on a statue of Moses.
worked

Artists today still study the statue.
study

1. Michelangelo showed Moses as an old man with a long beard.
2. He began with a block of marble.
3. Michelangelo cut away pieces of the marble.
4. He carved the tiny details with smaller tools.
5. The figure of Moses appears thoughtful.

Independent Practice

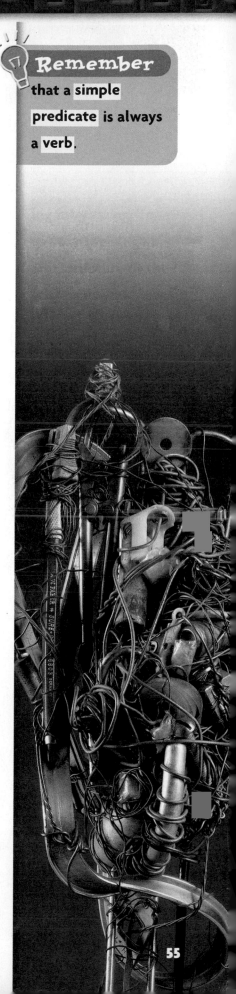

Remember that a simple predicate is always a verb.

B. Write each sentence. Underline the verb.

Examples: Anita creates colorful objects from old metal.
Anita <u>creates</u> colorful objects from old metal.

Her artwork makes people smile.
Her artwork <u>makes</u> people smile.

6. Anita saves steel and aluminum cans for her art.
7. One day she looked for junk metal.
8. She found a set of rusty garden tools.
9. She combined the parts in new ways.
10. Anita created a flock of metal birds.

C. Write each sentence. Use a verb from the box to complete each sentence, or use a verb or verbs of your own.

molds	chooses	creates	keeps
shapes	orders	produces	puts

Example: My friend Yoko _____ beautiful pieces of pottery.
My friend Yoko creates beautiful pieces of pottery.

11. Yoko _____ clay into beautiful bowls and mugs.
12. She _____ the clay moist and ready for use.
13. Yoko _____ the clay with skill.
14. Yoko _____ her colors carefully.
15. Then she _____ it back in the kiln for a final firing, or baking.

Writing Connection

Writer's Journal

Writer's Journal: Strong Verbs A strong verb is one that really makes a reader picture what is happening. Write several sentences with forms of the verb *go* (*go, goes, went*). Then rewrite the sentences using stronger verbs. Here is an example: *I **went** down the hill on my bicycle. I **sped** down the hill on my bicycle.* Start a list of strong verbs in your Writer's Journal.

Combining Sentences: Compound Predicates

A **compound predicate** is two or more predicates that have the same subject. The simple predicates in a compound predicate are usually joined by a **conjunction** such as *and, but,* or *or.*

Sometimes, two or more sentences have the same subject, but different verbs. You can combine the sentences into one sentence with a compound predicate. If there are three or more predicates in a compound predicate, use commas to separate them. Do not use a comma when there are only two predicates.

Separate Sentences with the Same Subject	Sentence with Compound Predicate
My sister paints pictures. My sister also draws cartoons.	My sister paints pictures **and** draws cartoons.
Sometimes Nick and I talk about art. Sometimes we shop for supplies. Sometimes we visit museums.	Sometimes Nick and I talk about art, shop for supplies, **or** visit museums.

Guided Practice

A. Each of these sentences has a compound predicate. Tell what shorter sentences were combined to form each sentence.

Example: Nick made a vase and entered it in the art show.
Nick made a vase. Nick entered it in the art show.

1. My friend went to the museum without me but met me afterward.
2. I went to the museum later and enjoyed my visit.
3. I copied patterns from ancient Greek vases or changed them to suit my style.
4. My friend Midori paints and makes jewelry.
5. Her glass vases win prizes and are popular as gifts.

Independent Practice

B. Combine each pair or group of sentences. Underline the verbs in each compound predicate.

> **Example:** My brother and I stopped at a gift shop. We bought postcards. We went to an art show.
>
> *My brother and I <u>stopped</u> at a gift shop, <u>bought</u> postcards, and <u>went</u> to an art show.*

6. An art gallery displays art. An art gallery has art for sale.
7. The gallery displayed masks. The gallery sold beautiful jewelry.
8. I looked at some jewelry. I enjoyed the colorful Greek masks.
9. Artists created masks for Greek plays. Artists made each one different.
10. I took my brother. I showed him the masks.

C. Write each sentence, correcting the errors. If there is no error, write *Correct*.

> **Example:** Tom works carefully, and makes fine pottery.
>
> *Tom works carefully and makes fine pottery.*

11. Tom makes bowls, but keeps only a few for himself.
12. Tom and I might hold an art show or open an art school together.
13. Tom and I found the perfect place and soon opened a school.
14. We bought materials set up classrooms and started classes.
15. We displayed student art, and offered more classes.

Remember

that **compound predicates** are joined by a **conjunction**. If there are more than three predicates, they must be separated by commas.

Writing Connection

Writer's Craft: Choosing a Form Write about a talent or skill that you would like to develop. Would you like to be an artist, a musician, a ballplayer? Choose your own form, such as a paragraph, a letter, a diary entry, or a poem. Use at least two compound predicates.

Extra Practice

A. **Write each sentence. Draw a line between the complete subject and the complete predicate. Underline the simple predicate.** *pages 52–53*

Example: The Italian word *terra-cotta* means "burnt earth."
The Italian word terra-cotta | *means* "burnt earth."

1. Terra-cotta is a clay with many uses.
2. Ancient Greeks and Romans made tiles from this baked clay.
3. They covered whole buildings in terra-cotta tiles.
4. Museums display terra-cotta dishes, pots, and tiles.
5. Artists made terra-cotta clay into many shapes.
6. People make flowerpots today from terra-cotta.
7. Terra-cotta pots break easily.
8. A terra-cotta flowerpot breaks after a fall.
9. Artists glaze terra-cotta for color and design.
10. Unglazed terra-cotta is a lovely color.

B. **Write each sentence. Underline the verb or verbs in each sentence.** *pages 54–55*

Example: Sculptors design large works for outdoor use.
Sculptors *design* large works for outdoor use.

11. Rain, snow, heat, and cold can damage outdoor sculptures.
12. A green color forms on bronze and copper statues.
13. The copper Statue of Liberty has turned green.
14. People rub some bronze statues for luck.
15. The human touch may keep parts of such statues bright for years.
16. The gold on some statues can fade with time.
17. Artists sometimes freshen the statues with new coats of gold.
18. In time, rain harms even stone and marble statues.
19. Sculptors today protect statues from the weather.
20. Sometimes people move statues indoors.
21. Some statues, however, must remain outdoors.
22. The Great Sphinx in Giza is a huge statue in the Egyptian desert.
23. Workers built it more than 4,500 years ago.
24. This statue has a lion's body and a human face.
25. The Sphinx has suffered weather damage.

> **Remember**
> that a complete predicate includes all the words that tell what the subject of the sentence is or does. The simple predicate is the main word or words in the complete predicate.

DID YOU KNOW?
The largest piece of architecture in the world is the Great Wall of China. The wall covers 4,000 miles, took 2,000 years to build, and was built entirely by hand!

For more activities with predicates, visit *The Learning Site:*

www.harcourtschool.com

C. Combine each pair or group of sentences to form one sentence with a compound predicate. *pages 56–57*

Example: I design animal puppets. I sew animal puppets.
I design and sew animal puppets.

26. I drew a bear on paper. I pinned the paper to brown cloth.
27. My sister Amy cut the cloth. She pinned the pieces together.
28. I sewed the bear. I attached button eyes. I gave it to Amy.
29. Amy liked the bear. Amy called him Bill.
30. Amy wrote a thank-you note. She asked for another puppet.

D. Rewrite each sentence, correcting the errors in punctuation. *pages 52–57*

31. An artist must get tools clear space and think of ideas.
32. Some artists work with metal, but practice with wood and clay.
33. They may also sculpt bars of soap, or cut paper sculptures.
34. I built a wire frame put papier-mâché on it and let it dry.
35. I will paint the sculpture cover it with glitter or leave it plain.

Writing Connection

Real-Life Writing: Headlines Newspaper headlines are not written as sentences, but they often contain subjects and verbs. Look at some examples of headlines. Then imagine that you have become a great success at something, now or in the future. Write the headlines of some articles about yourself that might appear in newspapers. Use strong verbs in your headlines.

Chapter Review

For items 1 through 3, find the simple predicate of the sentence. Choose the letter below it.

1. The <u>Statue</u> of Liberty <u>stands</u> at the <u>entrance</u> to
     A   **B**   **C**
  <u>New York Harbor</u>.
      D

2. The <u>statue</u> <u>was</u> a gift <u>from</u> the <u>people</u> of France.
      F   **G**   **H**   **J**

3. <u>Frédéric Bartholdi</u> <u>designed</u> the <u>statue</u> in the <u>1800s</u>.
        A   **B**   **C**   **D**

For items 4 and 5, find the sentence that best combines the two sentences into one.

TIP Notice when the directions ask for the *best* way to do something. The right answer will have no mistakes. It will also be the clearest way to express the idea.

4 *The statue holds a torch. The statue welcomes visitors.*

  F The statue holds a torch, and welcomes visitors.

  G The statue holds a torch or welcomes visitors.

  H The statue holds a torch and welcomes visitors.

  J The statue holds a torch, but welcomes visitors.

5 *Carlos visited the Statue of Liberty. He climbed the stairs.*

  A Carlos visited the Statue of Liberty or climbed the stairs.

  B Carlos visited the Statue of Liberty but climbed the stairs.

  C Carlos visited the Statue of Liberty and climbed the stairs.

  D Carlos visited the Statue of Liberty, or climbed the stairs.

6 Find the sentence that is complete and is written correctly.

  F Is inside the statue.

  G Visitors climb the stairs.

  H Climbing the stairs to the crown.

  J A long, winding staircase.

For additional test preparation, visit *The Learning Site:*

Adjusting Speech for Audience and Purpose

How do you feel about speaking to an audience? Do you get nervous or excited? Or do you feel calm? Perhaps your reaction depends on the audience itself. An audience can be a room of people listening to a speech. It can also be a person to whom you are talking about your homework. You are always changing your speaking style for your audience.

Since your goal is to be understood, you should speak as clearly and correctly as possible. Choose words that mean exactly what you want to say. Other things about your speech will vary, depending on your audience and purpose. They include

- your **rate** of speech, or how quickly you speak. For example, when you explain something, you need to give people time to understand what you are saying.

- your **volume**, or how loudly you speak. You might need to increase your volume when you talk in a room filled with many people.

- your **pitch**, or the highness or lowness of your voice. If you feel nervous, take a deep breath before speaking to keep your pitch normal.

- your **tone** of voice, or the emotion suggested by your voice. Your tone may be one of confidence, sadness, or anger.

YOUR TURN

DISCUSSION With a partner, discuss how you would adjust your rate, volume, pitch, and tone for each of the following occasions. Think about the audience and your purpose for speaking in each case. Be prepared to share your ideas with the class.
- a discussion with friends about a movie that you all have seen
- a speech contest at your school
- a welcome to new children at camp that includes a list of the camp rules
- a pep talk to your teammates before you play the championship game

TIP
Remember to think of your audience when you are speaking, both in formal situations and in informal ones.

Simple and Compound Sentences

A sentence that expresses only one complete thought is a simple sentence. A compound sentence is made up of two or more simple sentences.

The subject or predicate in a simple sentence may be simple or compound.

Examples:

Simple Sentences

Many artists illustrate children's books.

Writers and artists create children's books. (compound subject)

They create the books and give book talks. (compound predicate)

A compound sentence is made up of two or more simple sentences joined by *and, or,* or *but.* Notice that a comma comes before *and, or,* or *but.*

Compound Sentence

Many artists illustrate children's books, but other artists work with computer graphics.

Guided Practice

A. Identify each sentence as *simple* or *compound.*
 Explain your answer.

> **Example:** Some artists go to art school, but others teach
> themselves to draw. *compound*

 1. One artist began drawing in high school.
 2. At first she wanted to illustrate science books, but
 her interests changed.
 3. She went to art school, and she decided on a new
 goal.
 4. She enjoyed designing cards and went to work for a
 greeting card company.
 5. She designed greeting cards, and she learned about
 business.

Independent Practice

B. Write each sentence. Draw one line under each complete subject. Draw two lines under each complete predicate. Tell whether the sentence is simple or compound.

Example: Some art is displayed in museums, but commercial art is used in business. *compound*

6. Commercial art is different from the art in museums.
7. Advertising art is one kind of commercial art.
8. Advertising companies hire commercial artists, but other businesses hire them, too.
9. Many commercial artists work for large companies, but others work on their own.
10. Commercial artists can be painters, or they can be photographers.
11. Food photographers and fashion illustrators are commercial artists.
12. Few people were commercial artists before 1900, but commercial art is a popular career now.
13. Early commercial artists taught themselves to draw.
14. Another kind of commercial artist designs product packages.
15. Commercial artists design advertisements.
16. They choose the pictures, but others write the words.
17. The ads must be attractive and also send a message.
18. The illustration must match the message.
19. The people in a food ad must look satisfied, and the setting must be pleasant.
20. Commercial artists must be good at art, and they must be able to deal with people.

Remember

that a **simple** **sentence** expresses one complete thought. A **compound** **sentence** is made up of two or more simple sentences.

Writing Connection

Real-Life Writing: Message Write the message for a birthday card for someone you know. Start by writing in simple sentences. You might compliment the person or suggest ways to celebrate. Then combine some of the simple sentences into compound sentences by using *and*, *or*, or *but*.

Coordinating Conjunctions	
and	for
but	so
or	yet

Conjunctions in Compound Sentences

The simple sentences that make up a compound sentence are usually joined by a coordinating conjunction.

The conjunctions most often used to join simple sentences are *and*, *but*, and *or*.

A coordinating conjunction shows the relationship between two sentences. *And* joins two sentences that are closely related. *Or* joins two sentences that are about choices. *But* joins two sentences that tell about difference.

Examples:
Commercial artists design Websites, **and** they illustrate computer programs.

Commercial artists design Websites, **or** they develop new packaging.

Commercial artists design Websites, **but** they don't teach classes about the Internet.

Notice that a comma is used before the conjunction that joins the main parts of a compound sentence.

Guided Practice

A. **Identify the coordinating conjunction in each sentence.**

Example: Website designers must be creative, and they must understand computers, too. *and*

1. Websites can give information, or they can sell products and services.
2. Website designers must create attractive sites, and they must be sure the information is clear.
3. These designers get some ideas from other Websites, but they must use their own ideas, too.
4. Website designers must understand art, and they must know what attracts people to visit Websites.
5. Some Website artists first sketch out ideas on paper, but others design on the computer.

Independent Practice

B. Write each sentence. Underline the conjunction that joins the simple sentences.

Example: Some commercial artists draw on paper, but others draw with computers.

Some commercial artists draw on paper, <u>but</u> others draw with computers.

6. Pictures drawn with computers can be called illustrations, or they can be called computer graphics.
7. Some computer programs create bar graphs, but others make circle charts.
8. Some artists use computers to illustrate books, and the results are very attractive.
9. Artists must have fast computers, or the graphics software will not work well.
10. Graphics are used in television programs, and commercial artists design these graphics.

C. Write each sentence. Choose the conjunction that best fits each sentence.

11. Computer graphics are often designed for news programs, (but, or) other programs also include graphics.
12. Commercial artists understand computer graphics, (or, and) they know what television viewers like.
13. Computer graphics can be colorful, (but, or) they can be in black and white.
14. Billboards must catch people's attention, (and, or) they must get across a message quickly.
15. Billboards must have few words, (and, or) drivers will not be able to read them.

Remember

to use *and* when you join two sentences that are closely related. Use *or* to join two sentences that are about choices. Use *but* to join two sentences that tell about a difference.

Writing Connection

Real-Life Writing: Help-Wanted Ad Imagine that you run a small business and need to hire a commercial artist. Think about the work an artist would do for your business. Write a help-wanted ad to find a commercial artist. Use compound sentences to tell about the work the person would do.

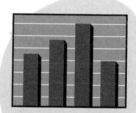

USAGE AND MECHANICS

Combining Sentences: Semicolons and Conjunctions

Conjunctions or semicolons may be used to combine sentences.

Most of the time, the conjunctions *and*, *or*, and *but* are used to join simple sentences. When the relationship between the sentences is clear without a conjunction, you can use a semicolon to join them. Using semicolons adds variety to your sentences. When you use a semicolon, do not use a conjunction.

Examples:

Many books have illustrations, **but** children's book illustration is a special art.

Some illustrations in children's books are black and white; others are printed in color.

Guided Practice

A. Tell how the two simple sentences are joined in each compound sentence.

Example: This book has beautiful pictures, and they help tell the story. *comma and the conjunction* and

1. Artists first read the story, and then they create illustrations.
2. Illustrations make books attractive, and they provide information.
3. Math textbooks usually have more charts, but reading textbooks have more drawings.
4. Science books may show drawings of the solar system, or they may include photographs of plants.
5. Textbook illustrations cannot look old-fashioned; students will not like them.

BASEBALL
IN THE
BARRIOS

HENRY HORENSTEIN

Independent Practice

Remember

that simple sentences can be joined by a **conjunction** or by a **semicolon**.

B. Use a conjunction or a semicolon to combine each pair of sentences to form one compound sentence. Choose the method that you think combines the sentence in the best way.

> **Example:** Illustrating picture books is an interesting job. It requires many skills.
> *Illustrating picture books is an interesting job, and it requires many skills.*

6. Each artist's style is special. No two pictures look alike.
7. Some characters look real. Others look like cartoon characters.
8. Artists draw a character's looks. They also draw the character's actions.
9. Sometimes a bright cover helps sell a book. The story is the important part.
10. Stories can be told in words. They can be told with only pictures.
11. Book illustrators usually draw and paint. They may sometimes use computer graphics.
12. We learn about characters from illustrations. We learn more from the story.
13. Books are made in different sizes. Illustrations are made to fit.
14. Illustrators often work at home. Some illustrators work in studios.
15. Illustrators may work on one book. They may work on a series of books.

Writing Connection

Technology: Speech-to-Text Feature Write four compound sentences, using conjunctions and semicolons. If speech-to-text software is available, read them to the computer. Did the computer punctuate them correctly? As an alternative, write a paragraph to explain which sentences might be difficult for the software and why.

Extra Practice

A. Write each sentence. Draw one line under each complete subject and two lines under each complete predicate. Then write whether the sentence is simple or compound. *pages 62–63*

Example: Some commercial artists work for fashion magazines.

<u>Some commercial artists</u> <u><u>work for fashion magazines.</u></u> simple

1. Commercial artists illustrate new styles of clothing.
2. Some fashion illustrations are used in magazines, but others are used in newspapers.
3. Fashion artists must make the clothing look attractive.
4. They draw the piece of clothing, and they show details.
5. People want to see details, or they will not buy the clothing.
6. Fashion artists show how the clothing fits and make it look attractive.
7. Fashion illustrators must know a lot about clothing.
8. Fashion artists can show a whole outfit, or they can show only certain pieces.
9. A fashion artist may draw shoes for a newspaper advertisement.
10. Fashion illustrators enjoy what they do, but they work hard.

B. Write each sentence. Choose the conjunction or punctuation in parentheses that best fits each sentence. Add commas as needed. *pages 64–67*

11. Commercial artists make pictures on paper (and, but) commercial photographers make pictures on film.
12. Some photographers take pictures of people (or, ;) they are called portrait photographers.
13. Some commercial photographers take pictures of sports (and, or) they only shoot photos of games.
14. Sports photographers attend many games (and, but) they are too busy to cheer for the teams.
15. Photographers may develop their own pictures (and, or) they may take their film to labs.

For more activities with simple and compound sentences, visit *The Learning Site:* www.harcourtschool.com

C. Use a conjunction or semicolon to combine each pair of sentences. Write one compound sentence.

pages 66–67

Example: Designers are like commercial artists in some ways. They are different in other ways.
Designers are like commercial artists in some ways, but they are different in other ways.

16. Some designers create things for homes. They may design furniture for offices.
17. Toys are designed to be colorful. Furniture is designed to be comfortable.
18. Toys must be fun. They must be safe.
19. Furniture designers must make a chair comfortable. People will not buy it.
20. Designers make models. Models help them see whether their ideas work.

D. Write each sentence, correcting the errors.

pages 62–67

21. Many companies hire commercial artists and hire more each year.
22. Some commercial artists work in office buildings but others work at home.
23. Commercial artists must have art tools, or they must also have good light.
24. Many commercial artists have computers in their studios but, not all of them do.
25. Some artists need quiet to work, others are not bothered by noise.

Writing Connection

Writer's Journal: Recording Memories Think of something that happened recently that you would like to remember. Write about what happened. Choose a form for your writing, such as a diary entry, a paragraph for a scrapbook, a news story, or a poem. Use at least one compound sentence.

Chapter Review

Read the group of words in the box. There may be a mistake in sentence structure. If you find a mistake, choose the answer that is written most clearly and correctly. If there is no mistake, choose *Correct as is*.

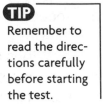

TIP
Remember to read the directions carefully before starting the test.

---

1 Maurice Sendak is known for his children's book illustrations and his writing is also well known.

A Maurice Sendak is known for his children's book illustrations and, his writing is also well known.

B Maurice Sendak is known for his children's book illustrations, and his writing is also well known.

C Correct as is

---

2 You may know his book *Where the Wild Things Are* or you might remember *Chicken Soup with Rice*.

F You may know his book *Where the Wild Things Are*, but you might remember *Chicken Soup with Rice*.

G You may know his book *Where the Wild Things Are*, or you might remember *Chicken Soup with Rice*.

H Correct as is

---

3 He started drawing in high school and later he went to the Art Students League.

F He started drawing in high school, or later he went to the Art Students League.

G He started drawing in high school; later he went to the Art Students League.

H Correct as is

---

4 He published his first book at age nineteen or he has continued writing and illustrating ever since.

A He published his first book at age nineteen, or he has continued writing and illustrating ever since.

B He published his first book at age nineteen, and he has continued writing and illustrating ever since.

C Correct as is

For additional test preparation, visit *The Learning Site:*

www.harcourtschool.com

Analogies

An **analogy** expresses a relationship between words or ideas. In an analogy question, a pair of words appears with a colon between them, followed by a double colon. Then another word appears. You are given choices to complete the analogy. Decide how the first two words are related. The second two words must have the same relationship. In the first pair below, *shovel* is a tool used to do an action, *dig*. *Pencil* is also a tool. What does a pencil do? Look at the possible answers. You know that a pencil is not used to stir, and "crayon" is not an action. *Write* must be the correct answer.

shovel : dig :: pencil :

   A. stir   B. write   C. crayon

Here are some possible relationships among analogy words:	
Relationship	Examples
Word : Synonym	happy : joyful :: tired : sleepy
Word : Antonym	warm : chilly :: hot : cold
Cause : Effect	cloud : rain :: fire : smoke
Object : Use	pot : cook :: shovel : dig
Whole : Part	tree : branch :: body : arm
Product : Producer	egg : chicken :: milk : cow

YOUR TURN

Choose the correct word to complete each analogy.

1. heat : fire :: cold :
   A. water B. ice C. flame

2. bread : bakery :: milk :
   A. cheese B. farm C. dairy

3. large : small :: huge :
   A. tiny B. gigantic
   C. enormous

4. bed : sleep :: bathtub :
   A. wet B. dry C. bathe

5. book : chapter :: movie :
   A. film B. scene C. review

TIP Find the relationship between the first two words in an analogy. Then you will be able to choose the word that shows the same relationship between the second two words.

Writing Workshop

LITERATURE MODEL

In a personal narrative, the writer tells about an event that he or she experienced. In this narrative, a boy tells about his experiences playing baseball. As you read, notice how he shows the order of events and his feelings about the game.

Baseball in the Barrios

by Henry Horenstein

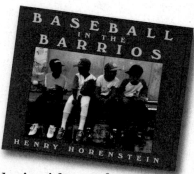

At night as I fall asleep I imagine the sound of fans cheering: "Hubaldo! Hubaldo! Hubaldo!" There are two outs; the count is 1 and 2; and the score is tied 1–1. The pitch is tough—high, inside, and fast. But I don't back away. With one smooth stroke, I send the ball over the left field fence. I trot around the bases. My teammates greet me as I tag home plate. We win the game— and the national championship.

73

Personal Narrative

Chico Carrasquel

Luis Aparicio

I'm called Hubaldo (oo-BAL-doh), but my full name is Hubaldo Antonio Romero Páez. Antonio is my middle name, just like Anthony in English. My father is Pedro Romero and my mother is Carmen Páez, so Romero and Páez are my family names. In Venezuela, where I live, we use both our parents' family names and our mother's goes last.

The most popular sport here is baseball—or *béisbol* in Spanish. My mom says baseball has been played in Venezuela almost as long as in the United States. That makes it an *all*-American sport— played in North *and* South America.

To be a good ballplayer, you must start early, and in Venezuela there are many opportunities to play organized baseball, even at a very young age. When I was four years old, I started playing with the Semillitas, which means little seeds. The idea is that seeds will grow into big ballplayers. We won the city championship, and there was a picture of me with my friends Romni and Rodni and the rest of our teammates in *El Nacional*, one of the largest newspapers in Caracas.

Semillitas work out at least once a week. They run around the field to get in shape. Then they take fielding and hitting practice. They even play formal games, though they need a lot of help from grown-ups. I remember my first hit. I was so surprised that I ran right to my mother instead of to first base.

In Venezuela, each team has a god-mother, or *madrina*. She watches the game and cheers for her team, bringing it good luck. The *madrina* is usually about the same age as the team she represents—even for the Semillitas.

As I got older I played with the Preparatories and the Preinfantils. Now I'm with the Infantils, which is the league for ten- and eleven-year-olds. We practice three times a week and play formal games once a week, usually on Friday nights.

My team is called los Trompos, which means tops—and we are. So far, we're in first place, mostly because of Romni's excellent hitting—he leads the league in home runs—and Rodni's outstanding pitching. I play shortstop, like the great Carrasquel and Aparicio. I hit pretty well, but if I make it to the major leagues it'll

be because I'm a good fielder and I'm fast. Very few ground balls get past me, and I try to steal a base whenever I can.

My friends and I practice a lot with tennis balls. They don't cost much and they don't break windows as easily as baseballs. Whenever we don't have a formal game, I meet Romni and Rodni and we go to the nearest playground and play ball. We laugh a lot, but we're pretty serious about it. Sometimes we play for hours. Then we sit around and talk about the next los Trompos game and our favorite professional players.

When I get home, I'm exhausted and ready for bed. Unfortunately, on most nights I haven't done my homework. I try to explain to my parents that I need my sleep for tomorrow's game, but they won't budge. They always say I need my studies more. "Even major leaguers need to read and write well," they say.

Later, as I close my eyes to go to sleep, I imagine myself on second base. I look into the dugout and nod at Rodni. I see the legendary Chico Carrasquel standing next to him. The game is tied 1–1, and it's the bottom of the ninth inning. Romni is up and looks my way as he steps into the batter's box. The pitch comes in—fast, high, and inside. Romni goes with it and lines a single to right field. I'm off at the crack of the bat. I know it'll be a close play at home, so it's a good thing Dad has taught me to slide around the tag. After all, if I beat the throw, we win the game—and the World Series.

76

Analyze THE Model

1. How does Hubaldo feel about baseball?
2. Why do you think the writer tells Hubaldo's story in the first person?
3. What words or phrases in the narrative show time order?
4. Why did the writer begin and end the story with scenes from Hubaldo's imagination?

READING — WRITING CONNECTION

Parts of a Personal Narrative

"Baseball in the Barrios" is the story of a boy who loves baseball. Now, look at a narrative written by a student who loves kite flying. Pay attention to the way Claudia tells her story.

MODEL

topic ——

first event ——

next event ——

viewpoint ——

next event ——

Flying High

My love of kites began one day last March. I was sketching a robin in my backyard when a loud noise startled me. An eagle was swooping down from the sky. As it fell, it screamed "Waaah!" I leaped to my feet and ran. It lay still. The eagle was made of painted paper! Then I heard the sound again behind me: "Waaah!" Turning, I saw Tommy, the seven-year-old who lives next door. He was crying.

"Is it broken, Claudia?" he asked through tears.
"I don't know," I said. "What happened?"
"It hit a tree and fell."

I lifted the toy and studied it. The round wooden stick that supported the kite was broken.

"It's broken, isn't it?" Tommy sobbed.
"Shh! We can fix it." I said aloud. To myself I thought, "How, Claudia?"

Then the idea came to me. The round stick looked like one of the curtain rods on the kitchen windows. I asked Mom if she had any spare rods. With her permission, I took one. I removed the broken stick and attached the curtain rod to the paper. Tommy and I spent the next two hours flying the kite. He was so excited, and I couldn't believe the fun I was having!

The next day I went to the library and borrowed two books about kites. Kites are fascinating. I decided to make my own kite. Kite making was a perfect blend of art and science, my favorite subjects.

From my new hobby, I've learned about other cultures and about science. I've made new friends who also enjoy flying kites. Most of all, I'm having fun!

next event

next event

viewpoint/ending

Analyze THE Model

1. **What is Claudia's purpose for writing?**

2. **What words and details show Claudia's feelings?**

3. **What metaphor does Claudia use at the beginning? Why?**

4. **Why do you think Claudia included dialogue?**

Summarize THE Model

Make a list of the main events and ideas in Claudia's personal narrative. Then use your list to write a summary of her narrative. Be sure to include the events in the correct time order. Leave out the details.

Writer's Craft

Personal Voice The details Claudia chooses and the feelings she expresses help create her personal voice and style. How is Claudia's narrative different from your summary of her narrative? Which is more interesting to read? Why?

Prewriting

Purpose and Audience

You probably enjoy telling friends about activities you like to do. In this chapter, you will share an experience by writing a personal narrative.

WRITING PROMPT Think of a favorite activity. Write a personal narrative telling your classmates about something that happened when you were participating in the activity. For example, you might tell how you discovered the activity or how you learned something from it.

Begin by thinking about your audience and purpose. What would interest your classmates? What events do you want to tell them about?

MODEL

Claudia began by thinking of an activity that she enjoyed—kite flying. She decided to tell her classmates how she discovered the activity and why she enjoys it. She made this flowchart to organize her thoughts:

Strategies Good Writers Use

- Decide on your purpose and audience.
- List events in the order they happened.

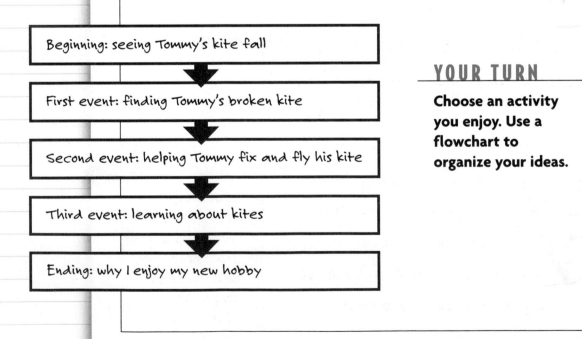

Beginning: seeing Tommy's kite fall

First event: finding Tommy's broken kite

Second event: helping Tommy fix and fly his kite

Third event: learning about kites

Ending: why I enjoy my new hobby

YOUR TURN

Choose an activity you enjoy. Use a flowchart to organize your ideas.

Organization and Elaboration

Use these steps to organize your narrative:

STEP 1 Get Your Audience's Attention
Introduce your topic in a way that makes your audience
want to read about it.

STEP 2 Write the Beginning of Your Narrative
Tell what happened first. Use specific details.

STEP 3 Write the Middle of Your Narrative
Put events in the order they happened.

STEP 4 Write the Ending to Your Narrative
End by explaining what you have gained or learned from
doing the activity.

MODEL

Read the beginning of Claudia's narrative. Notice how
she uses sound, sights, and a surprising discovery to make
her introduction vivid and interesting.

*My love of kites began one
day last March. I was sketching
a robin in my backyard when
a loud noise startled me. An
eagle was swooping down from
the sky. As it fell, it screamed
"Waaah!" I leaped to my feet
and ran. It lay still. The eagle
was made of painted paper!*

Strategies Good Writers Use

- Begin with an interesting topic sentence.
- Put the events in correct time order.
- Include a beginning, a middle, and an ending.

Use a computer to draft your essay. Double-space your work so that you can read and revise it more easily.

YOUR TURN

Draft your narrative. Use your flowchart from prewriting and the steps above. Use Claudia's and Henry Horenstein's narratives as models.

Revising

Organization and Elaboration

Reread your draft carefully. Ask yourself these questions as you read:

- How well have I introduced my narrative?
- How clearly have I ordered the events?
- How well have I revealed my feelings about the activity?
- Have I used vivid language, sensory details, and a variety of sentence types?

MODEL

Here is part of Claudia's original version of her narrative. Notice that in her revised version she combined sentences and added dialogue.

> "I don't know," I said. ~~I asked~~
> ~~Tommy~~ what happened. ~~Tommy~~
> ~~told me that the kite~~ hit a tree and
> fell.
>
> I lifted the toy and studied it.
> ~~There was a~~ The round wooden stick that
> supported the kite. ~~The stick~~ was
> broken. "It's broken, isn't it?"
> Tommy ~~asked~~ sobbed.

YOUR TURN

Revise your personal narrative to make sure that events are in the correct time order. Think about adding dialogue or figurative language.

Strategies Good Writers Use

- Place the events in correct time order.
- Add figurative language and sensory details.
- Combine sentences for variety.

Use the edit features on the toolbar to add details and combine sentences.

Proofreading

Checking Your Language

You proofread to find mistakes in grammar, spelling, punctuation, and capitalization. These errors can reduce the reader's enjoyment of your personal narrative.

MODEL

Here is another part of Claudia's personal narrative. After she revised her narrative, she proofread it. Notice how Claudia corrected errors in end punctuation. What other errors did she correct?

> Then the idea came to me. the
> round stick looked like one of the cur-
> tain rods on the kitchen windows. I
> asked Mom if she had any spare rods?
> With her permission, I took one. I
> removed the broken stick, and attached
> the curtain rod to the paper. Tommy
> and me spent the next two hours fly-
> ing the kite. He was so excited, and I
> couldn't believe the fun I was having!

Strategies Good Writers Use

- Check sentences for correct end punctuation.
- Check for correct conjunctions in compound sentences.

Editor's Marks
- ✗ delete text
- ∧ insert text
- ⟳ move text
- ¶ new paragraph
- ≡ capitalize
- / lowercase
- ◯ correct spelling

YOUR TURN

Proofread your revised narrative several times. Each time, do one of the following:
- **Check grammar.**
- **Check spelling and capitalization.**
- **Check punctuation, especially in compound sentences.**

You may want to trade papers with a partner and proofread each other's work.

Publishing

Sharing Your Work

Now you may publish your personal narrative. These questions can help you decide the best way to share your work:

1. Who is your audience? Which type of publishing would be best for them?

2. Should you print your narrative in manuscript or write it in cursive? To decide, think about your audience again. Your classmates can read cursive, but you would need to print by hand or from a computer for younger readers.

3. Would drawings or photographs make your narrative more lively and interesting? Look at the pictures in "Baseball in the Barrios." They may help you decide what kind of illustrations to add and where to place them.

4. Should you read your narrative aloud? If you do, use the information on page 85.

USING YOUR
Handbook

Use the rubric on page 506 to evaluate your personal narrative.

Reflecting on Your Writing

Using Your Portfolio What did you learn about your writing in this chapter? Write your answer to each question below.

1. How well did you complete all the parts of a personal narrative?

2. Using the rubric from your Handbook, how would you score your writing? Explain your answer.

3. What is one thing you would like to improve in your writing?

Place your answers and your personal narrative in your portfolio. Review your answers before you begin the next writing assignment.

Varying Pitch, Tone, Rate, and Volume

When Claudia finished her personal narrative, she decided to read it aloud to her class. You, too, can share your narrative with your classmates or another group. Use these steps as a guide:

STEP 1 Rehearse by reading your story at home in front of a mirror or to siblings or friends.

STEP 2 Speak clearly and confidently. Pronounce each word carefully.

STEP 3 Match your voice to the events in your narrative or the feelings you are expressing. Vary your voice by:
- pitch—highness and lowness
- tone—type of sound based on style or feeling (serious, happy)
- rate—speed
- volume—loudness

STEP 4 Make eye contact with your audience. Use gestures and facial expressions to show actions and emotions.

Strategies for Listening and Speaking

The strategies below will help you be an effective listener when your classmates read their stories.

- Pay attention to the speaker.
- Listen for time-order words.
- Be quiet and do not interrupt.

Sentences *pages 24–25*

A. If the group of words is a sentence, write *sentence*. If the group of words is not a sentence, write *not a sentence*.

1. The Industrial Revolution began in England in the 1700s.
2. Continued into the early 1800s.
3. Took more time to make goods by hand.
4. People bought goods made by machines.
5. They became interested in handicrafts again after World War II.
6. Was fought between 1939 and 1945.
7. Grew tired of machine-made things in the 1950s.
8. They all looked alike.
9. People began to look for ways to make things by hand again.
10. Sold kits for making handicrafts.

Four Types of Sentences *pages 26–27*

B. Write whether each sentence is declarative, interrogative, imperative, or exclamatory.

11. When did our local schools begin teaching crafts?
12. They offered those classes when people became more interested.
13. I made this statue of a horse and rider in my crafts class.
14. How talented you are!
15. Let me see that statue.

Punctuating Sentences *pages 28–29*

C. Identify each sentence by type. Write each sentence, adding the correct end punctuation.

16. What did people make from silver during colonial times
17. They made bowls and other dishes
18. They also produced beautiful pitchers
19. What beautiful patterns these pitchers have
20. Please buy this pitcher for me

Complete and Simple Subjects

pages 34–35

Unit 1
Grammar Review
CHAPTER 2
Subjects/
Nouns
pages 34–43

A. Write each sentence. Underline each complete subject. Circle each simple subject.

1. The art of glassblowing spread rapidly throughout the Roman Empire.
2. Glassware was common and inexpensive.
3. Glass objects are fragile.
4. Special ingredients change the color of the glass.
5. Glassmakers in Venice learned to make very thin glass.
6. Baskets are important in many cultures.
7. Handmade baskets are products of one of the oldest crafts.
8. People of long ago made baskets out of vines.
9. People around the world decorate their baskets differently.
10. Palm leaves make good baskets.

Nouns in Subjects *pages 36–37*

B. Write each sentence. Underline each noun. Circle the noun that is the simple subject.

11. The craft of bookbinding began centuries ago.
12. Today many bookbinders work to restore or repair old books.
13. Long ago bookbinders sewed leather covers onto books.
14. In 1825, the method of binding books changed.
15. The new process used glue to attach the covers to the pages.

Combining Sentences: Compound Subjects *pages 38–39*

C. Combine each pair of sentences to form one sentence. Use a conjunction to make a compound subject.

16. Libraries are good places to find books. Bookstores are good places to find books.
17. Adults enjoy reading books. Children enjoy reading books.
18. Hardback books are sold. Paperback books are sold.
19. Drawings appear in some books. Photographs appear in some books.
20. Short stories are fun to read. Mysteries are fun to read.

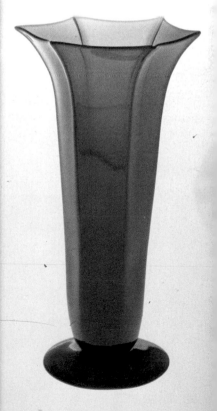

Unit 1
Grammar Review
CHAPTER 4
Predicates/
Verbs
pages 52–61

Complete and Simple Predicates

pages 52–53

A. Write each sentence. Draw a line between the complete subject and the complete predicate. Underline the simple predicate.

1. Our class visited an art gallery yesterday.
2. We saw a show of modern sculpture.
3. The artists used many interesting methods and materials.
4. Some sculptors carved statues from wood.
5. One artist nailed boards together in interesting ways.
6. The bronze statues reflected the light from the window.
7. Many sculptures begin as simple blocks of marble.
8. The artist cuts the marble with her chisels.
9. She keeps her tools in a special box.
10. Sculptors need sharp eyes and steady hands.

Verbs in Predicates *pages 54–55*

B. Write each sentence. Underline the verb.

11. Architects design buildings and bridges.
12. They learn their skills at school and on the job.
13. The bridge near our town crosses a large river.
14. A famous architect planned the new state capitol.
15. My aunt studied architecture in college.

Combining Sentences: Compound Predicates *pages 56–57*

C. Combine each pair of sentences to form one sentence. Use a conjunction to make a compound predicate.

16. One man made puppets. He sold them for ten dollars each.
17. Marge looked at puppets. She chose one to give to her sister.
18. A woman at the fair made tiny glass animals. She taught us about glassmaking.
19. Rosa bought a glass swan. She took it home.
20. We had a wonderful time. We went home tired.

Simple and Compound Sentences
pages 62–63

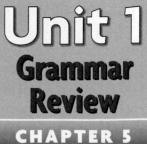

A. Write each sentence. Draw one line under the complete subject. Draw two lines under the complete predicate. Write whether the sentence is simple or compound.

1. Cartoons tell stories or express ideas.
2. Editorial cartoons encourage readers to think about important ideas and problems.
3. They are usually serious, but they are often funny at the same time.
4. Some cartoonists work for one newspaper, but others sell their work to many papers.

Conjunctions in Compound Sentences
pages 64–65

B. Write each sentence. Choose the conjunction in parentheses that best fits each sentence. Add commas as needed.

5. Some artists use computers, (or, and) some work by hand.
6. Many artists try new ways, (but, or) others continue working in the same ways.
7. Artists can ignore computers, (or, and) they can look at them as valuable tools.

Combining Sentences: Semicolons and Conjunctions
pages 66–67

C. Use a conjunction or a semicolon to combine each pair of sentences into one compound sentence. Choose the method that you think combines the sentences in the best way.

8. Many photographers work in advertising. Some of them specialize in food photography.
9. I want to be a commercial artist. I need to go to college first.
10. Commercial artists may work for magazines. They may work in television.

Story Quilt

Did you know that quilts can do more than keep us warm? They can also tell stories. Working with your class, create a quilt that tells the story of your current school year. Then use the quilt to help you write parts of the story.

Brainstorm Events

- Make a list of the interesting or important things that have happened so far this year. What has happened in class? What has happened in the news?

- Pick the event on your list that you remember best or liked best.

- Draw the event. You may use computer software if you like.

Make Your Square

- Cut out and glue together scraps of different colored construction paper to recreate the picture in your drawing.

- Glue the paper picture onto a square sheet of paper. Your teacher will provide it.

- Glue your square on a poster-sized sheet of paper with your classmates' squares.

Write the Story of Your School Year

- When you finish making your square, write the story it tells.

- Look at the other squares. Use one to help you write another story about your school year.

Publish Your Stories

- Publish your quilt stories in a scrapbook, or create a group time line. Arrange all the group members' stories in chronological order on the time line. Add to the time line and quilt throughout the year.

- Take a picture of your quilt, and scan it onto the school website.

Songs from the Loom
by Monty Roessel
NONFICTION
As Jaclyn learns the Navajo method of weaving on the loom, she also becomes aware of the history and culture of her people.

Weaving
by Susie O'Reilly
NONFICTION
Materials such as paper and yarn can be used to make beautiful weavings and other crafts.

Angela Weaves a Dream
by Michèle Solá
NONFICTION
Under the guidance of her grandmother, a young Mayan girl continues the tradition of weaving as she prepares to enter her first weaving contest.

Unit 2

| Grammar | **More About Nouns and Verbs** |
| Writing | **Informative Writing: Explanation** |

How to Build a Miniature Village

Diagram of Village

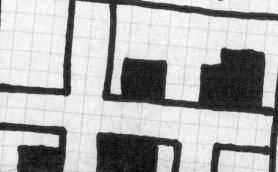

Materials:

400 1 inch x 1 inch x 4 inch blocks

100 1 inch x 1 inch x 1 inch blocks

Common and Proper Nouns

A **common noun** names any person, place, thing, or idea. A **proper noun** is the name or title of a particular person, place, or thing.

You have learned that the simple subject of a sentence is often a noun. Most sentences also contain other nouns. Any word that names a person, place, thing, or idea is a noun.

Example:
Europe and **North America** are both **continents**.

Notice that the nouns that name particular places are capitalized. A common noun begins with a lowercase letter. A proper noun begins with a capital letter. If a proper noun has more than one word, each important word begins with a capital letter.

Nouns	Person	Place	Thing	Idea
Common	pioneer	city	building	joy, sadness
Proper	Stephen Austin	Houston	Washington Monument	

Guided Practice

A. Identify the nouns in each sentence. Tell whether each noun is a common noun or a proper noun.

Example: The first people in North America came from Asia.
people (common), North America (proper), Asia (proper)

1. Spain had many ships, and the people were fine sailors.
2. Some explorers sailed to Africa and Asia.
3. These travelers claimed land for their rulers.
4. Christopher Columbus sailed across the Atlantic Ocean.
5. Columbus and his sailors reached the Americas.

Vocabulary Power

im·mi·grant
[iʹmə·grənt] *v.* A person who moves to a new land in order to live there.

Independent Practice

B. Write each sentence. Underline the common nouns. Circle the proper nouns.

Example: Spain sent other explorers to the new lands.
(Spain) sent other _explorers_ to the new _lands_.

6. The Aztecs were a group of Indians in Mexico.
7. They built cities as large as those in Europe.
8. A colony is made up of settlers who live in one land but are citizens of another nation.
9. Settlers from Spain traveled to Mexico and other areas.
10. Some immigrants built homes in the area now known as Texas.

C. Write each sentence. Add capitalization where needed.

Example: My family will drive to houston on thursday.
My family will drive to Houston on Thursday.

11. We visit my grandparents on thanksgiving.
12. The city of houston, texas, is named for sam houston.
13. My home town has an exciting fourth of july celebration.
14. Another fun and important event is called frontier days.
15. People dress like the settlers from spain.

Remember

that a **common noun** names any person, place, thing, or idea. A **proper noun** names a particular person, place, or thing.

Writing Connection

Writer's Journal: Specific Nouns Specific nouns, whether they are common or proper, make writing clearer and more interesting. The words _house, hut, mansion,_ and _residence_ all mean "a place where people live." However, each word is different from the others. Find the meanings in a dictionary, and use each word in a sentence that shows its meaning. Start a list of specific nouns in your Writer's Journal. See if you can think of other nouns naming places where people live or stay.

Some Irregular Nouns:	
Singular	**Plural**
woman	women
tooth	teeth
mouse	mice
child	children
foot	feet
ox	oxen
scissors	scissors
moose	moose
deer	deer
sheep	sheep
trout	trout

Singular and Plural Nouns

A singular noun names one person, place, thing, or idea. A plural noun names more than one person, place, thing, or idea.

Most nouns are regular. They become plural when you add *s* or *es*. Nouns that end in *s*, *x*, *z*, *sh*, and *ch* need the ending *es*. Most nouns ending in a consonant + *o* need *es*.

beach ⟶ beaches   potato ⟶ potatoes

Some nouns need a spelling change before the ending is added.

life ⟶ lives   mystery ⟶ mysteries
leaf ⟶ leaves   colony ⟶ colonies

Some irregular nouns have a special spelling in the plural form. Other irregular nouns have the same spelling for both the singular and plural forms. If you are not sure about the correct plural form of any noun, look it up in a dictionary.

Guided Practice

A. **Choose the correct plural form of each noun in parentheses. (If you need to, look in a dictionary.) Be ready to explain your answers.**

Example: Spanish rulers made a fortune from their American (colonys, colonies).
colonies

1. (Colonists, Colonistes) sent metal (boxs, boxes) filled with gold and silver to Spain.
2. French and English sailors explored new (territorys, territories).
3. They discovered new land (masses, mass).
4. They also found (schooles, schools) of (fish, fishies).
5. Fishing took place in North American (waterwaies, waterways).

Independent Practice

B. Write each sentence. Use the correct plural form of each noun in parentheses.

6. Many furry (animales, animals) lived in the woods.
7. French (gentlemen, gentlemans) liked to wear fur hats.
8. (Furs, Fures) were popular with French (ladys, ladies).
9. Native Americans traded hides from (beaveres, beavers) and (foxs, foxes) for metal goods.
10. The metal items may have been (kettles, kettls) and (dishes, dishs).
11. Fur trading was one of the most important colonial (activities, activitys).
12. Some fur traders rode (horse, horses) to hunt.
13. They sometimes hunted (deers, deer) for food.
14. Soldiers built (fortresss, fortresses) for protection.
15. We read a book about early American (heroes, heros).

C. Write each sentence. Change each underlined singular noun to the correct plural form.

Example: <u>Animal</u> roamed the woods.
Animals roamed the woods.

16. Native American and French <u>woman</u> often married fur traders.
17. Their <u>husband</u> often gave up hunting to become farmers.
18. These farmers may have used <u>ox</u> to pull <u>plow</u>.
19. Other settlers started fishing and logging <u>business</u>.
20. French settlers built <u>community</u>.

Writing Connection

Social Studies Work with a small group. Imagine you are explorers. Brainstorm a list of supplies that you might need from a trading post. Organize the list into categories, such as food items and clothing items. Have each group member choose a category and write a sentence using some nouns from that list. Proofread each other's sentences, checking for the correct forms of plural nouns.

Remember that some nouns form their plural in special ways. If you are uncertain about the correct plural form, look in a dictionary.

97

Special abbreviations for states are used in addresses. These are made up of two capital letters with no period. You can find these postal abbreviations on page 525, and in reference sources in print and on the Internet.

USAGE AND MECHANICS

Abbreviations

An **abbreviation** is a shortened form of a word.
Use a period after most abbreviations.

Begin the abbreviation for a proper noun with a capital letter.

Titles		Addresses		Days		Months	
Ms.	Sr.	St.	Dr.	Sun.	Thurs.	Jan.	Sept.
Mrs.	Dr.	Rd.	Rt.	Mon.	Fri.	Feb.	Oct.
Mr.	Rev.	Ave.	Blvd.	Tues.	Sat.	Mar.	Nov.
Jr.				Wed.		Apr.	Dec.
						Aug.	

Abbreviations for metric measurements are always written without periods. Abbreviations for English units of measure may be written with or without periods, but always use a period after the abbreviation for *inch*.

Times		English Units		Metric Units	
A.M.	before noon	in.	inch(es)	m	meter(s)
P.M.	after noon	ft. *or* ft	feet	cm	centimeter(s)
		lb. *or* lb	pound(s)	g	gram(s)
min. *or* min	minutes	oz. *or* oz	ounce(s)	kg	kilogram(s)
sec. *or* sec	seconds	gal. *or* gal	gallon(s)	l *or* L	liter(s)

Use A.M. and P.M. and abbreviations for titles of people in all your writing. Use most other abbreviations only in addresses, in tables and charts, in recipes, and in notes or announcements.

Guided Practice

A. Identify the abbreviation that correctly replaces each underlined word.

Example: <u>October</u> 12, 1492 (Oct., Oct) *Oct.*

1. <u>Doctor</u> Andrews (Dr., DR.)
2. 500 Maple <u>Avenue</u> (Av., Ave.)
3. 15 <u>centimeters</u> (cm, cm.)
4. <u>Sunday</u> (Sun.,Sun), <u>December</u> 7, 1941 (Dec, Dec.)
5. 2:00 <u>in the afternoon</u> (PM, P.M.)

Independent Practice

B. Write the abbreviation that could be used in place of each underlined word or words.

6. 12 <u>feet</u> (ft., FT)
7. 10 <u>minutes</u> (min, mn)
8. 8 <u>pounds</u> (lb., lbs.)
9. John Newport, <u>Junior</u> (Jr, Jr.)
10. 27 <u>centimeters</u> (cm, cms)
11. <u>Sunday</u>, Feb. 10 (Snd., Sun.)
12. 2 <u>liters</u> (L, L.)
13. San Jose, <u>California</u> (CAL, CA)
14. <u>August</u> 20 (Aug., aug.)
15. 7:00 <u>in the morning</u> (am, A.M.)
16. 3 <u>ounces</u> (oz., oc)
17. 10 <u>seconds</u> (sec., Sec.)
18. Portland, <u>Maine</u> (ME, Me)
19. Fifth <u>Avenue</u> (Av., Ave.)
20. <u>Mistress</u> Jones (Mrs., Mtr.)

C. Write each sentence. Use the correct abbreviation to replace the underlined word or words.

Example: The gate is 4 <u>feet</u> 8 <u>inches</u> high.
The gate is 4 ft (or ft.) 8 in. high.

21. The address on the envelope was 44 Circle <u>Drive</u>.
22. <u>Mister</u> Jenkins introduced <u>Doctor</u> Ramos.
23. The date on the invitation was <u>Friday</u>, <u>April</u> 12.
24. The party will begin at 4:00 <u>in the afternoon</u>.
25. The newborn baby weighed 7 <u>pounds</u> 12 <u>ounces</u>.

Remember to capitalize the first letter in an abbreviation of a proper noun or title. Periods follow most abbreviations. Use all capital letters and no period when abbreviating state names in addresses.

Writing Connection

Real-Life Writing: Sharing a Recipe Find a recipe to share with your friends. Write it on an index card, making sure that the steps make sense. If amounts are spelled out, use abbreviations. If amounts are abbreviated, write the word for which each abbreviation stands. Trade recipes with a partner to proofread.

Extra Practice

A. Write each sentence, capitalizing any proper nouns you find. Then underline each noun in the sentence.
pages 94–95

Example: The colonists from britain believed that people had certain rights.
The <u>colonists</u> from <u>Britain</u> believed that <u>people</u> had certain <u>rights</u>.

1. These colonists wanted to choose their own leaders.
2. Settlers in virginia wanted their leaders to make laws.
3. This group of lawmakers was called the house of burgesses.
4. There was a plan of government in colonial new england.
5. The people agreed to certain rules of behavior.

B. Write each sentence. Change each underlined singular noun to the correct plural form. If the plural form is the same as the singular form, write *no change*.
pages 96–97

Example: <u>Waterway</u> were important travel routes.
Waterways were important travel routes.

6. Colonists usually settled in <u>valley</u> near rivers.
7. Their <u>ship</u> could remain in the <u>harbor</u>.
8. Cattle and <u>sheep</u> could graze in the fertile <u>pasture</u>.
9. River fish such as <u>trout</u> were a source of food.
10. <u>Child</u> helped gather <u>nut</u> that fell from trees.
11. The settlers needed water to wash pants and <u>dress</u>.
12. <u>Dish</u> also had to be washed with soap and water.
13. Rivers and streams served as <u>highway</u> in a land without <u>road</u>.
14. Settlers used <u>canoe</u> or other <u>boat</u> to travel between towns.
15. People used <u>ox</u> and <u>wagon</u> to move heavy loads.

For more activities with nouns and abbreviations, visit *The Learning Site:*
www.harcourtschool.com

C. Write each item, using abbreviations.

pages 98–99

Example: Sacramento, California *Sacramento, CA*

16. 2 meters
17. Doctor Lax
18. Texas
19. Wednesday
20. Mistress Ortega
21. January
22. gallon
23. Alan Stone, Senior
24. Mister Wu
25. feet
26. title for a woman
27. Illinois
28. 14 grams
29. Palm Street
30. 55 seconds

D. Write each sentence, correcting the errors in capitalization and noun usage. pages 94–99

31. French immigrants settled in acadia, a colony in northeastern north america.
32. When Acadia came under British Rule, ten thousand Acadian were forced to leave their homes.
33. Many acadians moved south to make new home in louisiana.
34. La is the postal abbreviation for louisiana.
35. *Evangeline* tells about the journies of two Acadian.

Writing Connection

Writer's Craft: Using Nouns Imagine that you have moved to a Spanish, French, or British colony. Write a diary entry about a day in your life as a colonist. Use specific nouns to make your writing interesting. Exchange diary entries with a partner, and mark any common and proper nouns, plural forms of irregular nouns, and abbreviations that you find.

Chapter Review

Look for mistakes in capitalization and noun usage in the sentences below. When you find a mistake, write the letter of the part containing the mistake. Some sentences do not have any mistakes at all. If there is no mistake, choose the letter beside *No mistakes*.

TIP Read the directions carefully. Notice what kinds of mistakes you might find.

1 A William penn arrived in
   B Pennsylvania, the colony he founded,
   C in October 1682.
   D (*No mistakes*)

2 J Penn treated Native Americans
   K fairly and signed peace
   L treatys with them.
   M (*No mistakes*)

3 A Many settlers came to his
   B Colony because Penn promised
   C to respect their beliefs.
   D (*No mistakes*)

4 J Penn planned the first
   K city in Pennsylvania and
   L named it philadelphia.
   M (*No mistakes*)

5 A Benjamin Franklin moved to Philadelphia
   B from colonial massachusetts
   C as a young man.
   D (*No mistakes*)

6 J This trip was one of many
   K journey that Franklin would
   L make in his lifetime.
   M (*No mistakes*)

7 A Friends in Philadelphia and
   B Europe called him dr. Franklin
   C because they respected his learning.
   D (*No mistakes*)

8 J Franklin was a famous writer,
   K editor, publisher, leader,
   L and scientist.
   M (*No mistakes*)

Listening to Gain Information

There are many things that you can learn if you keep your ears open! Use the following strategies to become an effective listener.

- Identify the speaker's purpose. Is the speaker's purpose to inform, to persuade, to entertain, or to give directions?

- Identify the speaker's main idea. It is often stated at the beginning. It may be repeated during the presentation or restated near the end.

- Listen for important details that support the main idea.

- Ask yourself as you listen, "Do I agree with the speaker's main idea? Do the reasons or details support the main idea?"

- Pay attention to verbal and nonverbal messages. A speaker sometimes uses hand gestures or facial expressions to show the importance of ideas. A speaker also may change the pitch, tone, rate, or volume of his or her voice to stress an important point.

- Take notes as you listen. Politely ask questions if you do not understand the speaker's message or want to know more details.

YOUR TURN

ACTIVE LISTENING **Invite a guest speaker to talk to the class. The speaker might be a history teacher or a local historian who could talk about the first settlers in your area. The day before the talk, write down questions about the topic that you would like answered. Take notes during the talk. Ask questions based on your notes after the speaker has finished. After the talk, form a group with two or three classmates. Discuss the answers to these questions:**

1. What was the speaker's purpose?
2. What was the speaker's main idea or message?
3. What facts did the speaker give to support the main idea?
4. How did the speaker use his or her voice, face, and hands to make important points?

TIP Pay special attention to the speaker at the beginning of a presentation. If you talk or daydream before you settle down to listen, you might miss the main idea and be unable to follow the rest of the speech.

Singular Possessive Nouns

A possessive noun shows ownership. A singular possessive noun shows ownership by one person or thing.

A noun can tell what someone or something owns or has. To make a singular noun possessive, add an apostrophe and an *s*. Place the apostrophe and *s* after the last letter of the noun, even when that letter is *s*.

Examples:
Chris's book is about life in colonial New England.

Each **colonist's** home was a place for work and play.

A **settler's** house was made of wood and mud.

Vocabulary Power

ap•pren•tice
[ə•pren′tis] *n.* A person who works for another person in order to learn a trade or business.

Guided Practice

A. **Identify the possessive nouns in the sentences below. Some sentences have more than one possessive noun.**

Example: In colonial Massachusetts, the father was the family's head. *family's*

1. The father's job was to take care of his family.
2. A man's time often was divided between farming and hunting.
3. The mother's jobs were usually cooking, cleaning, and sewing.
4. A child's education often took place at home.
5. A son's lessons were in farming and repairing the family's tools.
6. It soon became each Massachusetts town's duty to start a school.
7. A colonial school's lessons included spelling, reading, writing, arithmetic, and religion.
8. A student's lessons were often written on a hornbook.
9. Charles's book from the library tells more about colonial life.
10. Mrs. Morris's class is studying colonial life.

Independent Practice

B. Write each sentence. Underline the possessive noun.

> **Example:** The house's heat came from fireplaces.
> *The <u>house's</u> heat came from fireplaces.*

11. A colonial family's first house often was made of logs.
12. A nice brick home might be a wealthy merchant's.
13. A colonist's mattress might be stuffed with straw or cornhusks.
14. Such a mattress might become a mouse's nest.
15. The bed's cover was a quilt.

C. Write the sentence. Add an apostrophe to each singular possessive noun.

16. A persons bed was sometimes stuffed with feathers.
17. Bed curtains gave the colonists a warm nights rest.
18. A colonists dining area sometimes had fancy dishes and rugs.
19. The homes best furniture often was a grandfather clock.
20. Two people often would share a bowls contents at the familys table.
21. A childs breakfast was usually mush and meat.
22. The days main meal was at noon.
23. The familys noon meal was often a stew.
24. A persons main tool for eating was a spoon.
25. A womans work included making butter and cheese.

Writing Connection

Writer's Journal: Showing Possession Write a sentence using each of the following types of nouns in the singular possessive form: (1) a person, (2) an animal, (3) an object, (4) the name of your school. Then rewrite each sentence, showing possession without using the possessive form of the noun—for example, *the ball belonging to Adam, the pages of the book.* Tell which sentences you think are more effective and why.

Plural Possessive Nouns

A plural possessive noun shows ownership by more than one person or thing.

You have learned that many nouns form their plurals by adding *s* or *es* to the singular form. To form the possessive of a plural noun that ends in *s*, add only an apostrophe.

Examples:

The **Smiths'** farm was the largest in the county.

Colonists' clothing was very different from what we wear today.

You also know that some plural nouns are irregular. These include the nouns *children, men, women, mice,* and *deer.* To make plural nouns such as these possessive, add an apostrophe and an *s.*

Examples:

Many **people's** clothes were made of linen and wool.

The **children's** wool caps kept them warm.

Guided Practice

A. **Identify the plural possessive nouns in these sentences. Tell whether each possessive noun is regular or irregular.**

Example: Making clothes usually was women's work.
women's, irregular

1. Men's clothes included long shirts and woolen pants.
2. Some people's outfits included wigs that had braids.
3. Wigs' lengths ranged from very long to short.
4. Wealthy people's clothes were made from fine fabrics.
5. Women's clothes were often trimmed with lace.
6. Colonists' shoes sometimes had silver buckles.
7. Linen caps covered most adults' heads.
8. Boys' headgear was sometimes a cap.
9. Babies' dresses often reached the ground.
10. Adults' and older children's clothes were similar.

Independent Practice

B. If the plural possessive noun in the sentence is used correctly, write *correct*. If the plural possessive noun is not used correctly, write the sentence using the correct form.

Example: During the early years of settlement, the American colonists energies were focused on survival.

During the early years of settlement, the American colonists' energies were focused on survival.

11. Before long, colonists' attention turned to the arts.

12. Writers interests ranged from religion to the classics.

13. *Poor Richard's Almanack* by Benjamin Franklin was among colonial readers favorite books.

14. Some colonial poets work was well known.

15. Colonial portrait painter's work was soon popular.

C. Write each sentence. Use the plural possessive form of the noun in parentheses.

Example: Travel on the (colony) roads was difficult.
Travel on the colonies' roads was difficult.

16. (Horse) hooves created paths through the woods.

17. (Traveler) wagons could be seen on paths through the forests and fields.

18. By 1760 several (settlement) highways were well known.

19. People called post riders sometimes delivered the (settler) mail.

20. Colonists waited patiently for their (friend) letters.

Writing Connection

Technology Search the Internet for a work of art depicting a person or scene from early American history, such as *Washington Crossing the Delaware*. Try using *American art* as keywords for your search. Keep track of the steps you use to find the artwork. Then write a brief description of the artwork, and tell how you found it on the Internet. Use possessive nouns as needed to help make your writing concise and clear.

that when you form the **possessive** of a **plural noun** that ends in s, add only an apostrophe. When you form the possessive of a plural noun that does not end in s, add an apostrophe and an s.

USAGE AND MECHANICS

Apostrophes in Possessive Nouns

Always use an apostrophe to signal a possessive noun. Do not use an apostrophe in a noun that is simply plural.

As you are writing, you must decide whether a noun that ends in *s* is plural or possessive. Here are some tips:

- Think about the meaning of the sentence. Does the sentence need a singular noun or a plural noun?

- Decide whether the noun shows ownership. If it is singular and shows ownership, add an apostrophe and an *s*.

  If the noun is plural and ends in *s,* add an apostrophe. If a noun is plural and does not end in *s,* add an apostrophe and an *s*.

Examples:
Many colonists were **farmers**. (plural)

A **farmer's** crops might include corn, wheat, and rice. (singular possessive)

Farmers' tools often were homemade. (plural possessive)

Guided Practice

A. **Choose the correct form of the noun in parentheses.**

Example: Farming was most (colonists', colonists) way of life.
colonists'

1. (Farmers, Farmers') planted the same crop in a field year after year.
2. After several (year's, years') use, these fields produced less food.
3. A (farmers', farmer's) tools were an ax, a hoe, and a plow.
4. (Blacksmiths', Blacksmiths) made tools such as the hoe and the plow.
5. A (blacksmith's, blacksmiths) apprentice helped make the tools.

Independent Practice

B. Identify the correct form of the two in parentheses. Write the sentence, using the correct form.

> **Example:** Many (colonists, colonists') jobs involved fishing.
> *Many colonists' jobs involved fishing.*

6. Coastal Massachusetts and Cape Cod were (center's, centers) of fishing.
7. Several (ports, ports') were well known for whaling.
8. One (whale's, whales') body produced gallons of oil.
9. Other important colonial (businesses, businesses') specialized in timber and shipbuilding.
10. (Settlers', Settlers) built homes, fences, and barrels from wood.
11. A (ship's, ships') mast was also made of wood.
12. The pines of (New Englands', New England's) forests made excellent ships.
13. (Builders', Builders) also used oaks and maples.
14. Many of (Englands, England's) ships, in fact, were made in the colonies.
15. To pay for goods or services, (colonists', colonists) offered goods or services in exchange.
16. A (farmers', farmer's) payment for a silver dish might be food from his farm.
17. (Markets, Market's) were places where goods could be exchanged, or bartered.
18. (Native Americans, Native Americans') goods for barter usually were furs and animal hides.
19. Some colonial (business's, businesses') ships carried goods to Europe.
20. The ships returned to North America with furniture, china, and other (supplies, supplies').

Remember

always to use an apostrophe to show possession. Be sure to place the apostrophe to show whether the possessive noun is singular or plural.

Writing Connection

Writer's Craft: Explain a Diagram Make a diagram of an object related to American history, such as a ship, a statue, or a flag. Label the parts. Then write a few sentences explaining the diagram. Be sure to use apostrophes in possessive nouns.

Extra Practice

A. Write each sentence. Underline the possessive noun. Write whether the possessive noun is singular or plural. *pages 104–107*

Example: England's earliest attempts to settle North America were not successful.
England's earliest attempts to settle North America were not successful. singular

1. One early settlement's story is not known.
2. The colonists' settlement on Roanoke Island was deserted a year after it was begun.
3. Historians' efforts to learn what happened have produced no answers.
4. The London Company's settlement at Jamestown was started in 1607.
5. This was Virginia's first colony.
6. The colonists' hardships were many.
7. The winter's freezing weather made life difficult.
8. A supply ship's arrival in the spring was a welcome sight.
9. North America's second successful English settlement was at Plymouth.
10. The colony's settlers were called Pilgrims.

B. If the possessive noun in a sentence is used correctly, write *correct*. If it is not used correctly, write the sentence, using the correct form.
pages 104–107

Example: The Pilgrims's main reason for leaving England was to find religious freedom.
The Pilgrims' main reason for leaving England was to find religious freedom.

11. The settlers' knowledge of farming was limited.
12. With the Native Americans help, they learned to grow corn.
13. Thanksgivings' history began with the feast that the Pilgrims shared with Squanto and his people.
14. Englands' next settlement was called the Massachusetts Bay Colony.
15. After 1660, a kings charter created six more colonies.

Remember

that a singular possessive noun ends with an apostrophe and an *s*. A plural possessive noun that ends in *s* has only an apostrophe. A plural possessive noun that does not end in *s* has an apostrophe and an *s*.

For more activities with possessive nouns, visit *The Learning Site:*
www.harcourtschool.com

C. **If the nouns in a sentence are written correctly, write *correct*. If any noun is incorrect, write the sentence correctly.** *pages 104–109*

> **Example:** Like European society, the colonists society was divided into classes.
> *Like European society, the colonists' society was divided into classes.*

16. The wealthier peoples class was called the gentry.
17. A communitys' elected officials were often members of the gentry.
18. Churches best seats were reserved for members of the gentry.
19. The "middling class" included a towns shopkeepers.
20. In the middle class, a family's income was produced by both the husband and the wife.

D. **Write each sentence. Choose the correct form of the two in parentheses.** *pages 104–109*

21. The (Wallaces, Wallaces') trip to New England was enjoyable.
22. Their son (James, James') gave me a book on colonial life in New England.
23. I walked their (dogs, dogs') while they were away.
24. The (dogs, dogs') leashes hung by the front door.
25. Mrs. (Morris, Morris's) class will enjoy reading my book.

Writing Connection

Real-Life Writing: Store Names The names of stores and businesses often include possessive nouns. Think of a few from your community, and write them down. (You may want to refer to the yellow pages of a phone book.) Then imagine that you are starting a business of your own. Think of a name for your business that includes a possessive noun, and write a few sentences about what you would sell or what service you would provide.

Chapter Review

Read the passage and choose the word that belongs in each space. Mark the letter for your answer.

Colonial children played with toys. A favorite __(1)__ toy was a kite. Often, a parent would make a __(2)__ kite at home. Sometimes the __(3)__ would make dolls from the outer leaves of corn. __(4)__ toys included hoops, marbles, and balls. A child might play with toys sent by the __(5)__ friends in England. The children played games, too. A popular way to spend an afternoon was watching the various farm __(6)__ activities. Colonial children had fewer toys and games than __(7)__ children. They enjoyed playing with the __(8)__ they had, just as children of today do.

STANDARDIZED
TEST PREP

TIP Remember to read the directions and make sure you understand them before trying to answer the test questions.

1 A childrens
  B children's
  C children
  D childrens'

2 F child's
  G childs
  H childrens'
  J children's

3 A girls
  B girl's
  C girls'
  D girl

4 F Boys
  G Boy's
  H Boy
  J Boys'

5 A parents
  B parent
  C parents'
  D parent's

6 F animals
  G animal
  H animals'
  J animal's

7 A today
  B today's
  C todays
  D todays'

8 F toy's
  G toys
  H toy
  J toys'

For additional test preparation, visit *The Learning Site:*
www.harcourtschool.com

Using Card Catalogs

The materials in a library include books, magazines, audiotapes, videotapes, and compact disks. Books are grouped as fiction and nonfiction. On the shelves, fiction books are organized alphabetically by the author's last name. Nonfiction books are organized by special numbers called call numbers. A book's call number is based on the Dewey Decimal System.

Dewey Decimal System	
000–099	General Works (such as encyclopedias)
100–199	Philosophy
200–299	Religion
300–399	Social Science
400–499	Language
500–599	Pure Science
600–699	Applied Science, Technology
700–799	Arts and Recreation
800–899	Literature
900–999	History, Geography

Library books can be listed in two kinds of card catalogs. A traditional card catalog is a group of drawers with cards that are arranged in alphabetical order. Many libraries also have electronic card catalogs. A computer helps a user find a book in an electronic card catalog. In traditional and electronic card catalogs, books are organized in three ways: by author, title, and subject.

Look at this catalog card. What facts does it include?

Title	John Glenn : space pioneer /
Author	Angel, Ann, 1952-
Edition	1st ed.
Publisher	New York : Fawcett Columbine, 1990, c1989.
Description	120 p. : ill. ; 20cm.
Notes	"For middle school readers" -- T.p. verso. Bibliography: p. [121].
Summary Results	Traces the life of John Glenn, the first American to orbit the earth, and discusses his accomplishments as a Marine pilot, an astronaut, and a U.S. senator.
ISBN	0449903958 (pbk.) :
Subjects	Glenn, John, 1921- Astronauts--Biography.

YOUR TURN

SUBJECT SEARCH Think of a subject you want to know more about. Using a traditional or an electronic card catalog, find the most recent book the library has on that subject. Check out the book if you wish. Then tell or write about how you found it. Give some advantages and disadvantages of the kind of card catalog you used.

TIP To do a subject search, think of a word or words that tell about the subject. If you can't find the book you want under one subject heading, try another.

Writer's Craft

Paragraphing

INFORMATIVE WRITING Every time you tell someone a fact or explain how to do something, you are giving **information**. Giving information in a written form is called **informative writing**.

Read the following passage from *Have a Happy* . . . by Mildred Pitts Walter. Notice how the author explains the steps Chris followed to make a tiny rocking chair out of clothespins.

LITERATURE MODEL

Carefully he turned the pins so the indentations for the spring wires made interesting lines. He mixed and matched the varying shades of wood to make contrasts. When all the parts were glued, he had a real rocking chair.

He looked at it. Something was missing.

He figured out what to do. He took four pieces from two pins and placed them with the thinner part at the bottom, so the space that held the wire faced the back of the chair. He spread them to look like a Chinese fan, then glued them together. When the glue dried, he stuck them onto the back of the chair. It looked like a granny rocking chair. *Ah, my best piece ever.*

Analyze THE Model

1. Do you think the writer did a good job of explaining what Chris did? Why or why not?

2. How can you tell in what order Chris did the steps?

3. Why do you think the writer used more than one paragraph to explain the steps Chris followed?

Vocabulary Power

tran•si•tion
[tran•zish′ən] *n.* A signal word that shows how the ideas expressed in different sentences and different paragraphs connect to each other.

If you are writing to explain a short or simple activity, you may need to write only one paragraph. Often, however, you will need to write more paragraphs, as Mildred Pitts Walter did when she explained how Chris made the chair.

The chart on page 115 tells more about **paragraphing**.

Examples

Write a **topic sentence** for each paragraph, and give **details** that relate to it.

Topic sentence: Empty plastic milk containers have many uses.
Details: You can cut them down to make bird feeders. You can also put soil in them and plant seeds.

Give information in the correct order, or **sequence**.

Glue the ends, and let the glue dry. Then paint the outside.

Use **transitions** and other signal words such as **first, then, last, so, because,** and **also** to show how ideas connect to each other.

Measure one inch from the end and mark your measurement. **Then** cut on the mark **so** the piece will be the right size.

YOUR TURN

ANALYZE INFORMATIVE WRITING With two or three class-mates, look through a book or magazine for an article that explains how to do something. Notice how the information is divided into paragraphs. Discuss the article with your group.

Answer these questions:

1. What is the writer's purpose?

2. What is the main idea of each paragraph, and how do you know?

3. What details does the writer include in each paragraph?

4. Does the writer present ideas in a sequence that makes sense? Explain.

5. How does the writer use transitions to show connections between ideas?

6. Can you follow these directions easily? Why or why not?

Topic Sentence and Details

A. Read these two topic sentences. Then read the paragraph that follows. Choose the best topic sentence for the paragraph. Write the complete paragraph.

Topic Sentences:

The public library is just a short walk from our school.

The public library lends videotapes and compact discs as well as books.

Turn left down Maple Street in front of the school. Walk two blocks to the corner of Maple and Pine. Cross the street at the light, and walk one block on Pine Street, past the video rental store. You will see the library two doors down, on the same side of the street as the video store.

Sequence

B. Read the following directions for a science experiment. Put the steps in time order so that the experiment makes sense. Then write the sentences in paragraph form on your paper.

- Put a sewing needle on the floating newspaper.
- Add a drop of liquid detergent at the edge of the bowl to break the surface tension and sink the needle.
- Float the square of newspaper on the water in the bowl.
- The needle will continue to float on the surface of the water.
- Fill a bowl with water, and cut a small square of newspaper.
- Gently push down the edges of the newspaper square until it sinks.

Using Transitions

C. Write the paragraph below on your paper. Add transition words and phrases from the box so that the sentences read smoothly and make sense. Remember to capitalize the first word of each sentence.

next	first	finally
for example	after	so

Paint a mural with your classmates. _____, meet in a group to decide on a subject and to plan your mural. _____, draw the mural on a large sheet of paper. You will want to sketch lightly _____ you can erase and make changes. _____, you may want to add something or correct the proportions. _____ you are satisfied with the drawing, you can paint your mural. _____, hang the completed mural where everyone can admire it!

Writing and Thinking

Write to Record Reflections Have you ever had difficulty understanding the directions for playing a new game, doing a craft, or completing a homework assignment? Why is it important for written directions to be clear and easy to understand? Write your reflections in your Writer's Journal.

Writer's Journal

Writing Directions

Chris used clothespins to make a little rocking chair. Antonio likes to make things from scrap materials, too. Antonio wrote some paragraphs to tell his classmates how to make a refrigerator magnet. Read the directions that he wrote.

MODEL

topic sentence ———
details ———

You can make your own refrigerator magnet. You will need a small plastic lid and a picture small enough to fit inside the lid. You will also need a pencil, scissors, a small square magnet, and some glue.

topic sentence/
transition ———
details ———
sequence ———

First, make sure the picture you want to use will fit. Lay the lid on the picture, and trace around it. Then, cut out the picture.

transition/sequence ———
sequence ———
sequence ———
sequence ———

Next, glue the picture to the top of the lid. After the glue has dried, turn the lid over. Now glue the magnet to the underside of the lid. Let the glue dry, and then you can use your new refrigerator magnet.

Analyze THE Model

1. Would you be able to follow Antonio's directions? Why or why not?

2. Why is Antonio's first sentence a good topic sentence?

3. Does the sequence of the steps make sense to you? Explain your answer.

4. How does Antonio use transitions to show connections between paragraphs and between sentences in a paragraph?

WRITING PROMPT Think of a craft you like to do or a game you like to play. How can you explain this craft or game to your classmates? Write two paragraphs to give directions for doing the craft or playing the game.

STUDY THE PROMPT Ask yourself these questions:

1. What is your topic?
2. Who is your audience?
3. What is your purpose for writing?
4. What writing form will you use?

Prewriting and Drafting

Organize Your Ideas Begin by writing down in order the steps you want to include in your directions. Then use a chart like this one to plan your paragraphs.

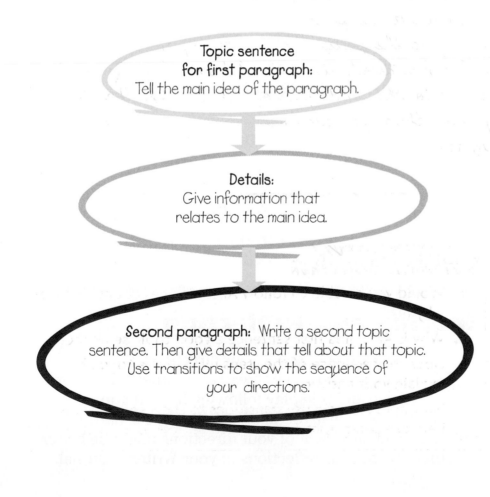

Topic sentence
for first paragraph:
Tell the main idea of the paragraph.

Details:
Give information that
relates to the main idea.

Second paragraph: Write a second topic
sentence. Then give details that tell about that topic.
Use transitions to show the sequence of
your directions.

USING YOUR
Handbook

Use the Writer's Thesaurus to find words that you can use to make smooth transitions and to help your reader understand the sequence of events.

Editing

Read over the draft of your directions. Is there any information you would like to add, leave out, or express more clearly? Use this checklist to help you revise your directions:

☑ Will your reader be able to follow the directions?
☑ Have you begun each paragraph with a topic sentence?
☑ Are the steps in the right sequence?
☑ Have you used transitions to help your reader understand the connections between paragraphs and between sentences within a paragraph?

Use this checklist as you proofread your paragraph.

☑ I have used capitalization and punctuation correctly.
☑ I have used singular and plural nouns correctly.
☑ I have used apostrophes correctly in possessive nouns.
☑ I have indented the first line of each paragraph.
☑ I have used a dictionary to check my spelling.

Editor's Marks

𝒚 delete text
∧ insert text
ᵔ move text
𝓠 new paragraph
≡ capitalize
/ lowercase
◯ correct spelling

Sharing and Reflecting

Writer's Journal

Make a final copy of your directions, and share them with a partner. Read each other's directions aloud, and role-play following the directions. Discuss what you like best about your partner's directions and how each of your directions might be better next time. Write your reflections in your Writer's Journal.

Giving Directions Orally

Now that you have written a set of directions, think about times when you have given directions orally. Can what you have learned about writing directions help you give better spoken directions?

Study the Venn diagram to compare and contrast writing directions with giving them orally.

Written Directions
divided into paragraphs;
reader can go back
and reread

Both
should be clear;
should be given in
sequence;
should use transitions
to make them easier
to understand

Spoken Directions
listener needs to
remember directions
or ask speaker to
repeat them

YOUR TURN

Now you can work with a small group to practice giving spoken directions. Follow these steps:

1. Brainstorm a list of simple subjects for which you might give directions. Here are some ideas to get you started.

   - Give directions from your classroom to the principal's office, the media center, or the gym.

   - Give directions for doing a task, such as looking up a word in a dictionary or using an electronic card catalog.

2. Have group members take turns choosing a subject from your list and giving a clear set of directions.

3. Other group members should listen carefully and try to visualize following the directions.

4. Discuss strategies that your group members used for giving good spoken directions. Discuss how you can use this skill in your everyday lives.

Strategies for Listening and Speaking

Use these strategies to help you give, as well as understand and follow, spoken directions:

- Speakers should remember to adjust rate, volume, pitch, and tone to fit their audience and purpose.

- Listeners should listen carefully to identify and remember the sequence of steps.

Action Verbs

An action verb is a word that tells what the subject of a sentence does, did, or will do.

You know that a verb is the main word in the predicate of a sentence. It is a word or words that express action or being. Action verbs can express physical actions (*run, jump, play*) or mental actions (*see, hear, think*).

Many times, a sentence with an action verb has a **direct object**—a word that receives the action. This word is most often a noun. The direct object answers the question *Whom?* or *What?* after the verb.

Examples:

Subject	Action Verb	Direct Object (whom or what)
A doctor	treats	patients.
An author	writes	books.
People	learn	different <u>skills</u>.
We	heard	a <u>speech</u> on careers.

Guided Practice

A. **Identify the action verb in each sentence. Identify the direct object if the sentence has one.**

Example: People often choose challenging careers.
choose, careers

1. Some people talk to career counselors.
2. They need help in choosing careers.
3. Students prepare for future careers.
4. They attend classes every day.
5. I dream of becoming an astronaut.
6. My brother wants a career in sports.
7. One entrepreneur started a magazine.
8. Another started an online business.
9. I visited my grandparents at their craft shop.
10. They sell many interesting items.

Independent Practice

B. Write each sentence. Underline each action verb. Some sentences have more than one action verb.

Example: The right job makes a person happy.
The right job <u>makes</u> a person happy.

11. Some people enjoy charity work.
12. Others think mainly about a big paycheck.
13. Your career reflects your personal interests.
14. Everyone desires enjoyable work.
15. Workers expect fair wages.
16. A few people enter show business and plan for fame.
17. People sometimes choose careers based on interests.
18. Perhaps your favorite subjects suggest a future career.
19. Anita and Kim went to the career center.
20. Career counselors talked to them and gave them advice.

C. Write each sentence. Underline the action verb. Circle the direct object.

Example: They explored many possibilities before choosing careers.
They <u>explored</u> many (possibilities) before choosing careers.

21. The students discussed their career plans.
22. People often learn new skills in school.
23. Business courses offer valuable help.
24. Many organizations provide information about careers.
25. Success usually takes hard work, however.

Writing Connection

Real-Life Writing: Board Game Work with a group of classmates to make up a board game called "The Perfect Job." First, brainstorm some jobs and think about how people find good jobs. Next, sketch a gameboard. Then write step-by-step instructions on how to play the game. Use action verbs in your instructions to show that the game is lively and interesting.

Common Linking Verbs

be	look
appear	seem
become	smell
feel	sound
grow	taste

Linking Verbs

A linking verb links the subject of a sentence to a word or words in the predicate.

All verbs are either action verbs or linking verbs. Linking verbs show being or tell what something is like. A linking verb is never followed by a direct object. Instead, it is followed by a word or words that rename or describe the subject.

Examples:

My mother **is** a doctor.

(*Doctor* is another name for *mother*.)

She **seems** happy with her job.

(*Happy* describes *she*.)

I **am** very proud of her.

(*Proud* describes *I*.)

Some verbs can be either action verbs or linking verbs, depending on how they are used.

Examples:

The cook *tastes* the soup. (action verb)

The soup *tastes* good. (linking verb)

Guided Practice

A. Identify the linking verb in each sentence. Tell what word or words are connected to the subject by the linking verb.

Example: Years ago, many jobs were not open to women.
were, open

1. Most women in the United States became homemakers during the 1800s.
2. Their work was very important.
3. Many frontier women were also hunters.
4. Those days seem distant to us today.
5. Later, factory and office jobs became possible for women.

Independent Practice

B. Write each sentence. Underline the linking verb. Draw an arrow from the subject to the word or words in the predicate that rename or describe the subject.

Example: Guilds were important in the history of Europe.

Guilds <u>were</u> important in the history of Europe.

6. Merchants were eager to sell their goods.
7. A guild was a group of workers in the same craft.
8. A modern trade union seems similar to a guild.
9. Workers felt stronger as part of a guild.
10. An apprentice was a beginner in a trade.
11. Apprentices appeared young and foolish to their masters.
12. An apprentice became a journeyman, or traveling worker, after many years of practice.
13. Masters were craftspeople with their own shops.
14. Guilds grew very important in local government.
15. The merchant guilds were powerful throughout Europe.

C. Write each sentence. Use the linking verb from the box that best completes each sentence. Underline the words that each linking verb connects.

am	were	became	was	seemed

16. A guild _____ responsible for training young workers.
17. Many masters _____ kind to their apprentices.
18. An apprentice _____ a journeyman after long training.
19. I _____ sure that I would not want to be an apprentice.
20. The future probably _____ an impossible dream to a young apprentice.

Writing Connection

Art Find a painting or a photograph that shows one or more persons doing some kind of work. Imagine yourself in the scene, and write a few sentences describing it. Use several linking verbs to help your description appeal to the senses.

125

USAGE AND MECHANICS

Using Forms of the Verb *Be*

The most common linking verbs are forms of the verb *be*. Always use the form of *be* that agrees with, or matches, the subject in number.

Be is a verb with many forms. *Am*, *is*, and *are* tell what a subject is or is like now. *Was* and *were* tell what a subject was or was like in the past.

Rules for Using *Be*	Examples
Use *am, is,* or *was* with a singular subject.	I **am** an entrepreneur. Sam **is** pleased about the job. She **was** a student, but now she **is** a teacher.
Use *are* or *were* with *you* and with a plural subject.	We **are** in a hurry. You **were** late today. They **are** at the job fair. The workers **were** tired.
Use *be* in a command, or an imperative sentence.	Please **be** on time. **Be** sure to write your report on careers tonight.

Guided Practice

A. **Identify the form of *be* that is used as a linking verb. Identify the word it agrees with, and tell whether that word is singular or plural.**

Examples: Sometimes baby-sitting is difficult.
is, baby-sitting, singular

Good baby-sitters are patient and kind.
are, baby-sitters, plural

1. I am a member of the baby-sitting club.
2. My sisters are the founders of the club.
3. It is important to arrive on time.
4. The baby was asleep when I arrived.
5. The parents were home by nine o'clock.

Independent Practice

B. Write each sentence. Use the form of the linking verb in parentheses that agrees with the subject.

> **Example:** Most people in my family (is, are) pleased with their jobs.
> *Most people in my family are pleased with their jobs.*

6. My uncle (are, is) the owner of a farm.
7. He (was, were) a farmer for more than twenty years.
8. His main crops (are, is) corn and soybeans.
9. We (was, were) happy to help with the chores.
10. My grandmother (was, were) a doctor.
11. Some of her children (are, is) doctors, too.
12. One of my cousins (are, is) a nurse.
13. Her favorite subject in school (was, were) science.
14. My father (are, is) a forest ranger.
15. I (am, is) a student for now.

C. Choose the correct form of the verb *be* for each sentence. Then write the sentence.

> **Example:** All kinds of workers _____ present at the job fair yesterday.
> *All kinds of workers were present at the job fair yesterday.*

16. It _____ a great opportunity to talk with workers.
17. Drilling _____ one job in the oil industry.
18. Mining _____ more dangerous in the past than today.
19. The construction workers at the fair _____ strong.
20. I learned that all lawyers _____ college graduates.

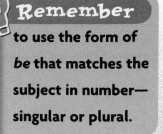

Remember to use the form of *be* that matches the subject in number—singular or plural.

JOB FAIR

FARMING

BUSINESS
OPEN

ART

SCIENCE

Writing Connection

Writer's Craft: Verb Variety *Be* is a useful verb, but your writing will be stronger if you do not use it too much. Choose three sentences from the exercises in this lesson, and rewrite them using a different verb. For example, item 6 could be written, *My uncle owns a farm.* Then look at a piece of your own writing for forms of *be*, and find a sentence to revise.

Extra Practice

A. Write each sentence. Underline the action verb and circle the direct object. One sentence has two action verbs. *pages 122–123*

Example: Most jobs require a high school diploma.
Most jobs require a high school (diploma).

1. Students learn basic job skills in school.
2. Many people continue their education after high school.
3. Colleges offer four-year programs in many subjects.
4. Many jobs involve special training.
5. Workers with a good education deserve higher wages.
6. Employers often send workers for more job training.
7. My cousin studies business in college.
8. She enjoys her courses.
9. Her boss sees the results of her hard work and pays her school costs.
10. How my cousin loves her job!
11. Mr. Wilson studied science in high school.
12. He liked chemistry best of all.
13. Mr. Wilson took a job as a chemist after college.
14. He performs research at work.
15. Sometimes he discovers new information.
16. My aunt took classes in computer science.
17. She attended a technical school.
18. She found a job writing software for computers.
19. There she learned new information about computers.
20. Now she teaches computer science at the technical school.

B. Write the verb in each sentence. Then write *action* or *linking* to identify the kind of verb. *pages 122–125*

Example: Ms. Brown loves plants. *loves, action*

21. She owns several greenhouses.
22. We felt hot in the greenhouse.
23. We felt the moisture in the air.
24. The gardener grew some amazing tomatoes.
25. We grew hungry and thirsty.

Remember

that action verbs tell what the subject of a sentence does, did, or will do. Linking verbs connect the subject to a word or words in the predicate.

For more activities with action verbs and linking verbs, visit *The Learning Site:*
www.harcourtschool.com

C. Write each sentence. Underline each linking verb. Draw an arrow from each subject to the word or words in the predicate that rename or describe it. *pages 124–127*

Example: My neighbor is a scientist.

My neighbor <u>is</u> a scientist.

26. Biology is the study of life.
27. Biology sounds difficult to some people.
28. Scientists are responsible for many discoveries.
29. They often are busy in their laboratories all day.
30. Many scientists become teachers.
31. Sometimes they grow tired of the laboratory.
32. They feel glad when they are in the classroom.
33. My science teacher was happy with my science project.
34. Engineering is a career that interests me.
35. A career in biology also seems possible.

D. Write each sentence. Choose a form of *be* from the box to complete each sentence. *pages 126–127*

am	is	are	was	were

Example: I ____ a person who works well with others.
I am a person who works well with others.

36. Some people ____ comfortable in an office.
37. I ____ a very good worker.
38. As a young man, my grandfather ____ an entrepreneur.
39. Long ago, he and his brother ____ partners.
40. My future career ____ still unknown.

Writing Connection

Writer's Journal: Listen and Write Do you know someone who has an interesting job? Talk to the person about his or her job. Ask questions such as these: "What is a regular workday like? How and when did you choose your work? What kind of training did you need?" Take careful notes as you listen to the person's answers. Use your notes to write about the person's job in your Writer's Journal. Use specific verbs.

Chapter Review

Read the passage and choose the word that belongs in each space. Write the letter for your answer.

> Many interesting jobs __(1)__ available in the visual and performing arts. Workers in the arts __(2)__ thoughts and feelings through their creative efforts. Photography __(3)__ one of the visual arts. Visual artists __(4)__ beautiful things for people to enjoy. For some people, acting __(5)__ a good career choice. Dance, music, and theater __(6)__ performing arts. They __(7)__ as popular in ancient times as they are today. The theater __(8)__ popular long before the invention of movies and television.

STANDARDIZED
TEST PREP

TIP Read a fill-in-the-blank sentence all the way through before thinking of an answer. Then try to think of an answer. See whether your answer is one of the choices.

1 A be
　B am
　C are
　D is

2 F become
　G grow
　H appear
　J express

3 A were
　B is
　C are
　D been

4 F seem
　G creates
　H make
　J are

5 A be
　B make
　C is
　D been

6 F is
　G be
　H am
　J are

7 A been
　B was
　C were
　D is

8 F was
　G are
　H am
　J were

For additional test preparation, visit *The Learning Site:*

Prefixes and Suffixes

A prefix is a word part added to the beginning of a base word. A suffix is a word part added to the end of a base word. Prefixes and suffixes change the meaning of the base word. A suffix almost always changes a word's part of speech, too. Knowing the parts of a word can help you understand its meaning.

Examples: non- ("not") + fiction = nonfiction ("not fiction")
fix + -able ("capable of") = fixable ("capable of being fixed")

Study the examples in this chart.

Prefix	Base Word	Suffix	New Word
pre- ("before")	view		preview
out- ("greater, better")	run		outrun
un- ("not")	able		unable
	happy sad	-ness ("state of being")	happiness sadness
	quiet lucky	-ly ("in a certain way")	quietly luckily
	bright	-en ("to make")	brighten

YOUR TURN

WORD MIXTURE Use the prefixes, suffixes, and base words below to build as many words as you can. Remember that the spelling of the base word may change when you add a suffix.

TIP Check that all of your combinations are real words by looking them up in a dictionary.

Prefixes
in-, un-, out-, pre-, over-, co-

Base Words
active, confident, happy, live, decided, pay, achieve, do, exist

Suffixes
-ness, -able, -en, -ly, -less

131

Vocabulary Power

in•au•gu•ra•tion
[i•nô′gyə•rā′shən] *n.*
A ceremony installing
a person in an office.

Verb Phrases

When a verb includes two or more words, it is called a verb phrase.

You know that a verb is a word or words that express action or being. A verb phrase is a verb in which two or more words work together.

Examples:

Citizens **are voting** for the next President.

They **will cast** their votes for President on Tuesday.

Voters **must go** to their assigned voting location.

Sometimes the words in a verb phrase are separated. In a question, the subject often comes between words in the verb phrase. The negative *not* can also come between words in a verb phrase.

Sentence	Verb Phrase
Do the candidates **plan** to debate?	Do plan
Some people **will** not **see** it.	will see

Guided Practice

A. Identify the verb phrase in each sentence.

Example: Voting has always been an important part of citizenship. *has been*

1. We have been learning about the election process.
2. U.S. voters have always voted by secret ballot.
3. Each citizen over the age of eighteen can vote.
4. The candidates must explain their ideas to the voters.
5. Voters must get information about the candidates.
6. Each person will vote for his or her preferred candidate.
7. The President's inauguration will happen in January.
8. Our teacher has assigned homework about past Presidents.
9. Students are researching on the Internet.
10. Our school is not holding a mock election this year.

Independent Practice

B. Write the verb phrase in each sentence.

> **Example:** We have learned about President Theodore Roosevelt.
> *have learned*

11. In the late 1800s, the United States was becoming a world power.
12. Theodore Roosevelt had become President in 1901.
13. Before that, he had been governor of New York State.
14. He had worked as a rancher in the Dakota Territory.
15. People are still quoting his words about foreign policy.
16. Roosevelt had also made a name for himself as a nature lover.
17. During his presidency, he had created 150 national forests.
18. He was supporting other causes as well.
19. Roosevelt's efforts did help farmers and business owners.
20. Americans have not forgotten his contributions.
21. Voters can choose members of Congress.
22. Many people are listening to the speeches of candidates.
23. The writers of the Constitution have created a separation of powers.
24. The legislative branch can pass new laws.
25. Selecting federal judges might not be an easy job for any President.

Remember

that a **verb phrase** is two or more words that express action or being.

Writing Connection

Writer's Craft: Action Verbs Imagine you are a news reporter at the scene of an exciting event. Write a few sentences to tell what is happening—for example, *The helicopter is landing on top of the building.* Use several verb phrases with action verbs.

Main Verbs and Helping Verbs

The main verb is the most important verb in a verb phrase. A helping verb works with the main verb to tell about an action.

You know that the words in a verb phrase work together as the simple predicate of a sentence. The helping verb comes before the main verb.

Example:
Congress **has passed** many laws.

Helping Verbs	Usually with this Main Verb Ending	Example
am, is, are, was, were	*ing* ending	Tina **was** help**ing** her grandmother.
have, has, had	*ed* ending	I **have** help**ed** her.
do, does, did, can, could, will, would, should, must	no change in the verb	Rishi **will** help his grandfather.

Sometimes other words, such as *not*, *always*, or *never*, come between a helping verb and a main verb.

Example:
The Supreme Court **has** not always **had** nine justices.

Guided Practice

A. **Identify the verb phrase in each sentence. Tell which verb is the main verb.**

Example: The Supreme Court has made many important decisions. *has made, made*

1. Courts do not decide all legal questions.
2. A law must not conflict with the Constitution.
3. The court can reject a law.
4. How does it do this?
5. The court has played an important role in our government.

Independent Practice

B. Write each sentence. Underline each verb phrase. Circle each main verb.

> **Example:** Court justices have made important legal decisions.
> *Court justices <u>have</u> (made) important legal decisions.*

6. Can the President appoint anyone to the Supreme Court?
7. Yes, but the person must win approval by the Senate.
8. Have you heard of Justice Sandra Day O'Connor?
9. She had been a state senator in Arizona.
10. Usually the President will choose someone with a career in law.

C. Choose the helping verb in parentheses that best completes the verb phrase. Write the sentences. Underline the verb phrase.

> **Example:** All courts in the United States (must, have) follow decisions of the Supreme Court.
> *All courts in the United States <u>must follow</u> decisions of the Supreme Court.*

11. This requirement (is, can) provide equal justice.
12. Even the Supreme Court usually (will, may have) follow its past decisions.
13. The court (has, does) not review every legal question.
14. It (will, have) accept only cases about important issues.
15. At least four of the nine justices (are, must) agree to hear a case.

Writing Connection

Social Studies Work with a partner to role-play an interview with a famous President, such as George Washington or Abraham Lincoln. (You might need to find out more about some important events in the person's life.) Write down some of your questions and answers. Use helping verbs as needed to make your meaning clear. Identify the ones you used.

USAGE AND MECHANICS

Contractions with *Not*

A **contraction** is the shortened form of two words.
The negative *not* is often combined with a verb in a
contraction.

The verb that is combined with *not* is often a helping
verb in a verb phrase.

Example:
Without George Washington, the United States **wouldn't** be
what it is today. [The verb phrase is *would be*.]

Notice that one of the contractions below, *won't*, involves a
change in the spelling of the verb. In all the contractions, an
apostrophe takes the place of the *o* in *not*.

Common Contractions	
is + not = isn't	are + not = aren't
does + not = doesn't	do + not = don't
has + not = hasn't	have + not = haven't
can + not = can't	could + not = couldn't
will + not = won't	would + not = wouldn't

Guided Practice

A. Identify the contraction and the verb phrase in
each sentence.

Example: Washington didn't receive much formal education.
didn't, The verb phrase is *did receive.*

1. Washington's mother wouldn't send him to England
for schooling.
2. After age fifteen, Washington wasn't attending
school.
3. His abilities didn't go to waste, however.
4. He hadn't received any military training, but he
asked for a place in the army.
5. Washington wouldn't shrink from hardship or
danger.

Independent Practice

B. Write the contraction in each sentence. Underline the verb that was combined with *not* in each contraction.

> **Example:** Washington hadn't campaigned for the office of President, but he was elected. *hadn't*

6. Washington served in the colonial legislature, but we don't believe that he made many speeches.
7. He hadn't been there long before he met Patrick Henry and Thomas Jefferson.
8. He learned that he couldn't pass laws without patience.
9. He wasn't neglecting his home life during this time.
10. He wouldn't give up his time with his stepchildren and his wife, Martha.

C. Rewrite each sentence. Use the contraction that is formed from the words in parentheses.

> **Example:** We (can not) imagine how our country would have managed without George Washington.
> *We can't imagine how our country would have managed without George Washington.*

11. He (did not) take much part in the debate over the new government.
12. At the convention, however, he (would not) let the delegates give up.
13. Washington (was not) sure that he should accept the presidency.
14. The other candidates, however, (had not) won nearly as many votes.
15. The people's choice (could not) have been wiser.

> **Remember**
> that verbs can be combined with the negative *not* to form **contractions**. Most of these contractions are spelled by replacing the *o* in *not* with an apostrophe.

Writing Connection

Technology: Sending E-Mail Figure out how to send e-mail to the White House or to a state or local government office. Then write directions to explain the process to a classmate. You might also give some advice. Include at least one example of what *not* to do and why. Use negative contractions where possible.

Extra Practice

A. Write the verb phrase in each sentence. *pages 132–133*

Example: George Washington had been a military man
before he became President. *had been*

1. Before his presidency, Dwight Eisenhower had pursued a military career.
2. Early in his career, "Ike" Eisenhower had shown great skill with people.
3. He had led people from different nations.
4. In 1948, he had taken a position as a university president.
5. He did not yet feel ready for politics.
6. Two years later, he had returned to the military.
7. He was doing a different job this time.
8. Eisenhower still was enjoying great popularity.
9. To his political party, he would be the perfect candidate.
10. He would win two terms as President easily.

B. Write each sentence below. Underline each verb phrase. Circle each main verb. *pages 134–135*

Example: James Earl "Jimmy" Carter has been a successful
farmer as well as a politician.
*James Earl "Jimmy" Carter has (been) a successful
farmer as well as a politician.*

11. Carter had dreamed of a naval career.
12. In 1942, he was starting his naval career.
13. He soon had chosen submarine duty.
14. In 1953, Carter was doing well in the navy.
15. His family was asking for his help with the family farm in Georgia, however.
16. Before long, he had left the navy.
17. The family farm and business were growing quickly under Carter's management.
18. People were encouraging Carter's interest in the field of politics.
19. By 1962 his political career in the Georgia state senate had begun.
20. Fourteen years later, the voters would elect him President.

Remember

that the most
important word in a
verb phrase is the
main verb. Other
words in the verb
phrase are helping
verbs.

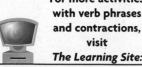

For more activities
with verb phrases
and contractions,
visit
The Learning Site:
www.harcourtschool.com

C. Rewrite each sentence. Use the contraction that is formed from the words in parentheses. *pages 136–137*

Example: Historians (can not) ignore Woodrow Wilson.
Historians can't ignore Woodrow Wilson.

21. He (was not) just a champion of world peace.
22. As president of Princeton University, he (did not) shrink from change.
23. Wilson (could not) push through all his ideas.
24. It (is not) surprising that he left to work in politics.
25. His years at Princeton (were not) a handicap.
26. Without his powerful speeches, he (would not) have been elected governor of New Jersey.
27. He (had not) been governor long before he ran for President.
28. At his inauguration, Wilson saw that people (were not) allowed near him.
29. Wilson (did not) want the people held back.
30. Many of his ideas (have not) lost their importance.

D. Rewrite each sentence, correcting the errors.
pages 136–137

31. Before 1920, most women still could'nt vote.
32. Presidents and members of Congress didnt' think the issue was important.
33. Women such as Elizabeth Cady Stanton and Susan B. Anthony hadnt given up.
34. U.S. history woul'dnt be the same without Stanton and Anthony.
35. Their efforts wont' be forgotten.

Writing Connection

Writer's Journal: Writing Ideas Brainstorm a list of things you know how to do or make. Exchange lists with a partner. Choose two topics on your partner's list that you would be interested in reading about. Write a few sentences to explain your choices to your partner. Use helping verbs as needed to make your meaning clear. Be sure to put apostrophes in any contractions you use.

Chapter Review

For Numbers 1, 2, and 3, find the word or words that best complete the sentence.

1 Next month, the people of our community ＿＿＿ a new mayor.

    A were electing   **C** will elect

    B had elected   **D** did elect

2 We ＿＿＿ the issues, and we have chosen the best candidate.

    F will study   **H** are studying

    G have studied   **J** is studying

3 The city's fire and police services ＿＿＿ important issues lately.

    A becoming   **C** have become

    B will become   **D** are become

For Numbers 4, 5, and 6, find the words that best complete the sentences.

Leaders in a city or county __(4)__ for today and tomorrow. They __(5)__, for example, whether to fix the roads this year or next year. The roads __(6)__ in good condition for drivers.

4 **F** does always plan
    G has always planned
    H was always planning
    J are always planning

5 **A** were decided
    B has decided
    C have decided
    D must decide

6 **F** has been
    G should be
    H are being
    J did been

STANDARDIZED
TEST PREP

TIP Remember that you can usually recognize mistakes in grammar when you hear them. Say each choice to yourself before choosing the answer.

For additional test preparation, visit *The Learning Site:*
www.harcourtschool.com

Using Encyclopedias and Periodicals

Encyclopedias and periodicals are sources of information that you use to find facts about a subject. Periodicals are publications that appear monthly, weekly, or daily. They include magazines and newspapers.

An **encyclopedia** is a good place to start if you have a broad or general topic. It is organized alphabetically. An encyclopedia also has an index that lists all the topics alphabetically. Some encyclopedias come in computer versions. On the computer, you can do a **key word search**. The computer uses key words to find articles that are related to your topic.

For narrower topics, especially current events, you may not find information in an encyclopedia. **Magazines** and **newspapers** are good resources for topics about current events. There are guides to periodicals that list articles by subject. Computerized guides are organized like a card catalog. If your library does not have a computerized guide, you may use a printed guide.

Each listing in a guide to periodicals gives the following information about an article: title, author, source (title of newspaper or magazine), date, volume, and page numbers. Ask a librarian to help you find the articles you need.

YOUR TURN

RESEARCHING On a sheet of paper, write each of the topics below. List your best guess about where to find information on each topic. Then go to the library and check your guesses.

- **Abigail Adams**
- **a review of a new movie**
- **the Declaration of Independence**
- **the Library of Congress**

TIP Different reference materials have different purposes. When you are looking for information, try more than one reference source. If you need help finding the right source, ask a librarian.

In this novel excerpt, Laura Ingalls Wilder tells what one family had to do to complete the fall cleaning. As you read, think about how she describes the steps of the job.

LITTLE TOWN
ON THE
PRAIRIE

by Laura Ingalls Wilder
illustrated by Garth Williams

Laura Ingalls Wilder described the frontier life she lived with her family in the series known as the Little House books. In this scene, Laura's parents have left to take older sister Mary to college in a wagon driven by a neighbor boy. This leaves Laura in charge of her younger sisters.

They stood there in their own house and felt nothing around them but silence and emptiness. Mary was gone.

Grace began to cry again, and two large tears stood in Carrie's eyes. This would never do. Right now, and for a whole week, everything was in Laura's charge, and Ma must be able to depend on her.

"Listen to me, Carrie and Grace," she said briskly. "We are going to clean this house from top to bottom, and we'll begin right now! When Ma comes home, she'll find the fall housecleaning done."

How-to Essay

There had never been such a busy time in all Laura's life. The work was hard, too. She had not realized how heavy a quilt is, to lift soaked and dripping from a tub, and to wring out, and to hang on a line. She had not known how hard it would be, sometimes, never to be cross with Grace who was always trying to help and only making more work. It was amazing, too, how dirty they all got, while cleaning a house that had seemed quite clean. The harder they worked, the dirtier everything became.

The worst day of all was very hot. They had tugged and lugged the straw ticks outdoors, and emptied them and washed them, and when they were dry they had filled them with sweet fresh hay. They had got the bedsprings off the bedsteads and leaned them against the walls, and Laura had jammed her finger. Now they were pulling the bedsteads apart. Laura jerked at one corner and Carrie jerked at the other. The corners came apart, and suddenly the headboard came down on Laura's head so that she saw stars.

"Oh, Laura! Did it hurt you?" Carrie cried.

"Well, not very much," Laura said. She pushed the headboard against the wall, and it slid down swiftly and hit her anklebone. "Ouch!" she couldn't help yelling. Then she added, "Let it lie there if it wants to!"

"We have to scrub the floor," Carrie pointed out.

"I know we have to," Laura said grimly. She sat on the floor, gripping her ankle. Her straggling hair stuck to her sweating neck. Her dress was damp and hot and dirty, and her fingernails were positively black. Carrie's face was smudged with dust and sweat, and there were bits of hay in her hair.

"We ought to have a bath," Laura murmured. Suddenly she cried out, *"Where's Grace?"*

They had not thought of Grace for some time. Grace had once been lost on the prairie. Two children at Brookins, lost on the prairie, had died before they could be found.

"Here I yam," Grace answered sweetly, coming in. "It's raining."

"No!" Laura exclaimed. Indeed, a shadow was over the house. A few large drops were falling. At that moment, thunder crashed. Laura screamed, "Carrie! The straw ticks! The bedding!"

They ran. The straw ticks were not very heavy, but they were stuffed fat with hay. They were hard to hold on to. The edge kept slipping out of Laura's grasp or Carrie's. When they got one to the house, they had to hold it up edgewise to get it through the doorway.

"We can hold it up or we can move it. We can't do both," Carrie panted. Already the swift thunderstorm was rolling overhead, and rain was falling fast.

"Get out of the way!" Laura shouted. Somehow she pushed and carried the whole straw tick into the house. It was too late to bring in the other one, or the bedding from the line. Rain was pouring down.

The bedding would dry on the line, but the other straw tick must be emptied again, washed again, and filled again. Straw ticks must be perfectly dry, or the hay in them would smell musty.

"We can move everything out of the other bedroom into the front room, and go on scrubbing," said Laura. So they did that.

For some time there was no sound but thunder and beating rain, and the swish of scrubbing cloths and the wringing out. Laura and Carrie had worked backward on hands and knees almost across the bedroom floor, when Grace called happily, "I'm helping!"

She was standing on a chair and blacking the stove. She was splashed from head to foot with blacking. On the floor all around the stove were dribbles and splotches of blacking. Grace had filled the blacking box full of water. As she looked up beaming for Laura's approval, she gave the smeared stove top another swipe of the blacking cloth, and pushed the box of soft blacking off it.

Her blue eyes were filled with tears.

Laura gave one wild look at that awful house that Ma had left so neat and pretty. She just managed to say, "Never mind, Grace; don't cry. I'll clean it up." Then she sank down on the stacked pieces of the bedsteads and let her forehead sink to her pulled-up knees.

"Oh Carrie, I just don't seem to know how to manage the way Ma does!" she almost wailed.

That was the worst day. On Friday the house was almost in order, and they worried lest Ma come home too soon. They worked far into the night that night, and on Saturday it was almost midnight before Laura and Carrie took their baths and collapsed to sleep. Sunday the house was immaculate.

Analyze THE Model

1. What difficulties do Laura and Carrie have in doing the housecleaning?

2. In what kind of order did Laura Ingalls Wilder tell about the parts of the job?

3. How does the reader know the steps needed to complete each part?

READING — WRITING CONNECTION

Parts of a How-to Essay

Laura Ingalls Wilder described how to clean a house in the time and place that Laura and her family lived. Read this how-to essay, written by a student named Pablo. Look carefully for the parts of the essay.

MODEL

Stamp Collecting

introduction of topic

If you are looking for an interesting hobby, you might find it right in your mailbox. Stamp collecting is popular all over the world. You can learn about different countries, famous people, and special events from the pictures on stamps. It is easy to start your own collection.

step 1

First, think about what kind of stamps you would like to collect. There are hundreds of new stamps each year. You can collect one country's stamps or stamps with a favorite theme. For

details

example, you might collect stamps about all kinds of transportation or about one kind, such as ships.

step 2

Next, get a few simple materials. You will need a stamp album and some stamp hinges, special papers with glue to attach stamps

materials

to the album's pages. You won't damage your stamps if you handle them with tweezers, and a magnifying glass will

transition

help you look at details. Now you are ready to start collecting.

146

Finally, here are ways to obtain stamps. One source is the post office. Check the display area for new stamps. You can also look in travel magazines or on the Internet for stamp offers. You can buy packets or bags containing many different stamps to sort through. Don't forget to tell your friends, neighbors, and family members that you are a stamp collector. They can give you stamps from the mail they receive.

Now that you know how to begin, you can start anytime. Stamp collecting is a fascinating hobby that can take you on a trip across the United States or around the world.

step 3

details

conclusion

Analyze THE Model

1. What is the purpose of Pablo's essay?

2. How does Pablo use details to explain how to collect stamps?

3. Would you put the steps in the same order as Pablo did? Why or why not?

Summarize THE Model

Use a graphic organizer like the one shown here to explain how to start a stamp collection. Write the topic sentences. Leave out the details. Then write a summary of Pablo's how-to essay.

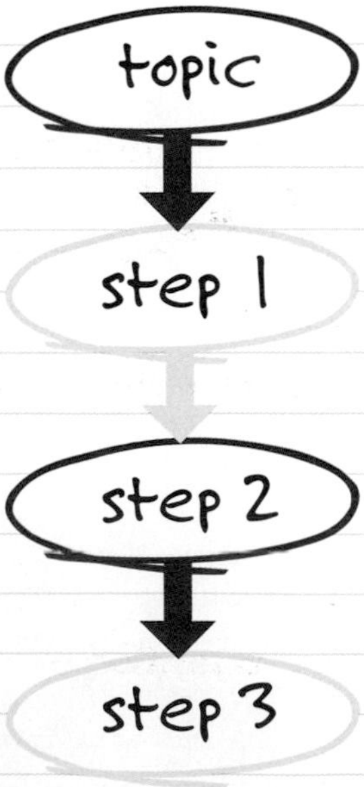

topic

↓

step 1

↓

step 2

↓

step 3

Writer's Craft

Paragraphing Pablo put his paragraphs in time-order sequence. Tell why this is important in a how-to essay. List the time-order words Pablo uses. Then list the transition sentences or phrases in the essay.

Prewriting

Purpose and Audience

Think of new activities or hobbies that you or your friends might enjoy. In this chapter, you will explain how your classmates can begin a new activity or hobby.

WRITING PROMPT Write a how-to essay telling your classmates how to start a new hobby or activity. State your topic in the introduction, and list all the steps. Include details and examples to explain the steps.

Begin by thinking about your purpose, audience, and topic. What would you like to tell your classmates about? What do you know how to do that not everyone knows about?

MODEL

Pablo began by thinking of something he could teach someone to do. He decided to explain to his classmates how to start a stamp collection. He made this chart to organize his thoughts.

Purpose: to explain how to start a stamp collection
Audience: my classmates

Topic: Stamp collecting is an interesting hobby.

Steps: 1. Decide what kind to collect.
2. Get the materials you need.
3. Obtain stamps from different sources.

YOUR TURN

Choose an activity that you can teach someone. Use a chart to organize your ideas.

Organization and Elaboration

Follow these steps to help you organize your essay.

STEP 1 Grab Your Audience's Attention
Introduce your topic in an interesting way. Tell why your audience might want to try the activity.

STEP 2 Tell What Materials Are Needed
List all materials and equipment needed. Explain items that may be unfamiliar to your audience.

STEP 3 Describe Each Step in a Paragraph
Look at the chart you made. Turn each step into a topic sentence for a separate paragraph. Then add details and examples to help explain the topic sentence.

STEP 4 Write a Concluding Paragraph
Restate your topic. Tell your audience that now they can try the activity.

MODEL

Here is the beginning of Pablo's draft of his essay. How does he get his audience's interest? What does he include in his introductory paragraph?

> *If you are looking for an interesting hobby, you might find it right in your mailbox. Stamp collecting is popular all over the world. You can learn about different countries, famous people, and special events from the pictures on stamps. It is easy to start your own collection.*

YOUR TURN

Now draft your essay. Follow the steps above. Reread your prewriting notes. Use Pablo's essay as a model.

Strategies Good Writers Use

- Introduce your topic in an interesting way.
- Present the steps in order.
- Make each step a topic sentence.
- Include details to explain each step.

 Go to the drop-down Format menu and choose Paragraph. Change your draft to double line spacing so that you will have enough room to mark changes.

Revising

Organization and Elaboration

Begin editing your essay by rereading it carefully.

- Have I listed all the materials that are needed?
- Are my paragraphs in the most logical order? Did I include time-order words?
- Have I included details that do not support the topic sentence? Do I need to delete anything?
- How well have I kept my audience in mind? Is there anything they might not be able to do or understand?

Strategies Good Writers Use

- Take out words that don't support the topic.
- Use transitions between paragraphs.
- Ask another writer to suggest improvements.

 You can use the button for bullets or numbers if you want to list materials separately.

MODEL

Here is part of Pablo's essay. Notice that he took out information that did not support the topic. He also added a time-order word and a detail.

First
^ Think about what kind of stamps you would like to collect. There are hundreds of new stamps each year. ~~I collect stamps with pictures of places in the United States.~~ You can collect ~~one country's~~ stamps ~~or stamps~~ with a favorite theme. For example, you might collect stamps about all kinds of transportation or about one kind. ^such as ships

YOUR TURN

Revise your essay to make sure that your paragraphs have topic sentences and supporting details that explain each step. Add time-order words if needed.

Checking Your Language

When you proofread, look for mistakes in grammar, spelling, punctuation, and capitalization. If you do not correct these errors, readers may find your instructions unclear or confusing.

MODEL

Here is another part of Pablo's essay. After he revised his essay, he proofread it. Look at how Pablo corrected a possessive noun. What other errors did he correct?

> Next, get a few simple materials. You
> will need a stamp album and some
> stamp hinjes. ~~Special~~ papers with glue to
>   *hinges*
> ~~attech~~ stamps to the album's pages. You
> *attach*
> won't damage your stamps if you handle
> them with tweezers, and a magnifyng
> glass will help you look at detales. Now
>   *details*
> you are ready to start collecting.

YOUR TURN

Proofread your revised essay several times. Look for one type of error each time:
- errors in grammar
- errors in spelling
- errors in punctuation and capitalization

Trade essays with a classmate and proofread each other's work.

Strategies Good Writers Use

- Check for capitalization of proper nouns.
- Check for correct usage of the verb _be_.
- Check for apostrophes in possessive nouns.

Editor's Marks

ℐ	delete text
∧	insert text
⌒	move text
¶	new paragraph
≡	capitalize
/	lowercase
○	correct spelling

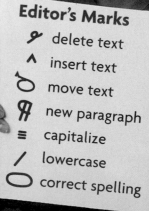

How-to Essay

Publishing

Sharing Your Work

Now you will publish your how-to essay. Answer these questions to help you decide on the best way to share your work:

1. Who is your audience? What is the best way to publish your essay so that your audience will see or hear it?

2. Should you write your essay in cursive or print it in manuscript? If your audience is your classmates, you should write in cursive. If you are writing to teach something to younger children, you would choose manuscript so that they could read it. If you are using a word processor, you might use a larger type size for younger readers than for older ones.

3. Are there diagrams or illustrations that you can add to make your essay easier to understand?

4. Should you read your essay aloud? Use the information for speakers on page 153.

USING YOUR
Handbook

- Use the rubric on page 507 to evaluate your essay.

Reflecting on Your Writing

Using Your Portfolio What did you learn in this chapter about your writing? Write your answer to each question below.

1. Do you think your essay fulfilled its purpose? Explain your answer.

2. Use the rubric in your Handbook to evaluate your writing. How would you score it? What things made it strong? What things made it weak?

Add your written answers and your essay to your portfolio. Then review your portfolio. Write a sentence that tells what you think is the strongest part of your writing. Then set a goal for making your writing better.

Listening to Follow Directions

After Pablo finished his essay, he decided to read it aloud. He knew that his classmates would have to listen carefully to learn about the topic. Here are some tips for listening to follow directions:

☑ Focus your attention on the speaker's words. Don't let your mind wander.

☑ Identify the topic. Think of what you already know about it.

☑ Identify the main ideas or steps. Listen for time-order words, short pauses, or transition sentences that signal a new idea or step.

☑ Keep track of the order of the steps. If possible, take notes to remember each step and when it should be done.

☑ Identify the details that support each main idea. Listen for descriptive words or specific examples.

☑ If something is not clear, make a note to ask about it. Wait until the speaker is finished before you ask questions.

Strategies for Listening and Speaking

When you are the speaker, use these strategies to make your presentation clear and effective:

• Practice reading your essay.

• Speak clearly and loudly.

• Make eye contact with your audience.

• Ask for questions when you finish.

Common and Proper Nouns *pages 94–95*

A. Write each sentence. Draw one line under each common noun and two lines under each proper noun.

1. Four northern American colonies were called New England.
2. Roger Williams founded Rhode Island, which was a part of that group.
3. The colony called Georgia was in the southern region.
4. James Oglethorpe started the colony of Georgia.
5. The middle region included New York and Pennsylvania.

Singular and Plural Nouns *pages 96–97*

B. Write each noun. Write *singular, plural,* or *both* next to it. Then write the plural form of each singular noun.

6. colony
7. cattle
8. forest
9. deer
10. child
11. turkey
12. fish
13. potatoes
14. ox
15. mouse

Abbreviations *pages 98–99*

C. Write the correct abbreviation for each of the following words.

16. second
17. Tuesday
18. February
19. Avenue
20. Doctor

Singular Possessive Nouns pages 104–105

A. Write each sentence. Change the underlined group of words to a phrase that contains a singular possessive noun.

1. The colonists were not prepared for the <u>extreme cold of winter</u>.
2. The <u>wind of the snowstorm</u> howled all afternoon.
3. The <u>surface of the pond</u> froze overnight.
4. In the cold air, the children could see the <u>breath of the horse.</u>
5. A woman stored the <u>food of the family</u> in a root cellar.
6. A man fixed the <u>broken runner of the sled</u>.
7. The <u>roof of the cabin</u> needed repair.
8. The <u>branches of the tree</u> were gathered for firewood.
9. The family enjoyed the <u>warmth of the fire</u>.
10. They talked about the <u>work of the day</u>.

Plural Possessive Nouns pages 106–107

B. Read each sentence. If the plural possessive noun is used correctly, write *correct*. If the plural possessive noun is incorrect, write the sentence using the correct form.

11. The animals' work on the farm was important.
12. The oxens strength was useful to the farmer.
13. The children enjoyed drinking the goats milk.
14. The settlers' cats kept their houses free of rats.
15. The children checked the chickens nests for eggs.

Apostrophes in Possessive Nouns

pages 108–109

C. Choose the correct form of the noun in parentheses. Write the sentence.

16. Some (colonist's, colonists') houses were made of logs.
17. All of the (settlers, settlers') fields were planted.
18. The (farmer's, farmers) friends helped him fix his barn.
19. They repaired the (barns', barn's) leaking roof.
20. One (carpenters, carpenter's) skills came in handy.

Unit 2
Grammar Review

CHAPTER 10

Action Verbs
and Linking
Verbs

pages 122–131

Action Verbs *pages 122–123*

A. Write each sentence. Underline each action verb.

1. Most people worked in their own homes before the Industrial Revolution.
2. People took jobs in factories.
3. Workers made cloth in textile factories.
4. Francis Cabot Lowell built a textile factory in Waltham, Massachusetts.
5. Workers spun cotton thread on large machines.
6. Henry Ford started the assembly line in his automobile factories.
7. Workers in factories labored long hours.
8. They wanted shorter hours and better pay.
9. Today computers do some of the work in factories.
10. Some factories even have robots for certain jobs.

Linking Verbs *pages 124–125*

B. Write each sentence. Underline each linking verb. Draw an arrow from the subject to the word in the predicate that renames or describes the subject.

11. Mr. Wilson was young when he chose his career.
12. He became a teacher at an early age.
13. Our teacher seems happy to see us each morning.
14. We are pleased to see him, too.
15. I grew curious about teaching because of Mr. Wilson.

Using Forms of the Verb *Be* *pages 126–127*

C. Write each sentence with the correct form of the verb *be*.

16. My grandparents _____ teachers before I was born.
17. My grandfather _____ a history teacher before he retired.
18. My mother _____ a teacher, too.
19. Some of her students _____ soccer players.
20. I _____ a fifth grader this year.

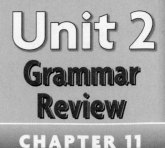

Verb Phrases *pages 132–133*

A. Copy each sentence. Underline the verb phrase.

1. People had known little about Abraham Lincoln before his election as President.
2. His parents were living in Kentucky before Abraham's birth.
3. They would move to Indiana in 1816.
4. There they could buy land directly from the government.
5. They must build a cabin immediately.
6. By the time Lincoln was fourteen, he had not spent much time in school.
7. On the frontier, people could not find paper and books easily.
8. Lincoln was always borrowing books to read.
9. He would walk long distances for books.
10. He did say that *Life of Washington* inspired him.

Main Verbs and Helping Verbs

pages 134–135

B. Write each sentence. Underline each main verb once. Underline each helping verb twice.

11. What have you heard about the new community center?
12. Teams will play basketball there.
13. The center will not open until spring.
14. The mayor has talked about it on television.
15. I must learn more about the new center.

Contractions with *Not* *pages 136–137*

C. Write each sentence. Include the contraction that is formed from the words in parentheses.

16. My grandmother (is not) qualified to run for President of the United States.
17. She (was not) born in this country.
18. She (did not) come here until she was twelve.
19. (Would not) it be fun to be the President's grandchild?
20. I (can not) imagine what that would be like!

A Colonial Scene

How was life in colonial times different than it is today? Work with a group to find out. Then act out a scene from colonial daily life for your class. The steps below will help you.

Research Your Topic

- Review what you have learned about colonial life in this unit.

- Do an Internet search on colonial life in North America. Also check the card catalog for books on the subject.

- Ask some questions as you read:

  - Where did colonial people live? What were their homes like?

  - What was school like?

  - What jobs did people do?

  - How was life different for men and for women?

  - What kinds of clothes did people wear?

Write and Publish a Report

- With a group, pick several questions from the list above. Write a report that answers the questions.

- Download or copy pictures to illustrate your report.

- Bind your report and display it in your classroom.

Practice and Perform a Scene from Colonial Life

- Use the information you learned about colonial life to write a scene.

- Decide where your scene takes place and what parts to play. Draw a setting on the board and find or make simple props. Practice acting out your parts.

- Perform your part for the class. Tell them who you are, what you are doing, and other important facts about your life.

Ben and Me
by Robert Lawson

HISTORICAL FICTION

The many adventures of Benjamin Franklin
are told by Amos, a mouse who shares
Ben's home.

Lewis Carroll Shelf Award

Ride of Courage
by Deborah Felder

HISTORICAL FICTION

Molly must overcome her fear of her
neighbor's huge Arabian horse in order to
warn the local patriot soldiers that the British
soldiers are landing.

Shh! We're Writing the Constitution
by Jean Fritz

NONFICTION

Writing the Constitution for the United States
wasn't an easy job, and those chosen to write it
had many important issues to talk about.

ALA Notable Book

Four Types of Sentences *pages 24–29*

Write each sentence, and add the correct end punctuation. Then write *declarative*, *interrogative*, *imperative*, or *exclamatory*.

1. What do you know about totem poles
2. A totem pole is a carved and painted wooden post
3. Please show me a picture of a totem pole
4. How beautiful the carved animals on the totem pole are
5. Native American artists made this totem pole long ago

Subjects and Predicates *pages 34–39, 52–57*

Write each sentence. Draw one line under the complete subject and two lines under the complete predicate. Then circle the simple subject and the simple predicate, or verb.

6. A violin is a small, wooden musical instrument.
7. Three parts of a violin are the bridge, the strings, and the neck.
8. Miguel carefully removed his violin from its case.
9. The boy played his favorite musical composition.
10. Clear musical notes slowly filled the room.
11. Kirstin quietly listened to the music.
12. Some famous makers of violins lived in Italy.
13. These skilled people carved each piece of the instruments by hand.
14. The shiny brass trumpet is another musical instrument.
15. I play two other instruments.

Simple and Compound Sentences

pages 62–67

Write the compound sentences, and circle the conjunction that joins the two main parts of the sentence. If the item is a simple sentence, write *simple sentence*.

16. Maria can draw pictures, and she can print fancy letters.
17. This student wants to be a commercial artist.
18. These people study art, but they also learn about business.
19. That student will become a cartoonist, or he will design toys.
20. Movie studios and book companies hire commercial artists.

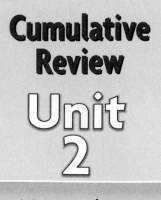
Nouns *pages 94–99*

List the nouns in each sentence. Write whether each noun is *common* or *proper* and *singular* or *plural*.

1. Mr. Jones drove his family to Williamsburg.
2. This city in Virginia is famous for its colonial houses and gardens.
3. Tourists can learn how a colonist from Great Britain lived.
4. Mrs. Jones and the children saw cabinetmakers, silversmiths, and a weaver.
5. Famous Virginians, like Patrick Henry and George Washington, visited this settlement.

Possessive Nouns *pages 104–109*

If each possessive noun in a sentence is used correctly, write *correct*. If a possessive noun is incorrect, write the sentence, using the correct form.

6. On the books' cover are pictures of colonists' clothes.
7. Mens' and boys' pants cover the upper legs and knees.
8. Mrs. Jones cape buttons at the neck and has a hood.
9. Captain Lewis' boots were made of leather.
10. A settler's diet usually included eggs and milk.

Verbs *pages 122–127, 132–137*

Write the verb or verb phrase in each sentence. Then write whether each verb is an action verb or a linking verb.

11. An astronaut travels on flights into space.
12. Most astronauts are scientists.
13. Space travelers should be very healthy.
14. Did you hear about Mae Jemison and Shannon Lucid?
15. These two women have flown on the space shuttle.
16. Dr. Lucid also lived in a space station for several months.
17. My uncle works in the space program.
18. Uncle Ted has not been able to go into space.
19. His job is important to the success of a space flight.
20. My uncle builds the spacecrafts' engines.

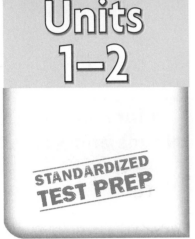
Language Use

Read the passage. Some sections are underlined. The underlined sections may be one of the following:

- Incomplete sentences
- Run-on sentences
- Correctly written sentences that should be combined
- Correctly written sentences that do not need to be rewritten

Choose the best way to write each underlined section and mark the letter for your answer. If the underlined section needs no change, mark the choice "Correct as is."

TIP A run-on sentence is two sentences with no punctuation between them.

Thomas Jefferson was born in Virginia in 1743. (1) Jefferson wrote the Declaration of Independence he also was the third President of the United States. This brilliant Virginian is famous for other reasons. (2) Jefferson designed his home, Monticello. Planned its gardens. Jefferson also founded the University of Virginia. (3) On his orders, the university accepted students who could not afford to pay. (4) In his spare time, Jefferson read books. Jefferson wrote letters and he invented things.

---

1 A Jefferson wrote the Declaration of Independence, and became President of the United States.

B Jefferson wrote the Declaration of Independence, he also was the third President of the United States.

C Jefferson wrote the Declaration of Independence. He also was the third President of the United States.

D Correct as is

2 F Jefferson designed his home, Monticello, he planned its gardens.

G Jefferson designed his home, Monticello, and he planned its gardens.

H Jefferson designed his home, Monticello, but he planned its gardens.

J Correct as is .

3 A On his orders, the university accepted students. Who could not afford to pay.

B On his orders. The university accepted students who could not afford to pay.

C On his orders, the university accepted students, but who could not afford to pay.

D Correct as is

4 F In his spare time, Jefferson read books, wrote letters, and invented things.

G In his spare time. Jefferson read, wrote letters, and invented things.

H In his spare time, Jefferson read books. Wrote letters and invented things.

J Correct as is

Written Expression

Read the paragraph. Then read the questions that follow the paragraph. Choose the correct answer. Write the letter of the answer you have chosen.

> The objects a potter makes include bowls, pitchers, and vases. Glassblowers also make vases. The potter's art is called pottery. Pottery is an ancient art form. The Egyptians made pottery thousands of years ago. So did the Chinese. Ancient potters formed their objects by hand. Many modern artists use a potter's wheel to help them shape objects. The first potters left objects in the sun to bake.

1 What is the purpose of this paragraph?

A to persuade

B to entertain

C to inform

D to give directions

2 Which of these would be the *best* topic sentence for this paragraph?

F Egyptians have always made fine pottery.

G A potter makes objects by shaping and baking clay.

H A potter's wheel is a useful invention.

J Bowls have many uses.

3 Which of these sentences does not belong in this paragraph?

A The Egyptians made pottery thousands of years ago.

B The potter's art is called pottery.

C The first potters left objects in the sun to bake.

D Glassblowers also make vases.

4 Which of these would go *best* after the last sentence in this paragraph?

F Later, potters learned to heat objects in special ovens, called kilns.

G Baking objects in the sun can be a long, slow process.

H Clay cups sometimes were made this way.

J Today businesses use machines to shape clay into objects.

5 How can sentences 5 and 6 of the paragraph *best* be combined?

A The Egyptians made pottery thousands of years ago, and so did the Chinese.

B The Egyptians and the Chinese made pottery thousands of years ago.

C The Egyptians made pottery thousands of years ago, but so did the Chinese.

D The Egyptians or the Chinese made pottery thousands of years ago.

Unit 3

Grammar More About Verbs

Writing Persuasive Writing

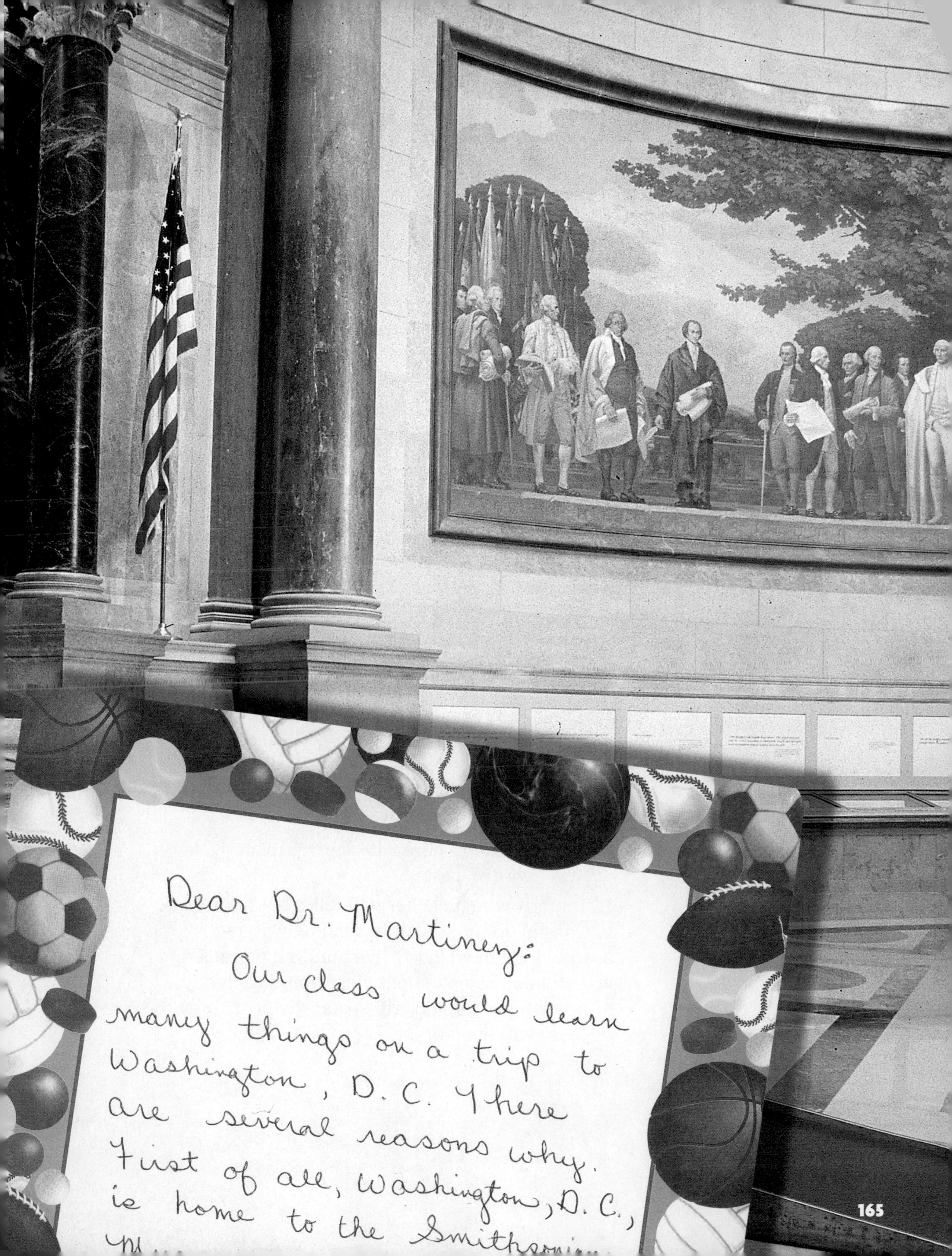

Dear Dr. Martinez:
	Our class would learn
many things on a trip to
Washington, D.C. There
are several reasons why.
First of all, Washington, D.C.,
is home to the Smithson...

Past, Present, and Future Tense

The **tense** of a verb shows the time of the action or state of being. There are three basic verb tenses: present tense, past tense, and future tense. These are called the **simple tenses**.

A verb in the present tense shows that an action is happening now or that it happens over and over. A verb in the past tense shows that an action happened at a definite time in the past. A verb in the future tense shows that the action will happen at a time yet to come.

Examples:	
Present Tense	Water **covers** much of the earth's surface.
Past Tense	Many changes in the oceans **happened** over time.
Future Tense	Scientists **will study** more forms of ocean life in coming years.

Guided Practice

A. **Identify each verb. Tell whether the verb is in the present tense, the past tense, or the future tense. Explain how you know.**

Example: I visited a huge saltwater aquarium.
visited, past

1. Tomorrow my teacher will talk about dolphins.
2. Coastal dolphins stay in shallow waters.
3. One dolphin weighed five hundred pounds.
4. A dolphin sleeps about eight hours each day.
5. A newborn dolphin will spend the next three to six years with its mother.

Vocabulary Power

a•quar•i•um
[ə•kwâr′ē•əm] *n.*
A building where a collection of water animals and plants is displayed.

Independent Practice

B. Write each sentence. Underline each verb and write its tense.

Example: The tides will carry food to some fish.
The tides will carry food to some fish.   future

6. High tide will return tomorrow.
7. Many interesting creatures live in the ocean.
8. Clams dwell on the ocean floor.
9. Clams filter tiny bits of food from the water.
10. This manta ray grew to a large size.
11. Water flows into the mouth of a manta ray.
12. Soon the water will pour out through slits.
13. The slits in the ray's head serve a special purpose.
14. Sharks swim at high speeds.
15. That shark hunted in shallow water.

C. Write each sentence. Use the verb and tense given.

Example: Explorers first _____ penguins in 1497. (_see_, past)
Explorers first saw penguins in 1497.

16. Eighteen kinds of penguins _____ in the Southern Hemisphere. (_live_, present)
17. Sailors once _____ penguins for food. (_hunt_, past)
18. The emperor penguin _____ almost four feet tall. (_stand_, present)
19. Many penguins _____ squid and fish. (_eat_, present)
20. Next year, scientists _____ the life cycle of the king penguin. (_study_, future)

Writing Connection

Writer's Journal: Amazing Facts Find an encyclopedia article on a form of ocean life. Look at how the present and past tenses are used in the article. Find interesting facts in the article, and write them in your Writer's Journal. (Be sure to include the source.) Identify the tenses in the sentences you wrote, and explain why you used these tenses.

that the tense of a verb tells you the time of its action—present, past, or future.

Present Tense

A present tense verb shows that an action is happening now or that it happens over and over.

When the subject of a present tense verb is *I, you,* or a plural word, the verb needs no ending:

Examples:

I **enjoy** my aquarium.

Many people **enjoy** aquariums.

The following chart shows how to form the present tense when the subject of the verb is singular and is not *I* or *you.*

Add *s* to most verbs.	work–works
For verbs ending in *s, ch, sh, x,* or *z,* add *es.*	guess–guesses fix–fixes catch–catches buzz–buzzes push–pushes
For verbs ending in a consonant and *y,* change the *y* to an *i* and add *es.*	try–tries apply–applies

Remember that the verb *be* has special forms in the present tense.

Present Tense Forms of Be

Singular	Plural
I am	we are
you are	you are
he, she, it is	they are

Guided Practice

A. Tell which of the present tense verbs in parentheses ( ) correctly completes each sentence, and explain your choice.

Example: Some scientists (explore, explores) the quality of ocean water. *explore*

1. Marine biologists (collect, collects) seawater in bottles.
2. The scientist and her assistant (empty, empties) the contents into test tubes.
3. They (watch, watches) for uncommon results.
4. These scientists (look, looks) for dangerous substances in the seawater.
5. Many tiny animals (is, are) in the water.

Independent Practice

B. Write each sentence. Use the correct present tense form of the verb in parentheses ( ).

Remember

If the subject is singular and is not *I* or *you*, form the present tense by adding *s*, adding *es*, or changing *y* after a consonant to *i* and adding *es*.

Example: A student _____ different kinds of ocean life. (classify)

A student classifies different kinds of ocean life.

6. The ocean _____ food for fish and people. (provide)
7. Fishers _____ trout for sale in stores. (catch)
8. Scientists _____ the ocean as a farm. (use)
9. A scientist sometimes _____ information into a notebook. (copy)
10. One kind of marine snail _____ a medicine for muscles. (produce)
11. Doctors and nurses _____ this medicine to sick patients. (give)
12. Fish farmers _____ shellfish in the ocean. (harvest)
13. The ocean also _____ us with minerals. (supply)
14. Scientists _____ energy from ocean tides. (harness)
15. The moon _____ ocean tides. (affect)

C. Write the paragraph. In each sentence, fill in the proper form of a present tense verb. Choose from the following list of verbs. Use each only once.

> collect   come   explore   be   sell

16–20.   Many companies __16__ the ocean. In South Africa, a miner __17__ diamonds on the ocean floor. Companies __18__ these diamonds all over the world. The oceans __19__ full of many natural resources. Even household sponges __20__ from the ocean.

Writing Connection

Science Why is it important for people to know about the oceans and ocean life? Using present tense verbs, state at least two reasons as clearly as you can. Then compare your reasons with those of a partner. Work with your partner to write a paragraph that tells why learning about the ocean is important.

USAGE AND MECHANICS

Subject-Verb Agreement

Having singular and plural subjects and verbs that match is called subject-verb agreement.

You know that some subjects are singular and some are plural. When you are writing with present tense verbs, always use the verb form that agrees with, or matches, the subject in number. Remember to use the plural form of the verb to agree with a compound subject using *and*.

Examples:

subject   verb
A humpback **whale likes** shallow waters.

compound subject   verb
The **whale** and its **calf swim** together.

subject   verb
The **people** on the boat **watch** the whales.

Guided Practice

A. **Identify the subject and verb in each sentence. Tell whether the subject is singular or plural. If the subject and verb do not agree, tell the correct verb form.**

Example: The visitor watch for humpback whales from his boat.
visitor (singular), watch; watches

1. The tourist boat pass near a humpback whale.
2. A humpback whale dives in the Pacific Ocean.
3. Its white flippers looks like wings.
4. The male humpback sings his song over and over.
5. The sound carries a long way through the water.
6. The visitor and her daughter hears the sound.
7. A whale's slow heartbeat save oxygen during a dive.
8. Many whales breathes through a blowhole.
9. The blowhole opens wide for air.
10. Powerful muscles close the blowhole.

Independent Practice

B. Decide whether each verb agrees with the subject. If the subject and verb do not agree, write the sentence correctly.

> **Example:** Whales lives in a mysterious watery world.
> *Whales live in a mysterious watery world.*

11. A female humpback whale weighs more than 40 tons.
12. A humpback defend itself in various ways.
13. That whale lash at an enemy with its tail.
14. One whale spurts clouds of bubbles.
15. This tourist rush for her camera.
16. Baby humpbacks come up to the surface for air.
17. That mother humpback hurry to her calf.
18. These whales produces milk for their babies.
19. Some baby whales gains more than 100 pounds a day.
20. A whale's ribs and backbone is similar to those of other mammals.

C. Write each sentence. Use the correct present tense form of the verb in parentheses ( ).

> **Example:** Many whales _____ just off the coast. (live)
> *Many whales live just off the coast.*

21. One of the whales ___ beside the boat. (swim)
22. The killer whale's body ___ up to 30 feet. (stretch)
23. These whales ___ prey with their teeth. (capture)
24. Most whales with teeth ___ fish or squid. (eat)
25. Thick blubber ___ whales warm and helps them float. (keep)

Writing Connection

Writer's Craft: Concise Captions Captions—words that identify or explain an image—are often placed beneath photographs or pictures. Captions should be brief, correct, and interesting. Find an action picture, and write a caption for it. Describe the action; if possible, tell where or when the picture was taken. Check carefully for subject-verb agreement.

Remember

that the tense of a
verb shows the time
of the action or
state of being—past,
present, or future.
Remember, too, that
a verb must agree
with its subject in
number.

Extra Practice

A. Write each sentence. Underline each verb. Then
write whether the verb is in the present tense, the
past tense, or the future tense. *pages 166–167*

Example: Florida adopted the sailfish as the official state
saltwater fish in 1975.
*Florida adopted the sailfish as the official state
saltwater fish in 1975. past*

1. We use the ocean for recreation.
2. Vacationers will crowd the beaches next summer.
3. Many tourists visit beaches in Florida, California,
and Texas every year.
4. Some lighthouses welcome visitors.
5. The National Park Service moved the Cape Hatteras
Lighthouse farther away from the shore in July 1999.
6. This North Carolina lighthouse traveled 950 yards
inland.
7. This surfer swims very well.
8. Many surfers enjoy the waves in Hawaii.
9. The beaches on this island are beautiful.
10. Waikiki Beach is a favorite spot with many surfers.
11. Tomorrow the lifeguards will watch the surfers.
12. The waves rolled across the water.
13. The largest waves are as high as tall buildings.
14. Some wave-riders plunge fifty feet.
15. Surfers often tie their boards to their ankles.
16. Soon these surfers will paddle into a giant wave.
17. Easky, Ireland, held a surfing contest in April 1984.
18. Newcastle, Australia, hosted a contest in March
2000.
19. A sailboat docks at a marina.
20. Stormy seas kept the sailors on shore yesterday.

B. Write each sentence. Use the correct form of the present tense verb in parentheses. *pages 168–169*

Example: A surfer _____ a great deal of time on the beach. (spend)

A surfer spends a great deal of time on the beach.

21. Surfers and tourists _____ to California and Hawaii. (flock)
22. The North Shore of Oahu, Hawaii, _____ many surfers every year. (attract)
23. People _____ on beaches all over the world. (surf)
24. A surfer _____ exact timing and good reflexes. (need)
25. Strong waves _____ across the ocean. (hurry)
26. One wave _____ over a surfer. (crash)
27. A surfer and his surfboard _____ under a giant wave. (fall)
28. The wave _____ the surfboard into two pieces. (split)
29. Sometimes surfers _____ on the surfboard. (sit)
30. This surfer _____ on the board. (stand)

C. Write whether the subject in each sentence is singular or plural. Then write the form of the verb in parentheses that agrees with the subject. *pages 170–171*

Example: Scientists _____ the ocean. (explore)

plural, explore

31. Ocean exploration _____ today. (continue)
32. Satellites _____ the earth. (circle)
33. They _____ data about the oceans. (collect)
34. Several nations _____ a research station in Antarctica. (operate)
35. These countries _____ researchers to Antarctica. (send)

Writing Connection

Real-Life Writing: Advertisements Find a magazine advertisement that contains an ad with a picture of the ocean. Write about how the picture adds to the message of the words. Tell how the ad tries to make people feel. Check your writing for appropriate verb tenses and for subject-verb agreement.

Chapter Review

Read the passage and choose the word or group of
words that belongs in each space. Write the letter for
your answer.

TIP Read and think
about all of the answers
before choosing one of
them.

> We rarely __(1)__ about the world's smallest ocean, the
> Arctic. I __(2)__ to find out more about it. I learned that in
> the winter, ice __(3)__ nearly all of the Arctic Ocean. The
> ice __(4)__ about 160 feet thick at the North Pole. Few
> plants __(5)__ in the Arctic Ocean, because of the cold and
> the lack of sunlight. However, many seals, whales, and
> fish __(6)__ there.
>
> Researchers __(7)__ to study the Arctic Ocean. Airplanes,
> submarines, research stations, and satellites help them
> gather information. Hopefully, this research __(8)__ to bet-
> ter conservation programs for the north polar region.

1 A heard

  B will hear

  C hear

  D hears

2 F will decide

  G decided

  H decides

  J deciding

3 A covered

  B will cover

  C cover

  D covers

4 F is

  G was

  H will be

  J are

5 A grow

  B grew

  C grows

  D will grow

6 F lives

  G will live

  H lived

  J live

7 A continues

  B will continue

  C continued

  D continuing

8 F lead

  G leads

  H will lead

  J led

For additional test
preparation, visit
The Learning Site:

www.harcourtschool.com

Analyzing Advertisements

Literacy is the ability to read and write. If you are literate, you can look at the words in a sentence and understand the writer's message.

The images in a picture are like the words in a sentence. We can put these images together to understand the artist's message. We call the ability to understand the artist's message **visual literacy**.

As you view a picture, ask yourself questions like these: What is the setting of the picture? Are there any people in it? What is happening? How do the people feel about what is happening? What objects are in the picture? What do these objects tell me? Use the words and definitions in the Viewing Vocabulary to help explain your answers.

My Favorite Snack!

Fruits Are Delicious and Nutritious

Great-tasting fruits are chock-full of vitamins and minerals.
They keep you looking and feeling your best.

Have you eaten fruit today?

YOUR TURN

TALK ABOUT OR WRITE your answers to these questions:

What is the center of interest in Advertisement 1? How do you know this?

In what way does Advertisement 2 look different from Advertisement 1?

How do the advertisements use highlighting, emphasis, or symbols in their messages?

Who is the audience for each advertisement?

Which advertisement is more likely to persuade you to buy fruit? Why?

TIP Hint: Create a two-column chart with the headings *Ad 1* and *Ad 2.*

Past Tense and Future Tense

A verb in the past tense tells what the subject did some time ago. A verb in the future tense tells what the subject will do at a time to come.

This chart shows the patterns that many verbs follow to form the past tense.

Add *ed* to most verbs.	jump → jumped
If a verb ends in *e*, drop the *e* and add *ed*.	smile → smiled
If a verb ends in a consonant plus *y*, change the *y* to *i* and add *ed*.	hurry → hurried
If a one-syllable verb ends with a consonant-vowel-consonant, double the final consonant and add *ed*.	flip → flipped
To ask a question in the past tense, add the helping verb *did* to most verbs. Put the subject between *did* and the main verb.	**Did** the cubs **chase** each other yesterday?

To form the future tense, add the helping verb *will*.

Guided Practice

A. **Identify the verb in each sentence. Tell whether it is in the past tense or the future tense.**

Example: Tomorrow the games will start again.
will start, future

1. Many animals played games in their younger days.
2. These games will continue into their adult life.
3. The two lion cubs jumped on each other.
4. Did the scientist study the lions?
5. The scientist studied lions in the outdoors.

Independent Practice

B. Write each sentence. Use the verb and the tense given in parentheses. Some sentences have two verbs.

Example: Yesterday the parrots (toss) pebbles into the air. (past)
Yesterday the parrots tossed pebbles into the air.

6. Elephant calves sometimes (charge) at each other. (past)
7. They (use) their trunks in another game. (future)
8. They (need) their trunks to find food. (future)
9. That lamb (play) alone. (past)
10. The lamb (jump) over stones. (past)
11. In the coming weeks these monkeys (grow) larger. (future)
12. That monkey (carry) a ball around for hours. (past)
13. Playful bear cubs (turn) into clever hunters. (future)
14. Some scientists (study) animal behavior. (past)
15. One scientist (spy) a polar bear at play. (past)
16. One polar bear cub (tip) another one over. (past)
17. When these cubs finish swimming, they (rest). (future)
18. Yesterday at the zoo we (watch) the animals. (past)
19. The chimpanzee (look) in the mirror. (past)
20. Then he (drop) it on the ground. (past)

Writing Connection

Writer's Craft: Choosing Tenses Write a paragraph that describes animals playing. You might use some verbs from the Guided Practice and the Independent Practice to tell what they do. Put the verbs in the present tense. Then exchange paragraphs with a partner. Rewrite your partner's paragraph in the past tense. Discuss the difference between the two versions.

Principal Parts of Verbs

The principal parts of a verb are forms that help it express time and action. The four principal, or main, parts are called the present, the present participle, the past, and the past participle.

Principal Parts of Verbs			
Present	Present Participle	Past	Past Participle
climb	(is, are, was, were) climbing	climbed	(have, has, had) climbed
carry	(is, are, was, were) carrying	carried	(have, has, had) carried
live	(is, are, was, were) living	lived	(have, has, had) lived

To form the future tense, use verbs from the Present column with **will** or **shall.** You can use helping verbs with participles to make other tenses. For the present participle, use forms of the helping verb *be.* For the past participle, use forms of *have.*

Examples:

She is **using** her pencil again today. *present participle*

She had **used** her pencil yesterday. *past participle*

Notice that only the helping verb agrees with the subject and shows tense. The participle stays the same.

Guided Practice

A. Identify the principal part used in the verb in each sentence, and tell the kind of part it is. One sentence has two verbs.

Example: The scientist has arrived in the tropical forest.
arrived, past participle

1. She pitched her tent and looked around.
2. Now she observes a band of spider monkeys.
3. They are jumping from tree to tree.
4. They have paused for a snack.
5. They have lived here for many years.

Independent Practice

B. Write each sentence, and underline the verb or verb phrase. Write the kind of principal part used in the verb. Some sentences have two verbs.

> **Example:** The zoologist had stayed in the tropical forest.
> *The zoologist <u>had stayed</u> in the tropical forest.*
> *past participle*

6. She prepared for her return to North America.
7. "The animals here have amazed me," she noted in her journal.
8. She has taken some beautiful photographs.
9. She has recorded information in her journal.
10. "Now, a different forest awaits me."
11. Soon she will sketch raccoons at a pond.
12. The zoologist has photographed otters.
13. Three otters are playing by the river.
14. "Have they encountered humans before?" she wondered.
15. Soon she will publish a wildlife book.

C. Rewrite each sentence. Use the correct form of the verb in parentheses. Some sentences have two verbs.

> **Example:** The zoologist is _____ animals in their habitats. (study)
> *The zoologist is studying animals in their habitats.*

16. The zoologist is _____ two bears. (watch)
17. They have _____ very close to the river. (walk)
18. Tomorrow they _____ somewhere else. (hunt)
19. Yesterday the zoologist had _____ owls. (observe)
20. She has _____ valuable information. (gather)

Remember

that every verb form comes from a **principal part**. Four principal parts are the **present**, the **present participle**, the **past**, and the **past participle**.

Writing Connection

Technology: Compare Websites Find two websites about wild animals. Is one more appealing than the other? Write some information about the two sites for a classmate. Tell the classmate whether or not to visit the sites. Check the forms of your verbs.

USAGE AND MECHANICS

Using *Do* and *See* Correctly

Use the forms of *do* and *see* that correctly express your meaning.

This chart shows the special ways that *do* and *see* form their principal parts.

Present	Present Participle	Past	Past Participle
do	(is, are, was, were) doing	did	(have, has, had) done
see	(is, are, was, were) seeing	saw	(have, has, had) seen

Incorrect:	Jessica **done** a report about animals
Correct:	Jessica **did** a report about animals.
	Jessica **has done** a report about animals.
Incorrect:	We **seen** amazing pictures in her presentation.
Correct:	We **saw** amazing pictures in her presentation.
	We **have seen** amazing pictures in her presentation.

Guided Practice

A. Tell which verb form in parentheses is correct.

> **Example:** Tia once (seed, saw) a chameleon change color.
> *saw*

1. The chameleon (did, done) that to hide.
2. Animals (do, does) many things to stay safe.
3. Perhaps you have (seen, saw) rabbits running away.
4. A shark (sawed, saw) an octopus and went after it.
5. The octopus has (seen, saw) the shark and squirted an inky cloud.

Independent Practice

Remember

to use *done* and *seen* with *have* or *had*.

B. Write each sentence using the correct verb form of the two in parentheses.

> **Example:** The opossum played dead when it (saw, seen) a dog.
> *The opossum played dead when it saw a dog.*

6. Paul has (seed, seen) a moth whose wings look like eyes.

7. That moth is (doeing, doing) nothing to hide because mimicry will protect it.

8. If you (see, sees) a twig, it might be an insect called a walking stick.

9. Mimicry has (doed, done) a good job of protecting viceroy butterflies.

10. Birds that have (seen, saw) viceroys usually have left them alone.

C. Find the verb form in the box that correctly completes each sentence. Write the completed sentence.

saw	seen	did	done

11. I have _____ pictures of the snowshoe rabbit, which turns white in the winter.

12. The lion _____ a herd of zebras.

13. Because the zebras looked like swirling stripes, the lion _____ nothing.

14. Zoologists have _____ much research about how animals protect themselves.

15. What have people _____ to protect animals?

Writing Connection

Real-Life Writing: Classified Ad In newspapers, many brief ads are grouped (or *classified*) on a few pages. These ads invite people to apply for jobs, find lost pets, and buy used furniture and other items. Read a classified ad in a newspaper. Then write a classified ad of your own. Use at least one form of *do* and one form of *see* in the ad. Be sure to use the forms correctly.

Extra Practice

A. Write each sentence. Use the verb and the tense in parentheses. *pages 176–177*

Example: President Theodore Roosevelt _____ more than fifty bird refuges. (create, past tense)
President Theodore Roosevelt created more than fifty bird refuges.

1. Some refuges _____ endangered animals and plants. (protect, present tense)
2. American bison almost _____. (disappear, past tense)
3. Conservation efforts _____ them. (help, past tense)
4. Today, they _____ on refuges in the Great Plains. (prosper, present tense)
5. Visitors _____ seeing the bison. (enjoy, future tense)

B. Write each sentence. Underline the verb or verb phrase. Then write the kind of principal part used in the verb (present, present participle, past, or past participle). *pages 176–179*

Example: Roosevelt created this nation's first bird sanctuary.
Roosevelt <u>created</u> this nation's first bird sanctuary.
past

6. This sanctuary protected pelicans.
7. Roosevelt's idea has developed into the National Wildlife Refuge System.
8. Today, more than 500 wildlife refuges exist.
9. Refuges are protecting many wild animals.
10. The United States Fish and Wildlife Service runs many of these refuges.
11. Private groups have started other refuges.
12. Refuges have protected bald eagles, whooping cranes, and trumpeter swans.
13. In the future, refuges will play an important part in conservation.
14. Other countries have joined efforts to conserve wildlife.
15. These refuges are saving some species.

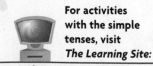

Jasmine Archie   April

C. Each sentence contains an error in verb use. Write each sentence, correcting the error. *pages 176–181*

Example: The duck has see a fox.
The duck has seen a fox.

16. At the wildlife refuge, visitors seen and learned about some rare birds.
17. These snow geese flies south for the winter.
18. When does they return?
19. Bird-watchers have seed these geese fly in a V-formation.
20. The birds flaped their large wings.
21. These geese have travel far this year.
22. During the winter these emperor penguins will remains in Antarctica.
23. They have live on this icy continent for centuries.
24. These birds have did a lot of swimming every day.
25. Penguins' thick fat will protects them during the freezing winter.

D. Write a sentence with each verb form. *pages 180–181*

26. saw   27. seen   28. did   29. done   30. doing

Remember
the principal parts of *do* and *see* are *do, doing, did, done; see, seeing, saw, seen.*

Writing Connection

Writer's Journal: Stating an Opinion Read the letters to the editor in a magazine or newspaper. Find examples of sentences that state the writer's opinion. Choose one that you think is especially effective, and copy it. Then think of an opinion of your own. State it two different ways, and tell which you think would be better for a letter to the editor. Make sure you use correct verb forms and spelling.

DID YOU KNOW?
The San Diego Zoo is home to more than 1,600 mammals, 1,700 birds, and 850 reptiles and amphibians.

183

Chapter Review

Read the passage and choose the word or group of words that belongs in each space. Write the letter for your answer.

TIP Read all directions very carefully before you start the test.

Have you ever (1) a white bullfrog or a white kangaroo? Occasionally a naturally colorful animal is born all white or with very pale markings. Scientists (2) studies on this kind of unusual animal. They (3) these animals *albinos*. White rabbits and white mice are albinos.

In general, albino parents (4) their unusual coloring on to their children. This baby mouse, for example, (5) white hair and red eyes. If the mother has more children, she (6) these coloring patterns to all of her offspring.

---

1 A seed
  B saw
  C see
  D seen

2 F have done
  G doing
  H does
  J done

3 A is calling
  B call
  C will call
  D had called

4 F has passed
  G passing
  H pass
  J passes

5 A is developing
  B develop
  C will developed
  D is developed

6 F passing
  G pass
  H has passed
  J will pass

For additional test preparation, visit *The Learning Site:*
www.harcourtschool.com

Using E-mail

E-mail is short for "electronic mail." E-mail is as fast as making a phone call, but it costs less. You can send the same message to several people at the same time.

Your E-mail Address

An e-mail address is similar to a postal address. Every e-mail address has three parts:

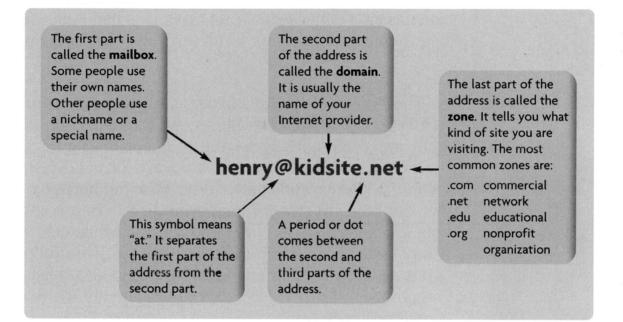

The first part is called the **mailbox**. Some people use their own names. Other people use a nickname or a special name.

The second part of the address is called the **domain**. It is usually the name of your Internet provider.

The last part of the address is called the **zone**. It tells you what kind of site you are visiting. The most common zones are:

.com commercial
.net network
.edu educational
.org nonprofit organization

henry@kidsite.net

This symbol means "at." It separates the first part of the address from the second part.

A period or dot comes between the second and third parts of the address.

E-mail Safety

When you e-mail to a company or a person that you do not know, be careful. Remember these rules.

- *Do not give personal information* about yourself or your family.
- *Do not agree to meet anyone.*
- *Do not reply to scary or upsetting messages.* Tell your parents or teacher about them.

YOUR TURN

Read an article in a newspaper or magazine about a recent event. Write an e-mail message to a partner. In your message, tell about the article and give an opinion about the event. Send your e-mail message to your partner. When you receive an e-mail from your partner, read the message and write a reply.

Writer's Craft

Elaboration

PERSUASION Suppose you want to skate, but your friend wants to play video games. You might try to **persuade** your friend to skate with you. **Persuasion** means trying to get someone to do or think something.

Read the following passage from the book *Ola Shakes It Up* by Joanne Hyppolite. Ola's family is moving to a new house, but she wishes she could persuade them not to move. Notice the reasons she gives for not liking the new house.

LITERATURE MODEL

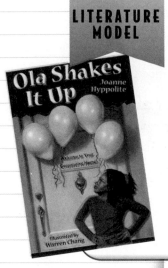

There were too many corners and too many white walls. Aeisha would be able to find a million places to hide and read her books without me pestering her to come out and live a little. (If it wasn't for me, Aeisha would be the world's only twelve-year-old hermit.) We wouldn't be able to sit together in the kitchen doing our homework while Dad prepared for one of his classes and Mama hummed under her breath. We wouldn't be able to lie down on Mama and Dad's bed all squashed together to watch TV. This house was so big we would never see each other.

Analyze THE Model

1. What is Ola's opinion of the new house?

2. What are Ola's reasons for wanting to persuade her family not to move there?

3. What details does Ola give to support her reasons?

When you write to persuade, you want your reader to do something or to agree with your point of view. You can persuade more effectively by using **elaboration**. Elaboration is adding details and reasons to explain your ideas. Study the chart on the next page.

Ways to Elaborate	Questions to Ask Yourself	Strategies to Use
Identify your purpose and audience.	• What opinion do I want to express? • Whom do I want to persuade?	• Choose words and ideas to fit your purpose and your audience.
Use reasons and details.	• What reasons can I give to show why others should agree with my opinion? • What details can I give to support each of my reasons?	• Put your reasons in an order that makes sense. • Give details, facts, and examples for each reason.
Stay on the topic.	• Do all of my reasons and details clearly support my opinion?	• Leave out extra information that doesn't relate directly to your topic.

YOUR TURN

ANALYZE PERSUASIVE WRITING Work with two or three classmates. Look for an example of persuasive writing, such as a newspaper editorial, a letter to the editor, a TV or movie review, or an advertisement. Talk about how the writer elaborates ideas.

Answer these questions:

1. What opinion does the writer express?

2. Does the writing fit the purpose and audience? Why or why not?

3. What reasons does the writer use to persuade you?

4. What details does the writer use to support his or her reasons?

5. Does the writer stay on the topic? Explain your answer.

Identifying Purpose and Audience

A. Identify the purpose and audience for each of the following paragraphs.

1. Come to the Smith School fair for exciting games and delicious refreshments. All students are guaranteed a great time!

2. I received the telescope I ordered from your company. When I opened the package, the telescope was broken. I hope you will send me a new telescope to replace the broken one.

3. I think we should have a car wash to raise money for our scout troop. People like to have clean cars, and we can have fun doing it.

Using Reasons and Details

B. Write each opinion. Then write one reason and one detail to develop each opinion.

Example
Opinion: Our school needs a new cafeteria.
Reason and Detail: The old cafeteria is too small and overcrowded. Students bump into each other because there isn't enough room.

4. **Opinion**: Many students would enjoy reading this book.
5. **Opinion:** Mr. Morris is a good principal.
6. **Opinion:** People should eat more vegetables.
7. **Opinion:** Kara is a superb athlete.
8. **Opinion:** We need a traffic light on this corner.

Staying on the Topic

C. Read the opinions and reasons below. Write each opinion, and then write the reason that should be left out because it does not stay on the topic.

OPINION
School uniforms are a good idea.

REASON
Students don't have to waste time in the morning deciding what to wear.

REASON
Many sports teams wear colorful uniforms.

REASON
Uniforms help students feel that they belong to a group.

OPINION
School uniforms are not a good idea.

REASON
Students, teachers, and parents all worked together at our school clean-up day.

REASON
Uniforms may be too expensive for some families.

REASON
Students enjoy choosing their own clothes.

Writing and Thinking

Writer's Journal

Write to Record Reflections When you learn about ways to persuade others, you also learn how others may try to persuade you. How do you think understanding persuasive techniques may help you in your daily life? Write your reflections in your Writer's Journal.

Letter to the Editor

Ola wished she could persuade her family not to move to a new house. Melissa wants to persuade people in her community not to build a new parking lot. She wrote a letter to the editor of her local newspaper. As you read Melissa's letter, notice how she develops ideas.

MODEL

heading —

> Richmond School
> City, State zip
> date

inside address —

> The City Herald
> 456 Stevens Street
> City, State zip

greeting —

> To the Editor:

body of letter —

> I have been reading about the plan to build a new parking lot on Lodge Street. I agree with those who have spoken out against this plan.
>
> To build the parking lot, it will be necessary to cut down quite a few trees. Trees are important because they help protect us from air pollution and reduce noise pollution.
>
> Another reason not to build the parking lot is that there is already too much traffic in that area. I walk by there every day and often see traffic jams and minor accidents.
>
> I hope the readers of this newspaper will ask their representatives on the city council to vote against this plan.

closing —

> Sincerely,

signature —

> Melissa Martino

Analyze THE Model

1. What opinion does Melissa express in her letter?
2. What is her purpose for writing? Who is her audience?
3. What reasons does Melissa give to support her opinion? What details does she give to develop her reasons?
4. Does Melissa stay on the topic? Explain your answer.
5. In what ways is a business letter like this one different from a friendly letter?

YOUR TURN

WRITING PROMPT Imagine that a community group is planning to give your school a fresh coat of paint and to plant flowers and shrubs. Write a letter to the editor of your local newspaper to persuade other members of the community to volunteer for this project. Give reasons and details to support your request.

STUDY THE PROMPT Ask yourself these questions:

1. What is your purpose for writing?
2. Who is your audience?
3. What writing form will you use?
4. What will you try to persuade your audience to do?

Prewriting and Drafting

Organize Your Ideas Make a list of reasons and details to support your request. Then use a flowchart like this one to help you organize your ideas.

> **OPINION**
> Write a sentence that states your opinion.

> **REASONS AND DETAILS**
> Give two or three reasons to support your request. Give facts and details to develop each reason.

> **OPINION**
> Restate your opinion in different words.

USING YOUR
Handbook

Use the Writer's Thesaurus to find forceful words that will help you persuade your readers.

Editing

Reread the draft of your letter to the editor. Can you revise your letter to make it more persuasive? Use this checklist to help you revise your work:

☑ Did you state your opinion clearly?
☑ Did you keep your audience in mind?
☑ Are there details you should take out because they don't stay on your main topic?
☑ Do you want to put your details in a different order?
☑ Should you add more reasons and details to elaborate on your opinion?

Use this checklist as you proofread your paragraph:

☑ I have used capitalization and punctuation correctly.
☑ I have used correct verb tenses.
☑ I have made sure that subjects and verbs agree.
☑ I have used a dictionary to check my spelling.
☑ I have used correct business letter form.

Editor's Marks

� delete text
∧ insert text
ↄ move text
¶ new paragraph
≡ capitalize
／ lowercase
◯ correct spelling

Writer's Journal

Sharing and Reflecting

Make a final copy of your letter to the editor, and share it by trading with a partner. Read and discuss each other's letters. Tell what you like best about your partner's letter and what he or she could do better next time. Ask whether your own letter meets its purpose. Write your reflections in your Writer's Journal.

Persuasive Discussion

When people with different opinions discuss a subject and try to persuade each other, they are having a persuasive discussion. Think about how a persuasive discussion might be similar to and different from persuasive writing. Study the Venn diagram.

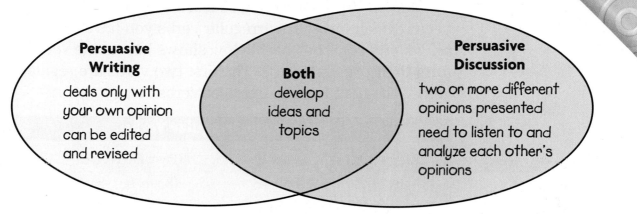

Persuasive Writing

deals only with your own opinion

can be edited and revised

Both
develop ideas and topics

Persuasive Discussion

two or more different opinions presented

need to listen to and analyze each other's opinions

YOUR TURN

Role-play a persuasive discussion with a small group of classmates. Follow these steps:

STEP 1 Choose a topic about which many students have opinions.

STEP 2 Decide what opinion each speaker will express.

STEP 3 Plan and practice your discussion. As you role-play, use the Strategies for Listening and Speaking.

STEP 4 Present your persuasive discussion to classmates.

STEP 5 Afterward, ask your audience for comments about your persuasive discussion.

Strategies for Listening and Speaking

Use these strategies to help you have a good discussion:

• As you speak, remember to choose your words and adjust your rate, volume, pitch, and tone to fit the audience and setting. Stay on your topic.

• As you listen, identify the speaker's main ideas and supporting details. Interpret each speaker's message, purpose, and perspective.

• As you respond, use reasons and details to develop your ideas.

Regular and Irregular Verbs

Regular verbs end with *ed* in the past and past-participle forms. **Irregular verbs** have past and past-participle forms that are spelled in other ways.

Most of the verbs you have learned about so far have been regular verbs. The irregular verbs you have studied are *be, do,* and *see.* The chart below shows how some verbs form their principal parts. The first two verbs are regular verbs. The next five are irregular verbs.

Regular and Irregular Verbs		
Present	**Past**	**Past Participle**
help	helped	(have, has, had) helped
study	studied	(have, has, had) studied
sit	sat	(have, has, had) sat
know	knew	(have, has, had) known
come	came	(have, has, had) come
give	gave	(have, has, had) given
think	thought	(have, has, had) thought

Guided Practice

A. **Identify the verb in each sentence. Include any helping verbs. Then tell whether each main verb is a regular verb or an irregular verb.**

Example: William Mitchell had studied the stars for years.
had studied, regular

1. His young daughter, Maria, often helped him.
2. He had encouraged her interest in mathematics and science.
3. As an adult, Maria Mitchell worked as a librarian.
4. Maria was also her father's assistant at his observatory.
5. Few people knew about their librarian's interest in astronomical studies.

Independent Practice

B. Read each sentence. Write each verb. Then write whether the verb is regular or irregular. Some sentences have two verbs.

> **Example:** The father and daughter had seen great things in the night sky. *had seen, irregular*

6. The Mitchells' research earned the respect of other scientists.
7. One night in 1847, Maria Mitchell had seen something through the telescope.
8. She thought it looked like a new comet.
9. Scientists agreed, and they gave her credit for the discovery.
10. The king of Denmark awarded her a gold medal.
11. Soon scientists around the world knew of Mitchell's work.
12. She had become the first woman astronomer in the United States.
13. Maria Mitchell worked as a professor of astronomy.
14. She studied the sun and took photographs of its surface.
15. Astronomers respected her and her studies.
16. Long ago, people thought that the sun traveled around Earth.
17. In 1543 Copernicus proposed that Earth traveled around the sun.
18. Galileo studied the stars with a telescope.
19. Before 1781 astronomers had known of only six planets.
20. Telescopes in orbit around the Earth have given scientists more knowledge.

Writing Connection

Writer's Journal: Interesting Quotes Find and copy a quotation about space that includes past or past-participle forms. Look in a book of quotations under a topic related to space. Identify the regular and irregular verbs in the quotation.

More Irregular Verbs

Irregular verbs do not end with *ed* in the past and past-participle forms. Those forms are spelled in other ways.

More Irregular Verbs		
Present	**Past**	**Past Participle**
bring	brought	(have, has, had) brought
say	said	(have, has, had) said
make	made	(have, has, had) made
go	went	(have, has, had) gone
write	wrote	(have, has, had) written
begin	began	(have, has, had) begun
teach	taught	(have, has, had) taught
take	took	(have, has, had) taken
fly	flew	(have, has, had) flown
ride	rode	(have, has, had) ridden

Examples:

The reporter **writes** about space travel. (present form of irregular verb)

The reporter **wrote** about space travel. (past form of irregular verb)

The reporter **has written** about space travel. (past-participle form of irregular verb)

Guided Practice

A. Name the past form of the verb. Then name the past-participle form.

Example: give
   gave, given

1. say
2. go
3. take
4. bring
5. fly

6. teach
7. make
8. write
9. begin
10. ride

Independent Practice

Remember that irregular verbs have special spellings for their principal parts.

B. Write the correct past or past-participle form of the verb in parentheses.

> **Example:** Juan (make) a wish for a tour of the solar system.
> *Juan made a wish for a tour of the solar system.*

11. The space age (begin) in 1957.
12. That year the first satellite (go) into orbit.
13. Some spacecraft, called probes, (fly) without pilots.
14. They (gather) information to send to Earth.
15. Some (take) photographs of other planets.
16. One United States space probe (fly) to the planet Jupiter.
17. Later, astronauts (ride) in new kinds of spacecraft.
18. President Kennedy (say) the United States would send a person to the moon.
19. U.S. astronauts (go) to the moon in 1969.
20. Astronauts (make) six moon landings.
21. They (bring) back samples from the moon's surface.
22. Engineers (begin) to build space shuttles.
23. Space shuttles have (make) many trips into space.
24. People have (live) in a space station for many months.
25. They had (take) supplies to last a long time.
26. The space station crews have (do) scientific experiments.
27. Trainers (teach) astronauts how to stay fit in space.
28. Crew members have (ride) exercise bikes.
29. They have also (bring) books and computer games with them.
30. Astronauts have (make) life on a space station as normal as possible.

Writing Connection

Writer's Craft: Giving Reasons What reasons might an astronaut give to encourage people to travel into space? Imagine that you are the astronaut. Write two sentences about your past experiences in space, using some irregular verbs. Then write one reason why others should try space travel. With a partner, take turns reading your sentences aloud.

Examples

Students **sit** on benches in the classroom. *(rest)*

The teacher **sets** the benches in rows. *(puts)*

Don't **lie** in the sun too long. *(rest)*

Lay your towel under the umbrella. *(put)*

USAGE AND MECHANICS

Commonly Misused Verbs

Avoid confusing the following verb pairs: *sit/set, lie/lay, can/may, teach/learn, rise/raise*, and *let/leave*.

Some verb pairs are easy to confuse. These verbs are similar in meaning but are not quite the same. Knowing the exact meanings of these verbs can help you use them correctly.

Verb Pairs			
sit	"to rest, as in a chair"	*set*	"to put or place something"
lie	"to rest, as on a bed"	*lay*	"to put or place something"
can	"to be able to do some thing"	*may*	"to be allowed to do something"
teach	"to give instruction"	*learn*	"to receive instruction"
rise	"to go upward; to get up"	*raise*	"to lift up"
let	"to permit or allow"	*leave*	"to go away from; to let stay in place"

Guided Practice

A. Identify the word in parentheses that completes each sentence correctly. Explain your choice.

> **Example:** A new student (teaches, learns) her classmates about astronomy. *teaches*

  1. A star map (lies, lays) on that shelf.
  2. I will look at the map and then (lie, lay) it back in its place.
  3. The teacher (lets, leaves) us alone to work on our star maps.
  4. My teacher (can, may) let us look through the telescope.
  5. We look at the stars after the moon (rises, raises).

Independent Practice

B. Write the verb choice that correctly completes each sentence.

> **Example:** "(Teach, Learn) us about gravity today," the students say.
> *Teach*

Remember
to avoid confusing one verb with another verb that seems similar.

6. Some science textbooks (teach, learn) students about planet Earth.
7. The students (teach, learn) the difference between planets and stars.
8. The sun is a star that (rises, raises) every morning.
9. The student (lies, lays) a star map on his desk.
10. The students (let, leave) the telescope in the classroom.
11. New telescopes (let, leave) scientists see objects in more detail.
12. Computer printouts (lie, lay) near the telescope.
13. Astronomers (lie, lay) their books aside to study the sky.
14. They can (teach, learn) much by observation.
15. Astronauts (can, may) float in space because there is no gravity.
16. On Earth special trainers (teach, learn) them about this natural force.
17. NASA does not (let, leave) untrained people fly into space.
18. Powerful engines (rise, raise) the spacecraft off the launch pad.
19. Astronauts (sit, set) when the spacecraft takes off.
20. Astronauts (can, may) not leave the spacecraft without a good reason.

Writing Connection

Real-Life Writing: Safety Rules Write two safety rules for conducting a science experiment. Use some verbs from the commonly confused verb pairs to state what students should or should not do. Exchange your rules with a partner and check each other's verbs.

Extra Practice

A. Write each sentence. Underline each verb. Then write whether the verb is a regular verb or an irregular verb. Some sentences have two verbs.
pages 194–197

Example: I have seen several planets through my telescope.
I <u>have seen</u> several planets through my telescope. *irregular*

1. Last month I studied the planets with my classmates.
2. I taught my classmates about Mars.
3. The name of the planet came from Roman mythology.
4. The Romans gave Mars its name to honor their god of war.
5. They thought that the planet's reddish color looked like blood.
6. Last night I saw the planet Venus near the moon.
7. I looked at the moon's craters.
8. People have seen animal shapes in the moon's shadows.
9. Some astronauts traveled to the moon.
10. They came back to Earth with moon rocks.
11. Many comets have moved through our solar system.
12. People have seen comets more clearly through telescopes.
13. Halley's Comet came near Earth again in 1986.
14. One comet collided with the planet Jupiter in 1994.
15. Have you ever wondered about the craters on the moon?
16. We made a model of the moon.
17. Our teacher had brought photographs of the moon.
18. We used clay and shaped it into craters.
19. I learned the names of some of the craters.
20. I already knew the names of all the planets.

B. Write each sentence. Use the correct past or past-participle form of the verb in parentheses.
pages 194–197

Example: I have (think) about space travel for a long time.
I have thought about space travel for a long time.

21. Last night I dreamed that I (go) to visit a space station.
22. I had (ride) a space shuttle to get there.
23. The builders had (make) the space station look like a city.
24. A tour guide (give) me a tour.
25. Soon I (fly) out of my dream and back home.

C. Write each sentence, using the correct verb or verb form of the two in parentheses. One sentence has two verbs. *pages 198–199*

Example: I have (thinked, thought) a lot about Mars lately.
I have thought a lot about Mars lately.

26. (Raise, Rise) the telescope, and you will see Mars.
27. (Can, May) I tell you about Earth's nearest neighbor?
28. (Let, Leave) me (learn, teach) you some interesting facts.
29. Ice caps (set, sit) on the northern and southern poles of Mars.
30. Does water (lay, lie) beneath the Martian soil?

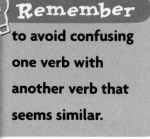

Remember
to avoid confusing one verb with another verb that seems similar.

DID YOU KNOW?
In 1998, seventy-seven-year-old John Glenn became the oldest person ever to go into space. He was on the crew of the space shuttle *Discovery*.

Writing Connection

Technology: Website On the Internet, find NASA's website for kids. You can use *NASA* and *kids* as search words. Find out about a topic that interests you. Then write two sentences to answer each of these questions: What did you see on the site? What did you know about the topic before? What did you learn? Be sure to use the correct forms of irregular verbs.

For more activities with irregular verbs, visit
The Learning Site:
www.harcourtschool.com

Chapter Review

Read each sentence. Look at the underlined word or words. There may be a mistake in verb usage. If you find a mistake, choose the answer that is the best way to write the underlined section of the sentence. If there is no mistake, choose *Correct as is*.

STANDARDIZED
TEST PREP

TIP Before beginning, think of one verb. Use it as an example to review the principal parts.

1 Let's <u>lay</u> on the quilt and watch for shooting stars.
   A lie
   B laid
   C lying
   D Correct as is

2 Many people <u>have written</u> about the moon.
   F has written
   G have writed
   H have wrote
   J Correct as is

3 Neil Armstrong <u>sit</u> foot on the moon on July 20, 1969.
   A sitted
   B sat
   C set
   D Correct as is

4 Astronauts <u>bringed</u> back samples of soil and rock from the moon.
   F brings
   G brought
   H has brought
   J Correct as is

5 People once <u>thinked</u> that parts of the moon were covered with water.
   A thought
   B have thinked
   C thinks
   D Correct as is

6 Now we <u>knowed</u> that there is no water there.
   F knew
   G know
   H have known
   J Correct as is

7 Last week we <u>beginned</u> to read about other planets.
   A had began
   B begin
   C began
   D Correct as is

8 My friend <u>gave</u> me a book about astronomy.
   F gived
   G had gave
   H gives
   J Correct as is

For additional test preparation, visit *The Learning Site:*

www.harcourtschool.com

Listening for Facts and Opinions

Speakers try to persuade by using both facts and opinions. Listening carefully to hear the difference can help you make good decisions.

A fact is information that can be proved. You may already know a fact to be true, or you may know where to research to find out. Speakers sometimes include supporting information to prove their facts. An opinion, however, cannot be proved. Statements of opinion often begin with words like *I believe, I think,* or *personally.* Opinions can also include emotional words like *terrific, terrible,* or *best.*

News stories use facts to tell about people and events. Advertisements often use emotional words to convince listeners, but facts are also included. Here are some active listening steps to decide whether a statement is a fact or an opinion.

- Give careful attention to the speaker.
- Listen for key words and phrases.
- Listen for supporting information.
- Take brief notes, but continue to listen.
- Note words that are used with opinions.
- Ask yourself, "Can this statement be proved?"

YOUR TURN

WRITE AN ADVERTISEMENT In a small group, work together to write the words for a television advertisement. Imagine a product that you are trying to sell. You may want to listen to advertisements for similar products to practice telling fact from opinion. First, list some facts about the product. Make sure that the facts are statements that could be proved. Next, write several opinion statements about the product. Use emotional words and words that introduce opinions. Then, decide on the most persuasive order for the statements. Be creative!

Vocabulary Power

me•te•or•ol•o•gist
[mē´tē•ə•rol´ə•jist] *n.*
A scientist who studies
weather, winds, and the
air around the earth.

Present Perfect and Past Perfect Tenses

There are three perfect tenses—present perfect, past perfect, and future perfect. The perfect tenses use the past participle with a form of the helping verb *have*.

Present Perfect Tense:

We **have watched** the sky all morning. (present tense of helping verb)

Past Perfect Tense:

We **had seen** the movie before. (past tense of helping verb)

A verb in the **present perfect tense** shows action that started to happen at some time before now. The action may continue into the present. A verb in the **past perfect tense** shows action that happened before a specific time in the past and has stopped.

This chart shows the difference between the simple tenses and the perfect tenses.

	Simple Tenses	Perfect Tenses
Present	Dry weather **hurts** farm crops.	Dry weather **has hurt** farm crops this year.
Past	Clouds **gathered** in the afternoon.	By 8:00 P.M., clouds **had gathered**.

Guided Practice

A. Identify the verb in each sentence. Tell whether each verb is in the present perfect tense or the past perfect tense.

Example: The meteorologist has predicted rain for Tuesday.
has predicted, present perfect

 1. The heat wave has lasted for two weeks.
 2. We have expected rain all week.
 3. I have watered the garden every day.
 4. By evening, rain had started to fall.
 5. The heat wave had finally ended.

Independent Practice

Remember
that a verb in the **present perfect tense** shows action that started to happen before now and may be continuing. A verb in the **past perfect tense** shows action that happened before a specific time in the past.

B. Write the perfect tense verb in each numbered sentence. Write whether it is in the present perfect or past perfect tense.

> **Example:** Evan had written one letter to Derek before the storm.
> *had written, past perfect*

Dear Derek,

(6) I had planned to write you sooner. (7) I'm sure you have heard all about the hurricane. (8) We have been very busy since it passed through. We were ordered to evacuate our home before the storm. (9) When we returned, the wind had blown the roof off my clubhouse. (10) The doghouse and a section of fence had disappeared completely. (11) The wind had also ripped several branches from the maple trees. (12) We had boarded up our house, and it was fine. (13) We had really expected more damage. (14) According to the rain gauge, it had rained only five inches.

(15) Since we returned, the weather has been beautiful. (16) We have enjoyed being back home. (17) We have even enjoyed cleaning up the yard. (18) We had thought we might not see our house again. (19) We have started building Ginger a new house. (20) She has watched us every minute.

Please write soon.

> Your friend,
>
> Evan

Writing Connection

Writer's Craft: Strong Verbs Imagine that you are a news reporter telling about a summer storm. What might have happened during this storm? List some strong verbs that a news reporter could use. Then write a few sentences to report on the storm. Include some verbs in either the present perfect or the past perfect tense.

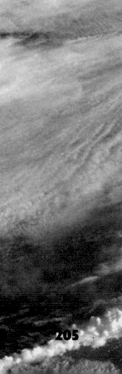

Future Perfect Tense

The future perfect tense is formed by adding the help-ing verbs *will have* to the past participle form of the main verb.

You know that the future tense shows action that will hap-pen at a time to come. The future perfect tense shows action that will start and finish before a future time.

Future Tense	Future Perfect Tense
At 6:30 the farmer **will watch** the weather report.	By 7:00, the farmer **will have watched** the weather report.
I **will water** the garden this afternoon.	I **will have watered** the garden by supper time.

Guided Practice

A. **Identify the verbs in these sentences. Tell whether each verb is in the future tense or the future perfect tense.**

Example: The weather will have improved by the weekend.
will have improved, future perfect

1. Lower temperatures will give us a welcome change.
2. An air mass, or large body of air, will arrive from Canada.
3. This air mass will have reached our area by midnight.
4. By Thursday evening, those winds will have pushed out the hot air.
5. The temperature will have dropped 20 degrees by Friday morning.
6. The humidity, or amount of moisture in the air, will fall throughout the day Thursday.
7. The winds will have calmed by Thursday evening.
8. The chance of rain will have dropped by half.
9. The sun will shine brightly over the weekend.
10. The heat wave will have passed before Thursday evening.

Independent Practice

B. Write each sentence. Use the verb in the tense shown in parentheses after the sentence.

Example: Farmers (prepare) their fields for dry conditions in advance. (future perfect)
Farmers will have prepared their fields for dry conditions in advance.

11. It (rain) here tomorrow. (future)
12. The rain (start) by the middle of the afternoon. (future perfect)
13. Some neighborhoods (receive) more rain than others. (future)
14. Dark clouds (form) in the sky before dawn. (future perfect)
15. Water in the clouds (become) very heavy. (future)
16. Around noon, the first drops (fall). (future)
17. The water (reach) the earth as rain. (future)
18. The rain (stop) by the time school is out. (future perfect)
19. Soon the ground (soak) up the rain. (future perfect)
20. By 8.00 the sun (set). (future perfect)
21. I hope the weather (be) nice for our trip. (future)
22. This weekend a cold front (move) through. (future)
23. The air pressure (rise). (future)
24. By Saturday night, the air (cool) about twenty degrees. (future perfect)
25. By that time we (arrive) at our grandparents' house. (future perfect)

Writing Connection

Writer's Journal

Writer's Journal: Writing Advice List some things that you have been told to do (or not to do) because they are good (or not good) for you. Choose one item from your list, and write a paragraph of advice for classmates. Be persuasive. Explain what will happen in the future if someone does or does not follow your advice. Use at least one verb in the future perfect tense.

Remember that a verb in the **future perfect tense** shows action that will start and finish before a specific time in the future.

Sequence of Tenses

Use the verb tense that accurately shows the time of the verb's action.

Within a sentence or a paragraph, the verb tenses need to be in a sequence that makes the order of events clear. Here are some tips to remember:

- Think about the meaning of the sentence. What time or times are being described?
- Look at all the verbs in the sentence. If actions happen at different times, the verbs should be in different tenses.
- Be especially careful with perfect tense verbs. They are often used with verbs in other tenses. Choose the perfect tense verb that shows when the action happened in relation to other actions.

Example:

Incorrect: Reports **have promised** only rain, but a tornado **struck** during the night.

Correct: Reports **had promised** only rain, but a tornado **struck** during the night.

Guided Practice

A. Identify which verb tense in parentheses is correct.

Example: A hurricane (forms, had formed), and it grew rapidly.
had formed

1. Last night, the storm (strengthened, strengthens).
2. Meteorologists (hope, had hoped) that the hurricane would stay at sea, but it (changes, changed) direction.
3. Now the storm (crossed, has crossed) the Gulf of Mexico and is approaching Texas.
4. People along the Texas coast (have helped, had helped) one another as everyone (will prepare, prepares) for the storm.
5. After the storm, we learned that the winds (have reached, had reached) 100 miles per hour.

Independent Practice

B. Identify which verb tense in parentheses is correct. Rewrite the sentence, using the correct form.

6. We had feared a tornado even before the storm (breaks, broke).
7. Earlier this afternoon thunderclouds (darkened, have darkened) the sky.
8. Next (came, will have come) thunder, louder and louder.
9. Now a funnel-shaped cloud (formed, has formed) in the distance.
10. We look to see which way it (went, will go).
11. We watch, amazed, as the tornado (kicked, kicks) up a cloud of dust.
12. The funnel cloud (has been, will be) visible for ten minutes now.
13. In a moment we (will go, went) into the storm cellar.
14. We (added, add) the storm cellar last year.
15. A tornado (damages, damaged) a neighbor's house a month before we built our cellar.
16. People have called tornadoes "twisters" because the winds (turn, turned) in a circle.
17. Strange things (happened, have happened) during last year's tornadoes.
18. A boy said that he (has seen, had seen) a car fly past him.
19. We (stored, had stored) supplies in case a storm came.
20. You never (know, knew) when a tornado will strike.

Writing Connection

Technology With a partner, find a weather forecast on the Internet and a weather forecast in a newspaper. You and your partner can each write a summary of one forecast for the next day. Be sure to use the correct sequence of tenses. Check the weather report the next day, and see which forecast was more accurate.

For more activities
with verb
tenses, visit
The Learning Site:
www.harcourtschool.com

Extra Practice

A. Write each sentence, and underline each perfect tense verb. Write whether the tense of the verb is past perfect, present perfect, or future perfect.
pages 204–207

Example: Many areas have experienced droughts, or long
periods of time with little or no rainfall.
*Many areas <u>have experienced</u> droughts, or long
periods of time with little or no rainfall.*
present perfect

1. The Great Plains has been a productive farming area of the United States for many years.
2. The Great Plains has suffered many droughts since the early 1930s.
3. This region had been dry even before the droughts.
4. By 1934, topsoil had turned to dust.
5. Many farmers had lost their crops before the end of the drought.
6. In just a few years, the drought had destroyed many farms.
7. Ever since then, people have called that area the Dust Bowl.
8. Despite this nickname, the area has recovered from the disaster.
9. People have remembered that event.
10. Forecasters have compared recent droughts to that famous one.
11. However, none of the recent droughts has been as bad as the drought in the 1930s.
12. Still, some people have predicted another drought soon.
13. Many cities will have prepared for drought.
14. Some places have limited water usage in the dry months.
15. Other communities have increased education on water conservation.

B. Write each sentence, and underline each verb. Write whether the verb is in the future or the future perfect tense. *pages 206–207*

Example: By the end of September, fall will have arrived.
*By the end of September, fall <u>will have arrived</u>.
future perfect*

16. The days will become cooler.
17. Nights will have grown longer.
18. A few leaves will have changed colors.
19. Then other leaves will drop to the ground.
20. By November most trees will be bare.

C. Decide which verb tense in parentheses is correct. Rewrite the sentence, using the correct form.

pages 204–209

Example: Until the storm ends, we (had stayed, will stay) inside.
Until the storm ends, we will stay inside.

21. Before any raindrops fell, storm sirens (sound, had sounded).
22. The storm (drenched, will have drenched) our town soon.
23. Lightning (will have flashed, has flashed) overhead for the last ten minutes.
24. We hear thunder each time the lightning (strikes, had struck).
25. All day we (have wanted, want) to run outside with our dog.

DID YOU KNOW?
To measure the distance between you and a bolt of lightning, count the number of seconds between the lightning flash and the thunder that follows. Then divide the number of seconds by five to find out how many miles away it is. For example, five seconds is one mile, and ten seconds is two miles.

Writing Connection

Real-Life Writing: Storm Safety Poster Suppose that you want to tell people how to be safe during a severe thunderstorm. In a small group, discuss some ideas for making a poster that explains what to do during lightning and heavy rain. List at least three safety tips. Use a sheet of paper to make a draft of the poster. Be sure your poster can be read quickly and easily.

Chapter Review

Look for mistakes in verb usage in the sentences below. When you find a mistake, write the letter of the line containing the mistake. Some sentences may not have any mistakes. If there is no mistake, choose the letter beside *No mistakes*.

TIP Before you begin, read the directions carefully to see what kinds of mistakes you are expected to find. After you read a test item, mark only one letter for your answer.

1 A   Miguel and Kim learned about *Sputnik*
  B by the time they had finished
  C their Internet research on satellites.
  D *(No mistakes)*

2 J   The United States has planned to be
  K the first country to launch a satellite, but the
  L Soviet Union launched one on October 4, 1957.
  M *(No mistakes)*

3 A   Since the 1950s, satellites had watched
  B the world's weather. They continue to give
  C scientists and farmers helpful information.
  D *(No mistakes)*

4 J   By the beginning of the 1990s,
  K thousands of satellites had been launched
  L to watch the weather.
  M *(No mistakes)*

5 A   Satellites have taken
  B accurate pictures of the earth
  C and had sent them back to scientists.
  D *(No mistakes)*

6 J   Jaime had not found the astronomy book
  K when Mrs. Po asked for it. She will have wanted it
  L to teach us about the stars.
  M *(No mistakes)*

For additional test preparation, visit *The Learning Site:* www.harcourtschool.com

Searching Online

The Internet offers exciting ways to find facts about a subject. By **searching online** you can research information from many sources. Learning important skills can make your online search successful.

A **search engine** is the tool you use to locate information. There are several search engines on the Internet. A librarian may be able to help you select a good search engine, or you might want to try more than one search engine. Use the search engine to find websites on a topic. A website is a group of linked screens, or "pages." When you get information from a Web page, make a note of the page's name and Web address.

All search engines have a search box. You type one or more **keywords** in the search box. Search engines then look for sites that have your keywords. To expand or narrow your search, click on the search engine's help button to find information about how to search. Suppose you want to find information about tornadoes designed for students your age. Here is how you might search.

YOUR KEYWORDS

kids tornadoes	**SEARCH**

YOUR RESULTS

Websites on
- tornadoes and other storms
- books for children about weather
- kids' weather pages
  . . .more

The top matches for your search will appear first. Click on a site that interests you. Use the *Back* button at the top of the screen to return to the list and choose another site.

YOUR TURN

SEARCH ONLINE With a partner, do an online search. First, choose a topic about the weather, such as a type of weather or weather in a certain place. List possible keywords to use. Enter the keywords in a search engine. How many websites did the search engine find?

If necessary, narrow or expand your search. Then choose the two sites that are the most interesting or helpful. Record the Web address and examples of the kind of information on each site.

TIP Remember to make a list of keywords before you search online. Use the search engine's *help* feature to find out how to expand or narrow your search.

213

Writing Workshop

You know that persuasive writing tries to convince someone to believe or to do something. In this article, Brian Ward tries to persuade readers to exercise regularly. As you read, think about the reasons he uses to support his opinion.

LOOKING and FEELING
YOUR BEST

by Brian Ward

Why do you need to exercise? What are the benefits of feeling fit? The two go together. Without exercise, you certainly won't either feel or be fit, and fitness is one of the foundations of good health.

Good health is not just the absence of illness. It is the combination of being physically fit and feeling good. There is no doubt that if you are feeling healthy you will be happier and more confident and able to cope better with school and other activities.

Regular exercise is the best way of keeping in shape. It helps you stay at a proper weight, improving your muscle tone and posture.

Exercise also helps to avoid stress. Stress is a problem that affects both young and old because of pressures at home, at school, or at work. During a session of vigorous exercise, you take your mind off your everyday problems. Afterwards, you will be pleasantly relaxed. Another benefit is that you will sleep better and wake up feeling refreshed.

The body works more efficiently when it is fit and can operate at its peak. Fitness is a combination of three important things: **suppleness, strength** and **stamina.**

Suppleness allows you to bend and twist freely and stay more active as you get older. Strength is something you need all the time—to climb stairs, to push, pull, and lift things. Stamina gives your muscles staying power and keeps you from feeling tired. You can only be truly fit if you exercise regularly to develop each of these three things.

There are no shortcuts to fitness. It doesn't have to cost much—it may even be free if you choose to exercise at home or go walking or running. What fitness does take is time, the right kind of exercise, and some determination to keep yourself physically active.

Best of all, fitness is fun. The more you exercise, the easier it gets and the more you will enjoy it. Why not start exercising today?

Analyze THE *Model*

1. How does Brian Ward show his feelings about fitness in the first paragraph?

2. What reasons to exercise does Ward give? How does he support each one?

3. Do you find this article convincing? Why or why not?

READING — WRITING CONNECTION

Parts of a Persuasive Essay

Brian Ward tried to persuade his readers to exercise. Study this persuasive essay, written by a student named Kelly. Pay attention to the parts of the essay.

MODEL

Run for Your Life!

statement of opinion — Do you exercise? Many people don't. They think that staying fit means having to work out at a gym, buy weights, or join an aerobics class. Actually, exercise can be simple. One great way to get or stay fit is running.

first reason — For one thing, running is inexpensive. You may already have a pair of comfortable shoes.

details — If you do, running will cost you only some time. Each run should last at least twenty minutes. You can use that time, though, to listen to music, to get to know your neighborhood better, or just to think.

second reason — Running is also a wonderful way to build your muscles. Like many activities, running makes muscles stronger. Running is especially

details — good for training muscles to keep going without getting tired. That staying power helps you when you play sports or work hard.

third reason — Most important, running makes your heart stronger. When your heart is strong, it can do a better job of pumping blood throughout your body. Your blood carries oxygen and nutrients to different parts of your body. Your blood also carries away waste. Your blood will do those jobs well only if your heart is strong.

Running is a simple way to improve your fitness. Have a coach or another adult runner help you get started safely. Then run for your life!

details

restatement of opinion/ call to action

Analyze THE Model

1. What is Kelly's purpose? Explain your answer.

2. Who do you think Kelly's audience might be? Why do you think so?

3. Why does Kelly restate her opinion at the end?

Summarize THE Model

Write Kelly's opinion and reasons in a web like the one shown here. Then use the web to write a summary of Kelly's persuasive essay. Be sure to include all the important points. Leave out the details.

opinion

reason   reason   reason

Writer's Craft

Elaboration Kelly used elaboration to develop her ideas about the topic. List the reasons in Kelly's essay. Then list the details that support each reason. Tell why Kelly put her strongest reason last.

Prewriting

Purpose and Audience

You probably have opinions on many topics that matter to you. In this chapter, you will share an opinion with your classmates by writing a persuasive essay.

WRITING PROMPT Write a persuasive essay urging your classmates to do (or keep doing) something that you think is good for them. State your opinion, and give good reasons to persuade your classmates to agree with you. End your essay by asking your classmates to take action.

Begin by thinking about your purpose, audience, and topic. Who will your readers be? What opinion will you persuade them to share?

MODEL

Kelly began by thinking of activities that were good for her. She decided to encourage her classmates to run for exercise. She made this web to organize her thoughts.

Strategies Good Writers Use

- Decide on your purpose.
- Think about your audience.
- Brainstorm reasons that will persuade your audience.

My audience: classmates

My purpose: to persuade my classmates to run for exercise

My Opinion: Running is good exercise.

inexpensive

makes your heart stronger

builds your muscles

YOUR TURN

Choose a topic you feel strongly about. Make a web to organize your ideas.

Organization and Elaboration

Follow these steps to help you organize your essay:

STEP 1 **Get Your Audience's Attention**
Introduce your topic in a way that makes your audience want to read about it.

STEP 2 **State Your Opinion**
Give your opinion clearly and directly.

STEP 3 **Provide Your Reasons**
Organize your reasons, putting the strongest one last to emphasize it. Use details to strengthen each reason.

STEP 4 **Conclude with a Call to Action**
Restate your opinion. Conclude with a call to action, urging your audience to do something.

MODEL

Here is the beginning of Kelly's draft of her essay. How does she try to get her audience's attention? What is Kelly's opinion? Where does she state it?

> Do you exercise? Many people don't. They think that staying fit means having to work out at a gym, buy weights, or join an aerobics class. Actually, exercise can be simple. One great way to get or stay fit is running.

YOUR TURN

Now draft your essay. Use the steps above. Remember to look back at your prewriting web. Use Brian Ward's article and Kelly's essay as models.

Strategies Good Writers Use

- Begin by getting your audience's attention.
- Add supporting facts and details for each reason.
- Put your strongest reason last.

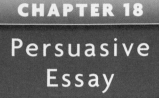 Use a computer to draft your essay. You can use the click-and-drag feature to rearrange your reasons.

Revising

Organization and Elaboration

To begin editing, reread your draft thoughtfully.

- How well did I organize my reasons into paragraphs?
- Have I strengthened my reasons with enough details? (If not, you should add more details.)
- Have I used interesting words and a variety of sentence patterns to keep my writing interesting?
- Have I kept to my topic? Do I need to delete anything that does not relate to the topic?

Strategies Good Writers Use

- Replace weak words with strong ones.
- Ask another writer to suggest improvements.

Save a copy of your first draft before you revise it. That way you can go back to your original if you don't like your revisions.

MODEL

Here is part of Kelly's essay. Notice that she added stronger words and additional details to support her reasons. She also used a variety of sentence patterns.

Running also is a wonderful way to build your muscles. Like many activities, running makes muscles stronger. Running is especially good at training muscles to keep going without getting tired.

For one thing, Running is inexpensive. The main thing is good shoes, and you may already have a pair of comfortable shoes. If you do, running will cost you only some time. Each run should last at least twenty minutes. You can use that time, though, to listen to music or just to think, to get to know your neighborhood better,

That staying power helps you when you play sports or work hard.

YOUR TURN

Revise your persuasive essay to make your reasons as powerful and interesting as you can. Think about adding more details and using stronger words.

Checking Your Language

When you proofread, you look for mistakes in grammar, spelling, punctuation, and capitalization. If you do not correct these mistakes, readers may find your essay less persuasive.

MODEL

Here is another part of Kelly's essay. After she revised her essay, she proofread it. Look at the way Kelly corrected her spelling mistakes. What other errors did she fix?

> *running*
> Most important, ~~runing~~ makes your heart stronger. When your heart is strong, it can do a better job of pumping blood *throughout* ~~through out~~ your body. Your blood carries oxygen and ~~nutriants~~ *nutrients* to ~~differant~~ *different* parts of your body. Your blood also carries away waste. your blood will do those ~~jobes~~ *jobs* well only if your heart is strong.
>
> Running is a simple way to ~~improove~~ *improve* your fitness. Have a coach or another adult runner help you get started ~~safeley~~ *safely*. Then run for you life!

Strategies
Good Writers Use

- Check for subject-verb agreement.
- Check spellings of irregular verbs, including commonly misused verbs.
- Look up spellings if you are unsure of them.

YOUR TURN

Proofread your revised essay. You may want to proofread several times to
- check grammar.
- check spelling.
- check punctuation and capitalization.

Editor's Marks

႒	delete text
∧	insert text
ꝺ	move text
ℛ	new paragraph
≡	capitalize
/	lowercase
◯	correct spelling

Publishing

Sharing Your Work

Now you are ready to publish your persuasive essay. Answer these questions to help you decide on the best way to share your work:

1. Who is your audience? How can you publish your essay so your audience will see it?

2. Should you write your essay in cursive or print it from a computer? If you are publishing your work along with that of classmates—for example, making a class magazine or combining your essays into a book—you would all want to use the same method.

3. Should you read your essay aloud? To give an oral presentation, use the information on page 225.

USING YOUR
Handbook

- Use the rubric on page 508 to evaluate your essay.

Reflecting on Your Writing

Using Your Portfolio What did you learn about your writing in this chapter? Write your answer to each question below.

1. Did your writing meet its purpose? Why or why not?

2. Using the rubric from your Handbook, how would you score your own writing? Explain your answer.

Add your answers and your essay to your portfolio. Then take some time to review your portfolio. How well are you meeting the goals you set earlier? Set one new goal for improving your writing.

Making an Oral Presentation

After Kelly finished her essay, she decided to make an oral presentation to her class. You, too, can share your opinions with your classmates this way. Follow these steps:

STEP 1 Write an outline of your essay on notecards. Use neat, large print so you don't lose your place while speaking.

STEP 2 Think about whether multimedia aids, such as pictures, video segments, or music, would make your presentation more powerful.

STEP 3 Prepare any multimedia aids in advance, and decide when you will use them in your presentation.

STEP 4 Relax, and give your presentation! Speak in a loud, clear voice, and make eye contact with your classmates as much as possible.

STEP 5 When you have finished, answer any questions your classmates may have.

Strategies for Listeners

As your classmates give their presentations, use these strategies to gain information and make judgments:

- Think about the speaker's message, purpose, and viewpoint.
- Identify the speaker's opinion and main reasons. Notice whether the reasons are supported by facts.
- Consider the speaker's reasons fairly.

Unit 3
Grammar
Review

CHAPTER 13

The Simple
Tenses
pages 166–175

Past, Present, and Future Tense

pages 166–167

A. Rewrite the following sentences. Use the tense of the verb given in parentheses.

Example: Many tourists (past tense of *sail*) around coral reefs this year.
Many tourists sailed around coral reefs this year.

1. Coral reefs (present tense of *surround*) Hawaii.
2. Many coral animals (past tense of *create*) coral reefs.
3. Scientists (past tense of *study*) life in the coral reef.
4. Reefs (present tense of *provide*) fish with food.
5. They also (present tense of *protect*) fish from predators.
6. Human activity (past tense of *pollute*) waters.
7. Many people (present tense of *worry*) about the health of coral animals.
8. Some coastal areas (future tense of *be*) off limits.
9. These protected areas (future tense of *grow*) in number.
10. These areas (present tense of *serve*) as popular tourist attractions.

Present Tense *pages 168–169*

B. Rewrite the following sentences. Change the verb to the present tense.

11. Sea exploration technology will change every year.
12. Scientists learned more about sea life.
13. Scientists have captured some sea creatures.
14. No sunlight reached the deepest parts of the ocean.
15. Some sea creatures were on display in aquariums.

Subject–Verb Agreement *pages 170–171*

C. Correct any errors in subject-verb agreement. Write *correct* for any sentences that have no errors.

16. My brother and sister knows how to sail a boat.
17. Tourists collects shells along the seashore.
18. Sea turtles hatches on the beach and crawl to the water.
19. One of the turtles crawl the wrong way.
20. These turtles swim at night.

Past Tense and Future Tense

pages 176–177

A. Rewrite each sentence. Choose the correct verb form in parentheses.

1. Gray wolves (will be, were) a topic of debate soon.
2. Gray wolves (will prowl, prowled) the West for centuries.
3. Long ago, wolves sometimes (will kill, killed) settlers' livestock.
4. Wolves once (will hunt, hunted) coyotes in the West.
5. Coyotes (will grow, grew) in number now that the wolves are gone.

Principal Parts of Verbs pages 178–179

B. Rewrite the following sentences. Change the verb in parentheses to the past, present-participle, or past-participle form.

Example: Long ago, animals (live) in every part of this country.
Long ago, animals lived in every part of this country.

6. The bald eagle (become) America's national bird in 1782.
7. By 1970 few bald eagles (remain) in the United States.
8. The government (place) many plants and animals on a special list.
9. The list (help) to protect these plants and animals.
10. The number of bald eagles has (increase).
11. Scientists have just (take) the bald eagle off the list.
12. Some people have (say) that the bald eagle should still be protected.
13. Certain states have (write) laws to protect bald eagles.
14. Bald eagles are (soar) in the sky.
15. Many eagles have (return) to their nests.

Using *Do* and *See* Correctly

pages 180–181

C. Rewrite the sentences below. Use the correct verb form of the two in parentheses.

16. Last week we (seen, saw) many animals at the zoo.
17. The tiger (done, did) a good job of hiding in tall grass.
18. Now I have (seen, saw) an elephant.
19. All the monkeys were (doing, done) leaps and jumps.
20. We have (done, did) reports about the zoo.

Regular and Irregular Verbs
pages 194–195

More on Irregular Verbs pages 196–197

A. Write each sentence using the past tense of the verb in parentheses. Write whether the verb is regular or irregular.

Example: Many inventions (begin) in the early days of the space program.
Many inventions began in the early days of the space program. irregular

1. The space age (start) when the first satellite was launched.
2. In 1957 the first satellite (go) into space.
3. Astronauts and probes (gather) information about space.
4. In 1969 Neil Armstrong (walk) on the moon.
5. The astronauts (make) a perfect landing on the moon.
6. Astronauts from the United States (place) a flag on the moon.
7. Many Americans (watch) them on television.
8. They (wear) spacesuits when they walked on the moon.
9. Astronauts from the United States (make) six trips to the moon between 1969 and 1972.
10. They (come) back to Earth four days later.

Commonly Misused Verbs pages 198–199

B. Rewrite the following sentences. Use the correct verb in parentheses.

11. Kim will (let, leave) us borrow the telescope.
12. (Can, May) we ask the astronaut to show us the stars?
13. The astronauts (sit, set) in the command module.
14. The spacecraft (sets, sits) on the launch pad.
15. Rockets (can, may) lift the spacecraft into the air.
16. The spacecraft (rises, raises) very quickly.
17. Soon it (lets, leaves) Earth's atmosphere.
18. Because they are weightless, astronauts cannot (lie, lay) down.
19. (Can, May) we search the Internet for more information on space travel?
20. (Sit, Set) the astronomy book on the shelf.

Unit 3
Grammar Review

CHAPTER 17

The Perfect
Tenses
pages 204–213

Present Perfect and Past Perfect Tenses *pages 204–205*
Future Perfect Tense *pages 206–207*

A. Write whether the tense of the underlined verb is present perfect, past perfect, or future perfect.

Example: This hurricane <u>had formed</u> over the ocean near the equator. *past perfect*

1. The storm <u>has grown</u> to be 200 miles wide.
2. Over the ocean, its winds <u>had whirled</u> at tremendous speeds.
3. The winds <u>have hit</u> land with massive force.
4. Waves, wind, and rain <u>will have pounded</u> the beach before noon.
5. All day people <u>have listened</u> for warnings on the radio.
6. People living near the shore <u>had boarded</u> up their windows.
7. Before the winds hit, people <u>will have tied</u> down items that are not secure.
8. Winds from hurricanes <u>have torn</u> down trees in the neighborhood.
9. Severe floods <u>will have damaged</u> buildings by the storm's end.
10. The hurricane <u>has caused</u> much trouble for the town.

Sequence of Tenses *pages 208–209*

B. Rewrite each sentence. Choose the correct verb tense in parentheses.

11. We (have read, will have read) about hurricane Mitch in class this week.
12. It (has caused, had caused) much damage in 1998 and left one million homeless.
13. Mitch (has stayed, had stayed) near Honduras for four days before it left.
14. We (will have learned, have learned) about hurricane George by Tuesday.
15. It is likely that many storms (had hit, will have hit) the country before next year.

Your Opinion Counts

What endangered species live in your region? Should people protect them? The steps below will help you write an editorial expressing your opinion.

Research the Species in Your Region

- Visit the library or check the Internet to get a list of local endangered species.

- Choose one endangered species, and find out as much as you can about it. Research these questions:

  - Does the species harm people or the environment? Does it benefit them?

  - What would it take to save this species? What are the problems that might occur? What are the costs?

Plan Your Editorial

- Watch TV news shows to see what a TV editorial looks like.

- Write a short speech to persuade people of your point of view about protecting the species you have researched. Be sure to

  - describe the species.

  - estimate how many members of it are left in the wild.

  - explain how it became endangered.

  - give reasons why people should or should not protect the species.

Present and Publish Your Editorial

- Practice your editorial until you can read it without having to look down at it often. If you have a video camera, have a friend tape your editorial, and show the tape in class. Otherwise, set up a mock news magazine set in your classroom. Present your editorial.

- Submit your editorial to the school newspaper or class newsletter. (TV editorials make good written editorials, too.)

Come Back, Salmon
by Molly Cone
NONFICTION
A group of students adopt a creek near their school, clear away the garbage, and repopulate it with salmon.
Notable Social Studies Trade Book; Teacher's Choice; Outstanding Science Trade Book

The Gray Whales Are Missing
by Robin A. Thrush
REALISTIC FICTION
Spencer's class studies the possible reasons the whales haven't been seen in the ocean near San Diego, California.

Unit 4

232

To Black Rock Cave

Take Old Mountain
Highway two miles
to the fork. Then
turn left, and
follow Route 44
until you reach
the river. N

Subject Pronouns

A **pronoun** is a word that takes the place of one or more nouns. A **subject pronoun** takes the place of a noun or nouns as the subject of a sentence.

In the example below, the subject pronoun *he* takes the place of *Cara's father*.

Example:
Cara's father is a chef. ~~Cara's father~~ taught Cara to cook.
He

He is an example of a subject pronoun. A subject pronoun is in the **subjective case**. This chart shows the subject pronouns. Always capitalize the pronoun *I*.

Subject Pronouns		
Person	**Singular**	**Plural**
First person (person speaking)	I	we
Second person (person spoken to)	you	you
Third person (person or thing spoken about)	he, she, it	they

Guided Practice

A. Identify the subject pronoun in each sentence. Tell whether it is singular or plural.

Example: We should eat different kinds of foods. *We, plural*

1. I enjoy fruits and vegetables.
2. He brought a tuna sandwich for lunch.
3. It is high in body-building proteins.
4. With every meal, she drinks milk.
5. She knows that milk is high in calcium.
6. It builds strong teeth and bones.
7. He chooses lowfat milk.
8. One day we asked Tim about cheeses.
9. "They contain calcium and protein," Tim said.
10. Tomorrow we will share some cheese and fruit.

Vocabulary Power

nu•tri•tion
[n(y)o͞o•trish′ən] *n.* The process used by a body to take in and use food as energy.

Independent Practice

B. Write each sentence. Underline the subject pronoun. Write whether that pronoun is singular or plural.

Example: With every meal, we take in nutrients.
With every meal, we take in nutrients. plural

11. They keep the body working properly.
12. It uses nutrients for growth and energy.
13. We also use nutrients to help repair the body.
14. I listen to the doctor and eat a balanced diet.
15. "The body needs many nutrients," she says.
16. "It gets these nutrients from different foods."
17. I also listen to the health teacher at school.
18. He says that some foods have more vitamins than others.
19. We saw a helpful poster of the food groups.
20. They were arranged in a chart called the Food Guide Pyramid.

C. Rewrite each sentence, using the subject pronoun that best replaces the underlined word or words.

Example: My mother is a food scientist, or nutritionist.
She is a food scientist, or nutritionist.

21. Nutritionists created the Food Guide Pyramid.
22. The Food Guide Pyramid shows six basic food groups.
23. Fruits make up one group on the Food Guide Pyramid.
24. My brother likes oranges and bananas best.
25. My sister and I like apples.

Remember

that a **pronoun** stands for one or more nouns. A **subject pronoun** is used as the subject of a sentence.

Writing Connection

Real-life Writing: Menu Work with a small group or a partner to make a short menu for a fast-food restaurant that serves healthful foods. Display your menu, and invite classmates to come and "order" from your restaurant. Take turns role-playing the order taker and the customer. Use language that is appropriate to the situation, including the correct forms of subject pronouns.

Object Pronouns

An object pronoun takes the place of a noun after an action verb, such as *see* or *tell*, or after a preposition, such as *about, at, for, from, in, of, to,* or *with*. An object pronoun is in the **objective case**.

This chart shows the object pronouns.

Object Pronouns		
Person	**Singular**	**Plural**
First person	me	us
Second person	you	you
Third person	him, her, it	them

You know that a direct object often follows an action verb. The direct object may be a noun or an object pronoun. An object pronoun may also follow a preposition.

Examples:
Anita surprised **him.** (direct object of verb)
Anita often reads to **him.** (pronoun after a preposition)

Sometimes we use *I* or *me* together with a noun or another pronoun. *I* or *me* should always follow the noun or other pronoun.

Examples:
He and *I* like broccoli. (pronouns as part of subject)
Broccoli is good for *him* and *me*. (pronouns after a preposition)

Guided Practice

A. Identify the object pronoun in each sentence. Tell whether it is singular or plural.

Example: Vegetables are good for me.
me, singular

1. Vegetables in our diet keep us healthy.
2. Carrots have vitamin A in them.
3. A tomato has vitamin C in it.
4. Tell him about the importance of minerals.
5. Vegetables are good for Eric and me.

Independent Practice

B. Write the object pronoun used in each sentence. Tell whether the pronoun is singular or plural.

Example: Kris met me near the nutrition booth at the health fair. *me, singular*

6. We found it by looking for the Food Pyramid sign.
7. The nutritionist spoke to us.
8. Kris talked with him about a well-balanced diet.
9. Fats, oils, and sweets are a food group, but we get few nutrients from them.
10. Vegetable oil, however, has vitamin E in it.

C. Choose one of the pronouns in parentheses to complete each sentence. Write the sentence.

Example: Do bread, cereals, rice, and pasta have fiber in (they, them)?
Do bread, cereals, rice, and pasta have fiber in them?

11. What does fiber do for (me, I)?
12. Fiber helps (us, we) get rid of waste material.
13. How does protein benefit Caitlin and (I, me)?
14. Protein helps (you, we) grow, heal, and fight diseases.
15. Fish is one excellent source of (it, they).
16. Can you tell Caitlin and (me, I) about other sources of protein?
17. Meat, eggs, and nuts provide (us, we) with protein.
18. White beans can supply (she, her) with protein and calcium.
19. Tell (him, he) what we learned.
20. A well-balanced diet will help (them, they) enjoy life.

> **Remember**
> that an **object pronoun** replaces a noun or nouns after an action verb or a preposition.

Writing Connection

Real-Life Writing: Note Write a note inviting a friend to go somewhere with you and another person. Be sure to use object pronouns where they are needed and to use *I* and *me* last with other nouns and pronouns.

USAGE AND MECHANICS

Pronoun-Antecedent Agreement

The antecedent of a pronoun is the noun or nouns to which the pronoun refers. A pronoun must agree with its antecedent in number and gender.

When you use a pronoun, you need to know its antecedent. Ask yourself whether the antecedent is singular or plural. If it is singular, decide whether it is masculine, feminine, or neuter. Use a pronoun that agrees with the antecedent.

Example: antecedent   pronoun
People bring recipes with **them** to new homes.

Other words come between a pronoun and its antecedent. A pronoun and its antecedent may even be in separate sentences. Pronoun-antecedent agreement helps readers know what the pronoun stands for.

Example:
Miguel helped Anna make this soup. **He** did an excellent job. (*He* refers to Miguel, not Anna.)

Guided Practice

A. **Identify the pronoun or pronouns in each sentence. Name the antecedent of each pronoun. Be prepared to tell how you know the antecedent.**

Example: People have traditions, and special foods are one of them. *them, traditions*

1. The Pilgrims had little food when they arrived in New England.
2. A Native American leader met the Pilgrims, and he felt pity.
3. Native Americans brought food and shared it with the newcomers.
4. The Pilgrims thanked the Native Americans and learned from them.
5. The Native Americans helped the Pilgrims by showing them how to grow corn, pumpkins, and beans.

Independent Practice

B. Write each sentence. Underline the pronoun. Draw an arrow to the pronoun's antecedent.

Example: The United States is a big country, and it has several regions.
The United States is a big country, and *it* has several regions.

6. Many people came to the United States, and they settled in different regions.
7. People brought their own recipes with them.
8. Often a family tasted a food made by another group and liked it.
9. All people contributed to the diet of the region where they lived.
10. Fried chicken began as a Southern favorite, but it is enjoyed everywhere today.

C. Add a pronoun to complete each sentence. Write the sentence. Underline the pronoun's antecedent.

Example: Southwestern food is popular wherever _____ is served.
Southwestern *food* is popular wherever it is served.

11. When the Spanish came, _____ learned many recipes from Native Americans.
12. These foods often have beans and peppers in _____.
13. Texans are famous for the beef cattle that _____ raise.
14. Your neighbor may use a Texas beef recipe when _____ prepares a meal.
15. A cook in any state might use beef when _____ makes a regional dish.

Writing Connection

Writer's Craft: Clear Pronouns Choose a piece of your writing, and look at the way you used subject and object pronouns. Is it clear what each pronoun stands for? Have you used the correct subject and object forms? Make any improvements in pronoun use that would help you communicate more clearly.

Extra Practice

A. Identify the pronoun in each sentence. Write whether it is a subject pronoun or an object pronoun. One sentence has two pronouns. *pages 234–237*

Example: I eat three pieces of fruit every day.
   I, subject pronoun

1. We should plan a diet that meets the body's needs.
2. Maria gave him a copy of the Food Guide Pyramid.
3. Leon and she discovered the nutrition chart in a health book.
4. The Food Guide Pyramid has been useful to them.
5. If I want to plan a well-balanced diet, the nutrition chart can help me.

B. Write each sentence. Underline the pronoun. Draw an arrow from the pronoun to the antecedent. *pages 238–239*

Example: People use energy as they work and play.

   People use energy as <u>they</u> work and play.

6. "The amount of energy people have comes from what they eat," said Maria.
7. "The foods that a person eats can be grouped together, and they are called the person's diet."
8. "Wait a minute," Brian interrupted. "I thought that diets were for people who want to lose weight."
9. "No, Brian," Maria replied. "You probably have a diet."
10. "Most people have some kind of diet—a group of foods that they eat often," Maria continued.
11. "Diet is important because it may affect a person's health."
12. "Protein can help repair body parts if they have been injured."
13. "Some foods have nutrients in them that can help prevent certain diseases."
14. Rochelle wants to be a nutritionist like Maria so that she can help people.
15. Rochelle said, "Eric, you should read this book about nutrition."

For more activities with pronouns, visit *The Learning Site:*
www.harcourtschool.com

C. **Choose the correct pronoun in parentheses. Write the sentence. Some sentences have more than one pronoun.** *pages 234–239*

Example: Some people must follow a special diet because (they, them) are ill.
Some people must follow a special diet because they are ill.

16. (I, me) read Rochelle's book about diet.
17. Good nutrition can help (we, us) lead healthy lives.
18. A healthful diet does not guarantee that (we, us) will always be well.
19. People with some diseases may follow a special diet that can help (them, they).
20. (They, Them) may need to eat certain foods.
21. These people must avoid a food if (he, it) makes (they, them) sicker.
22. Eric and Caitlin told Hiroshi and (me, I) about a disease called diabetes.
23. (I, Me) listened to (they, them) with interest.
24. People with diabetes should visit a doctor; (he or she, him or her) can help (them, me).
25. Like all of (we, us), (they, them) should eat vegetables, fruits, and whole-grain foods.
26. People with diabetes should avoid foods with refined sugar in (it, them).
27. Eating meals at the same time every day is good for (they, them).
28. Regular exercise helps all of (we, us), and (it, you) is very good for diabetics.
29. The doctor gave Amy and (I, me) some advice.
30. He told (we, us) girls to drink lowfat milk every day.

Writing Connection

Writer's Craft: Vivid Adjectives Think of all the green vegetables you can name. Choose three of them to describe. Write sentences that use vivid adjectives and other descriptive details to tell how the vegetables are similar and how they are different. Be sure to use the correct forms of subject and object pronouns.

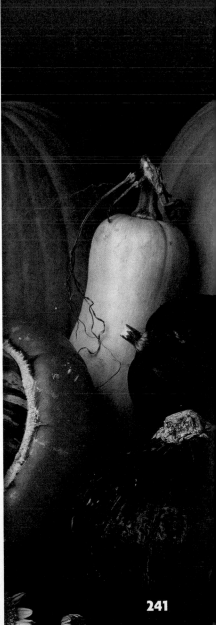

Chapter Review

Read the passage and choose the pronoun that belongs in each space. Write the letter for your answer.

Yesterday in school my class learned about nutrition. Our teacher, Ms. Jordan, told __(1)__ many interesting facts. __(2)__ explained how the foods __(3)__ eat affect our bodies. The body needs nutrients, and it finds __(4)__ in food. Nutrients help the body work and grow. The body also uses __(5)__ to repair injuries.

Today my brother pulled a muscle while playing ball. What will nutrients do for __(6)__? The doctor talked to my mother and __(7)__ about nutrition. He told __(8)__ that when a muscle is hurt, nutrients help heal the muscle.

STANDARDIZED TEST PREP

TIP If you are not sure of the correct answer, read the sentence, using each of the possible answers. Then rule out the answers that do not make sense.

1 A her
  B they
  C it
  D us

2 F He
  G It
  H She
  J Her

3 A she
  B we
  C us
  D they

4 F them
  G they
  H it
  J him

5 A it
  B us
  C they
  D them

6 F she
  G he
  H him
  J you

7 A he
  B me
  C I
  D it

8 F I
  G she
  H us
  J we

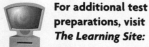
For additional test preparations, visit *The Learning Site:*

www.harcourtschool.com

Homophones and Homographs

Homophones are words that are pronounced alike but are spelled differently and have different meanings.

Examples:

Did you go to <u>sea</u>? (Did you travel on the ocean?)
Did you go to <u>see</u>? (Did you go to look?)

Some Common Homophones			
buy—by	hour—our	sea—see	for—four
know—no	hear—here	meet—meat	their—there—they're
week—weak	hole—whole	right—write	to—too—two

Homographs are words that are spelled alike but have different meanings. They may or may not be pronounced differently.

Examples:

I enjoy the rides at the **fair**.
That's not **fair**!
Her **fair** skin does not tan easily.

Throw me that ob'ject. (Throw me that thing.)
I ob·ject' to what he said. (I do not like what he said.)

Some Common Homographs		
hide (noun)—hide (verb)	well (noun)—well (adjective/adverb)	treat (noun)—treat (verb)
des'ert (noun)—de·sert' (verb)	ob'ject (noun)—ob·ject' (verb)	tire (noun)—tire (verb)

YOUR TURN

WORD PLAY A pun is the humorous use of a homophone or a homograph to suggest two meanings at the same time. For example, a magazine article about a young writer comments that she has "the write stuff." Puns are often used in jokes, in humorous poetry, and in newspaper headlines. Find an example of a pun to share with classmates, or make up your own. Tell whether your pun uses a homophone or a homograph.

TIP This sentence can help you remember that homophones sound alike: "I hear the sound of a *phone ringing*."

243

Possessive Pronouns

A **possessive pronoun** shows ownership and takes the place of a possessive noun.

There are two kinds of possessive pronouns. One kind is used before a noun. In the example below, the pronoun *her* stands for the possessive noun *Tammy's*. Both *Tammy's* and *her* come before the noun *book* and tell whose book it is.

Example:

I found **Tammy's** exercise book. I found **her** book.

The other kind of possessive pronoun is not used before a noun. It often comes after a form of the linking verb *be*.

Example:

This book is **Tammy's**. This book is **hers**.

Both kinds of possessive pronouns are said to be in the possessive case. This chart shows all the forms.

Possessive Pronouns Used Before a Noun		Possessive Pronouns That Stand Alone	
Singular	**Plural**	**Singular**	**Plural**
my	our	mine	ours
your	your	yours	yours
his, her, its	their	his, hers	theirs

Guided Practice

A. **Identify the possessive pronoun in each sentence. If the possessive pronoun is used before a noun, name the noun.**

Example: Masahiko wants to know how to build strength in his arms. *his arms*

1. We all need to care for our bodies.
2. I must choose my exercises carefully.
3. The exercise program you choose may not be the same as mine.
4. Carlos does his aerobics after school.
5. Tanya does hers three mornings a week.

Vocabulary Power

aer•o•bics [âr•ō′biks]
n. Vigorous physical exercises designed to increase the body's capacity to take in and use oxygen.

Independent Practice

B. **Write each sentence. Underline the possessive pronoun.**

Example: I practice my aerobics three times a week.
I practice <u>my</u> aerobics three times a week.

6. Different people approach their aerobic exercise in different ways.
7. The choice of activity is theirs.
8. Jevon says, "My favorite exercise is swimming."
9. "Mine is running," says Sarah.
10. Elena and Marta practice their soccer dribbling skills together.
11. John needs strong arms for his job.
12. He lifts weights to keep his muscles strong.
13. Joanne lifts weights to keep hers strong.
14. John said to Joanne, "Lift your weights carefully."
15. Sandra needs a strong heart and strong lungs in order to run her long races.

C. **Write each sentence. Replace the possessive noun in parentheses with a possessive pronoun.**

Example: (The players') coach teaches them the best exercises.
Their coach teaches them the best exercises.

16. Sandra uses aerobic exercise to meet (Sandra's) goal.
17. George uses different exercises to meet (George's).
18. Football players must keep (players') muscles strong.
19. A basketball team depends on the ability of (team's) players to think fast.
20. Gina says, "I exercise to improve (Gina's) dancing."

Remember

that a **possessive pronoun** shows ownership and takes the place of a possessive noun. Some possessive pronouns are used before a noun, and others are not.

Writing Connection

Real-Life Writing: Note Write a note inviting a friend to meet you somewhere for an activity that involves exercise. Tell the friend where to meet you and what to bring. You might also tell what you will bring. Use several possessive pronouns. Work with a classmate to identify the kinds of pronouns you used.

Reflexive Pronouns

A reflexive pronoun refers back to a noun or pronoun. A reflexive pronoun agrees with its antecedent in gender and number.

Compare the meanings of these sentences. Which pronoun refers to *Alma and Jonathan?*

Alma and Jonathan gave **themselves** a reward.
Alma and Jonathan gave **them** a reward.

Themselves is a reflexive pronoun that refers back to *Alma and Jonathan. Them* is an object pronoun that refers to other people. Here are the reflexive pronouns. Notice that some have gender.

Singular: myself, yourself, himself, herself, itself
Plural: ourselves, yourselves, themselves

Reflexive pronouns end in *-self* or *-selves*, depending on whether the antecedent is singular or plural.

A reflexive pronoun should not be used in place of a subject pronoun.

Incorrect: John, Ellen, and **myself** exercise together.
Correct: John, Ellen, and **I** exercise together.

Guided Practice

A. Identify each reflexive pronoun and its antecedent(s). The antecedents may be nouns or pronouns.

Example: Athletes need to push themselves harder than most people do. *themselves, athletes*

1. Young athletes have often proved themselves to be winners.
2. Women basketball players in the United States organized themselves into a successful league.
3. A young athlete who wants to excel makes herself practice every day.
4. You can practice and develop yourself to achieve a goal.
5. Many world champions probably tell themselves that practice makes perfect.

Independent Practice

Remember

that a reflexive pronoun refers back to a noun or pronoun. It should match its antecedent in gender and number.

B. Find the reflexive pronoun in each sentence. Write the reflexive pronoun and its antecedent(s). The antecedent may be a noun or a pronoun.

> **Example:** We need to push ourselves a little each time we exercise. *ourselves, We*

6. Justin wore himself out by running too hard.
7. You may want to find yourself an exercise partner.
8. My brother enjoys himself more in group activities.
9. My brother chooses team sports for himself.
10. Regina keeps herself fit by training for soccer.
11. Training builds the strength she needs to make herself better at the sport.
12. The team members work themselves hard during games.
13. One girl places herself in front of the other team's goal.
14. The other players arrange themselves in position.
15. Each team earns a point for itself by kicking the ball into the goal.

C. Choose a reflexive pronoun to complete each sentence. Then write the sentence.

> **Example:** You owe it to _____ to exercise regularly.
> *You owe it to yourself to exercise regularly.*

16. Studies have shown that people who exercise protect _____ from heart disease.
17. Miguel paces _____ during his aerobics.
18. Certain exercises help us protect _____ against bone loss.
19. You should choose the right exercise for _____.
20. Jogging, swimming, and riding a bicycle are aerobic exercises I can do by _____.

Writing Connection

Writer's Craft: Clear Pronouns Write a short paragraph about an activity you like to do by yourself or for yourself. Explain what you like about the activity. Be sure to use the first-person pronouns *I, me, my,* and *myself* correctly.

USAGE AND MECHANICS

Contractions with Pronouns

Subject pronouns are often used with verbs in contractions, as in *we're*.

A contraction is the shortened form of two words. An apostrophe takes the place of one or more letters that are left out.

The contractions and possessive pronouns in the following chart are sometimes confused with each other. Remember that only the contraction has an apostrophe.

Contractions	Possessive Pronouns
you're	your
it's	its
they're	their

Examples:
It's (It is) time to go to exercise class.
Its pace is just right for me.

Some Pronoun Contractions

I + am	=	I'm
you + are	=	you're
he + is	=	he's
she + will	=	she'll
we + have	=	we've
they + are	=	they're

Guided Practice

A. **Identify each contraction. Give the two words the contraction replaces.**

Example: I'm ready to start exercising. *I'm, I am*

1. They're already exercising.
2. It's important to warm up before exercising.
3. Stretch when you're ready to exercise.
4. I feel good after I've stretched.
5. We begin our exercise slowly after we've stretched.
6. Consuela is a swimmer, so she's in good condition.
7. She'll cool down slowly after swimming.
8. We're stronger now that we run often.
9. They'll slow down to a walk after their run.
10. They're walking to relax their muscles.

Independent Practice

B. **Write each sentence. Replace the words in parentheses with contractions.**

Example: (He is) learning about exercise and body fat.
He's learning about exercise and body fat.

11. (I am) reading what one expert writes about fitness.
12. (He has) studied the effects of exercise on the body.
13. (You are) healthier without extra body fat.
14. (It is) important to keep the percentage of body fat in the right range.
15. (She is) exercising to keep her body fat in the range of twelve to thirty percent.
16. (It is) not a healthy range for a young man, though.
17. (He had) better exercise if his body is thirty percent fat.
18. Exercise works best if (it is) aerobic.
19. (He is) trying to keep his body fat between five and twenty percent.
20. (He will) feel better after exercising.

C. **Write each sentence. Choose the correct word of the two in parentheses.**

Example: (Your, You're) keeping yourself healthy by exercising.
You're keeping yourself healthy by exercising.

21. Exercise can help if (you're, your) sad.
22. (It's, Its) good for people's moods.
23. (Their, They're) often more relaxed after exercising.
24. (They're, Their) sleeping habits are better, too.
25. Doing many kinds of exercise makes all (your, you're) muscles stronger.

> **Remember**
> that subject pronouns and verbs join together to form **contractions**. Avoid confusing the contractions *you're, it's,* and *they're* with possessive pronouns.

Writing Connection

Writer's Journal: Using Different Styles

Write a paragraph to a friend about a book or movie that you especially liked. Use informal language, including contractions, to make your paragraph sound natural. Then rewrite your paragraph in more formal language, as it might appear in a newspaper. Remember not to use contractions.

Extra Practice

A. Write each sentence. Replace the possessive noun in parentheses with a possessive pronoun.
pages 244–245

Example: The boy was late for (the boy's) soccer game.
The boy was late for his soccer game.

1. Soccer has made (soccer's) mark in the world.
2. People in more than 140 countries spend (people's) time playing soccer.
3. Blanca says, "Soccer is (Blanca's) favorite sport."
4. Julio plays soccer with (Julio's) team.
5. Bruno and I plan (Bruno's and my) time around soccer games.
6. Julio always says, "Please come to (Julio's) game."
7. We tell Julio, "We will be at (Julio's) game."
8. Kathy is the best player in (Kathy's) soccer league.
9. Players may pass the ball to (players') teammates.
10. Fans cheer for (fans') favorite teams.

B. Choose a reflexive pronoun to complete each sentence. Then write the sentence. *pages 246–247*

Example: You will be running the race by _____.
You will be running the race by yourself.

11. We can all keep _____ healthy by exercising.
12. I keep _____ in shape by jogging.
13. You may prefer to keep _____ fit by walking.
14. Joggers should pace _____ so they can talk and still breathe easily.
15. Serious runners usually push _____ harder than joggers do.
16. Both runners and joggers should buy _____ the right type of shoes.
17. Sarah protects _____ from foot injuries by wearing the right shoes.
18. Robert is careful to protect _____ from muscle strain.
19. He and Sarah guard _____ against joint injury.
20. Robert and Sarah said, "We always prepare _____ by stretching before running."

C. Write each sentence. Replace the words in parentheses with contractions. *pages 248–249*

Example: (I am) a believer in the importance of exercise.
I'm a believer in the importance of exercise.

21. (We are) healthier when we exercise regularly.
22. (You are) sure to grow stronger if you exercise a little bit every day.
23. (It is) possible to hurt yourself exercising, however.
24. (You are) wise to exercise carefully.
25. People sometimes have muscle pain when (they are) exercising too much.
26. (It is) a sign that they should rest.
27. (They will) be healthier if they rest their muscles for a day or two.
28. (It is) not good to push ourselves too much.
29. The human body is not the machine (we would) sometimes like it to be.
30. (You will) feel better if you take care of your body.

D. Write each sentence. Choose the word in parentheses that correctly completes each sentence. *pages 244–249*

31. People need to exercise so (they're, their) in good health.
32. Hassan pushes (hisself, himself) hard when he exercises.
33. Michelle and Hassan practice (they're, their) aerobics every day.
34. You always need to pay attention to (your, you're) body.
35. (Its, It's) important to stop when you feel pain.

Writing Connection

Technology Search the Internet for a review of a book you have read or some computer software you have used. Try searching by the title of the book or by the keywords *children's books* or *children's software*. Write whether you agree or disagree with the reviewer's opinion, and explain why. Be careful not to confuse pronoun contractions and possessive pronouns.

For more activities with possessive and reflexive pronouns and contractions, visit *The Learning Site:*
www.harcourtschool.com

Chapter Review

Read the passage and choose the word that belongs in each space. Write the letter for your answer.

> I hope (1) planning to run the race with me. (2) going to be a great race. Nancy and I will be running in (3) first race. Alice and Vince have decided (4) not going to run. Alice hurt (5) leg while training. Vince says he bought (6) new shoes for the race. He ran in last year's race, and the trophy was (7) . This year I hope the trophy will be (8) .

STANDARDIZED
TEST PREP

TIP Read the directions carefully. Then read all the possible answers before you choose the best one.

1 **A** your
   B you're
   C yourself
   D you

2 **F** It
   G Its
   H It's
   J Itself

3 **A** our
   B ours
   C ourselves
   D mine

4 **F** they
   G their
   H there
   J they're

5 **A** her
   B hers
   C herself
   D their

6 **F** him
   G himself
   H hisself
   J he

7 **A** he
   B his
   C himself
   D hisself

8 **F** I
   G myself
   H my
   J mine

For additional test preparation, visit *The Learning Site:*
www.harcourtschool.com

Evaluating Film and Television

A media message includes both words and visual images. **Media literacy** is the ability to view and listen critically to media messages. People use this ability to form opinions about the messages they receive from movies and TV. These opinions can guide people in making decisions. Because media messages can reach millions of people, the entire culture may be affected.

It is important for all of us to be media literate so that we can make wise decisions. You can improve your media literacy by asking yourself questions as you watch a movie or television program. Here are some questions you can use.

1. What are you watching, and what is it about?

2. How true or accurate is the information given? How can you tell?

3. Whose point of view is shown? Is it dependable? Why do you think so?

4. What is the message? Do you agree? Why or why not?

5. What is the purpose of the program or movie? How might this affect your opinion?

6. How might the message affect our culture?

YOUR TURN

EVALUATE A MESSAGE Make your own chart or list of the six questions. Use it to analyze a television program or a movie. Think carefully as you answer each question. Then bring your work to class and share your answers and opinions with your classmates.

TIP Think about the purpose of the movie or program. Ask yourself, "Is the purpose to *inform*, to *persuade*, or to *entertain*?"

Writer's Craft

Effective Sentences

CONTRASTING Contrasting means telling how things are different from each other. Read the following passage from the book *Leonardo da Vinci* by Diane Stanley. Notice how the writer uses contrast to give information about her subject.

Over the years Leonardo da Vinci filled thousands of pages with the outpourings of his amazing mind. There were drawings of grotesque faces, drafts of letters, sketches for future paintings, lists of books he owned, plans for inventions . . . and observations of nature. On one page, for example, you can find geometry problems, a plan for building canals, and the note "Tuesday: bread, meat, fruit, vegetables, salad."

All this was written in a peculiar backward script, going from right to left. You must use a mirror to read it. This has led to the myth that he wrote that way to keep his notebooks safe from prying eyes. In fact, Leonardo was left-handed and found it much easier to write that way. When he really wanted to keep something secret, he wrote in code.

Analyze THE Model

1. How does the writer get your attention in the opening sentence?
2. Are the notes that Leonardo da Vinci wrote on one page all alike, or do they show a contrast? Explain your answer.
3. How does the writer show a contrast between a mistaken idea and what is true?

Vocabulary Power

gro•tesque [grō•tesk′] *adj.* Distorted or ugly in appearance or style.

We say that something is effective when it has the **effect**, or result, that we want. When you write to inform your reader, you want to give information in a clear and interesting way that holds your reader's interest. This is what effective sentences do.

Strategies for Writing Effective Sentences

Applying the Strategies

Write a good opening sentence.

Write a sentence that tells what you are writing about and sparks your reader's interest.

Combine sentences.

Look for places where you can use compound subjects and compound predicates. Combine simple sentences to write compound sentences.

Think about sentence variety.

Don't make all your sentences alike. Use statements, questions, and exclamations. Use simple sentences and compound sentences.

YOUR TURN

ANALYZE EFFECTIVE SENTENCES Work with two or three classmates. Look for examples of informative writing in newspaper or magazine articles or in chapters of your social studies or science textbooks. Discuss how the writers used effective sentences in their writing.

Answer these questions:

1. What is the writer's subject?

2. What is the writer's purpose?

3. Is the writer's opening sentence effective? Why or why not?

4. What different types of sentences does the writer use, and how does this make the article or chapter more interesting?

5. What are some examples in which the writer compares or contrasts things or ideas?

Opening Sentences

A. On your paper, write a good opening sentence for the paragraph below. Your sentence should state the main idea of the paragraph and spark your reader's interest.

In winter, the waterways would freeze often. Shipping was difficult. Sometimes the settlers had to wait until spring for supplies to reach them. In summer, however, great numbers of boats moved freely up and down the rivers.

Combining Sentences

B. Read each pair of sentences. Write a new sentence that combines each pair.

1. Japan is an island nation. The Republic of Indonesia is an island nation.
2. Japan is in eastern Asia. The Republic of Indonesia is in Southeast Asia.
3. Japan consists of four large islands. Japan also owns more than 1,000 small islands nearby.
4. Thousands of inhabited islands are part of Indonesia. Thousands of uninhabited islands are part of Indonesia.
5. My uncle has visited Japan. My uncle has only read about Indonesia.
6. A monarch is a type of butterfly. A swallowtail is a type of butterfly.
7. Butterflies can be found in woodlands and fields. Butterflies can be found in prairies.
8. Butterflies are insects. Moths are insects.
9. Some butterflies live on cold mountaintops. Some butterflies live in hot deserts.
10. Most butterflies have beautiful wings. Most butterflies have brightly colored wings.

Sentence Variety

C. **Read the following paragraph. Then rewrite it to include a variety of sentences. If you can, add a question, an exclamatory sentence, or an imperative sentence. Combine sentences to make them more effective.**

> Different people like different ways of living. Some people like to live in cities. Some people prefer living in the country. Some people enjoy excitement. They like the busy life of the city. Other people like peace and quiet. They like being close to nature. The country is a good place for them.

Writing and Thinking

Writer's Journal

Write to Record Reflections When you read an interesting piece of writing, do you ever take time to look at it from a writer's point of view? That means thinking about what makes the piece interesting and what you can learn from it that you can apply to your own writing. How can analyzing the effective writing of others, including your classmates, help you improve your own writing? Write your reflections in your Writer's Journal.

Paragraph That Contrasts

Diane Stanley, the author of *Leonardo da Vinci*, contrasted a mistaken idea about Leonardo's unusual handwriting with the true reason for it. Brian knew that life in Leonardo da Vinci's time was different from life in today's world. Read this paragraph that Brian wrote to contrast life then and now.

MODEL

opening sentence

contrast

compound subject

contrast

contrast

sentence variety

It is hard to imagine how different Leonardo da Vinci's life was 500 years ago from our lives today. Cars and airplanes did not exist back then. The printing press had just been invented, so most books were still written by hand. Leonardo was a great scientist, but he could not have dreamed of the technology we have today. What would he have thought of television, computers, and all the other wonderful inventions that are so much a part of our daily lives?

Analyze THE Model

1. What contrasts does Brian make in his paragraph?
2. Is Brian's opening sentence effective? Why or why not?
3. How does Brian vary his sentences?
4. Why are the words *different* and *but* important in this paragraph?

WRITING PROMPT Point out some differences between reading and watching TV. Write a paragraph that contrasts these two activities. Write a good opening sentence, and use effective sentences to make your paragraph interesting.

STUDY THE PROMPT Ask yourself these questions:

1. What is my purpose for writing?

2. Who is my audience?

3. What things will I contrast?

4. What writing form will I use?

Prewriting and Drafting

Plan Your Paragraph That Contrasts List ways in which reading and watching TV are different from each other. Then organize the information you will include in your paragraph. Use a chart like this one to help you plan the paragraph.

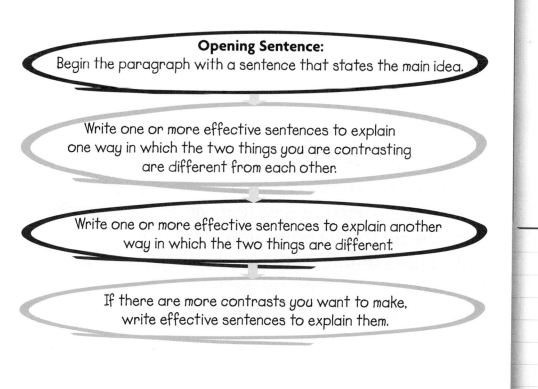

Opening Sentence:
Begin the paragraph with a sentence that states the main idea.

Write one or more effective sentences to explain one way in which the two things you are contrasting are different from each other.

Write one or more effective sentences to explain another way in which the two things are different.

If there are more contrasts you want to make, write effective sentences to explain them.

USING YOUR

Handbook

Use the Writer's Thesaurus to find interesting words that will help you write effective sentences.

Editing

Reread the draft of your paragraph that contrasts. Do you see ways to make your sentences more interesting and effective? Use this checklist to help you revise your paragraph:

☑ Have you given your reader enough information?

☑ Will your reader understand how the two activities are different from each other?

☑ Does your opening sentence state your main idea?

☑ Can you combine sentences to make them more effective?

☑ Have you varied the types of sentences you use?

Use this checklist as you proofread your paragraph:

☑ I have used capitalization and punctuation correctly.

☑ I have checked compound subjects and compound predicates to make sure that subjects and verbs agree.

☑ I have used conjunctions and punctuation correctly in compound sentences.

☑ I have used a dictionary to check my spelling.

Editor's Marks

✗	delete text
∧	insert text
ᵔ	move text
¶	new paragraph
≡	capitalize
/	lowercase
◯	correct spelling

Sharing and Reflecting

Writer's Journal

Make a final copy of your paragraph that contrasts, and share it with a partner. After reading each other's paragraphs, tell what you like best about your partner's paragraph. Point out effective sentences, and discuss how each of you could improve your writing. Write your reflections in your Writer's Journal.

Words That Signal Contrast

Certain words signal that a writer or speaker is expressing a contrast. Can you think of what some of these words might be? See if you can pick out words that signal contrasts in this conversation.

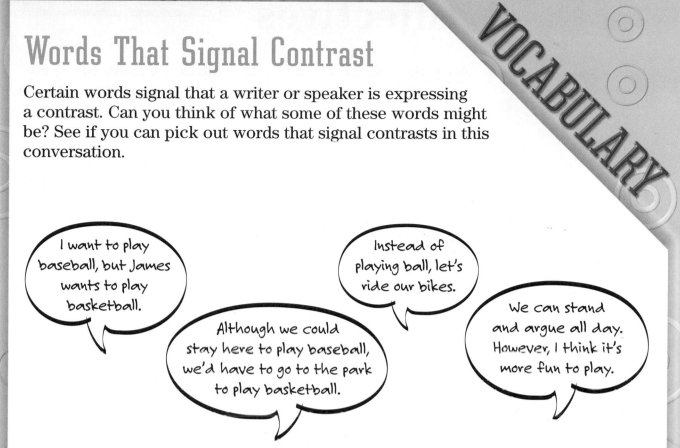

I want to play baseball, but James wants to play basketball.

Although we could stay here to play baseball, we'd have to go to the park to play basketball.

Instead of playing ball, let's ride our bikes.

We can stand and argue all day. However, I think it's more fun to play.

YOUR TURN

With a partner, go on a scavenger hunt for contrast words. Look all over your classroom for examples of words that show contrast. Here are some places you might look:

- textbooks
- magazine articles
- newspapers
- library books
- notices and messages in your classroom

Make a list of the words you find. Then compare your list with classmates' lists. Challenge each other to make up original sentences using contrast words from the lists.

Adjectives

An **adjective** is a word that modifies a noun or a pronoun. The adjectives *a*, *an*, and *the* are called **articles**. A **proper adjective** is formed from a proper noun.

Adjectives can tell *what kind, how many*, or *which one*. They usually come before the nouns they describe. They may also follow a verb such as *is, seems, feels*, or *appears*.

Example:
Tiny insects have **powerful** senses.

The article *the* refers to a particular person, place, thing, or idea. The articles *a* and *an* refer to any person, place, thing, or idea. Use *a* before a consonant sound, and use *an* before a vowel sound.

Example:
A sour lemon has **an** effect on your taste buds.

Always capitalize a proper adjective. Many proper adjectives are formed from place names. If you are not sure how to form a particular proper adjective, look in a dictionary.

Example:
A **German** scientist was one of the first to study the eye.

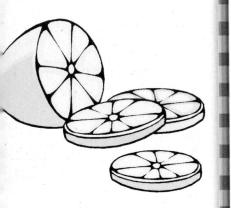

Vocabulary Power

stim·u·lus
[stim´yə•ləs] *n.*
Anything that stirs to action or greater effort. The plural of *stimulus* is *stimuli* [stim´yə•lī].

Guided Practice

A. Identify the underlined words as an adjective, a proper adjective, or an article.

Examples: <u>Famous</u> scientists have written about <u>the</u> senses.
adjective, article

<u>Chinese</u> scientists have studied <u>the</u> <u>five</u> senses.
proper adjective, article, adjective

1. Eyes are <u>sensitive</u> to <u>bright</u> light.
2. <u>Many</u> scientists have studied <u>the</u> eye.
3. People who are <u>blind</u> can read with their fingertips instead of their eyes.
4. <u>French</u> scientist Louis Braille lost his eyesight as <u>a</u> <u>young</u> child.
5. <u>The</u> <u>Braille</u> alphabet uses raised dots on paper that <u>the</u> fingertips can feel.

Independent Practice

B. **Write each sentence. Underline the adjectives in each sentence, including articles. Draw an arrow from each adjective to the word it modifies.**

Example: Joe took a long nap under the shady oak.

Joe took a long nap under the shady oak.

6. The warm afternoon was a perfect time for napping.
7. Today the sunshine is brilliant.
8. It is a beautiful day for a picnic.
9. There are many colorful birds in the park.
10. Our whole family hears their musical sounds.
11. We also watch playful ducks in the big pond.
12. Sometimes I take a morning swim in the large pool.
13. The water seems cool today.
14. I feel hungry when I smell Italian food.
15. Each day I use my five senses.

C. **Write each sentence. Underline all adjectives except articles and proper adjectives. Draw two lines under the articles. Circle the proper adjectives.**

Example: The science teacher has a garden of English roses.
The science teacher has a garden of English roses.

16. Several students visited the rose garden.
17. The nose is a powerful organ.
18. The human nose is not as sensitive as dog noses.
19. People enjoy the smell of fragrant flowers.
20. Some French perfumes smell like familiar flowers.

Remember

that **adjectives tell** *what kind, how many,* or *which one.* The adjectives *the, a,* and *an* are **articles**. Capitalize **proper** **adjectives**, which are formed from proper nouns.

Writing Connection

Technology: Making a Sensory Web Use a graphics software program to create a graphic organizer. Using the software, draw five circles on your screen. Then, place the name of one of the five senses (hearing, sight, smell, taste, touch) in each circle. For each sense, make a web of five adjectives that relate to the sense. As an alternative, you can draw a word web on a sheet of paper.

263

Adverbs

A word that modifies a verb is called an **adverb**.
An adverb often tells *how, when,* or *where*.

How?   Tia *gently* stroked the kitten's soft fur.

When?   The cat returned *yesterday*.

Where? The kitten looked *up*.

Many adverbs that tell *how* end in *-ly*. An adverb may
be placed before or after a verb that it describes. Negative
words such as *not* and *never* are adverbs that usually
describe verbs.

Examples:

Mrs. Choi **carefully** <u>prepared</u> her lesson on the five senses.

She <u>knows</u> **exactly** what she wants her students to learn.

Students **never** <u>arrive</u> **late** for her class.

<table>
<tr><th colspan="2">Common Negative Adverbs</th></tr>
<tr><td>not</td><td>rarely</td></tr>
<tr><td>never</td><td>hardly</td></tr>
<tr><td>nowhere</td><td>barely</td></tr>
</table>

Guided Practice

A. **Identify the adverb in each sentence, and tell what
word it describes. Explain whether the adverb tells
how, when, or *where*.**

Example: Jason eagerly volunteered for the first experiment.
eagerly, volunteered; how

1. He immediately went to the front of the class.
2. Jason walked to the table and stood there.
3. Mrs. Choi gently placed a clip on Jason's nose.
4. She then covered the student's eyes with a dark scarf.
5. Next, Jason reached for the object in Mrs. Choi's hand.
6. He rolled the object carefully between his hands.
7. Jason thought hard.
8. He said suddenly, "It's a grape."
9. He put it down with a smile.
10. "You have guessed correctly," replied Mrs. Choi.

Independent Practice

B. Write each sentence. Underline each adverb. Draw an arrow from the adverb to the verb that the adverb describes.

Example: Lena waited eagerly for the science lesson to start.
Lena waited eagerly for the science lesson to start.

11. Mrs. Choi taught each lesson thoroughly.
12. Today she wants us to think about the five senses.
13. "Do the brain and the eyes work together?" she asked.
14. Mrs. Choi repeated the question slowly.
15. Mrs. Choi then led a class discussion on the topic.
16. She explained, "Your two eyes look directly at the same object."
17. "Each eye focuses clearly on a different view."
18. "Each eye separately sends a picture of what it sees."
19. "The brain instantly forms one image from the two pictures."
20. The students looked up when Mrs. Choi wrote "three-dimensional effect" on the board.

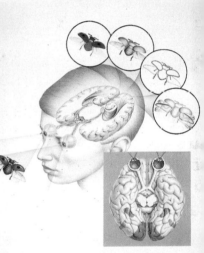

C. Add an adverb to describe the verb in each sentence. Write the new sentence.

Example: Birds depend on their vision.
Birds depend entirely on their vision.

21. We watched the sky.
22. Birds soared above us.
23. Birds hunt for food.
24. They drop to the ground at the sight of food.
25. One bird calls to another.

Writing Connection

Writer's Journal

Writer's Journal: Vivid Adverbs Make a list of at least five common verbs. (If you can't think of any verbs, just remember some of the things that you do every day, such as eating, drinking, running, and so on.) Then brainstorm a list of vivid adverbs that could describe the verbs on your list. Think of adverbs that are lively. Then write three sentences using your verbs and adverbs.

USAGE AND MECHANICS

Adjective or Adverb?

Whether a word is an adjective or an adverb depends on how it is used in a sentence.

Sometimes a sentence includes a word that could be either an adjective or an adverb. Ask yourself, "What does this word describe?" If the word describes a noun or pronoun, it is an adjective. If the word describes a verb, it is an adverb.

> Carpentry is a **hard** job. (The adjective *hard* describes the noun *job*.)
>
> Juan worked **hard**. (The adverb *hard* describes the verb *worked*.)

Many adverbs are formed by adding *-ly* to an adjective. Be sure to use the form you need.

> **Incorrect:**   Carla greeted her new teacher **cheerful**.
>
> **Correct:**   Carla greeted her new teacher **cheerfully**.
>
> (The adverb *cheerfully* tells how Carla greeted her teacher.)

A few words that end in *-ly* are commonly used as adjectives.

> Carla always speaks in a **friendly** manner. (The adjective *friendly* describes the noun *manner*.)

Guided Practice

A. **Tell whether the underlined word in each sentence is an adjective or an adverb. Tell how you know.**

Examples: A fire burns <u>nearby</u>.
adverb, describes "burns" and tells where

Call a <u>nearby</u> fire department.
adjective, describes the fire department

1. My brother and I eat <u>fast</u> at dinner time.
2. The smell of dinner is a <u>fast</u> way to build an appetite.
3. I can <u>easily</u> recognize the smell of bread baking.
4. We enjoy <u>lively</u> conversation at dinner.
5. The dishes clatter <u>noisily</u> while we wash them.

Independent Practice

B. Write each sentence. Draw an arrow from the under-lined word to the word it describes. Then write whether the underlined word is an adjective or an adverb.

Example: The sound of <u>soft</u> music filled the room.

The sound of <u>soft</u> music filled the room. adjective

6. An automobile drove <u>noisily</u> past the house.
7. An airplane flew <u>loudly</u> over the house.
8. Sound waves travel <u>quickly</u> through the air.
9. The waves bounce <u>everywhere</u>.
10. The sound <u>then</u> goes to the eardrum.
11. The eardrum is like a <u>little</u> trampoline.
12. Sound <u>always</u> makes the eardrum move.
13. The vibrations move <u>quickly</u> from the eardrum through the nerves.
14. Nerves carry <u>important</u> messages to the brain.
15. The brain make sense of the <u>different</u> noises we hear.

C. Choose the correct word in parentheses to complete each sentence. Then write the sentence.

Example: Birds are singing (cheerful, cheerfully) in the trees.

Birds are singing <u>cheerfully</u> in the trees.

16. Mike listens (careful, carefully) to their sounds.
17. The notes ring out (clear, clearly) in the stillness.
18. The birds seem (happy, happily).
19. Be (careful, carefully) not to scare them.
20. Oh no, a dog is barking (loud, loudly).

Remember

that some words can be either **adjectives** or **adverbs**. Many words that end in *-ly* are adverbs. However, some words that end in *-ly* are adjectives.

Writing Connection

Real-Life Writing: Lost-and-Found Notice Imagine that you have found someone's lost pet. The best way to get it back to its owner is to make a sign that describes it. Write a brief notice that describes the pet so that the owner will recognize it. Use adjectives and adverbs in your description. If you need help, look in the lost-and-found section of a newspaper for ideas on how to describe a lost pet.

Extra Practice

**A. Write each sentence. Underline all adjectives.
Draw two underlines under the articles.** *pages 262–263*

Example: The nose is the main organ for the sense of smell.
The nose is <u>the</u> main organ for <u>the</u> sense of smell.

1. Your nose has a tiny patch of nerves.
2. The ends of the nerves are sensitive to odors.
3. An odor causes a direct signal from the nerves to the brain.
4. The amazing brain has centers that identify odors.
5. A German scientist sorted different kinds of odors in 1916.
6. High temperatures can affect the strength of an odor.
7. The nose detects different odors at the same time.
8. The flavor of food is determined by our sharp sense of smell.
9. Some people do not like strong odors.
10. The brain works to identify the many odors.

**B. Write each sentence. Underline each adverb.
Draw two lines under the verb or verbs the adverb
describes.** *pages 264–265*

Example: The human body responds quickly to a stimulus.
The human body <u>responds</u> <u>quickly</u> to a stimulus.

11. You jump away from a hot stove.
12. You lose your balance after you step down from a roller-coaster ride.
13. Your body shivers when you go outside in winter.
14. You scratch constantly at a wool collar.
15. Your eye blinks immediately when dust gets in it.
16. Your knee jerks suddenly when the doctor taps it.
17. You cough often when you are around dust or dirt.
18. You might swallow water unexpectedly when you swim.
19. Your heart pounds rapidly when you are frightened.
20. Your body is working normally.
21. Your nerves always cause these reactions.
22. Your body moves instantly when it is in trouble.
23. The nerves react quickly to stimuli.
24. Signals pass directly from the nerves to the brain.
25. The brain processes sensory information rapidly.

Remember

that an **adjective**
describes a noun or
pronoun and an
adverb describes a
verb. Many, but not
all, adverbs end in
-ly. Some words can
be used both as
adverbs and as
adjectives.

For more activities
with adjectives and
adverbs, visit *The
Learning Site:*
www.harcourtschool.com

C. Write each sentence. Draw an arrow from each underlined word to the word it describes. Then write whether the underlined word is an adjective or an adverb. *pages 266–267*

Example: Mrs. Rojas is a popular teacher.
Mrs. Rojas is a popular teacher. adjective

26. Mrs. Rojas explained that the tongue can identify <u>four</u> kinds of tastes.
27. Each taste bud has a <u>hard</u> job.
28. Mrs. Rojas said, "Let's <u>quickly</u> draw a picture."
29. "Follow my instructions <u>carefully</u>," she said.
30. Each student sketched a <u>gigantic</u> face.
31. A <u>long</u> tongue poked out of the mouth.
32. The students drew tiny buds on <u>different</u> parts of the tongue.
33. The buds on the tip of the tongue <u>always</u> sense sweet tastes.
34. Only <u>bitter</u> tastes make buds on the back of the tongue react.
35. Buds on <u>both</u> sides of the tongue recognize sour tastes.

D. Write each sentence, choosing the word in parentheses that correctly completes the sentence. *pages 262–267*

36. The bird I saw was a (canada, Canada) *goose.*
37. I saw dolphins jump (playfully, playful) in the waves.
38. A dolphin makes (simply, simple) noises that bounce off underwater objects.
39. The sounds return to the dolphin like (an, the) echo.
40. The (playfully, playful) dolphins use sounds to "see."

Writing Connection

Writer's Craft: Descriptive Details Descriptive details, including adjectives and adverbs, can help you compare and contrast objects. Choose two objects, such as two kinds of fruit, and list words that appeal to the five senses. Use your list to write a paragraph or a poem about the objects. Trade descriptions with a partner. Circle the adjectives and underline the adverbs used.

Chapter Review

Look for mistakes in usage and capitalization in the sentences below. When you find a mistake, write the letter of the line containing the mistake. Some sentences do not have any mistakes at all. If there is no mistake, choose the letter beside *No mistakes*.

TIP The point of some tests is to identify errors. Look for simple mistakes when you take such tests.

1 A Ramon was reading
  B a interesting book
  C about the five senses.
  D (*No mistakes*)

2 J He regular
  K spends his Saturdays
  L reading at the library.
  M (*No mistakes*)

3 A Today he has selected
  B a book on the five
    senses
  C by an american
    scientist.
  D (*No mistakes*)

4 J Ramon tried hard
  K to understand
  L the material.
  M (*No mistakes*)

5 A He discovered
  B some fascinatingly
  C information.
  D (*No mistakes*)

6 J Food must be
  K complete chewed
  L in saliva.
  M (*No mistakes*)

7 A If a person eats quick,
  B he or she does not
    really
  C taste the full flavor.
  D (*No mistakes*)

8 J If you chew
  K your food slow,
  L it will taste better.
  M (*No mistakes*)

9 A Try eating an apple
  B carefully next time
  C to taste the difference.
  D (*No mistakes*)

10 J Enjoying a meal
    slowly
  K also helps the body
  L digest food easy.
  M (*No mistakes*)

For additional test preparation, visit *The Learning Site:*
www.harcourtschool.com

STANDARDIZED
TEST PREP

Using a Dictionary and a Thesaurus

The Dictionary

A **dictionary** lists words and gives their meanings. A dictionary also shows a word's history, its pronunciation, and its division into syllables and accents.

Each word listed in a dictionary is called an **entry word**. **Guide words** at the top of each page show which words are defined on that page. The guide word on the left is the first entry word on the page. The guide word on the right is the last entry word. All the words listed on the page come between the guide words alphabetically.

The Thesaurus

A **thesaurus** lists words and their **synonyms**. Synonyms are words that have the same or nearly the same meaning. Words in a thesaurus are listed in alphabetical order.

A thesaurus listing for the word *bad* might look like this:

> **bad** *adj.*
> | | |
> |---|---|
> | disobedient | harmful |
> | naughty | rotten |
> | evil | spoiled |
> | wicked | false |

A thesaurus can also show how words have positive or negative meanings. Look at the following advertisement. Notice how the meaning of the advertisement changes when different synonyms are used.

- **Small, old** house with **big** yard in **nice** neighborhood.

- **Petite, aged** house with **huge** yard in **agreeable** neighborhood.

- **Tiny, antique** house with **enormous** yard in **pleasant** neighborhood.

YOUR TURN

WORD PICTURES Write a sentence or two describing a scene. Use at least three common words that have synonyms. Use a dictionary or thesaurus to find some synonyms. Write the sentences two more times, using the synonyms. Next, find a partner and exchange sentences. Try to draw the scene described by each sentence. Compare your drawings.

TIP Use the right words in your writing to help your readers picture your ideas.

Other Kinds of Adverbs

An adverb can describe a verb. Adverbs can also describe adjectives and other adverbs.

You have learned that adverbs describe verbs by telling *how, when,* or *where.* When adverbs describe adjectives and other adverbs, they usually tell *how* or *to what extent.*

Examples:

Adverb Describing an Adjective

The human heart is a **very** strong organ. *(How strong, or strong to what extent?)*

Adverb Describing an Adverb

A healthy heart **almost** never skips a beat. *(To what extent?)*

The following adverbs can describe adjectives and other adverbs: *almost, incredibly, so, certainly, quite, too, extremely, really, unusually, hardly, slightly,* and *very.*

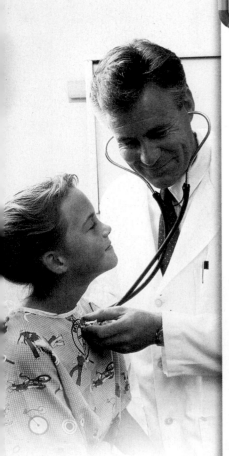

Guided Practice

A. Identify the adverb that describes each underlined adjective or adverb.

> **Example:** The human heart is an incredibly <u>powerful</u> pump.
> *incredibly*

1. The heart beats really <u>fast</u> during exercise.
2. Your heart pumps blood very <u>smoothly</u>.
3. The heart is an extremely <u>important</u> part of the circulatory system.
4. The three types of blood vessels have completely <u>different</u> jobs.
5. The work of blood vessels is certainly <u>important</u>.
6. Unusually <u>thin</u> tubes called capillaries connect the arteries to the veins.
7. The blood flows without too <u>much</u> trouble.
8. The heart and lungs work together quite <u>efficiently</u>.
9. We hardly <u>ever</u> think about how the body works.
10. People almost <u>always</u> take it for granted.

Independent Practice

Remember that an **adverb** can describe a verb, an adjective, or another adverb.

B. Write the adverb that describes each underlined adjective or adverb.

> **Example:** The respiratory system is very <u>important</u>.
> *very*

11. A healthy respiratory system works really <u>well</u>.
12. Breathing can be incredibly <u>rhythmic</u>.
13. When a person inhales, the lungs become quite <u>large</u>.
14. People breathe in unusually <u>deeply</u> when exercising.
15. The inside of the nose is extremely <u>moist</u>.
16. Almost <u>instantly</u>, the nose cleans and warms the air.
17. Air moves into the lungs through slightly <u>smaller</u> tubes.
18. The journey the air takes is not very <u>long</u>.
19. The lungs have totally <u>hollow</u> pockets that fill with air.
20. A person's chest expands rather <u>quickly</u> as the lungs fill.

C. Write each sentence, and underline each adverb. Some sentences have more than one adverb. Draw an arrow from each adverb to the verb, adjective, or adverb that it describes.

> **Example:** A person breathes quite rapidly during exercise.
> *A person breathes <u>quite rapidly</u> during exercise.*

21. The lungs release air very smoothly.
22. Oxygen from the air moves very quickly to the blood.
23. Carbon dioxide moves quite rapidly from the blood to the lungs.
24. You can see your breath in extremely cold weather.
25. When jumping, a person breathes rather quickly.

Writing Connection

Writer's Journal: Humor Experiment with writing opening sentences for funny poems. For example, a limerick might begin, *There once was a boy named Joe,/ Who by foot was extremely slow.* In each sentence, use at least one adverb that modifies an adjective or another adverb. Choose the opening you like best, and complete the poem.

Comparing with Adjectives and Adverbs

Adjectives and adverbs can be used to compare. Adjectives can be used to compare people, places, things, or ideas. Adverbs can be used to compare actions.

Add *er* to compare one thing with one other thing. Add *est* to compare one thing with two or more others.

More or *most* is used with many adjectives or adverbs of two or more syllables. Use *more* to compare one thing with one other thing. Use *most* to compare one thing with two or more other things.

Examples:	
Short Adjectives	A person's heart is **larger** than a frog's heart. The elephant's heart is **largest** of all.
Longer Adjectives	Kim is a **more athletic** soccer player than I am. Kim is the **most athletic** soccer player on the team.
Short Adverbs	Linda ran **farther** than Miguel. Henry ran the **farthest** of anyone in the race.
Longer Adverbs	Ellen learned the dance **more quickly** than her friends. Louis learned the dance **most quickly** of all.

Notice that *than* signals a comparison of two things. *Of all* often signals a comparison of three or more things.

Guided Practice

A. Decide which form of the adjective or adverb in parentheses is needed. Tell whether to use *er, est, more,* or *most.*

Example: The (small) animal with a circulatory system is the earthworm. *smallest*

1. The hummingbird has the (fast) heart rate of any animal.
2. A capillary is (thin) than a hair.
3. The heart lies (close) to the chest than to the back.
4. Kim is (active) than I am.
5. Athletes breathe (hard) of all when they run.

Independent Practice

B. Write each sentence. Use the correct comparing form of the adjective or adverb in parentheses.

Example: Our class worked (hard) than ever before to get ready for the Science Fair.
Our class worked harder than ever before to get ready for the Science Fair.

6. This is the (large) class project of the year.
7. Of all the projects, we were (excited) about the health project.
8. We chose the (interesting) subject of all.
9. Stefan's group worked (rapidly) of all.
10. I think our group worked (carefully) than his.
11. Our display showed that blood flows (slowly) in the tiny blood vessels than in the larger ones.
12. It also showed that some red blood cells carry oxygen to the lungs (late) than other red blood cells do.
13. White blood cells die (soon) than red blood cells.
14. In other words, red blood cells live (long) than white blood cells.
15. No one grinned (broad) than I did when the judges said my group had won.
16. Your heart beats (fast) when you run.
17. Hard work makes the heart (strong).
18. I check my pulse (carefully) than I used to.
19. The heartbeat of a sleeping person is (slow) than the heartbeat of someone who is exercising.
20. You can see the blue veins beneath the skin (clearly) than you can see other blood vessels.

Remember

to use *er* or *more* with adjectives and adverbs to compare one thing or action with another. Use *est* or *most* with adjectives and adverbs to compare three or more things or actions.

Writing Connection

Science Think about your heart and lungs. How are they the same when you exercise and when you are at rest? How are they different? Make a Venn diagram to compare and contrast these two states of your body. Then write four sentences based on your diagram. Use at least one comparing form in each sentence.

USAGE AND MECHANICS

Using *Good* and *Well*

Good and *bad* are adjectives. *Well* is an adverb unless
it means "healthy." *Badly* is always an adverb.

Examples:

The team played a **good** game despite the **bad** weather. Good
describes the noun game; bad *describes the noun* weather.

The team played **well**. Well *describes the verb* played.

Bill had a cold, but now he is **well** enough to play. Well *means*
"healthy" and describes the noun Bill.

The team plays **badly**. Badly *describes the verb* plays.

Some adjectives and adverbs have special forms.

	Comparing Two	More than Two
good, well	better	best
bad, badly	worse	worst

Examples:

This is a **good** book, but the other one is **better**.
The dog is behaving **badly**, but it has behaved **worse**.

Guided Practice

A. **Tell which word in parentheses correctly completes
each sentence. Then tell whether that word is an
adjective or an adverb in the sentence.**

Example: Swimming is (good, well) exercise. good, *adjective*

1. Running is (better, best) exercise than bowling.
2. It is the (worse, worst) track in the state.
3. Anita ran (better, best) than I did.
4. Geraldo was not (good, well); he had a cold.
5. The next day Geraldo ran (better, best) of all.

Independent Practice

B. Write each sentence. Use the word in parentheses that correctly completes each sentence. Then write whether the word is an adjective or an adverb.

6. The human voice is a (good, well) musical instrument.
7. With a drive to succeed, a singer may do (good, well).
8. A singer should not have a (bad, badly) voice coach.
9. Without proper training, a person may sing (bad, badly).
10. (Good, Well) singers control their breathing.
11. Today he sang (badly, worse) than yesterday.
12. He needs to take care of himself to stay (good, well).
13. Performers sing (good, well) when they practice.
14. The first practice session is often the (worse, worst) of all.
15. How (good, well) singers must feel after a great performance!

C. Write each sentence. Choose the correct form of the word in parentheses. Then write the word that your answer describes.

Example: This year we had a very (good, well) science fair.
This year we had a very good science fair. fair

16. Mario's exhibit about lungs was (better, best) than the other one.
17. You described it (good, well) in the school paper.
18. Julie's exhibit was judged the (better, best) at the fair.
19. No one made a (bad, badly) exhibit; they were all interesting.
20. The noise in the room, however, was the (worse, worst) I have ever heard.

Writing Connection

Technology: Compare Websites Find two health websites for kids. Use *children* and *nutrition* or *children* and *fitness* as keywords for your search. Write a paragraph in which you compare or contrast the websites. Tell which one you like better and why. Use several comparing forms of adjectives or adverbs.

Extra Practice

A. **Write each sentence and underline each adverb. Some sentences have more than one adverb. Draw an arrow from each adverb to the word that it describes.** *pages 272–273*

Example: Human blood takes a very interesting journey.
Human blood takes a <u>very</u> interesting journey.

1. Blood cells work rather hard.
2. They carry oxygen and later release it.
3. Oxygen is very important for the body.
4. The body's tissues finally receive the oxygen.
5. Blood cells also release carbon dioxide.
6. The lungs regularly release carbon dioxide.
7. Every breath does the job quite efficiently.
8. The body always replaces blood.
9. The whole cycle of the circulatory system begins again.
10. I think the respiratory and circulatory systems are really amazing.

B. **Write each sentence. Choose the correct comparing form of the adjective or adverb in parentheses.** *pages 274–275*

Example: Doctors perform some medical tests (often) than they do others.
Doctors perform some medical tests more often than they do others.

11. Blood tests are the (common) of all medical tests.
12. Computers do the blood tests (fast) than people do.
13. Today, doctors can spot unhealthy blood cells (precisely) than ever before.
14. Computers can check the blood samples (exactly) than the human eye.
15. Doctors can find blood diseases (easily) than before.
16. Today's labs process blood tests (fast) than the labs of twenty years ago did.
17. Doctor Ness is the (likable) doctor in the hospital.
18. He listens (carefully) to his patients than some other doctors do.
19. Doctor Ness is (busy) than the other cardiologists.
20. He wants his patients to get the (good) care possible.

Remember

that when you **compare** with **adjectives** or **adverbs**, you must use an *er* or an *est* ending, the words *more* or *most*, or special forms, such as *better, best, worse,* and *worst.*

DID YOU KNOW?
For an organ that pumps up to two gallons of blood every minute, the heart is not very heavy. In fact, the average human heart weighs only ten ounces.

For more activities with adverbs, visit *The Learning Site:*

www.harcourtschool.com

C. Write each sentence. Use the word in parentheses that correctly completes the sentence. Then write the word that your answer describes. *pages 276–277*

Example: This cold is (worse, worst) than the one I had last year.
This cold is worse than the one I had last year. cold

21. I breathe (good, well) when I don't have a cold.
22. My sore throat was (better, best) than before.
23. I was doing a (bad, badly) job of taking care of myself.
24. I slept (worse, worst) than I did the night before.
25. I did get a (good, well) rest that night.
26. I breathed much (better, best) after a few days.
27. I was finally (good, well) again.
28. Rest was the (better, best) treatment of all.
29. I play soccer (bad, badly) if I don't practice.
30. I'm glad that we played the last game so (good, well).

D. Rewrite each sentence, correcting the errors.
pages 272–277

31. Marissa did very good on the science test.
32. It was difficulter than the English test.
33. The last question was the difficultest of all.
34. She has never done bad on a science project.
35. It was her better project of the whole year.

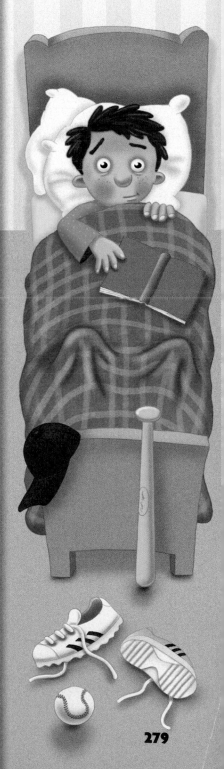

Writing Connection

Writer's Craft: Word Choice Think of a kind of physical exercise or activity that you either enjoy or do not enjoy. List several adjectives and adverbs that you could use to describe how you perform the exercise. Then write a short paragraph about the exercise. Do not state whether you enjoy the exercise; use the adjectives and adverbs to suggest your feelings. Exchange paragraphs with a partner. Have the partner find the adjectives and adverbs that help show how you feel.

Chapter Review

Look at the underlined words in each sentence. There may be a mistake in word usage. If you find a mistake, choose the answer that is the best way to write the underlined section of the sentence. If there is no mistake, choose *Correct as is*.

STANDARDIZED
TEST PREP

TIP Mistakes in word usage on standardized tests often include incorrect comparing forms of adjectives and adverbs. Carefully check any comparing forms you see.

1 Blood <u>moves quick</u> through the body.

   A moves quickly

   B moves quickest

   C moves quicker

   D Correct as is

2 The heart is the <u>most strong</u> muscle in the body.

   F more strong

   G strongest

   H more strongly

   J Correct as is

3 All other muscles tire <u>more sooner</u> than the heart.

   A soonest

   B most soonest

   C sooner

   D Correct as is

4 The heart is an <u>unusually strong</u> organ.

   F unusually stronger

   G unusual stronger

   H unusual strongly

   J Correct as is

5 The diagram of the heart <u>was drawn bad</u>.

   A was drawn good

   B was drawn badly

   C was drawn worst

   D Correct as is

6 It is the <u>worse illustration</u> in the book.

   F most bad illustration

   G more worse illustration

   H worst illustration

   J Correct as is

7 Doctors are finding <u>more better</u> ways to take care of the heart.

   A gooder

   B better

   C most good

   D Correct as is

8 Exercise is one way to stay <u>well</u>.

   F good

   G best

   H more well

   J Correct as is

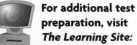

For additional test preparation, visit *The Learning Site:*

www.harcourtschool.com

Using Graphs and Maps

A **graph** is a visual aid that gives information in numbers. You can use graphs to show relationships and comparisons. The graph below is a bar graph. Each bar shows the same kind of information.

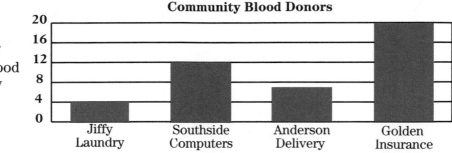

Community Blood Donors

Number of pints of blood donated by company

From this bar graph, you learn that Golden Insurance employees gave the most blood and that Jiffy Laundry employees gave the least. You also know how many pints the employees of each of the four companies donated.

A **map** is another kind of visual aid. It gives such information as where buildings, lakes, or parks are located. This map shows the community where the companies operate. What information do you learn from the map that is not given on the graph?

YOUR TURN

GRAPHING **Create a bar graph that shows information about things you study in your class. If possible, use computer software to help you. For example, you might graph the number of hours that your class spends studying one subject each day of the week. Provide a title and labels for your graph. Be ready to explain the comparisons you can make from the information.**

TIP Read carefully the captions and labels on graphs or maps to understand what information is being presented.

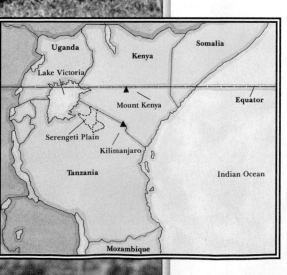

A writer can describe things by telling how they are similar and how they are different. Patricia Lauber tells about animals that live on the African plains. As you read, think about how she uses comparison and contrast to create a clear picture of the animals and how they live.

FUR, FEATHERS, and FLIPPERS

by Patricia Lauber

Much of East Africa lies on or near the equator. Here every day is hot because the sun rises high in the sky all year-round. Seasons are either rainy or dry. There are times when rains fall for weeks or months. There are times when little or no rains fall for three to eight months.

Grass grows better than other plants in a climate like this. During a dry season, grass dies back, but when the rains come again, grass springs up again, from its roots.

Most plants grow from the tips of leaves or shoots, but grass grows from the base of its leaves. This means it grows back quickly after being grazed.

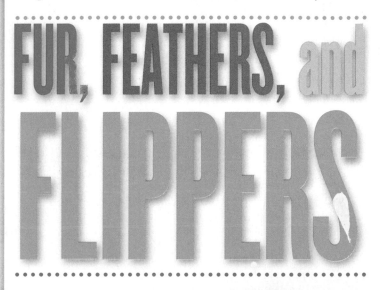

283

That is why the plains of East Africa are seas of green or golden grass, with scattered trees. That is why they are home to millions of grass-eating animals and to meat eaters that prey on the grass eaters.

The seas of grass are also home to the biggest herds of hoofed mammals in the world. In places, a million or more of these animals are moving about and feeding on grass. East Africa has more than sixty kinds of antelope, such as gazelles, wildebeests, topis, and elands. It has zebras. It has buffaloes. It has giraffes and elephants, which usually feed on the leaves of trees and bushes but also eat grass.

These many big grass eaters can share a habitat because they do not compete. Zebras, wildebeests, and topis may graze together. They eat the same kinds of grass, but they do not eat the same parts.

Zebras eat the tough, outer part of the stem. Then topis, which have pointed muzzles, can reach the lower parts. Wildebeests, which have square muzzles, bite off the leaves that grow sideways. Together these animals clip grass down to its base. Cutting grass causes it to grow. A few days later, Thomson's gazelles are nibbling the tender new growth.

Topis also eat grass that has reached its full height and dried out. New blades grow and are eaten by other animals. Elephants tear off long, tough grasses, leaving short grasses that other animals use.

Most of the big grass eaters move around to seek food, traveling as much as one thousand miles a year. Their long legs and small, hard hoofs are well suited to crossing the dry plains. Their long legs also make them speedy runners and help them escape from the meat eaters of the plains.

Lions are the chief hunters on the plains. They kill the biggest prey and harvest the most meat. These big cats eat antelope, buffaloes, zebras, and even

giraffes, but they usually take what they can easily catch.

Most often, lions hunt by night in groups of one or more families. They may stalk a zebra or a wildebeest through tall grass, taking hours to close in on one animal. To catch a speedy gazelle, they must take it by complete surprise in a short, quick dash.

The leopard is next in size to the lion. Leopards hunt alone at night, usually in forests or wooded places near the plains. They attack from hiding. After eating, a leopard may drag its catch up into a tree, to be finished later. When leopards do hunt on the plains, they feed on the new-born young of hoofed mammals. Many kinds of young are able to walk minutes after birth, but they cannot run fast enough to escape a leopard.

The cheetah is the third of the big cats. It hunts by day, first stalking a small antelope, then running it down. The cheetah is the fastest runner of all land animals.

Two other animals also prey on the grazing animals. One is the African hunting dog. Hunting dogs are long-distance runners that hunt in packs by day. Their leader chooses a prey animal, usually an antelope. The pack chases the animal until it tires; then the pack attacks. Hunting dogs are fierce; even a leopard will scramble out of their way.

The grass and the animals fit together. Grass grows best when it is cut or grazed. The hoofed mammals graze it. If their numbers multiplied and multiplied, they would graze too much and kill the grass. This does not happen, however, because the hunters keep down the number of grazers. If the hunters killed too many grazers, then they would run out of food. This does not happen either. The hunters never kill for sport, only for food. At times when food is scarce, many young meat eaters do not live to grow up. Therefore, the number of meat eaters is also kept in check, and the life of the plains is in balance.

Vocabulary Power

om•niv•o•rous
[om•niv′rəs] *adj.*
1. Eating both animal
and vegetable food.
2. Eagerly taking in
everything: an *omnivo-
rous* reader.

Analyze THE *Model*

1. What was Patricia Lauber's purpose for writing?
2. How did she introduce her topic?
3. How did Lauber organize her comparison and contrast of grass eaters and meat eaters?

READING — WRITING CONNECTION

Parts of a Comparison/ Contrast Essay

Patricia Lauber compared and contrasted two kinds of animals. Read this comparison/contrast essay written by a student named Phillip. Pay attention to the parts of the essay.

MODEL

Fun with Food

introduction

main idea

Do you know that you are omnivorous? That means that you can eat food from both plants and animals. Your body needs protein, carbohydrates, vitamins, minerals, and a small amount of fat to be healthy. You can't get all these things from any one food. In other words, being omnivorous means you can, and should, eat many kinds of food.

animal foods

Meat and milk products come from animals. Both are good sources of the protein your body needs to build muscles. Both can have a fairly high amount of fat in them. Animal foods can give your body important vitamins and minerals. For example, milk and cheese are good sources of calcium, which is important for your bones. Vitamin B6, which helps fight disease, is found in most meats.

similarities
of plant foods
and animal
foods

Foods from plants have some similarities to foods from animals. Nuts, whole grains, and some vegetables can provide protein. Quite a few plant foods can be, like meat and milk products, a source of fat. In addition, most of the vitamins and minerals that you get from animal foods can also be found in at least one plant food.

On the other hand, your body needs carbohydrates for fuel, and only plants can provide them. Also, some vitamins and minerals in fruits and vegetables, like vitamin C and beta-carotene, aren't found in food from animals. Finally, unlike animal foods, plants can provide fiber. This important material helps your body digest food better.

It takes work to make sure you get all the different things your body needs. However, being omnivorous is definitely more fun than eating hay for breakfast, lunch, and dinner!

differences between plant foods and animal foods

restatement of main idea

conclusion

Analyze THE Model

1. What was Phillip's purpose for writing?

2. Phillip presented the similarities and differences in animal and plant foods. How did he organize the information to make it easy for readers to follow?

3. What words or phrases did Phillip use that alert readers to similarities? To differences?

Summarize THE Model

Identify Phillip's topic and main ideas in a graphic organizer like the one shown here. Use the completed graphic to write a summary of Phillip's comparison/contrast essay. Include only the important points, not the supporting details.

topic

similarities   differences

Writer's Craft

Sentence Variety Phillip used a variety of sentences in his essay. What kinds of sentences did he use? Find an example of each. Tell why Phillip varied the sentences.

Comparison/ Contrast Essay

Prewriting

Purpose and Audience

You have probably noticed similarities and differences between many things. In this chapter, you will inform your classmates by writing a comparison/contrast essay.

WRITING PROMPT Write an essay about two outdoor activities that you enjoy. Compare and contrast the rewards and the challenges of the two activities. State your topic, and then explain the similarities and differences between the two activities. End your essay by restating your topic.

First, decide on your topic, purpose, and audience. What point will you be making by explaining the similarities and differences between the two activities? What audience might be interested in your ideas?

Strategies Good Writers Use

- Be clear about your purpose and audience.
- List similarities and differences.

MODEL

Phillip thought about the different kinds of foods people can eat. He decided to tell his classmates about how foods from animals and from plants are the same and how they are different. He used this diagram to organize his ideas.

My purpose: to tell my classmates why we need to eat different foods

My topic: animal foods and plant foods.

YOUR TURN

Choose two outdoor activities to compare and contrast. Use a diagram to organize your ideas.

similarities
nutrients from animals and plants:
    protein
    fat
    some vitamins and minerals

differences
nutrients only from plants:
    carbohydrates
    some vitamins and minerals
    fiber

Organization and Elaboration

Follow these steps to help you organize your essay:

STEP 1 Interest Your Reader from the Start
Begin your essay with an unusual fact or idea.

STEP 2 State Your Topic
State your topic clearly to introduce the two activities you will compare and contrast.

STEP 3 Compare and Contrast
Tell about the similarities and differences. Group them logically. For example, you may want to put the similarities in one paragraph and the differences in another.

STEP 4 Conclude by Restating Your Topic
Sum up your most important points.

MODEL

Here is the introduction of Phillip's essay. What fact does he use to get his audience's attention? What details does he use to lead into his topic statement?

> Do you know that you are omnivorous? That means that you can eat food from both plants and animals. Your body needs protein, carbohydrates, vitamins, minerals, and a small amount of fat to be healthy. You can't get all these things from any one food. In other words, being omnivorous means you can, and should, eat many kinds of food.

Write your first draft on a computer. The word count and line count features can help you keep track of how long your draft is.

YOUR TURN

Now draft your essay. Use the steps above, and look at your notes from prewriting.

Revising

Organization and Elaboration

Begin editing by rereading your draft thoughtfully.

- How well did I get my reader's interest?
- How have I varied my sentences? Have I repeated any words or phrases too often?
- Have I used words such as *for example* and *however* that help the reader follow my ideas?
- How logically have I arranged my ideas? Did I jump back and forth between similarities and differences?

MODEL

Here are the changes Phillip made to part of his essay. Notice how he moved one sentence so that all the similarities were grouped together.

> Meat and milk products come from animals. Both are good sources of the protein your body needs to build muscles. Both can have a fairly high amount of fat in them. ~~Like meat,~~ nuts, whole grains, and some vegetables can ~~also~~ provide protein. Animal foods can give your body important vitamins and minerals. For example Milk and cheese are a good source*s* of calcium, which is important for your bones. ~~Most meats are good sources of~~ Vitamin ~~vitemin~~ B6, which helps fight disease. is found in most meats.
> Foods from plants have some ~~other~~ similarities to foods from animals.

YOUR TURN

Revise your comparison/contrast essay to make the organization more logical. Add words and phrases to connect the ideas clearly.

Strategies Good Writers Use

- Vary the length and types of sentences.
- Use phrases such as <u>for example</u> or <u>on the other hand</u> to link ideas.
- Arrange ideas logically.

To revise a paragraph, copy it and paste the copy below the original. Make your changes on the copy, and then delete the original.

Checking Your Language

Check your work carefully for errors in spelling, capitalization, punctuation, and grammar. Mistakes like these can interrupt the flow of your ideas.

MODEL

After Phillip revised his essay, he proofread it carefully. Here is another part of his essay with the corrections he made. Phillip corrected two errors in agreement. What other corrections do you see?

> On the other hand, your body needs
> *carbohydrates*
> ~~carbahydrates~~ for fuel, and only plants
> *them*
> can provide ~~it~~. Also, some vitamins and
> minerals in fruits and vegetables, like
> *aren't*
> vitamin C and beta-carotene, ~~isn't~~ found
> in food from animals. Finally, unlike
> animal foods, plants can provide fiber.
> This important material helps your body
> digest food ~~most~~ better.

Strategies Good Writers Use

- Check comparing forms of adjectives and adverbs.
- Look for missing commas.
- Check pronoun-antecedent agreement.

Editor's Marks

- ℘ delete text
- ∧ insert text
- ○ move text
- ¶ new paragraph
- = capitalize
- / lowercase
- ○ spelling

YOUR TURN

Use this checklist to help you proofread your revised essay:
- **Check spelling, using a dictionary.**
- **Check punctuation and capitalization.**
- **Check grammar, especially pronoun-antecedent agreement.**

USING YOUR
Handbook

Use the rubric on page 509 to evaluate your comparison/contrast essay.

Publishing

Sharing Your Work

Now you are ready to publish your essay. Use the answers to these questions to help you decide how to share your work:

1. When you wrote the essay, what audience did you have in mind? How can you most easily reach that audience?

2. Should you print your essay in manuscript, write it in cursive, or produce your final copy on a computer? If you use a word processor to publish your essay, see the information on page 295.

3. What can you add to your published essay to make it more appealing? Would drawings or a collage of photos improve it? Should you add an illustrated cover?

Reflecting on Your Writing

Using Your Portfolio What did you learn about your writing in this chapter? Write your answer to each question below.

1. Do you think your writing was varied enough to keep your readers' interest? Why or why not?

2. How well did you connect the ideas in your essay? Give examples.

3. Did your writing meet its purpose? Explain your answer.

Add your answers and essay to your portfolio. Take some time to look through your past work. Write a sentence about something that you do well in your writing. In another sentence, tell about something you could do better. Based on your sentences, set a new goal for improving your writing. Have you made progress on your earlier goals?

Using a Word Processor

Phillip decided to use a word processor to format and print his essay for the class. You can use a word processor to publish your essay as well. Follow these steps:

STEP 1 Start the word processing program. Open a new document file. Save the new file, giving it a name that you can easily find again.

STEP 2 Type your document. Let the computer decide where to end one line and begin the next. Press the ENTER (or RETURN) key to start a new paragraph. Remember to save your work often.

STEP 3 Use the Spell Check feature to do a first proofreading. Then check the essay yourself for misspellings that the computer does not recognize (for example, *there* instead of *their*).

STEP 4 You can use the Format function to make certain words, such as your title, stand out. Use boldface, underlining, or italics.

STEP 5 Print your finished document. Check it carefully, type any changes or corrections, and print it again. You can repeat this step until you are satisfied. Always save your work.

Tips for Using a Word Processor

Experiment with your word processor. Here are some tips on what to try:

- Add pictures. Most computer systems offer pictures, called clip art, of people, symbols, and common objects.

- Add page numbers. Many word processing programs have a function that inserts page numbers automatically.

- Try changing margins and line spacing. You might even use double columns to make your writing easier to read.

Subject Pronouns *pages 234–235*

A. Write each sentence. Underline the subject pronoun.
Write whether that pronoun is singular or plural.

1. "We both want to be food scientists," said my friend, Carmen.
2. She is going to tell our science teacher, Mr. Payton.
3. He will be happy to hear about our plans.
4. Last night I told my parents about my career goal.
5. They were very interested in my choice.

Object Pronouns *pages 236–237*

B. Write each sentence. Underline the object pronoun.
Write whether the object pronoun is singular or plural.

6. When Sam talked to the grocery manager, he learned some valuable lessons from her.
7. She told him that people should always wash fresh vegetables.
8. Many fresh foods lose nutrients if we do not refrigerate them.
9. Most canned foods should be kept in the refrigerator after we open them.
10. Sam talked to Bonnie and me about what the grocery manager said.

Pronoun-Antecedent Agreement

pages 238–239

C. Write each sentence. Underline the pronoun. Circle the
noun that is the pronoun's antecedent.

11. Mr. Payton described digestion, and the students listened to him.
12. The body must break down foods before it can use nutrients.
13. The way the body breaks down foods is called digestion, and it begins in the mouth.
14. Luisa asked about how teeth help, and Mr. Payton told her.
15. Teeth begin the process as they break the food into tiny pieces.
16. Saliva moistens the food pieces and makes them easier to swallow.
17. Mr. Payton asked, "Peter, can you tell where swallowed food goes?"
18. Peter said that food goes from the mouth into a tube, and then it enters the stomach.
19. Mia said that she knew about the digestive juices in the stomach.
20. In the stomach, foods break down more before they move on.

Possessive Pronouns pages 244–245

Unit 4
Grammar Review

CHAPTER 20

More About
Pronouns
pages 244–253

A. Write each sentence. Replace the possessive noun in parentheses with a possessive pronoun.

1. Jean said, "Running makes (Jean's) muscles work hard."
2. Roberto asked, "Is that why (Jean's and Roberto's) legs get tired?"
3. Jean answered by nodding (Jean's) head.
4. They stopped running and checked (Jean's and Roberto's) heart rates.
5. Roberto found that (Roberto's) heart was beating faster than before.

Reflexive Pronouns pages 246–247

B. Write each sentence, replacing the word or words in parentheses with a reflexive pronoun.

6. Marta and Richard exercise to keep (Marta and Richard) healthy.
7. Marta exercises to keep (Marta) physically fit.
8. Richard said, "We can also use exercise to keep (Marta and Richard) feeling happy."
9. Marta's father runs to keep (Marta's father) in good shape.
10. During sleep, the body rests and repairs (the body).

Contractions with Pronouns

pages 248–249

C. Write each sentence. Replace the words in parentheses with contractions.

11. (You are) doing better than most people if you exercise regularly.
12. Only 41 percent of people between ages 18 and 64 say (they are) exercising.
13. Even fewer people over age 65 say (they have) been getting regular exercise.
14. (She is) wise to exercise regularly.
15. When we walk or jog between 20 and 30 minutes each day, (we are) exercising regularly.
16. Ravi says (he is) planning to start swimming.
17. Ravi said to Corrie, "(You have) been swimming for years."
18. Corrie said, "(I am) starting to swim more often."
19. "(We will) enjoy swimming together," said Ravi.
20. Corrie said, "(I will) meet you at the pool tomorrow."

Adjectives   *pages 262–263*

A. Write all of the adjectives, except for the articles, in each sentence. Then write the word or words that each adjective describes.

1. An eye can see distant objects.
2. An ear can hear faraway sounds.
3. Sight and hearing are similar in this way, but taste and touch are different.
4. Human skin must touch an object before a person can feel something.
5. The tongue must make direct contact with food before we can taste different flavors.

Adverbs   *pages 264–265*

B. Write each sentence. Underline each adverb. Draw an arrow from the adverb to the verb that the adverb describes.

6. The eagle sees clearly from high in the sky.
7. Eagles look down to hunt for small animals.
8. We must listen carefully to hear the faint sounds made by a giraffe.
9. Dogs easily smell scents that humans never notice.
10. Wolves usually stay with their pack to hunt.

Adjective or Adverb?   *pages 266–267*

C. Write each sentence. Underline each adverb. Circle all the adjectives. Do not circle articles.

11. Shari saw the bright flowers and laughed happily.
12. The girl bent down and gently turned a flower upward.
13. She breathed deeply and smelled the red and yellow roses.
14. Shari carefully avoided the sharp thorns.
15. Yesterday the raspberry bushes were heavy with berries.
16. Today Shari eagerly picked a handful of the red berries.
17. Their sweet flavor quickly brought a smile to her face.
18. Her family had worked hard to plant the young bushes.
19. Two crows chattered noisily in a tall tree.
20. A gray squirrel easily cracked the hard shell of a nut.

Unit 4
Grammar Review

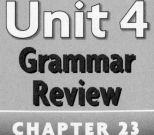

CHAPTER 23

More About
Adjectives and
Adverbs
pages 272–281

Other Kinds of Adverbs   *pages 272–273*

A. Write the adverb that describes each underlined adjective or adverb.

1. Our teacher suggested extremely <u>interesting</u> topics for our science fair projects.
2. Last year I worked almost <u>every</u> weekend on my project.
3. I started very <u>early</u> on this project.
4. I decided quite <u>recently</u> to show how the circulatory system works.
5. The model heart is slightly <u>larger</u> than a real one.
6. I worked an unusually <u>long</u> time to finish it.
7. This is not a totally <u>realistic</u> model.
8. A strip of red paper shows the blood's path really <u>well</u>.
9. We waited quite <u>impatiently</u> for the awards.
10. We were certainly <u>happy</u> when several of our projects won!

Comparing with Adjectives and Adverbs   *pages 274–275*

B. Write each sentence. Use the correct comparing form of the adjective or adverb in parentheses.

11. Mr. Williams is the (interesting) teacher I have ever had.
12. He said that people breathe (fast) when they exercise than when they rest.
13. The heart pumps much (hard) during exercise, too.
14. I worked (carefully) on this unit than on the last one.
15. My report was the (long) one in the class.

Using *Good* and *Well*   *pages 276–277*

C. Write each sentence. Use the word in parentheses that correctly completes each sentence. Then write whether *good* or *well* is an adjective or an adverb in the sentence.

16. I am a (good, well) student.
17. I usually perform (good, well) in class.
18. We found a (good, well) book on the respiratory system.
19. The team played (good, well) last night.
20. If you do not feel (good, well), you should see a doctor.

Unit 4
Wrap-Up

Writing Across the Curriculum: Health

An Exercise Journal

How often do you exercise? You may do it more or less often than you realize. The frequency may affect how you feel. One way to find out is to make an exercise journal.

Create Your Exercise Journal

- Write down all the exercise you have done so far today. How long did you do each kind of exercise? At bedtime, finish your list.

- On the back of the sheet, describe how you felt during the day. How did you feel before and after your exercise? How do you feel now?

- Keep your exercise journal for one week.

Make and Share a Graphic Organizer

- After seven days, use your journal to create a chart. What kinds of exercise did you do each day? For how long?

- Illustrate your chart with pictures of the kinds of exercise you did. Also include pictures of how you felt.

- Look over your chart. Do you see a pattern between your exercise habits and your feelings?

SUN.	MON.	TUES.	WED.	THURS.	FRI.	SAT.
Rode my bike for 1 hour	Played baseball for 2 hours	Jumped rope for 30 minutes	Walked my dog for 45 minutes	Played soccer for 1 hour	Rode my bike for 30 minutes	Walked my dog for 45 minutes

Write an Informative Essay

- At the end of the week, write an essay about your exercise experience. Explain how often you exercised. Tell if it affected your mood or energy level.

- If you wish, present your report in class. Share it with your doctor on your next visit.

Books to Read

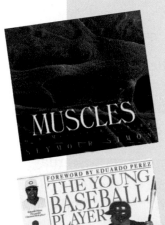

Muscles
by Seymour Simon
NONFICTION
Learn about the different muscles in the body, their jobs, and why exercise is important to good health.
Outstanding Science Trade Book

The Young Baseball Player
by Ian Smyth
NONFICTION
Hints on technique, teamwork, and strategies are included to help players improve their skills.

Four Types of Sentences *pages 24–29*

Write each sentence, and add the correct end punctuation. Then write *declarative*, *interrogative*, *imperative*, or *exclamatory*. If the group of words is not a sentence, write *fragment*.

1. Sapphires, emeralds, and rubies are three kinds of gems, or jewels
2. What color is a sapphire
3. A deep-blue gem
4. Show me a bright green emerald
5. What a brilliant red color that ruby is

Subjects and Predicates *pages 34–39, 52–57*

Write each sentence. Draw one line under the complete subject and two lines under the complete predicate. If the subject is compound, write *compound subject*. If the predicate is compound, write *compound predicate*.

6. The three fifth-grade classes visited an art museum yesterday.
7. Mrs. Rodriguez and Mr. Jordan went with us on the trip.
8. The group walked slowly and quietly around the large building.
9. Kevin and his classmates listened carefully.
10. The art stood on the floor, sat in glass cases, or hung on walls.

Simple and Compound Sentences

pages 62–67

Write each sentence. Choose the conjunction in parentheses that best fits each sentence. Add commas as needed. For each sentence, write whether it is *simple* or *compound*.

11. My family and I will visit the art museum on Saturday, (but, or) we will go to the crafts fair.
12. A painter draws pictures, (and, or) a sculptor makes statues.
13. The painter (and, or) the sculptor are both artists.
14. Juan enjoys mathematics, (and, but) he likes art better.
15. Juan will draw a funny cartoon (but, or) paint a pretty picture.

Nouns *pages 94–99*

List the common and proper nouns in each sentence. Add capitalization where needed.

1. King george III ruled england and its colonies in 1776.
2. In that year, colonists in north america declared their independence.
3. The Liberty Bell is in the city of philadelphia, pennsylvania.
4. The people of the united states celebrate their independence on the fourth of july.
5. Another name for that holiday is independence day.

Possessive Nouns *pages 104–109*

Rewrite each sentence. Change each underlined group of words to a phrase that contains the correct possessive noun.

6. The <u>family of Luis</u> visited a state park in New England.
7. The Sosas saw a <u>home of a colonist</u> in the state park.
8. <u>Dresses of women</u> and <u>toys of babies</u> were displayed inside the house.
9. The <u>clothing of everyone</u> was made by hand.
10. The <u>furniture of the colonist</u> was simple.
11. The <u>windows of the house</u> were small, but the <u>fireplace of the home</u> was large.
12. In the <u>yard of the family</u> was a vegetable garden.
13. The <u>chores of the children</u> included weeding the garden.
14. The <u>work of the people</u> was mainly farming.
15. The <u>home of the horse</u> was the barn.

Verbs *pages 122–127, 132–137*

Write each sentence. Underline the linking verb. Draw an arrow from the subject to the word or words in the predicate that rename or describe the subject.

16. These tools are examples of the blacksmith's work.
17. A horseshoe is attached to the horse's hoof.
18. The blacksmith's hammer seems very heavy.
19. The pounding of the hammer sounds loud.
20. The hot metal becomes cool in the tub of water.

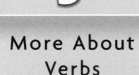

Cumulative Review
Unit 3

More About Verbs

Verb Tenses *pages 166–169, 176–177*

Write each sentence. Use the correct form of the verb in parentheses. Write the tense of the verb: *present*, *past*, or *future*.

1. Nine planets (travel) in orbits around the sun.
2. We (live) on Earth, the third planet from the sun.
3. People (name) the other eight planets after figures in mythology.
4. Stephen (study) astronomy in college next year.
5. Observatories (have) large telescopes through which the planets can be seen.

Commonly Misused Verbs *pages 198–199*

Write each sentence. Use the verbs in parentheses that correctly complete each sentence.

6. (Sit, Set) the astronomy book on the desk, and (sit, set) down.
7. Ms. Lee (teaches, learns) our science class, and we (have taught, have learned) about planets.
8. (Lie, Lay) the binoculars on the grass, and (lie, lay) down on the hilltop.
9. (Raise, Rise) the binoculars to your eyes; you will see stars (raise, rise) in the night sky.
10. (Let, Leave) your friend look through the binoculars before we (let, leave).

The Perfect Tenses *pages 204–207*

Write each sentence. Use the verb and tense shown in parentheses.

11. Astronomers ___ the planet Pluto since 1930. (observe, present perfect)
12. Earlier scientists ___ that Pluto existed. (predict, past perfect)
13. No one ___ the planet through a telescope until that year. (see, past perfect)
14. By the year 2030, astronomers ___ Pluto for one hundred years. (watch, future perfect)
15. I ___ a report on Pluto for my science class. (do, present perfect)

Subject and Object Pronouns

pages 234–239

Write each sentence. Choose the correct form of the pronoun in parentheses. Then write whether it is a *subject* pronoun or an *object* pronoun. Draw an arrow from a pronoun to its antecedent.

1. Robert knows that exercise is good for the body, and (he, him) walks two miles every day.
2. Laura enjoys swimming because (it, she) is fun.
3. The Smith twins run around the track after school, and several friends join (they, them).
4. Ishiro practiced soccer yesterday, and the coach gave (he, him) some help.
5. Kelly wants to be a nutritionist because (she, her) likes the field of food science.

Adjectives and Proper Adjectives

pages 262–263

Write the sentence, and underline each adjective except articles. Draw an arrow from the adjective to the word that it describes. If the word that you underline is a proper adjective, write *proper adjective.*

6. Cathy read an essay by an English scientist.
7. The human eye was the subject of the book.
8. The red rose in the vase has soft petals.
9. The fresh apple tasted sweet.
10. The band played a popular Irish song.

Adjective or Adverb? *pages 262–267, 272–273*

Write each sentence. Write whether each underlined word is an adjective or an adverb. Draw an arrow from the adjective or adverb to the word it describes.

11. The young man whistled <u>quietly</u>.
12. A lion makes a <u>very</u> <u>loud</u> roar.
13. The animal looked <u>up</u> and <u>eagerly</u> smelled the food.
14. The students follow the instructions <u>carefully</u>.
15. Our school's <u>best</u> runner <u>almost</u> <u>never</u> loses a race.

Language Use

Read the passage and decide which type of error, if any, appears in each underlined section. Mark the letter for your answer.

Have you seen the <u>Whitehead Science center's exhibit</u> about
(1)
the <u>planets? It includes</u> models of the planets. The four giant plan-
(2)
ets are <u>Jupiter Saturn Uranus, and</u> Neptune. Jupiter is so large
(3)
that <u>one thousand Earth's would</u> fit inside it. Saturn is the second
(4)
largest planet. Both planets <u>are very colorful, and are made</u> of
(5)
gases. I think <u>Saturn is the prettyest</u> because of its rings.
(6)

---

1 A Spelling error

   B Capitalization error

   C Punctuation error

   D No mistake

2 F Spelling error

   G Capitalization error

   H Punctuation error

   J No mistake

3 A Spelling error

   B Capitalization error

   C Punctuation error

   D No mistake

4 F Spelling error

   G Capitalization error

   H Punctuation error

   J No mistake

5 A Spelling error

   B Capitalization error

   C Punctuation error

   D No mistake

6 F Spelling error

   G Capitalization error

   H Punctuation error

   J No mistake

Written Expression

Here is the first draft of Brian's persuasive paragraph. There are several mistakes that need correcting.

> (1) No matter what season it is, it's always the right time to enjoy the outdoors. (2) You can have fun you can learn at the same time. (3) Nature wakes up your senses. (4) Nature has special colors, smells, and sounds. (5) Learn a lot by watching the plants and animals that live around you. (6) You can enjoy the natural world by taking walks, going camping, or playing outdoor sports. (7) Sometimes it is too cold to be outdoors, though. (8) The outdoors is waiting for you, and you can start your adventure now.

1 Choose the best way to write Sentence 2.

A You can have fun, you can learn at the same time.

B You can have fun and learn at the same time.

C You can have fun, and learn at the same time.

D Best as it is

2 Which of these best combines Sentences 3 and 4 into one sentence?

F Nature wakes up your senses because it has special colors, smells, and sounds.

G Nature wakes up your senses because they have special colors, smells, and sounds.

H Nature wakes up your senses and has special colors, smells, and sounds.

J Nature wakes up your senses, but it has special colors, smells, and sounds.

3 Select the best way to write Sentence 5.

A You have learned a lot by watching the plants and animals that live around you.

B You must learn a lot by watching the plants and animals that live around you.

C You can learn a lot by watching the plants and animals that live around you.

D Best as it is

4 Which is the best way to write Sentence 8?

F The outdoors is waiting for you, and you will start your adventure now.

G The outdoors is waiting for you, and you have started your adventure now.

H The outdoors is waiting for you, and we should start your adventure now.

J Best as it is

5 Which sentence does *not* belong in the paragraph?

A Sentence 1

B Sentence 4

C Sentence 6

D Sentence 7

Unit 5

Grammar Phrases and Clauses

Writing Research Report

Abraham Lincoln
born 1809, died 1865
born in Kentucky, lived in Illinois
16th President

Prepositions

A preposition is a word that tells the relationship of a noun or pronoun to another word in the sentence.

There are many prepositions. Here are a few:

about	by	of	to
across	during	off	until
after	for	on	up
at	from	over	with
between	in	throughout	within

A preposition can be almost anywhere in a sentence. Wherever it appears, it is followed by a noun or pronoun. Look at these examples.

Examples:
During the Ice Age, some ocean water froze.
The level **of** the oceans dropped.
A land bridge linked Asia **with** North America.
People could now travel **between** the continents.
Herds **of** large animals roamed **over** the land bridge.

Guided Practice

A. Identify the preposition in each sentence. Be ready to explain how you know that it is a preposition.

Example: Some anthropologists believe that the first settlers came from Asia.
from

1. They traveled across a land bridge.
2. After the Ice Age they moved south.
3. The hunters adapted to the warming climate.
4. Some groups still roamed with the herds.
5. The number of bigger animals grew smaller.
6. The hunters fished or made traps for smaller game.
7. Other groups settled in one place.
8. Over the years they learned farming skills.
9. When did the people split into different tribes?
10. Several hundred tribes developed within North America.

Independent Practice

B. Write each sentence. Underline each preposition.

> **Example:** Along the coast, tribes built small villages.
> *Along the coast, tribes built small villages.*

11. Fishing was important to most Northwestern tribes.
12. The Nootka tribe lived on Vancouver Island.
13. They stripped tree bark into long sheets.
14. They braved the open ocean in canoes.
15. Salmon was a major source of food.

C. Write each sentence. Choose the preposition in parentheses that makes sense.

> **Example:** The people made planks (from, under) cedars that reached heights (in, of) 300 feet.
> *The people made planks from cedars that reached heights of 300 feet.*

16. Totem poles were carved (until, for) different purposes.
17. Totems often represented events (in, on) people's lives.
18. The people used tools made (by, from) many things.
19. (Among, Along) the materials used were teeth, bones, shells, antlers, stone, and wood.
20. Tribes often held dances (across, during) the long winters.

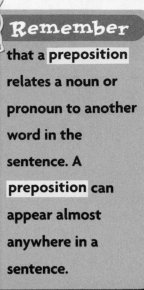
Writing Connection

Social Studies Imagine that you are meeting someone from another country or culture. What questions might that person ask about your culture? With a partner, write several questions and answers. You may want to role-play the conversation before you write. Underline the prepositions in your questions and answers.

Object of the Preposition

The noun or pronoun that follows a preposition is the object of the preposition. A prepositional phrase is made up of a preposition, the object of a preposition, and any words between them.

The object of a preposition can be either a noun or a pronoun. If the object is a pronoun, it is in the objective case.

Examples:

noun
The Anasazi people lived **in** <u>towns</u>.

pronoun
One **of** <u>them</u> had eight hundred rooms.

Words that come between the preposition and its object are part of a prepositional phrase, too. Study the examples below. The prepositional phrases are underlined, and the objects are circled.

Examples:

One town was built <u>on a sheer (cliff)</u>.
Dwellers climbed many feet <u>to the (mesa)</u>.

Guided Practice

A. **Each sentence contains one prepositional phrase. Identify the object of each preposition.**

Example: Toeholds in the rock are visible today. *rock*

1. The Anasazi were ancient people of the Southwest.
2. Mesa Verde held one of the largest towns.
3. Built on four stories, it had four hundred rooms.
4. The Anasazi people built rooms called kivas below the ground.
5. People entered kivas by ladder.
6. Many visitors came to Pueblo Bonito.
7. Traders came for the beautiful crafts.
8. Within the town lived skilled workers.
9. Were potters and jewelers among them?
10. Their work is interesting to me.

Independent Practice

B. Write the object of each preposition.

Example: Gardens lay outside the town walls. *walls*

11. Sandstone blocks were cemented with mud.
12. Builders made houses with many floors.
13. High above the square rose the central building.
14. Some parts of the Pueblo cultures remain today.
15. Anthropologists can only guess at others.

C. Write each sentence. Underline each prepositional phrase. Circle each object of a preposition.

Example: The Hopi and Zuñi peoples are descendants of the Anasazi.
The Hopi and Zuñi peoples are descendants of the (Anasazi).

16. Anasazi potters shaped clay into long, thin rolls.
17. They laid one clay roll upon another.
18. The potters coiled the rolls into a spiral.
19. With care, they smoothed and shaped the pots.
20. Finished pots dried in the sun.
21. The potters painted bold patterns on the pots.
22. Some pots were decorated with chunks of turquoise.
23. Turquoise came from mines 200 miles away.
24. Turquoise was also used in jewelry.
25. The Anasazi traded with people far away.

Remember

that the object of a preposition is a noun or pronoun that comes after the preposition. The preposition, its object, and any words between them form a prepositional phrase.

Writing Connection

Writer's Craft: Summarize Review the information about Native American buildings and artwork in this lesson. Write at least three sentences that summarize what you learned. Be sure to mention only the most important facts or ideas. Use several prepositional phrases. Then work with a partner to circle the objects of the prepositions.

GRAMMAR-WRITING CONNECTION

Expanding Sentences with Prepositional Phrases

Prepositional phrases may be at the beginning, in the middle, or at the end of sentences. They can expand sentences by adding details and examples. They can answer questions such as *where, what kind, which one, when,* and *how.*

Examples:

Northeastern Native Americans lived. *Where* did they live?
Northeastern Native Americans lived **in the woodland areas.**

The Iroquois raised crops. *What kinds* of crops were they?
The Iroquois raised crops **of corn and other vegetables.**

The corn is delicious. *Which* corn?
The corn **from this field** is delicious.

They held festivals. *When* did they hold festivals?
Throughout the year they held festivals.

The people worked. *How* did they work?
The people worked **in groups.**

Guided Practice

A. Read these sentences. Each prepositional phrase is underlined. Tell what question each phrase answers in the sentence.

Example: Many groups lived along the East Coast.
Where did they live?

1. People from the Great Lakes hunted and fished.
2. They gathered fruits, nuts, and berries in the woodlands.
3. The Iroquois farmed with great skill.
4. They grew more than sixty kinds of beans.
5. A planting festival took place in early spring.

Independent Practice

B. **Expand these sentences. Use the prepositional phrases in parentheses to add details.**

> **Example:** The Algonquian villages spread. (along the Atlantic coast)
>
> *The Algonquian villages spread along the Atlantic coast.*

6. The Algonquian people remained settled. (during the summer)
7. They pursued deer, bear, and other animals. (in the fall)
8. They built sturdy canoes using large sheets. (of birch bark)
9. They peeled the bark and placed it. (over the wooden frame)
10. Then builders sealed the seams. (with pine gum)

C. **Expand each sentence by adding at least one prepositional phrase.**

11. This book is interesting.
12. The picture shows a crowd.
13. The canoe floats.
14. The hunters hurry.
15. The women placed mats.

Writing Connection

Writer's Journal: Expanding Sentences Write for five minutes about a topic of your choice. Try not to use any prepositional phrases. Then write again on the same topic. This time, use prepositional phrases. Which version was easier to write? Which version would a reader prefer?

Extra Practice

A. Write the prepositions that appear in these sentences. Some sentences have two prepositions.
pages 310–311

Example: Woodland tribes enjoyed games of skill. *of*

1. One of their sports was a game called stickball.
2. Stickball players raced across a field with two sticks.
3. Players were sometimes injured by the sticks.
4. Another game involved a stone with a hole in the middle.
5. Players rolled the stone along the ground and guessed where it would stop.

B. Write each sentence. Underline each prepositional phrase. Circle each object of a preposition. Some sentences have two prepositional phrases. *pages 312–313*

Example: Symbols were important to the (people).

6. Dancers at a winter ceremony might wear bird masks.
7. At special times the chief wore a headdress.
8. The tribes of the Northeast Woodlands also made masks from wood.
9. The masks showed creatures from the forest.
10. People wore the masks during the healing ceremonies.
11. The Pueblo tribes in the Southwest were excellent craftworkers.
12. The Pueblo women decorated pottery with painted designs.
13. Southwestern Zuñi tribes often painted deer on their bowls.
14. Some tribes developed symbols for writing.
15. A Cherokee named Sequoyah invented a system of written signs called a *syllabary*.

Remember that a preposition is a word that relates a noun or pronoun to another word in the sentence. The noun or pronoun that follows the preposition is called the object of the preposition. A prepositional phrase contains a preposition, the object of the preposition, and any words between them.

C. Prepositional phrases are underlined. Tell what question each prepositional phrase answers. *pages 314–315*

Example: The Apache people traveled <u>to the Southwest</u>. <u>Where</u>?

16. Small groups moved <u>during the 1400s</u>.
17. They found shelter <u>in clever ways</u>.
18. The name "Apache" is a Pueblo word <u>for "enemy."</u>
19. <u>During the 1600s</u> some Apaches settled <u>in the Southwest</u>.
20. They became "the Apaches <u>of the fields</u>," or the Navajo.

D. Expand each sentence. Use the prepositional phrases in parentheses to add details to the sentence. *pages 314–315*

Example: The Navajo set up trading posts. (on the reservation)
The Navajo set up trading posts on the reservation.

21. The Navajo people moved. (with their herds in summer)
22. The Navajo lived in round homes called hogans. (during the winter)
23. A hogan is a wooden building. (with a hard earth cover)
24. Pueblo culture had a great influence. (on Navajo ways)
25. Traders saw their rugs. (as things of value)

Writing Connection

Technology Suppose you are going to make a film about Native American life. You want to have the important facts. On the Internet, find the home page of a Native American nation. Search by typing in the name of the nation, such as *Navajo* or *Cherokee*. Write a few sentences about the source you found. Use prepositional phrases to add information to your sentences.

Chapter Review

Read the passage. Choose the prepositional phrase or phrases that best complete each sentence. Write the letter of your answer.

Hiawatha was a Mohawk chief who wanted peace __(1)__. The League of the Iroquois resulted __(2)__ at peace-making. Another Native American leader, Powhatan chief Wahunsonacock, saved a group __(3)__. __(4)__, the settlers gave him a crown. Later the chief's daughter, Pocahontas, married one __(5)__, and their marriage sealed the peace __(6)__.

STANDARDIZED TEST PREP

TIP Before you finish a multiple-choice test, check your answers. Make sure that you have written the letters that match your answers.

1 A into the Native American tribes

  B under the Native American tribes

  C among the Native American tribes

  D from the Native American tribes

2 F at his efforts

  G from his efforts

  H to his efforts

  J before his efforts

3 A from settlers of starvation

  B before starving settlers

  C of settlers with starvation

  D of settlers from starvation

4 F From his kindness

  G In thanks for his kindness

  H With his kindness

  J Through his kindness

5 A of the settlers with her father's blessing

  B with her father's blessing, of the settlers

  C settler by her father's blessing

  D through the settlers, with her father's blessing

6 F after the settlers

  G for the Powhatan and the settlers

  H between the Powhatan and the settlers

  J to the Powhatan and the settlers

For additional test preparation, visit *The Learning Site:* www.harcourtschool.com

Making Outlines

Making an **outline** is a way to organize information that you are gathering for a research report. Use an outline to arrange information in the most effective order for your writing purpose.

Tips for Writing Outlines

1. Use Roman numerals for main ideas and capital letters for important details. Use a period after each. Indent each letter that appears below a numeral.

2. Keep entries brief. They do not need to be complete sentences.

3. Capitalize the first word of each entry.

4. Do not write a *I* without a *II* or an *A* without a *B*.

Title of Your Outline

   I. Main Idea
     A. Detail
     B. Detail

  II. Main Idea
     A. Detail
     B. Detail

YOUR TURN

Read the paragraphs below about the Hopi Indians. Apply the outlining tips to create a brief outline of the paragraphs. Your outline should have at least two Roman numerals with main topics and two letters with detail topics under each Roman numeral.

One group of Pueblo Indians is known as the Hopi. The Hopi were expert farmers who grew squash, melons, beans, and other fruits and vegetables. Their main crop was corn. The men also herded sheep, built houses, and made garments. The women usually made baskets and pottery, shared in the gardening, and helped with housebuilding.

In the late 1900s, there were about 6,000 Hopi people. Some of these Hopi lived in terraced houses in Oraibi. This village is located on a reservation in northeastern Arizona. Experts think that Oraibi is the oldest continuously occupied settlement in the United States. People have been living in this settlement since 1150 A.D.

Phrase or Clause?

A **phrase** is a group of closely related words that work together. A phrase does not contain a subject and a predicate. A **clause** is a group of words that has both a subject and a predicate.

You have learned about two kinds of phrases—verb phrases and prepositional phrases. These examples show the difference between a phrase and a clause.

Examples:

after the election	prepositional phrase—no subject and predicate
after <u>we</u> <u>won</u> the election	clause—has subject and predicate
<u>we</u> <u>won</u> the election	clause—has subject and predicate

Many clauses include phrases. In fact, a phrase in a sentence is always part of a clause.

My <u>parents</u> <u>voted</u>.	clause
My <u>parents</u> <u>voted</u> in the election.	clause containing prepositional phrase

Vocabulary Power

con·sti·tu·tion
[kon′stə·t(y)oo′shən] *n.*
A written plan of government that states the basic laws or rules.

Guided Practice

A. **Study each group of words. Tell whether it is a prepositional phrase or a clause. Which clause contains a prepositional phrase?**

Example: in the United States *prepositional phrase*

1. of government
2. according to the Constitution
3. the government has three branches
4. within each branch
5. senators and representatives are part of one branch
6. they write our laws
7. in the second branch
8. for the President
9. judges run the courts
10. if a person has broken a law

Independent Practice

Remember

that a **phrase** does not have a subject and a predicate. A **clause** has both a subject and a predicate.

B. Write whether each group of words is a prepositional phrase or a clause.

Examples: in a democracy *prepositional phrase*
the people choose their leaders *clause*

11. Congress writes laws
12. for the people
13. senators serve six-year terms
14. from each state
15. each state elects two senators
16. after six years
17. if they are not reelected
18. representatives serve shorter terms
19. because some states have more representatives
20. from each state

C. Write whether each underlined group of words is a phrase or a clause. Remember that a clause may contain phrases.

21. <u>Population is the number of people</u> who live in a place.
22. States <u>with bigger populations</u> can elect more representatives.
23. In 1999, California sent fifty-two representatives <u>to Congress.</u>
24. <u>Texas had thirty representatives in 1999.</u>
25. <u>After they have served for two years,</u> representatives must be reelected.

Writing Connection

Social Studies Talk with a partner about citizenship. What makes a person a good citizen? What responsibilities does a citizen have? With your partner, write five sentences about what you think makes people good citizens. Use phrases and clauses to add variety to your sentences.

Common Subordinating Conjunctions	
after	unless
although	until
because	when
before	whenever
if	where
since	while

Independent and Dependent Clauses

Some clauses can stand alone as sentences. These are called **independent clauses**. Other clauses cannot stand alone as sentences. These are called **dependent clauses**.

Examples:

Independent Clause
The colonists won independence from Great Britain.

Dependent Clause
when the colonists won independence from Great Britain

Notice the word that begins the dependent clause. *When* is an example of a **subordinating conjunction**. Many dependent clauses begin with the connecting words called subordinating conjunctions. When a clause begins with one of these words, it does not express a complete thought. It needs to be connected to an independent clause.

Example:

Independent Clause	**Dependent Clause**
A new nation was formed	when the colonists won independence from Great Britain.

Guided Practice

A. **Tell whether each underlined clause is an independent clause or a dependent clause. If the clause is dependent, name the subordinating conjunction.**

Example: The leaders shared ideas before they wrote the U.S. Constitution. *independent clause*

1. Before the Constitution was adopted, the United States had no President.
2. People liked the Constitution because it seemed fair.
3. When some people read the Constitution, they did not like it.
4. They would not support the Constitution unless the leaders added a Bill of Rights.
5. If certain rights were part of the Constitution, the government could not take them away.

Independent Practice

B. Write each sentence. Underline the independent clause.

Example: When the first Congress met, James Madison proposed new laws.
When the first Congress met, <u>James Madison proposed new laws.</u>

6. After Congress debated the laws, they became the Bill of Rights.
7. Congress presented twelve laws to the states.
8. The states approved ten of the laws.
9. After state governments approved the laws, they became part of the Constitution.
10. The First Amendment protects freedom of speech.

C. Write each sentence. Underline the dependent clause. Circle the word that begins the clause.

Example: The leaders improved the Constitution when they added the Bill of Rights.
The leaders improved the Constitution (when) <u>they added the Bill of Rights.</u>

11. Before the Bill of Rights was passed, many states had their own laws about rights.
12. Because we have the Bill of Rights, our freedoms are secure.
13. Police, for example, must have a good reason whenever they arrest someone.
14. If the government takes land, it must pay the owner.
15. Many people admire James Madison because he wrote the Bill of Rights.

> **Remember**
>
> that an **independent clause** can stand alone because it is a complete thought. A **dependent clause** cannot stand alone because it is not a complete thought. Look for a connecting word to help you identify a dependent clause.

Writing Connection

Writer's Journal: A Famous Sentence Find and read the Preamble to the Constitution. Notice that it is one independent clause that includes many phrases. In your Writer's Journal, write a long sentence with one clause. Underline the simple subject and the verb in your sentence.

323

Conjunction	Tells
after, before, until, when, whenever	when
where, wherever	where *or* which one
because, since, so that	why
if, unless, while	condition

GRAMMAR-WRITING CONNECTION

Combining Independent and Dependent Clauses

An independent clause expresses a complete thought and can stand alone as a sentence. You can expand that sentence by adding a dependent clause to it.

An independent clause states the main idea of a sentence. A dependent clause can add information about the main idea. When you add a dependent clause to a sentence, choose the connecting word carefully. The connecting word tells how the dependent clause is related to the main idea.

Examples: Senators must be fair *because* they write laws. (tells why)

Until I read the First Amendment, I did not understand its importance. (tells when)

Notice the comma in the last example. When the dependent clause comes at the beginning of the expanded sentence, it is followed by a comma.

Guided Practice

A. **Write the dependent clause in each sentence. Tell what kind of information it gives.**

Example: The President will decide after he has studied the facts. *after he has studied the facts; when*

 1. United States citizens can vote if they are at least eighteen years old.
 2. When people register to vote, they receive a voter identification card.
 3. Before they can vote, people must prove their age.
 4. Voters also must give the address where they live.
 5. The government needs this information because it must keep elections honest.

Independent Practice

B. **Write each sentence. Underline the dependent clause. Then write what kind of information it gives.**

Example: Washington, D.C., is the city where representatives work.
Washington, D.C., is the city <u>where representatives work</u>. (where)

6. If they want new laws, representatives must write bills.
7. Each bill needs to be revised before it is in final form.
8. Whenever the bill is ready, the writer will have other representatives read it.
9. Those representatives meet in a group so that they can offer suggestions.
10. Committee members approve the bill unless they disagree.

C. **Add a dependent clause to each sentence. You may want to give the kind of information shown in parentheses. Use a comma when necessary.**

Example: Laws affect us every day. (where)
Wherever we live, laws affect us every day.

11. We wrote a letter to the President. (why)
12. Adults should listen carefully. (when)
13. I can learn more about the Presidents of the United States. (condition)
14. I will read about the Constitution. (when)
15. I like to read. (condition)

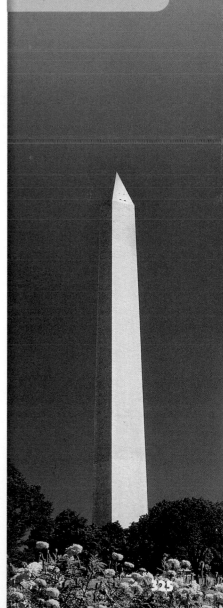

Writing Connection

Writer's Craft: Sentence Variety Choose a piece of writing you have done. Reread it to find sentences to expand by adding dependent clauses. Use the chart of subordinating conjunctions in this lesson for ideas. Rewrite some of the sentences.

Extra Practice

A. Write whether each group of words is a prepositional phrase or a clause. *pages 320–321*

Examples: thirteen states formed one country *clause*
of America *prepositional phrase*

1. the people formed a new government
2. because it seemed weak to them
3. at this Constitutional Convention
4. leaders from different states often argued
5. about the plan

Remember

that a phrase does not contain a subject and a predicate. A clause, however, has both. An independent clause can stand alone as a sentence, but a dependent clause cannot.

B. Write each sentence. Underline the independent clause. *pages 322–323*

Example: The Constitutional Convention of 1787 met in the city where the Declaration of Independence had been signed.
The Constitutional Convention of 1787 met in the city where the Declaration of Independence had been signed.

6. The leaders were called delegates because they were acting for the people.
7. Although James Madison had to travel a great distance, he was eager to attend the convention.
8. James Madison was thirty-six years old when he traveled to Philadelphia.
9. While he listened to the other delegates speak, Madison took notes.
10. We have excellent records of those meetings because Madison took such good notes.
11. Because every delegate respected General George Washington, he was chosen as the leader.
12. When the delegates met, Washington asked for a "wise and honest" plan of government.
13. Before the convention met, each state had one vote in Congress.
14. Since they had more people, large states found the idea unfair.
15. The argument might end if Congress had both a House and a Senate.

For more activities with phrases and clauses, visit *The Learning Site:*
www.harcourtschool.com

C. **For each item, connect the two clauses to write an expanded sentence. Add a connecting word that shows the kind of information named in parentheses.** *pages 324–325*

Example: (Condition) more people moved to a state, it could gain more votes in the House.
If more people moved to a state, it could gain more votes in the House.

16. (When) the basic agreement on Congress was reached, the delegates added details.
17. Both houses of Congress must approve of the wording (when) a law passes.
18. (Condition) the government wants a law to raise money, the House always writes the first draft.
19. The President cannot appoint a judge (condition) the Senate approves.
20. The delegates made other compromises (when) they worked on the Constitution.

D. **Add a dependent clause to each sentence. You may want to give the kind of information named in parentheses. Use a comma where necessary.** *pages 324–325*

Example: The delegates had many discussions. (why)
The delegates had many discussions because they did not always agree.

21. People wanted a Bill of Rights. (why)
22. A state has many votes in the House. (condition)
23. It is important to vote. (why)
24. The crowd cheered. (when)
25. I finished my research report. (when)

Writing Connection

Writer's Craft: Historical Fiction Imagine that you are a delegate to the Constitutional Convention of 1787. Write a paragraph about the meeting on the first day. Invent details to add to the facts you know. Use phrases and dependent clauses to help tell *why, when,* and *where.*

Remember
that a dependent clause often begins with a subordinating conjunction. A dependent clause that begins a sentence should be followed by a comma.

DID YOU KNOW?
Beginning in 1999 the United States government issued special sets of quarters. On the back of each set of quarters was a picture honoring one state. The sets of quarters were issued in the order that the states joined the Union.

The first coin honored Delaware, because it was the first state to approve the Constitution.

Chapter Review

Read the group of words in the box. There may be a mistake in sentence structure. If you find a mistake, choose the answer that is written most clearly and correctly. If there is no mistake, choose *Correct as is*.

1   Because the delegates disagreed at first it took time to finish work on the Constitution.

A   Because the delegates disagreed at first, it took time to finish work on the Constitution.
B   When the delegates disagreed at first, it took time to finish work on the Constitution.
C   Correct as is

2   The states had to approve the Constitution, after the delegates signed it.

F   The states had to approve the Constitution. After the delegates signed it.
G   The states had to approve the Constitution after the delegates signed it.
H   Correct as is

3   The first words of the Constitution, "We the people," should sound familiar and students learn them in school.

A   The first words of the Constitution, "We the people," should sound familiar unless students learn them in school.
B   The first words of the Constitution, "We the people," should sound familiar since students learn them in school.
C   Correct as is

4   When you read those words, you may remember the delegates' work.

F   When you read those words you may remember the delegates' work.
G   When you read those words. You may remember the delegates' work.
H   Correct as is

For additional test preparation, visit *The Learning Site:*
www.harcourtschool.com

Strategies Good Readers Use

Reading strategies can help you gather and organize information you need. Often you will find a large amount of information on a topic. Reading strategies that can help you find and sort through information include **skimming, scanning,** and **taking notes.**

Skimming is looking over a book or resource quickly to find the topic, sections, and headings. You may skim to find out if a resource has the information you need for a report or a project.

Scanning is looking quickly through a page or chapter to find a particular bit of information. For example, you might scan to find the definition of a word or the date when something happened.

Knowing the parts of a book can help you skim and scan. The **title page** tells the book's title, author, and publisher. The **table of contents** lists the titles and page numbers of the chapters. The **index** lists the book's topics in alphabetical order and shows their page numbers. The index is usually at the back of the book.

When you have located information, you can record it by **taking notes**. Write down ideas in your own words. Include the book's title and author. Writing your notes on index cards will make it easy to sort and organize information later. Use your notes to review information or organize it before you begin to write.

YOUR TURN

USE READING STRATEGIES Write the names of several interesting people, places, and things. Choose one topic to learn more about. Use skimming and scanning to choose a resource and find information. Take notes on what you find. Then tell a group of classmates what you learned.

Writer's Craft

Organizing Information

There are many different types of information you may give when you write to inform. You know that you might explain how to do something or how ideas are similar and different. Often you will write about subjects that you have researched.

Read the following paragraph from the book *Mountains* by Seymour Simon. Notice how the author presents information about his subject.

LITERATURE MODEL

Mountains are tall, but just how tall does one have to be to be called a mountain? The Himalayan Mountains in central Asia have at least fourteen peaks over 26,000 feet. Mount Everest in the Himalayas is the highest mountain above sea level in the world, 29,028 feet. That's five and a half miles above sea level, taller than the world's twenty-six tallest skyscrapers stacked one atop another.

Analyze THE Model

1. About what subject does the writer give information?

2. Is the paragraph organized in a way that makes sense to you?

3. What information that the writer gives could you check by looking it up somewhere else?

When you write to inform, you don't want to present just some scattered facts. Your facts should relate to each other and explain the topic you are writing about. It is important to organize your information, or arrange it in a way that will make sense to your reader. Look at the chart on the next page.

Strategies for Organizing Information	Applying the Strategies	Examples
Take notes.	• As you research your subject, jot down brief notes to help you remember important facts.	• Himalayas— 14 peaks over 26,000 feet

Make an outline.	• Organize your facts in an outline with main heads and subheads.	• I. Main head
		    A. Subhead
		    B. Subhead
		  II. Main head
		    A. Subhead
		    B. Subhead

Evaluate and document information.	• Determine whether your source is reliable. • Give the source of your information.	• Find out the author's qualifications. • Use other sources to confirm facts.

YOUR TURN

ANALYZE TEXT ORGANIZATION With a partner, examine a factual magazine article. Talk about how the writer organized and documented the information in the article.

Answer these questions:

1. What are the most important ideas that the writer presents? How are they organized?

2. How could you evaluate the information in the article?

3. Does the writer give any sources of information in the article or following the article? Explain.

Taking Notes

A. **On your paper, take notes on the information in each paragraph below. Remember to make your notes brief and to put them in your own words.**

1.   People dreamed of space travel long before that dream became a reality. In the second century A.D., a Greek named Lucian wrote about a trip to the moon. Several famous writers in the seventeenth and eighteenth centuries wrote exciting tales about imaginary space voyages. Jules Verne published *From the Earth to the Moon* in 1865. H. G. Wells published *The War of the Worlds* in 1898 and *The First Men on the Moon* in 1901.

2.   Mayan temples and other buildings were often built on mounds in the form of pyramids. The bases of the pyramids were made of earth or blocks of stone. The pyramids themselves were built in steps and were faced with stone. Both the insides and outsides of the buildings were painted in bright colors. The thick outer walls were richly decorated with sculptures and carvings. There were very few windows, and those were small and narrow.

Making Outlines

B. **Now use the notes you made in part A to make two outlines, one for each paragraph. Each outline should have one main head stating the specific topic of the paragraph. The subheads should give the important details.**

Evaluating and Documenting Information

C. Read the information and the questions that follow it. Write an answer to each question.

The book *Mountains*, from which you read a passage on page 330, was published in 1994 in New York by William Morrow & Company. The author, Seymour Simon, has written many books on scientific subjects. He is recognized as an expert, and his books have won many awards. In *Mountains*, the height of Mount Everest is given as 29,028 feet, a measurement made in 1954. However, in 1999, climbers used a satellite to measure Mount Everest again. Based on the information from the Global Positioning Satellite receiver, scientists discovered that the height of Mount Everest is 29,035 feet, seven feet higher than the previous measurement.

1. In light of this recent information, what can you conclude about the height of Mount Everest as stated in *Mountains*?
2. If you were to evaluate the information by checking an encyclopedia or a reference book published before the discovery in 1999, what would you find?
3. What sources might you use to find the most recent information?
4. If you used information from *Mountains* in a report, you might document it in a list of sources at the end of the report. Write an entry for *Mountains*, following the example on page 533 of your Handbook. Note the publisher and date in the paragraph above.

Writing and Thinking

Write to Record Reflections When you read information in a book, hear it on TV, or find it on a website, do you ever stop to ask yourself whether the information is accurate or true? Even if a writer or speaker believes that something is true, is it possible that he or she is mistaken? Think about these questions, and write your reflections in your Writer's Journal.

Paragraph of Information

Seymour Simon researched the subject of mountains. Then he wrote the book *Mountains* to share the information with young readers. Carla researched the subject of granite. She took notes and made an outline. Then she wrote a report to share with her classmates. Here is one paragraph from her report, along with a sample of her notes and the outline of the paragraph. Notice how she organizes her information.

MODEL

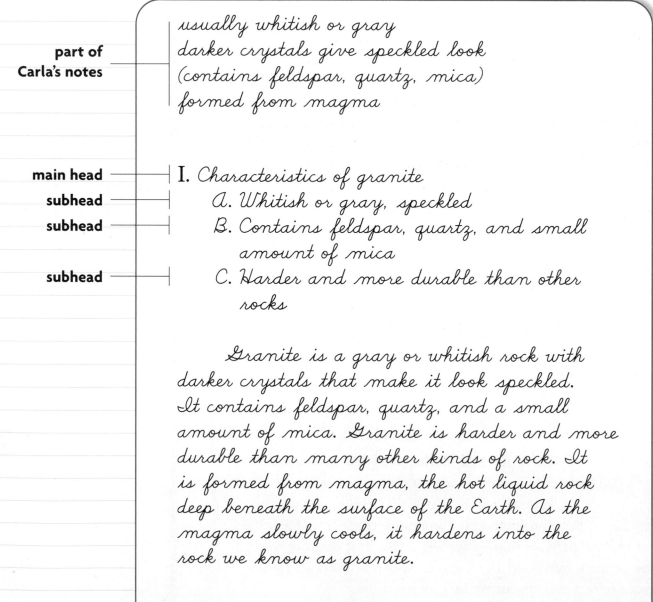

part of Carla's notes

usually whitish or gray
darker crystals give speckled look
(contains feldspar, quartz, mica)
formed from magma

main head
I. Characteristics of granite
subhead
   A. Whitish or gray, speckled
subhead
   B. Contains feldspar, quartz, and small amount of mica
subhead
   C. Harder and more durable than other rocks

   Granite is a gray or whitish rock with darker crystals that make it look speckled. It contains feldspar, quartz, and a small amount of mica. Granite is harder and more durable than many other kinds of rock. It is formed from magma, the hot liquid rock deep beneath the surface of the Earth. As the magma slowly cools, it hardens into the rock we know as granite.

Analyze the Model

1. Why didn't Carla use complete sentences when she took her notes?

2. What subheads did Carla use to organize the information in her outline?

3. Did Carla follow her outline when she wrote her paragraph? How can you tell?

4. Does Carla's paragraph explain the information in a clear and organized way? Explain your answer.

YOUR TURN

WRITING PROMPT Choose an important event that you have learned about in social studies. Use your social studies textbook and another source to research the event. Narrow the topic to one main idea that you can explain in a paragraph. Use your notes to make an outline. Then write a paragraph to share the information with your classmates.

STUDY THE PROMPT Ask yourself these questions:

1. What is your purpose for writing?

2. Who is your audience?

3. What writing form will you use?

4. What is your topic?

Prewriting and Drafting

Organize Your Information After you have chosen your topic, follow the steps below.

1. Take notes from two sources. Evaluate the sources.

2. Make an outline from your notes.

3. Use the outline to write a draft of your paragraph. Be sure to put information in your own words.

4. Document your information by listing your sources at the end of your paragraph.

USING YOUR
Handbook

Use the Writer's Thesaurus to help you restate information in your own words.

Editing

Now reread and evaluate the draft of your paragraph.
Are there details that you would like to add or leave out?
Use this checklist to help you revise your paragraph:

☑ Will your audience be able to understand the
  information in your paragraph?
☑ Do you need to change the order in which
  facts and details are given?
☑ Can you rewrite sentences to make them
  easier to understand?

Use this checklist as you proofread your paragraph:

☑ I have used capitalization and punctuation
  correctly.
☑ I have expanded sentences with prepositional
  phrases.
☑ I have combined independent and dependent
  clauses.
☑ I have used a dictionary to check my spelling.

Editor's Marks

✄ delete text
∧ insert text
ᵟ move text
¶ new paragraph
≡ capitalize
/ lowercase
◯ correct spelling

Sharing and Reflecting

Writer's
Journal

Make a final copy of your paragraph to share with a
small group of classmates. Tell what you like best
about each other's work and whether there is any
information you don't understand. Discuss how
taking notes and making an outline helped you organize your
information. Write your reflections in your Writer's Journal.

Evaluating Sources

There are many sources of information in our modern world. Look at the web below. Can you think of other sources in addition to the ones shown here?

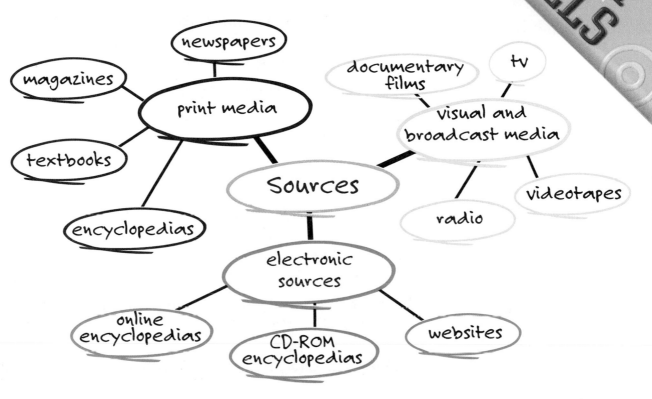

   Some sources are more reliable than others. It is always a good idea to check your facts, but in some cases you might also question the qualifications of the person giving the facts. Just because you see something in print, hear it on TV, or find it on a website does not necessarily mean it is true.

YOUR TURN

Work in a small group to rate each of the sources shown in the web. Discuss each source, and place it in one of the following categories:

- very reliable
- probably reliable
- may not be reliable

Create a chart or other graphic to show the results of your discussion. Then compare your ideas with those of other groups.

Compound and Complex Sentences

A complex sentence is made up of an independent clause and at least one dependent clause.

You know that an *independent clause* can stand alone as a sentence. Two or more independent clauses can be combined to form a **compound sentence**. These clauses are joined by a coordinating conjunction such as *and, but,* or *or.*

Example of compound sentence:
Some settlers farmed the land, **but** others tried ranching.

A *dependent clause* cannot stand alone as a sentence. In Chapter 26, you practiced combining dependent and independent clauses. The sentences you formed are called complex sentences. The dependent clause may be joined to the independent clause by a subordinating conjunction.

Example of complex sentence:
After the French and Indian War ended, many people moved west.

Guided Practice

A. **Tell whether each of the following sentences is compound or complex. If a sentence is complex, identify its dependent clause.**

Example: Although pioneers had a challenge ahead of them, they met it with courage.
complex; Although pioneers had a challenge ahead of them

1. People walked great distances, and animals carried their belongings.
2. Whenever they could, people made the long journey with friends and neighbors.
3. Life on the frontier was difficult, but the pioneers were hopeful.
4. After the Homestead Act was passed, many pioneers settled on public land.
5. If people farmed the land, it became theirs.

Independent Practice

B. Decide whether the sentence is compound or complex. Write each complex sentence. Underline each dependent clause.

> **Example:** If the land was heavily wooded, the settlers cleared away some trees.
>
> <u>If the land was heavily wooded</u>, *the settlers cleared away some trees.*

6. After the field was cleared, the settlers planted crops.
7. Pioneers changed the land as they cleared it for farms.
8. Settlers counted on each other if they needed help.
9. Neighbors helped out whenever a new family arrived.
10. Adults worked, and children attended school.
11. The hardy settlers continued their work when rain fell.
12. Before the day was over, a new cabin was built.
13. If troubles arose, some settlers found help at the fort.
14. Traveling teachers stayed for a few months, but then they moved to the next settlement.
15. Mail delivery became a problem as the frontier moved west.
16. The roads were terrible, and a stagecoach could take weeks to reach a small town.
17. The pony express, however, could travel where stage-coaches were unable to go.
18. Riders covered about fifty miles, and then they handed the mail over to other riders.
19. Although it was popular, the pony express did not make a profit.
20. As soon as tracks were laid, railroads could deliver mail to settlements.

> ## Remember
>
> that a **complex sentence** contains an independent clause and one or more dependent clauses.

Writing Connection

Writer's Journal: Reflecting Think about what you read in the practice exercises in this lesson. What personal qualities do you think people needed to make a new life on the frontier? To answer, write a few sentences. Use at least two complex sentences.

More About Complex Sentences

Dependent clauses can appear in different places in complex sentences. Depending upon its location, a dependent clause may or may not need to be set off with a comma.

As you know, a complex sentence includes at least one dependent clause. Most dependent clauses either begin or end complex sentences. A dependent clause that begins a sentence is followed by a comma. A dependent clause that comes at the end of a sentence usually does not have a comma before it.

Examples:

<u>When you think of frontier life</u>, what comes to mind?
<u>When you think of frontier life</u>, you may think of cowhands.
You may think of cowhands <u>when you think of frontier life</u>.

Guided Practice

A. **Identify the dependent clause in each of the following complex sentences. If a comma is needed, tell where it should be placed.**

Example: Although cowhands worked very hard they enjoyed life on the trail.
Although cowhands worked very hard; comma after hard

1. Longhorn cattle were common in the West because Spanish settlers had brought them to the Americas.
2. When longhorn cattle are full-grown their horns can measure up to eight feet across.
3. Because they can locate water from far away longhorns live successfully on the prairie.
4. When grass is scarce a longhorn will eat leaves.
5. A cowhand would say good-bye to loved ones before he began the long cattle drive to market.

Independent Practice

B. Write these complex sentences, and underline the dependent clauses. Add commas where needed.

Example: If the cowhands feared a stampede they slept in their clothes.

If the cowhands feared a stampede, they slept in their clothes.

6. A trail boss hired workers before a cattle drive began.
7. As you know a cook was an important member of the crew.
8. Even if the food tasted terrible the cowhands ate it.
9. A cowhand rode one horse while the other horses rested.
10. Because the work was hard cowhands grew tired.

C. Use the subordinating conjunction in parentheses to join each pair of sentences in a way that makes sense. Be sure to add commas where needed.

Example: Cowhands drank from a barrel. They were thirsty. (when)

Cowhands drank from a barrel when they were thirsty.

11. The supply of water ran low. A scout searched for more. (if)
12. The cowhands will travel all day. A storm comes. (unless)
13. The cattle could rest. They reached a place to stop for the night. (after)
14. The cattle would rest calmly. The cowhands sang. (while)
15. Horses were important to a cattle drive. The cowhands often sang songs about them. (because)

Writing Connection

Social Studies Write four sentences about things that happened every day on a cattle drive. Include at least two complex sentences. Read your sentences aloud to a classmate.

341

Examples:

Simple Sentences
The wagon trains started west in spring. They would arrive before winter.

Compound Sentence
The wagon trains started west in spring, and they would arrive before winter.

Complex Sentence
Because the wagon trains started west in spring, they would arrive before winter.

GRAMMAR—WRITING CONNECTION

Sentence Variety

To make your writing interesting and effective, vary the kinds of sentences you use.

One way that good writers keep their writing interesting is by using different kinds of sentences. For best effect, use some short sentences and some long ones. Use a combination of simple, compound, and complex sentences to keep your writing interesting.

Guided Practice

A. **Change the sentences as instructed. You may vary the order of words or clauses to make the new sentences more effective.**

Example: John Bidwell led a group of pioneers to California. He had never been west of Missouri before. (Rewrite as a complex sentence.)

Possible answer:
Although he had never been west of Missouri before, John Bidwell led a group of pioneers to California.

1. Bidwell's pioneer group was eager. No one knew the way to California, however. (Rewrite as a compound sentence.)
2. They found a mountain man named Thomas Fitzpatrick. They asked him for help. (Rewrite as a simple sentence.)
3. The party was frightened by a group of Cheyenne. The Cheyenne turned out to be quite friendly. (Rewrite as a complex sentence.)
4. The starving pioneers almost didn't make it, and they had to eat crows, a coyote, and even insects to survive. (Rewrite as two simple sentences.)
5. Bidwell and his followers reached California. They were very glad then. (Rewrite as a complex sentence.)

Independent Practice

B. Rewrite each set of sentences according to the instructions in parentheses. You may vary the order of words or clauses to make the new sentences effective. Add commas where needed.

Example: It was a difficult journey. More and more people from the United States traveled west. (Rewrite as a complex sentence.)

Possible answer:
Although it was a difficult journey, more and more people from the United States traveled west.

6. Rain turned the prairies to mud. Rivers overflowed their banks. (Rewrite as a compound sentence.)
7. Some of John Bidwell's pioneer group settled in Oregon. They found rich soil and a mild climate there. (Rewrite as a complex sentence.)
8. The settlers built homes from logs. They started schools in their new communities. (Rewrite as a compound sentence.)
9. The community grew large enough. After that, the settlers formed a government. (Rewrite as a complex sentence.)
10. The new constitution provided for jury trials. The new constitution provided for freedom of religion. (Rewrite as a simple sentence.)

Remember

that using different kinds of sentences can keep your writing interesting. Try to vary the length and structure of the sentences you write.

Writing Connection

Writer's Craft: Sentence Variety Choose a piece of writing that you have finished. Read it again to review the types of sentences you used. Mark each sentence to show its type. Find some sentences that you can rewrite or combine to add variety. Include simple, compound, and complex sentences.

Extra Practice

A. Read each sentence. Write whether it is a simple sentence, a compound sentence, or a complex sentence. If it is a complex sentence, write its dependent clause or clauses. *pages 338–343*

Example: The pioneers showed great courage when they traveled west.
complex; when they traveled west

1. Several families banded together and formed a wagon train.
2. If all went well, the westward journey could take almost seven months.
3. They faced many hardships, but most settlers were glad they made the trip.
4. They had little protection from the weather unless they had sturdy log houses.
5. Kit Carson, the famous frontier scout, was related to Daniel Boone.

B. Write each sentence, and underline the dependent clause. Add a comma where needed. *pages 340–341*

Example: Fremont felt honored when Senator Benton named him the leader of the western expedition.
Fremont felt honored <u>when Senator Benton named him the leader of the western expedition</u>.

6. John Fremont made a wise decision when he chose Kit Carson as his guide.
7. Fremont would not let anyone keep a diary because he planned a book of his own.
8. Many days passed before the expedition reached the Continental Divide.
9. When he was older Kit Carson became a general in the army.
10. While Fremont was exploring western lands Texas was not yet a state.

For more activities with compound and complex sentences, visit *The Learning Site:*
www.harcourtschool.com

C. **Rewrite each set of sentences as the type of sentence in parentheses. You may vary the order of words or clauses to make the new sentences effective. Add commas where needed.** *pages 342–343*

Example: John Fremont had served in the Senate. He ran for President. (complex sentence)
Possible answer:
After John Fremont had served in the Senate, he ran for President.

11. Texas won its independence from Mexico. It became a republic. (complex sentence)

12. Sam Houston became the republic's president. He encouraged people to settle in Texas. (compound sentence)

13. Many immigrants came to Texas. They came from France and Germany. (simple sentence)

14. Some Texans opposed statehood. Texas joined the Union in 1845. (complex sentence)

15. Today Texas is one of our largest states. Texas is also one of our most diverse states. (simple sentence)

16. The American frontier has disappeared. The pioneer spirit has continued. (compound sentence)

17. Today some pioneers study the ocean. Others study wilderness areas. (compound sentence)

18. Doctors talk about developing treatments for diseases. They often call themselves medical pioneers. (complex sentence)

19. Astronomers study outer space. They say it is the greatest frontier. (complex sentence)

20. They will continue exploring. They have the pioneer spirit. (complex sentence)

DID YOU KNOW?
The covered wagons traveling west carried many families and their belongings. The frames over the wagons were covered with light-colored fabric. Wagons that rumbled through tall prairie grasses looked like wooden ships with sails. These sailing ships were known as "schooners." As a result, the wagons were nicknamed "prairie schooners."

Writing Connection

Technology Search the Internet for more information about the frontier and westward expansion. Choose a keyword from the exercises in this lesson to find websites. Write one complex sentence about the topic from the information that you find. As an alternative, use an encyclopedia to find information.

Chapter Review

Read the passage. Some sections are underlined. Choose the best way to rewrite each underlined section, and write the letter for your answer. If the underlined section needs no change, write the letter for the choice "Correct as is."

(1) We usually think of pioneers as adults although, many pioneers were children. There was always work to be done on the farm or ranch. (2) The sun rose and the children got up and did chores. (3) The older children did big chores and the younger children helped with small tasks. Pioneer children did go to school, however. (4) They attended school in the winter. Because there was less farm work to do.

1 A Although we usually think of pioneers as adults many were children.

B Although we usually think of pioneers as adults. Many were children.

C Although we usually think of pioneers as adults, many were children.

D Correct as is

2 F The children got up and did chores, when the sun rose.

G When the sun rose, the children got up and did chores.

H When the sun rose the children got up and did chores.

J Correct as is

3 A The older children did big chores, the younger children helped with small tasks.

B The older children did big chores, and the younger children helped with small tasks.

C After the older children did big chores the younger children helped with small tasks.

D Correct as is

4 F Because there was less farm work to do in the winter they attended school.

G They attended school in the winter, but there was less farm work to do.

H They attended school in the winter because there was less farm work to do.

J Correct as is

Using Tables and Charts

Charts and **tables** organize and present information in an easy-to-understand way. A chart or table can show an idea that would need many words to explain.

A chart is a visual way of presenting information. Diagrams, flowcharts, time lines, and circle graphs are types of charts.

A table shows information in a way that makes the information easy to find and use. A table of contents, for example, lists the sections of a book and gives their page numbers. Information in tables often is arranged in rows and columns to make it clear and easy to compare.

Here are some guidelines to help you read or make a chart or table:

- Charts and tables have slightly different purposes. Charts often show how a process works. Tables are usually organized to compare facts.

- When you use a chart, look for extra information about how to read it. For example, look on the chart for arrows that you need to follow. Parts of the chart may be in different colors. Look for captions or notes that explain the chart.

- When you use a table, look at the headings across the columns and along the rows. To find a particular fact, decide which column heading and which row heading you need. The information should be in the space where the column and row meet.

A TABLE OF FIBER-RICH FOODS

Food	Serving	Fiber (grams)
Breads		
Bran muffin	1	4.0
Pumpernickel bread	2 slices	3.2
Whole-wheat bread	2 slices	3.2
Grains		
Brown rice	2/3 cup	3.0
Wheat bran	1 oz.	11.3
Cereals		
100% bran	1 oz.	8.4
Corn bran	1 oz.	5.3
Fruits		
Apple	1 medium	3.2
Banana	1 medium	3.0
Blueberries	1/2 cup	3.0
Vegetables/Legumes		
Broccoli, cooked	1/4 cup	5.0
Corn, sweet, cooked	1/2 cup	4.7
Green peas, cooked	1/2 cup	3.1
Nuts		
Almonds	1 oz.	5.0
Peanuts	1 oz.	5.0

YOUR TURN

Work with classmates to create a table or chart. Your table or chart should show facts about a state that was once a part of the American frontier. For example, you might present information about one of these topics:

- the state's capital
- the state's population at different times
- important dates in the state's history
- some things for which the state is known

Search for the information you need in an encyclopedia, in magazines, or on the Internet. Then design your table or chart. Include headings, captions, or notes to help explain the information. When you are finished, display and explain the table or chart in class.

Sentence Fragments

A sentence fragment is a group of words that does not express a complete thought.

Some fragments are missing a subject, a predicate, or both. Others may be dependent clauses that begin with a connecting word such as *because* or *after*.

You can correct some sentence fragments by adding the missing parts. If the sentence fragment is a dependent clause, it needs to be attached to an independent clause.

Sentence Fragment	Complete Sentence
Brought jobs to the city (needs subject)	A new cotton factory brought jobs to the city.
New markets for cloth (needs predicate)	New markets for cloth opened in the South.
When merchants shipped cloth (needs independent clause)	When merchants shipped cloth, they used the railroad.

Guided Practice

A. **Identify each group of words as a complete sentence or a sentence fragment. Tell how you know a group of words is a sentence fragment.**

Example: Developed a new magnifying glass.
sentence fragment

1. Walter Hunt invented a stove that used hard coal.
2. Also designed the first student lamp.
3. Because he had a creative mind.
4. Hunt worked in a shop in New York City.
5. Although his inventions seemed strange.
6. Hunt's best ideas.
7. Hunt invented a sewing machine.
8. In the early 1830s.
9. Tell me more about Hunt.
10. When inventors found different methods.

Vocabulary Power

in•dus•try [in′dəs•trē]
n. Businesses or manufacturing; also, a type of business, such as the clothing *industry*.

Independent Practice

B. Identify each group of words as a complete sentence or a sentence fragment.

11. Workers built the Erie Canal across the Appalachian Mountains.
12. On July 4, 1817.
13. Thousands of laborers worked on the canal.
14. A water route 363 miles long.
15. When farmers shipped their crops to market.
16. The canal connected Buffalo to the Hudson River.
17. New York businesspeople more than others.
18. The Erie Canal provided a quick passage for traders.
19. Since taking goods across land was expensive.
20. Sent crops to river docks in New Orleans.

C. Write *S* if the group of words needs a subject. Write *P* if it needs a predicate. Write *IC* if it needs an independent clause.

Example: After the dock workers loaded the boat. *IC*

21. Although the Erie Canal opened.
22. On November 4, 1825, the first passenger.
23. Shipped vegetables and flour on river barges.
24. With so many opportunities for trade.
25. Took eight days instead of twenty.
26. Lowered the cost of shipping.
27. As time passed.
28. The success of the Erie Canal.
29. Quickly got on the boat to Lake Erie.
30. Created the desire for more canals.

> **Remember**
> that a group of words without both a subject and a predicate is a **sentence fragment**.

Writing Connection

Writer's Craft: Elaboration Work with a partner to list ten inventions. You might list items such as a bicycle pump, an eraser, and a can opener. Then choose the one you think is the most important. On your own, write a paragraph about the invention. Describe what it does and why it is useful. Exchange paragraphs with your partner. Proofread your partner's paragraph. Correct any sentence fragments you find.

Run-on Sentences and Comma Splices

One common error is to write two sentences or independent clauses with no punctuation between them. This is called a **run-on sentence**. Another error is to use only a comma to join two sentences. This is called a **comma splice**.

Independent clauses should be separated by a period or other end punctuation, a semicolon, or a comma and coordinating conjunction.

Run-on sentences corrected:

In the 1800s the world was beginning to change not everyone wanted change.

New ways of farming and making tools were invented the inventions helped farmers.

Comma splices corrected:

With new tools farmers grew more crops, people began to leave farms for the factories.

Fewer goods were produced at home more and more were produced in factories.

Guided Practice

A. Write *RO* if the sentence is a run-on sentence. Write *CS* if it contains a comma splice. Write *correct* if it is correct. Explain your answer.

Example: Water is a good source of power, people used rivers to produce power for hundreds of years. *CS*

1. In the 1800s water was the main source of power a river was the best location for a factory.
2. A mill owner could buy part of a river, and the business would control its use.
3. Companies built manufacturing plants next to streams, the force of the water turned their mills.
4. The steam engine was invented it caught on slowly.
5. The steam engine needed coal to operate, coal was expensive.

Independent Practice

B. Write *RO* if the sentence is a run-on sentence. Write *CS* if it contains a comma splice. Write *correct* if it is correct.

Example: Richard Arkwright was an English inventor he designed the cotton-spinning machine.
RO

6. In the 1700s England was a world trade center, its cloth-making factories made huge profits.

7. People would buy American products English manufacturers would sell less fabric, thread, and cloth.

8. The English were afraid because they would lose money to American markets.

9. Spinners and weavers would lose their jobs; factories might have to shut down.

10. England passed laws to protect trade English merchants could not sell cloth-making machinery outside of England.

11. Inventors could not sell their designs to foreigners, even drawings could not leave the country.

12. Samuel Slater was English he escaped his country with plans for a cloth-making machine.

13. When Slater was fourteen, he worked in a cotton mill in England his job included operating cotton machines.

14. Eventually Slater moved to Rhode Island, then he built a cotton-spinning machine from memory.

15. The cotton-spinning machine was a success, and his company made money.

Samuel Slater

Writing Connection

Writer's Journal: Find Facts Find and write in your own words several interesting or surprising facts about a recent invention, an improvement to an existing invention, or a change in how a task is done. Check for run-on sentences and comma splices.

Writer's Journal

Punctuating Compound and Complex Sentences

Run-on Sentence

More iron became available people used it to make tools.

Comma Splice

More iron became available, people used it to make tools.

Run-on sentences and comma splices can be corrected in several ways. This chart shows how the sentences at the left can be corrected.

1. Place a period or other end punctuation between the two independent clauses.	More iron became available. People used it to make tools. (simple sentences)
2. Use a comma and a coordinating conjunction.	More iron became available, and people used it to make tools. (compound sentence)
3. Place a semicolon between the independent clauses.	More iron became available; people used it to make tools. (compound sentence)
4. Add a subordinating conjunction to make one of the clauses dependent.	As more iron became available, people used it to make tools. (complex sentence)

Guided Practice

A. Rewrite each run-on sentence and comma splice.

> **Example:** Most goods had been made by hand machines made the same goods more cheaply.
> *Most goods had been made by hand. Machines made the same goods more cheaply.*

1. In the 1700s America produced raw materials these included lumber, cotton, and wheat.
2. By 1800 machinery had improved manufacturers built more factories.
3. Samuel Slater worked out a factory system for his cloth-making mill, not all companies used the same method.
4. Sometimes a factory formed an assembly line people worked next to each other.
5. Each person completed a task, then the product moved to the next person for more work.

Independent Practice

B. Rewrite each statement correctly. If the sentence is correct, write _correct_.

Example: Francis Lowell had many new business ideas he wanted to improve working conditions in America. _Francis Lowell had many new business ideas. He wanted to improve working conditions in America._

6. Francis C. Lowell owned a cloth-making business it was located in Waltham, Massachusetts.
7. Lowell developed the Waltham System for his company; under this system, workers made fabric from cotton.
8. Waltham workers used a power loom to make cloth, all of the work was completed at the same place.
9. Lowell moved his factory to the Merrimack River he found a better place near the water.
10. Lowell's factory needed workers it was not located in a major town.
11. Lowell built a model factory town the town was called Lowell.
12. A rooming house was built for the women they needed a safe home.
13. Life at the factory was difficult, people worked more than ten hours a day, six days a week.
14. Workers attended factory social gatherings they published a monthly magazine.
15. Some of the workers came to the United States from Europe, they were eager to work.

Remember

that you can turn **run-on sentences** and **comma splices** into two separate sentences. You can also place a connecting word and appropriate punctuation between the clauses.

Writing Connection

Real-Life Writing: Catalog Work with a partner to invent a toy or another item that children might use. Sketch your invention. Write a description that might appear in a catalog, and include the price of the item. Include at least one compound or complex sentence. You might look at a toy catalog for ideas.

Extra Practice

**A. Identify each group of words as a complete sen-
tence or a sentence fragment. For each fragment,
write *S* if the sentence needs a subject, *P* if it needs
a predicate, and *IC* if it needs an independent
clause.** *pages 348–349*

Example: Before the Industrial Revolution in the United
States. *sentence fragment; IC*

1. Because many new inventions were developed.
2. Industry grew in the United States.
3. In 1800 the U. S. Patent Office received hundreds of
   requests for patents.
4. A patent, a license to use an invention.
5. Sixty years later 28,000 new patents.
6. Eli Whitney invented many useful devices.
7. The cotton gin took the seeds out of cotton.
8. Sold more cotton to cloth-making factories.
9. Increases cotton production in the South.
10. New harvesting machinery on the farm.
11. Farm machines increased the production of corn.
12. Unless a machine harvested the grain.
13. Was designed by Cyrus McCormick in 1831.
14. Later opened a factory to produce machines.
15. George Page invented a tool called the harrow.

**B. Write *RO* if the sentence is a run-on sentence.
Write *CS* if the sentence is a comma splice. Write
correct if it is correct.** *pages 350–351*

Example: Improvements in farm machines resulted in larger
crops, farmers sold more wheat. *CS*

16. In 1844 Samuel F. B. Morse introduced his electric
    telegraph, news traveled faster with this invention.
17. Morse sent the first telegraph message, and it trav-
    eled from Baltimore to Washington, D.C.
18. The sewing machine appeared two years later it was
    invented by Elias Howe.
19. Howe set up a demonstration, he challenged the
    fastest seamstresses to a race.
20. The new machine sewed only a straight line, but it
    was seven times faster than hand stitching.

For more activities
with fragments,
run-on sentences,
and comma
splices, visit
The Learning Site:

www.harcourtschool.com

C. Rewrite each sentence correctly. If the sentence is correct, write *correct*. *pages 352–353*

Example: Thanks to machines, farmers were more productive, they made more goods in less time.
Thanks to machines, farmers were more productive. They made more goods in less time.

21. Larger crops were harvested, farmers looked for better ways to get their goods to market.
22. Roads needed improvement, farmers could not always travel in bad weather.
23. It was difficult to ship goods to market over the poor roads.
24. Road trips were expensive, they also took a long time.
25. Businesses used wagons pulled by horses, the wagons hauled small loads.
26. As people looked for other ways to ship their goods, river canals were built.
27. Boats carried larger loads, they were quicker and cheaper than wagons.
28. Thomas Newcomen had invented the steam engine, Robert Fulton showed how to use it on steamboats.
29. At the same time, George Stephenson of England built a locomotive with a steam engine he called it the *Rocket*.
30. In 1829 the *Rocket* won a contest with other locomotives by going 36 miles an hour.

Remember

that you can fix run-on sentences and comma splices in several ways: (1) by correcting the punctuation, (2) by adding a coordinating conjunction, (3) by adding a subordinating conjunction.

DID YOU KNOW?
Having a patent means that no one else can make, use, or sell something that you invented unless you give permission. Patents have been granted to inventors in the United States since the late 1700s. Around 300 patents are issued every day.

Writing Connection

Social Studies Choose an event from United States history, and make a time line that shows when it happened in relation to other important events. For example, you might make a time line for the 1800s showing several important inventions. Write a few sentences to explain your time line.

Chapter Review

Read the passage. Some sections are underlined. Choose the best way to write each underlined section and mark the letter for your answer. If the underlined section needs no change, choose "Correct as is."

STANDARDIZED
TEST PREP

> **TIP** Read all the choices aloud in a quiet voice. Saying or hearing the choices can help you find the right one.

> (1) <u>The Baltimore and Ohio Railroad carried passengers and goods. South to Virginia and west to Chicago.</u> Merchants in Baltimore started the B & O Railroad. (2) <u>Do you know the name of the first steam locomotive for the B & O Railroad Company, it was the *Tom Thumb*.</u> *Tom Thumb* was designed by Peter Cooper. (3) <u>His train demonstrated its power. When it carried forty people at ten miles an hour.</u> Cooper had other business projects, too. (4) <u>Before he worked with trains. Cooper built horse-drawn coaches.</u>

1 A The Baltimore and Ohio Railroad carried passengers and goods, and south to Virginia and west to Chicago.

B The Baltimore and Ohio Railroad carried passengers and goods south to Virginia and west to Chicago.

C When the Baltimore and Ohio Railroad carried passengers and goods, south to Virginia and west to Chicago.

D Correct as is

2 F Do you know the name of the first steam locomotive for the B & O Railroad Company? It was the *Tom Thumb*.

G Do you know the name of the first steam locomotive, for the B & O Railroad Company? it was the *Tom Thumb*.

H Do you know the name of the first steam locomotive for the B & O Railroad Company it was the *Tom Thumb*.

J Correct as is

3 A His train demonstrated its power, and when it carried forty people at ten miles an hour.

B His train demonstrated its power, when it carried forty people at ten miles an hour.

C His train demonstrated its power when it carried forty people at ten miles an hour.

D Correct as is

4 F Before he worked with trains Cooper built horse-drawn coaches.

G Before he worked with trains, Cooper built horse-drawn coaches.

H Before he worked with trains; Cooper built horse-drawn coaches.

J Correct as is

For additional test preparation, visit
The Learning Site:

www.harcourtschool.com

Using Computer Graphics

Visuals can help explain your ideas in research reports. For example, suppose you want to compare and contrast inventors Isaac Singer and Elias Howe. You might explain how the two inventors are similar and different. Show your ideas by using a Venn diagram.

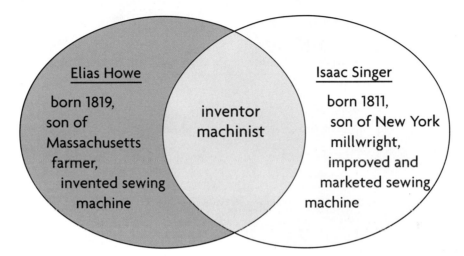

Elias Howe

born 1819, son of Massachusetts farmer, invented sewing machine

inventor machinist

Isaac Singer

born 1811, son of New York millwright, improved and marketed sewing machine

You can use your computer to create visuals like a Venn diagram. Graphics software helps you design charts, graphs, clusters, diagrams, and more. Here are some ideas for using such a program. Use the menu, keyboard, and tool bar on your computer to

- arrange words or other information on the page.
- call attention to the information with italics, underlining, and bold print.
- draw boxes and circles around the words to make them stand out.
- add color or shading to the boxes or circles.

YOUR TURN

Write a paragraph or two about an inventor or invention. Type your report on the computer. Add graphics. For example, if you compare two things, show your information in a Venn diagram. Work with a partner to revise your report. Ask your partner these questions: How can I improve my graphics? Are there any sentence fragments, run-on sentences, or comma splices in my writing? Is my explanation clear?

Writing Workshop

In this excerpt from the book *The World's Top Ten Deserts,* Neil Morris tells several facts about deserts. As you read, think about how the author makes the information easy to read and understand.

THE WORLD'S TOP TEN DESERTS

by Neil Morris

What is a Desert?

A desert is an area of land where very little rain falls. This means that the ground is dry nearly all the time. Most deserts are in warm parts of the world. We often think of them as being covered with endless sand dunes. There are many other desert landscapes, however, including rocky hills and flat, stony plains. Most scientists agree that any region that has less than 10 inches (25 cm) of rain a year can be called a desert.

Hot Deserts

Most of the world's largest deserts are very hot places. The largest desert of all, the Sahara in Africa, has temperatures that reach 122°F (50°C). In hot deserts the temperature usually falls very fast at night, sometimes by as much as 45°F (25°C).

In spite of their heat, temperature changes, and lack of water, deserts are not empty wastelands. Many kinds of plants and animals live in this difficult environment. Some people live in deserts, too.

Cold Wilderness

Not all deserts are as hot as the Sahara. The Gobi, in Mongolia, is also very cold in the winter. The Arctic and Antarctica can also be called deserts. These areas are so cold that there is little rainfall. Any water instantly freezes. The icy wastes around the North and South Poles get bigger in the winter and smaller in the summer.

The Sonoran Desert

North America's biggest desert is the seventh largest desert in the world. The Sonoran Desert runs across the border between the United States and Mexico. It covers parts of two states, Arizona and California, as well as three Mexican states, including Sonora.

Native American People of the Desert

Native Americans have lived in this area for 20,000 years. Five of these groups lived as herders and farmers in the Sonoran Desert. They are the Maricopa, Mohave, Papago, Pima, and Yuma.

Today 6,000 Native Americans live on the Papago reservation. They lead a modern life but have not forgotten their roots. They call themselves Tohono O'odham, or "desert people." When they lived by gathering food from the desert, their most important yearly festival was a rainmaking ceremony. Other groups have their own ceremonies, such as the deer dance of the Yaqui.

Giant Cactus

The Sonoran Desert has 300 different kinds of cacti, including the saguaro cactus, which is the largest cactus in the world. This giant can grow over 55 feet (17m) tall—about the height of nine people. Some desert birds find the cactus useful. Gila woodpeckers peck their way into saguaro cacti to make their nests. When they leave, the tiny elf owl takes its turn in the ready-made hole.

The roadrunner, on the other hand, spends its time on the ground. This bird, a relative of the cuckoo, runs away from danger and will chase anything that moves. It can run at speeds of up to 15 miles per hour (24 kph).

Desert
tortoise

**UNITED
STATES**

● **PHOENIX**

Colorado River

Elf
owl

Gila
woodpecker

Cottontail
rabbit

● **TUCSON**

The Modern Desert

The Sonoran Desert has many different kinds of landscapes. There are large areas of sand dunes, cactus forests, rocky wastes, Native American reservations, and national parks.

A highway runs across the northern part of the desert. It goes from the city of Tucson to Phoenix, the state capital of Arizona. There are about 430,000 people living in Tucson, and Phoenix has more than 2 million people. There are many other smaller towns within the desert region. Those who live there are the modern people of the desert.

MEXICO

Saguaro
cacti

**PACIFIC
OCEAN**

Gila
monster

Yucca
tree

Gulf of
California

Roadrunner

Living Deserts

Deserts are not vast wastelands of sand and rock. In fact, people live and work in deserts all over the world every day. Deserts are home to extremely diverse groups of plants and animals. They are essential pieces of the earth's ecosystem.

Rattlesnake

Vocabulary Power

en·vi·ron·ment
[in·vī′rən·mənt] *n.*
The conditions and
surroundings that
have an effect on the
development of a
person, animal, or plant.

Analyze THE *Model*

1. How does Neil Morris introduce his topic?

2. How do the heads help you follow the organization of ideas?

3. How can you tell that the writer includes facts rather than opinions?

4. Why do you think the writer repeats some information in the conclusion, or final paragraph?

READING — WRITING CONNECTION

Parts of a Research Report

Neil Morris wrote to inform readers about deserts. Read this research report by a student named Leslie. Look for the parts.

MODEL

introduction —

main idea —

details —

main idea —

details —

main idea —

details —

The California Gold Rush

When gold was discovered in California in 1848, the news spread around the world. By 1849 thousands of people had rushed to California dreaming of riches. These gold-seekers faced great difficulties, but most stayed, and California was changed forever.

Travel to California was laborious. Most people traveled by covered wagon. The trip covered thousands of miles and took months to complete. Other people made the long journey by ship. One route took them all the way around the tip of South America.

Prospecting for gold was hard work. People thought they would pick up gold from the ground. However, sand and gravel had to be washed with water in pans or special wooden boxes. Because the flakes of gold were heavy, they sank to the bottom. It took a long time to find a little gold.

Because of the gold rush, California's population grew rapidly. San Francisco and Sacramento had been settlements, but they soon became towns. There were 15,000 settlers in early 1848. There were more than 100,000 at the end of 1849. California had enough people to become a state in 1850.

All these people needed many things.
Businesses expanded or new ones were started.
Farmers supplied food. Miners bought supplies
and equipment at stores. Lumber mills provided
building materials. Government, transportation,
and industry also grew quickly.

Although most miners did not strike it rich,
many of them stayed in California. They
started farms and businesses, built cities and
roads, and helped California continue to grow
and change.

main idea

details

conclusion

Analyze THE Model

1. What was Leslie's purpose?

2. How do the four middle paragraphs, or body paragraphs, explain more about Leslie's topic?

3. Do you think Leslie's research report achieved her purpose? Why or why not?

Summarize THE Model

Use a graphic organizer like the one at the right to fill in Leslie's topic, main ideas, and conclusion. Then write a summary of her research report. You should not include details.

topic

main idea

main idea

main idea

main idea

conclusion

Writer's Craft

Organizing Information Leslie began each body paragraph with a topic sentence that states the main idea. Tell why you think Leslie put the body paragraphs in the order she did.

Prewriting

Purpose and Audience

In this chapter, you will share information about an important event by writing a research report.

WRITING PROMPT Write a research report for your classmates about an important or historic event that changed the world in some way. Use information from three sources. Draw your own conclusion about the topic. List your sources at the end of the report.

You may continue with the topic you wrote about in Chapter 27 or choose a new topic. List what you already know about your topic and what you would like to learn.

MODEL

Leslie wanted to learn more about the California gold rush. She took notes from three sources and then made this outline to organize her ideas:

I.   Introduction—beginning of the gold rush

II. Difficulties faced by the gold-seekers

    A. Hardships of travel

    B. Hard work of prospecting

III. How the gold rush changed California

    A. Rapid growth in population—California become a state

    B. Growth of business and industry

IV. Conclusion—what happened to the miners

YOUR TURN

Choose an event that changed history. Take notes from reliable sources. Make an outline for your report.

Strategies Good Writers Use

- Decide on your purpose and audience.
- Brainstorm ideas that may interest your audience.
- Evaluate sources of information.
- Take research notes and make an outline.

USING YOUR
Handbook

For help with taking notes, citing sources, and making an outline, see pages 530–531, 533, and 534.

Organization and Elaboration

Follow this flowchart to help you draft your research report:

Introduce the Topic
Explain why it is important or interesting.

Follow Your Outline
Each main idea might become a topic sentence for a paragraph.

Provide Supporting Details
In each paragraph, give facts and details that support the main idea. Put information from sources in your own words.

Provide a Conclusion
In the last paragraph, summarize briefly. State the most important idea you want your audience to remember.

Strategies Good Writers Use

- Begin by explaining the event.
- Put your paragraphs in the best order.
- Support each topic sentence with details and facts.
- Put quotation marks around any wording that is not your own.

MODEL

Here is the beginning of Leslie's report. Which sentence states the main idea of the entire report?

> When gold was discovered in California in 1848, the news spread around the world. By 1849 thousands of people had rushed to California dreaming of riches. These gold-seekers faced great difficulties, but most stayed, and California was changed forever.

 Use a computer to draft your essay. Use the click-and-drag or the cut-and-paste functions to rearrange details or paragraphs. See what order works best.

YOUR TURN

Draft your essay. Use the steps above. Look again at your prewriting notes. Remember to use Neil Morris's article and Leslie's report as models.

Revising

Organization and Elaboration

First, reread your draft carefully. Think about these questions:

- How well did I introduce my topic?
- How well do the facts and details support the topic sentence in each body paragraph?
- How effective is the order of the main ideas?
- How clearly did I state the most important idea at the end of the report?

MODEL

Here is part of Leslie's draft. Notice that she deleted some details that did not support the topic and some that were not facts. She also replaced two simple sentences with one complex sentence.

> Prospecting for
> ~~Finding~~ gold was hard work. ~~I think looking for gold must have been exciting, though.~~ People thought they would pick up gold from the ground. However, sand and gravel had to be washed with water in pans or special
> wooden
> boxes. ~~I saw a movie once about miners panning for gold.~~ Because The flakes of gold were heavy. ~~They~~ sank to the bottom. It took a long time to find a little gold.

Click on Select All in the drop-down edit menu. Then you can try different fonts to see which one looks best.

YOUR TURN

Revise your report to make it as interesting and factual as you can. Make sure each body paragraph has a topic sentence and supporting details. Think about using some compound and complex sentences.

Proofreading

Checking Your Language

When you proofread, look for mistakes in grammar, spelling, punctuation, and capitalization. When you correct these mistakes, it will be easier for your audience to enjoy and learn from your report.

MODEL

Here is a part of Leslie's revised draft. After she revised her report, she proofread it. Notice the spelling errors Leslie corrected. She also corrected a run-on sentence and a sentence fragment.

> Because of the gold rush, California's
> ~~poplation~~ _population_ grew rapidly. San Francisco and
> sacramento had been ~~settlemints~~ _settlements_. but They
> soon became towns. There were 15,000
> settlers in early 1848; there were more ~~then~~ _than_
> 100,000 at the end of 1849. _California_ had enough
> people ~~too~~ _to_ become a state in 1850.

YOUR TURN

Proofread your revised report several times. Check for one type of mistake each time.
- Check spelling and capitalization.
- Check grammar and punctuation.
- Check for sentence fragments, run-on sentences, and comma splices.

Strategies Good Writers Use

- Correct sentence fragments, run-on sentences, and comma splices.
- Check for commas in compound and complex sentences.

Publishing

Sharing Your Work

Now it is time to publish your research report. Answering these questions will help you choose the best way to share your work:

1. Who is your audience? What is the best way to show your work to the audience?

2. Should you print your report from a computer or write it in cursive?

3. Can you add any graphic aids, such as a chart, a graph, a diagram, a map, or a time line?

4. Should you publish your report as a multimedia presentation? What media (slides, music, video, or computer graphics) would work well?

USING YOUR
Handbook

- Use the rubric on page 510 to evaluate your research report.

Reflecting on Your Writing

 Using Your Portfolio What did you learn about your writing in this chapter? Write your answer to each of these questions:

1. Did your research report meet its purpose? Why or why not?

2. Use the rubric from your Handbook to score your own writing. How did you do?

Write your answers and add them to your portfolio, along with a copy of your report. Are you meeting the writing goals that you have set for yourself? Write one sentence about the strongest part of your writing. Write one sentence that sets a goal for improving your writing.

Giving a Multimedia Presentation

After Leslie finished her research report, she thought that her audience would enjoy it as a multimedia presentation. You can do a multimedia presentation, too. Here are the steps:

STEP 1 Reread your report. List facts, people, or places mentioned in your report. Choose ones that your audience might like. Could you show any through photographs, a map, a globe, or a poster?

STEP 2 Look in the library for audio or video recordings that would go well with your report. Search the Internet for images or sounds that you can use. Download or scan them into a computer. Prepare charts or graphs to explain facts.

STEP 3 Choose the items that you will use. Decide what equipment you will need, such as a VCR, an audio player, or a computer. Make sure they will be available.

STEP 4 Plan and practice your presentation. Mark your report with notes about when to stop and what to show or play. If you need help with the equipment, ask a classmate to assist you. Practice your presentation from beginning to end.

STEP 5 Relax, and let yourself enjoy presenting your report. Speak clearly and loudly, and look at your audience. Answer questions at the end.

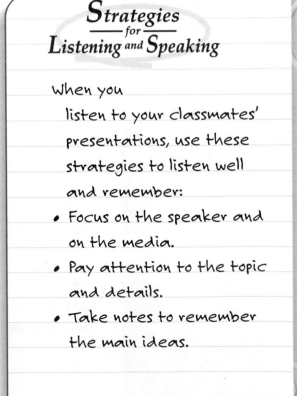

Strategies for Listening and Speaking

When you listen to your classmates' presentations, use these strategies to listen well and remember:

- Focus on the speaker and on the media.
- Pay attention to the topic and details.
- Take notes to remember the main ideas.

Prepositions *pages 310–311*

A. Write each sentence. Underline each preposition.

1. The word *Indian* was first used for Native Americans by Christopher Columbus.
2. Columbus thought that he had landed in the Indies.
3. Scientists think that people migrated across the Bering land bridge from Asia during the Ice Age.
4. Native American groups differ from one another in many ways.
5. The Anasazi culture thrived for hundreds of years.
6. Some Anasazi ruins are found at Chaco Canyon in New Mexico.
7. The Anasazi lived in adobe homes built around central plazas.
8. Native people of the Eastern Woodlands include the Iroquois.
9. The people of the Northwest are known for their beautiful wooden carvings.
10. During the winter, gifts were exchanged between neighboring villages at a ceremonial feast.

Object of the Preposition *pages 312–313*

B. Each sentence contains one or more prepositional phrases. Write each prepositional phrase, and underline the object of each preposition.

11. Native Americans gave many new foods to the world.
12. They grew maize, squash, and many kinds of beans.
13. Hunting and fishing were important activities in many Native American cultures.
14. Some Native Americans caught fish with nets and traps.
15. The Navajo used wool from their sheep for blankets.

Expanding Sentences with Prepositional Phrases *pages 314–315*

C. Expand these sentences by adding at least one prepositional phrase to each.

16. We learned about the traditions.
17. The students worked hard.
18. This article has interesting information.
19. The letter arrived yesterday.
20. We ate lunch.

Unit 5
Grammar Review
CHAPTER 26

Phrases and
Clauses
pages 320–329

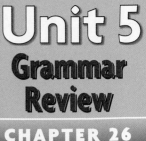

Phrase or Clause? *pages 320–321*

A. Write whether the underlined group of words is a prepositional phrase or a clause.

1. The American people fought a revolution because they
   wanted certain rights.
2. New leaders might take away those rights if they had too
   much power.
3. The delegates wrote "checks and balances" into the
   Constitution.
4. "Checks" limit the powers of each branch of the government.
5. "Balances" divide powers so that no branch can become too
   powerful.

Independent and Dependent Clauses *pages 322–323*

**B. Write each sentence below. Underline the dependent
clause.**

6. A bill is sent to the President after Congress passes it.
7. The President can veto the bill if he or she disagrees with it.
8. Because a President has this right, the power of Congress is
   checked.
9. Although Congress passes laws, courts can review the laws.
10. People can challenge a law in court when it seems unfair.

Combining Independent and Dependent Clauses *pages 324–325*

**C. Add a dependent clause to each sentence. You may want
to give the kind of information shown in parentheses,
using commas when necessary.**

11. A citizen has the right to vote. (when)
12. I will find out the election results. (when)
13. Candidates can be elected. (condition)
14. People watch the news on television. (why)
15. We can learn about our country's past. (condition)

Unit 5
Grammar Review

CHAPTER 28

Complex
Sentences
pages 338–347

Compound and Complex Sentences *pages 338–339*

A. Write whether each sentence is compound or complex. Write the dependent clause in each complex sentence.

1. As new trails were found, people began moving westward.
2. It was hard to build homes on the plains because few trees grew there.
3. Although the journey was long, many settlers headed for Oregon.
4. Some pioneers went to Oregon, but others chose California.
5. The trip was dangerous, and some people were afraid to go.

More About Complex Sentences

pages 340–341

B. Write each sentence. Underline the dependent clause. Add commas where needed.

6. Before the United States made the Louisiana Purchase this was a much smaller nation.
7. New territories opened in the west after the United States signed a treaty with England.
8. When the Mexican War was over Mexico had lost much of its land.
9. If Mexico had won the war it might have kept Texas.
10. Pioneers began to settle where no American citizens had lived before.

Sentence Variety *pages 342–343*

C. Rewrite each set of sentences to form the kind of sentence named in parentheses. You may vary the order of words or clauses. Add commas where needed.

11. California workers found gold in the American River. They were building a mill. (complex sentence)
12. Thousands of people arrived by land. Thousands more came by sea. (compound sentence)
13. Many people came to look for gold. The population of California grew. (complex sentence)
14. Towns grew into cities. California became a state. (compound sentence)
15. More than a billion dollars in gold was mined in California. Few people became rich. (complex sentence)

Sentence Fragments *pages 348–349*

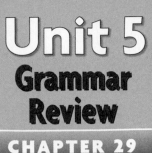

Unit 5
Grammar Review
CHAPTER 29

More About
Sentences
pages 348–357

A. Write whether each group of words is a complete sentence or a sentence fragment.

1. In Detroit, Michigan, a man named Henry Ford.
2. Was interested in designing and building cars.
3. When Ford started his own company.
4. The first cars were expensive and had problems.
5. Was a problem that needed to be solved.

Run-on Sentences and Comma Splices *pages 350–351*

B. Write *RO* if the sentence is a run-on sentence. Write *CS* if it contains a comma splice. Write *correct* if it is correct.

6. Henry Ford built his first car in 1896, and he founded the Ford Motor Company in 1903.
7. Ford developed the assembly line soon he was making many more cars.
8. The assembly line saved time and money, cars became less expensive.
9. Ford produced the first Model T in 1908, he sold fifteen million of them.
10. Henry Ford tried new ideas his company changed factory work.

Punctuating Compound and Complex Sentences *pages 352–353*

C. Rewrite each statement correctly. If the sentence is correct, write *correct*.

11. Henry Ford worked many years he did not retire until he was over 80 years old.
12. People remember Ford for his inventions he also changed factory work.
13. Although some people did not like it the assembly line changed how things were made.
14. Today fewer workers are needed in factories because many machines are run by computers.
15. Computers can do many things, companies will always need skilled workers.

Traces of the Past

Who settled your part of the country? Who lived there before the settlers came? Find out how those cultures affect your community today. Then write and present a group report.

Who Lived Here?

- Use a search engine, city home page, or encyclopedia to do your research. Visit a local history museum, if possible. Share your notes with classmates.

How Did Different Groups of People Affect Your Region?

- Consider the art, food, literature, music, place names, and holidays in your community. Are they connected to groups who lived there in the past?

Write and Present a Group Report

- Work with your classmates to write a report about what you discover.

- Create a diagram to show what kinds of people lived in your region. Provide pictures of the ways they have influenced your region and its culture.

- Present your report to the class. Each group member should take part in the presentation. Use the diagram to help present your ideas.

- As a class, create a website to show what you have learned about your region's history. Put information about different peoples on different pages. Then create links to show how they influenced your region.

Clambake: A Wampanoag Tradition
by Russell M. Peters

NONFICTION

Steven helps to prepare and celebrate a traditional Mashpee Wampanoag clambake with friends and family in Cape Cod, Massachusetts.

Notable Social Studies Trade Book; Teacher's Choice

The Indian School
by Gloria Whelan

HISTORICAL FICTION

Lucy learns many Native American traditions from Raven, a young girl at a mission school run by Lucy's aunt.

Award-Winning Author

Cities in the Sand
by Scott Warren

NONFICTION

A guide to the many ancient civilizations that used to inhabit the deserts of the Southwest shows how prehistoric people coped with the environment.

Unit 6

Grammar Usage and Mechanics

Writing Expressive Writing

Act I

Scene I

(The setting is the village, early in the morning. The townspeople enter noisily from all sides of the stage.)

Mayor: Good morning

Commas

Use a **comma** after each item in a series of three or more items. Use a comma to separate the independent clauses in a compound sentence.

This chart shows the rules for using commas in a series and in compound sentences.

Rule	Example
Use a comma to separate words in a series of three or more items.	An artist uses paints, brushes, canvas, and an easel.
Use a comma to separate three or more simple subjects in a compound subject.	Miguel, Kim, and Ben are using the brushes.
Use a comma to separate three or more simple predicates in a compound predicate.	We cleaned the canvas, mixed the paint, and set up the easel.
Use a comma to separate independent clauses in a compound sentence.	Some artists paint portraits, but others like to paint landscapes.

Guided Practice

A. Tell whether the comma usage in the sentence is correct. If it is not correct, tell where commas are needed.

Example: The earliest paintings show horses cattle deer and people.
The earliest paintings show horses, cattle, deer, and people.

1. Painting has not changed much from early times but the materials used by artists are very different.
2. Artists have painted on plaster, wood, and canvas.
3. Artists may get ideas sketch, and begin painting.
4. The Greeks and Romans painted murals with pictures of gardens buildings and people.
5. Some murals are painted on the outside of a building, but others are painted inside.

Independent Practice

B. If the sentence contains an error in comma usage, write the sentence. Add commas where they are needed. If the sentence is correct, write *correct*.

Example: Marc Chagall, Pablo Picasso and Paul Klee are famous modern painters.

Marc Chagall, Pablo Picasso, and Paul Klee are famous modern painters.

6. Paintings of fruit, flowers or dishes are called still-life paintings.

7. Still-life paintings do not show people or animals, but they can include plants.

8. Still-life painters gather arrange and set up the things they want to paint.

9. A painting of the outdoors is called a landscape but a painting of the sea or ocean is called a seascape.

10. Artists may paint a scene once or they may paint it several times.

11. Red, orange and yellow are known as the warm colors.

12. Some paints dry almost instantly, but others dry slowly.

13. Water, mineral spirits or turpentine makes the paint easy to use.

14. Many pigments are poisonous so painters have to be careful.

15. Paintings are made in many different ways, and there are many different tools you can use.

> **Remember** to use a **comma** to separate the two complete thoughts that make up a compound sentence. Also use a comma after each item in a series of three or more items.

Writing Connection

Art Imagine that you have been asked to design a large painting on a wall (a mural) for a school. Think of scenes to include in the mural. Write four sentences to describe the painting. List the colors you would use and the objects or people you would include. Be sure to use commas for items in a series.

More About Commas

Use a comma in direct address, in the greeting of a friendly letter, and after introductory words and phrases.

This chart shows the rules for using commas within a sentence and in the greeting of a friendly letter.

Rule	Example
Use a comma to set off the name of a person who is spoken to directly in a sentence.	A camera, Tino, is a simple machine that takes photographs.
Use a comma after an introductory word or phrase.	Yes, there have been many different kinds of cameras.
Use a comma after the last word in the greeting of a friendly letter.	Dear Gigi, I have a new camera!

Guided Practice

A. **Tell whether the comma usage in the sentence is correct. If it is not, tell where commas are needed.**

Example: Film comes in both black-and-white and color Aaron.
Film comes in both black-and-white and color, Aaron.

1. Yoko a camera works like the human eye.
2. Yes cameras see things that we cannot always see.
3. Of course photographs help us learn about people in other parts of the world.
4. Believe it or not the first camera was made in Italy in 1500.
5. Joseph Niepce took the world's first photograph in 1826 Kim.
6. Scott do you know who invented the first easy-to-use camera?
7. Well I think the inventor was George Eastman.
8. History students Brenda all remember Mathew Brady's pictures.
9. Brady's photographs help us learn about the Civil War José.
10. James please return the digital camera to Mr. Smith.

Independent Practice

Remember to use a **comma** after the last word in the greeting of a friendly letter.

B. Write each sentence, adding commas where they are needed.

Example: Carmen are you interested in photography?
Carmen, are you interested in photography?

11. Have you seen my new camera Arturo?
12. Believe it or not I have already taken many pictures.
13. Of course I have read several photography books.
14. Arturo an important part of the camera is the lens.
15. By the way the film is also important.

C. Rewrite these parts of letters. Add commas where they are needed.

16. Dear Mike
17. I saw a display of Ansel Adams's photographs. By the way do you like nature photography?
18. Well I think that nature photography is a great hobby.
19. What have you taken pictures of this summer Mike?
20. Of course I took pictures of my friends.

21. Dear Luis
22. Yes I'm learning to develop my film in a place called a darkroom.
23. Of course it is called a darkroom because there are no windows.
24. No the room is not completely unlit.
25. Luis people in darkrooms have to work by the light of a red bulb.

Writing Connection

Real-Life Writing: Questions Find a photograph that you think is interesting. Work with a partner to ask each other questions about the photograph you chose. Write down some of your questions and answers. Be sure to use commas with direct address and with introductory words and phrases.

USAGE AND MECHANICS

Using Commas with Appositives

An **appositive** is a noun or noun phrase that renames another noun or noun phrase. Use **commas** before and after an appositive.

An appositive usually comes immediately after the noun or noun phrase it renames. An appositive gives more information about the noun, but it does not change the meaning of the sentence.

> **Examples:**
>
> Mr. Allen, **the dance teacher,** knows how to tango.
>
> Do you think he could teach us the rumba, **a Latin dance**?

Guided Practice

A. Identify the appositive in each sentence.

> **Example:** We went to see a performance of *Swan Lake*, a ballet.
> *a ballet*

1. The first ballet, a great success, was performed for a wedding in Italy.
2. Ballet, a very formal dance, has complex steps.
3. A ballerina, a female ballet dancer, is very graceful.
4. Gina is dancing in my favorite ballet, *The Nutcracker*.
5. Mrs. Fox, her ballet teacher, owns a dance studio.
6. Isadora Duncan, one of the most famous dancers, danced in her bare feet.
7. John, a good dancer, will teach us the waltz.
8. We will be in the dance studio, a large room with mirrors.
9. There are two forms of the waltz, the three-step and the two-step.
10. The waltz was first performed in Vienna, the capital of Austria.

Independent Practice

B. Write each sentence. Underline the appositive.

Example: Mrs. Fox taught us the polka, a folk dance.
Mrs. Fox taught us the polka, <u>a folk dance</u>.

11. They danced the tango, a South American dance.
12. Gene Kelly, a dancer in many movies, was full of energy.
13. The fox-trot, a series of quick and slow steps, is hard to learn.
14. Our teacher, Mr. Morris, taught us an African dance.
15. Our class is also learning square dancing, a type of American folk dance.

C. Write each sentence. Add commas where they are needed.

Example: Musical comedy a type of play with music always tells a story.
Musical comedy, a type of play with music, always tells a story.

16. Dancing an important part of musical comedy helps tell the story.
17. *The Brook* one of the first musical comedies told a story about America.
18. Many musical comedies are performed on Broadway a well-known street in New York City.
19. Many shows hire a choreographer a person who makes up the dances.
20. George M. Cohan an actor and a composer wrote many musicals.

> **Remember**
>
> that an **appositive** tells more about the noun or noun phrase that it follows. An appositive is separated from the rest of the sentence by commas.

Writing Connection

Writer's Craft: Concise Wording Appositives help you be concise in your writing. With an appositive, you can tuck information into a sentence instead of writing a new sentence. Choose a story you have read recently, and write a one-paragraph summary. Use appositives to tell who the characters are or to summarize other information.

Extra Practice

A. Write each sentence. Add commas where they are needed. *pages 380–381*

Example: Some artists design wallpaper rugs and furniture.
Some artists design wallpaper, rugs, and furniture.

1. Drawings can be made with crayons markers or pens.
2. Photographs newspapers and magazines can be used to make collages.
3. Artists need paper brushes and paints to paint a portrait.
4. People nature and buildings are often the subjects of photographs.
5. A portrait photographer needs a camera film and lights.

B. Write each sentence. Add commas where they are needed. *pages 382–383*

Example: Of course the camera was a remarkable invention.
Of course, the camera was a remarkable invention.

6. Believe it or not many people were afraid that painting would come to an end when cameras were invented.
7. No it is not true that the invention of photography meant the end of painting.
8. Sarah do you know about Ansel Adams?
9. By the way the art museum displays some of his photos.
10. Of course he used black-and-white film.

C. Write each sentence. Add commas where they are needed. *pages 384–385*

Example: Michelangelo a great sculptor was famous.
Michelangelo, a great sculptor, was famous.

11. Mary Cassatt a well-known artist was an American.
12. Rembrandt the famous Dutch artist painted many portraits.
13. Mrs. Allen, the art teacher took us to the museum.
14. There we saw oil paintings by Degas a French painter.
15. My favorite paintings watercolors are also in the museum.

For more activities with commas, visit *The Learning Site:*
www.harcourtschool.com

D. Write each sentence. Add commas where needed.

pages 380–385

> **Example:** I enjoy photography, drawing and painting.
> *I enjoy photography, drawing, and painting.*

16. I use pencils pens, and chalk to draw.
17. Yes my brother enjoys drawing outdoor scenes.
18. What kinds of pictures do you draw Lisa?
19. Still-life drawings pictures of objects can be colorful.
20. Flowers vases, and furniture also appear in still-life drawings.
21. My art teacher draws paints, and builds sculptures.
22. By the way Julio and Hassan are in my art class.
23. We painted portraits and our teacher put them on the wall.
24. No she has not taken them down yet.
25. My painting, a seascape has many shades of blue.
26. What colors are in your painting Hassan?
27. My seascape is blue but yours has a lot of gray.
28. Julio likes to use green, yellow and brown for landscapes.
29. Julio's latest painting *A Field in Autumn*, won an award.
30. When do you want to go see it Hassan?

DID YOU KNOW?
Pop art was a form of art that began in the 1950s. Pop artists photographed or painted common, everyday objects, such as cans of food, road signs, or soft drink bottles.

Writing Connection

Writer's Journal: Writing Idea Picture in your mind a character for a character sketch. Draw a picture if you wish. Then paint a portrait of the character in words. Use items in a series to add details. Check your use of commas.

Writer's Journal

Chapter Review

Look at the underlined words in each item. There may be a mistake in punctuation or capitalization. If you find a mistake, choose the answer that is the best way to correct it.

STANDARDIZED TEST PREP

TIP When you see three items in a series, remember to add commas.

1 <u>Dear Anita</u>
  A dear Anita,
  B dear anita
  C Dear Anita,
  D Correct as is

2 <u>Well, ballet</u> classes are under way.
  F Well ballet
  G Well ballet,
  H Well, ballet,
  J Correct as is

3 We <u>stretch, bend and exercise</u> during warm-ups.
  A stretch bend and exercise
  B stretch, bend, and exercise
  C stretch bend, and exercise
  D Correct as is

4 My classmates include <u>Gregory, Leonie and Hassan</u>.
  F Gregory, Leonie and Hassan,
  G Gregory Leonie and Hassan
  H Gregory, Leonie, and Hassan
  J Correct as is

5 <u>Lisa enjoyed ballet but</u> now she is tap dancing.
  A Lisa enjoyed ballet, but
  B Lisa enjoyed ballet but,
  C Lisa enjoyed ballet. But
  D Correct as is

6 Gregory dances <u>the rumba, waltz and polka</u>.
  F the rumba, waltz, and polka
  G the rumba, waltz, and, polka
  H the rumba waltz and polka
  J Correct as is

7 <u>Milly the best dancer</u> will perform now.
  A Milly the best dancer,
  B Milly, the best dancer
  C Milly, the best dancer,
  D Correct as is

8 <u>By the way, our music teacher</u> will play the piano.
  F By the way, our music teacher,
  G By the way our music teacher,
  H By the way our music teacher
  J Correct as is

For additional test preparation, visit *The Learning Site:*
www.harcourtschool.com

Using Vocabulary Strategies

You already know what a clue is. It is an object or a fact that helps you find something out. What kind of clue is a context clue?

Think of *context* as another word for setting. Just as a story is set in a place and time, a word or phrase is set in a sentence and paragraph. The whole sentence or paragraph is the context for an unfamiliar word. This context helps you figure out the meaning of the word.

When you see a word you do not know, use context clues to help you define it. Think about its part of speech. Is it a noun, a verb, or an adjective? Look at the surrounding words in the sentence. Do they help define the word you do not know? Does the sentence provide clues to its meaning? Does this new word sound like or look like any words you already know? Once you have asked all these questions, you should have a good idea of what the new word means. Check a dictionary to see if you are correct.

Here is an example of how to use context clues.

An artist would paint a fresco on a plaster wall to show a scene or historic event. The paint was often applied to the plaster while the plaster was still wet.

What does the word *fresco* mean? The context tells you that it is a noun. You also know that it is a painting of a scene on a plastered wall. Since it is used to decorate a wall, you can guess that it is a kind of mural. When you check the dictionary, you will find that you were correct.

YOUR TURN

CONTEXT CLUES Play word detective with some classmates. On your own, each of you should find a written passage with some new or hard words in it. An older friend or family member can help you with this if necessary. The next day, get together with your classmates and listen as each person reads his or her passage aloud. Work together to use context clues to figure out the new and hard words. Check a dictionary to see how well you did.

TIP Look carefully at a sentence and paragraph to see if it defines the word for you.

Using Quotation Marks

A speaker's exact words are called a direct quotation. Use quotation marks before and after a direct quotation.

Sometimes the words that identify the speaker come before the quotation. Use a comma after them. Then use opening quotation marks and a capital letter to begin the quotation. After the quotation, put the correct end punctuation followed by closing quotation marks.

> **Example:**
> Mr. Brodsky said, "We will read three plays this semester."

Sometimes the words that identify the speaker come after the quotation. Use a comma, a question mark, or an exclamation point to separate the quotation from the rest of the sentence.

> **Example:**
> "Quiet, everyone!" shouted Mr. Brodsky.

Do not use quotation marks if a statement does not show a speaker's exact words.

> **Example:**
> Mr. Brodsky asked which plays the students wanted to read.

Guided Practice

A. Tell how to correct the punctuation and capitalization in each sentence.

Example: "Sophocles was an important writer of plays in ancient times" said Luisa.
add comma after times but before quotation marks

1. "The Greeks performed plays in large outdoor theaters called amphitheaters said Tom.
2. "We should put on a play this spring" said Yasmine.
3. "Let's make the audience laugh", said Emily.
4. "We could write the parts ourselves, she continued.
5. Yasmine said "this book can help us with ideas for costumes."

Vocabulary Power

play·wright
[plā′rīt] *n.* A person who writes plays.

Independent Practice

B. Write each sentence. Correct any capitalization and punctuation errors. If a sentence needs no corrections, write *correct*.

Example: "Which plays would you like to read" asked Mr. Brodsky?
"Which plays would you like to read?" asked Mr. Brodsky.

6. Acting was once considered a man's job only, so boys played the women's roles," Mr. Brodsky explained.
7. Tino said Women have sometimes played male roles, too."
8. "Did you know that a person who writes plays is called a playwright, Yasmine asked.
9. henrik Ibsen was a playwright who wrote great parts for women," said Luisa.
10. Nora is one of Ibsen's great characters. Can anyone name another playwright," asked Mr. Brodsky.
11. "George Bernard Shaw wrote plays," stated Trina.
12. he was born in Ireland," said Mr. Brodsky.
13. He went on, has anyone seen a musical play"
14. "I saw *Annie* at the high school, said Emily.
15. Musical plays are the main American gift to theater, said Mr. Brodsky.
16. He asked who can name some American musicals?"
17. We performed *Oklahoma* at drama camp" Tino replied.
18. "My brother and I liked *Cats* very much," said Tom.
19. Mr. Brodsky reminded him that *Cats* is not an American musical.
20. "*Cats* is a British play" agreed Jo.

Writing Connection

Writer's Journal: Specific Verbs Make a list of verbs that could be used instead of *said* in dialogue—for example, *yelled, cried, whispered, pointed out*. Then write two sentences that you or someone you know might say. Use two of the less common verbs from your list to help tell how the speaker spoke.

More About Quotation Marks

A quotation is sometimes interrupted by words that are not part of the quotation. This is called a **divided quotation**. Place quotation marks around the quoted words only.

If a divided quotation is all one sentence, use another comma after the speaker's name. If a divided quotation is two sentences, use a period after the words that interrupt.

Examples:

"Tell me what plays you want to read," said Mr. Brodsky, "and I'll list them on the board."

"I want to read *Julius Caesar*," said Rebecca. "We're studying him in history class."

Begin a new paragraph every time the speaker changes.

Example:

"After we read the plays," said Mr. Brodsky, "we'll choose one to perform for the school."

"Let's perform a comedy," said Teresa.

Guided Practice

A. **Tell how to punctuate each sentence. Be ready to explain your answers.**

Example: Will you tell us asked Ben which plays we will read?
"Will you tell us," asked Ben, "which plays we will read?"

1. I think answered Mr. Brodsky that we will read three plays
2. We would probably enjoy reading more he continued but there is not enough time.
3. There is one play he said that I know you will like.
4. Are you going to make us sing asked Arthur.
5. Don't worry said Mr. Brodsky you will not have to sing.

Independent Practice

B. Write each sentence, using correct punctuation.

6. William Shakespeare Mr. Brodsky said wrote many powerful plays.
7. Did you know Jo asked that most movies and books about Shakespeare are not true stories?
8. They are only some writers' ideas she continued of some things that might have happened.
9. Shakespeare's Globe Theatre explained Mr. Brodsky was rebuilt in London in the 1990s.
10. *Hamlet* is one of Shakespeare's most famous plays Trina said. What a long play it is!

C. Write each direct quotation as a divided quotation.

Example: "I'll bet that most people don't know where plays were first shown," said Luisa.
"I'll bet," said Luisa, "that most people don't know where plays were first shown."

11. "I know. The first plays were staged in Greece," said Tom.
12. Emily pointed out, "The Romans also enjoyed plays, and many Roman plays were based on Greek plays."
13. "During the Middle Ages, theater was very informal," said Tino.
14. He explained, "Actors traveled from town to town. They carried costumes and props with them."
15. Mr. Brodsky asked, "Do you know how they earned money? They performed at fairs and festivals."

Remember to set off interruptions to direct quotations with correct punctuation marks. The interruptions themselves should not have quotation marks around them.

Writing Connection

Writer's Craft: Vivid Adverbs Sometimes the words that identify the speaker, or speaker's tags, include adverbs to tell how the speaker spoke. Work with a partner to write "Tom Swifties"—speaker's tags with adverbs that make puns. Here is an example: *"I want to be a real boy," Pinocchio said* **woodenly**. You might start by making a list of vivid adverbs, such as *icily, hotly,* and *stonily*. Use one divided quotation.

**A Colon in a
Business Letter**

Dear Mr. Brodsky:

To Whom It May
Concern:

USAGE AND MECHANICS

Colons

Use a colon before a list of items, especially after expressions such as *the following* and *as follows*. Use a colon between the hour and the minutes when writing the time in numerals. Use a colon after the last word in the greeting of a business letter.

When a colon introduces a list, the list always appears at the end of the sentence. The colon should not come after a verb.

Examples:

Incorrect: The students who helped with the costumes were: Shirley, Barry, and Eva.

Correct: The students who helped with the costumes were Shirley, Barry, and Eva.

Correct: These students helped with the costumes: Shirley, Barry, and Eva.

Guided Practice

A. **Tell whether each sentence is punctuated correctly or needs a colon. If the punctuation is incorrect, tell how you would correct the sentence.**

Example: Next week, the students will rehearse on the following afternoons, Tuesday, Thursday, and Friday. *incorrect; Change the comma after <u>afternoons</u> to a colon.*

1. Mr. Brodsky asked the cast to meet at 320.
2. Mr. Brodsky began, "Here are the things we need to do today, rehearse Scene 1, read through Scene 2, and make a list of props."
3. "Mr. Brodsky," Luisa asked, "will all our performances be at 8:00?"
4. "Yes," he replied. "Before we start, though, I have the following three surprises a snack, an announcement, and a letter."
5. Emily read, "Dear Mr. Brodsky and Students, We are happy to loan you the costumes for your play."

Independent Practice

B. Write this business letter. Use colons where needed.

(6) Dear Ms. Andrews,

Since you direct our community children's theater group, I am writing to ask whether I may interview you. **(7)** I hope to write about the following, how your theater group began, how you choose your plays, and how you choose your actors. **(8)** We might also discuss these productions *Annie*, *Tom Sawyer*, and *A Christmas Carol*. **(9)** I thought we could meet at 3 30 on Friday afternoon for two hours. **(10)** Another possible time is Thursday at 415.

Sincerely,

Yasmine Davis

C. Write each sentence, using colons correctly. If a sentence does not need to be changed, write *correct*.

Example: The first three oral presentations were given by these students, Tino, Ben, and Yasmine.
The first three oral presentations were given by these students: Tino, Ben, and Yasmine.

11. Tino wrote the following titles on the board *Oklahoma*, *The King and I*, and *West Side Story*.

12. Tom thought, "I bet he won't finish until 4,30."

13. "It's almost 400," pointed out Mr. Brodsky.

14. Ben spoke about theater in three Asian nations: India, China, and Japan.

15. When Ben finished, Mr. Brodsky said, "Tomorrow we will hear from the following students Luisa, Jo, and Emily."

> **Remember**
> to use a **colon** before a list of items in a sentence, between the hour and the minutes when writing the time, and after the last word in the greeting of a business letter.

Writing Connection

Real-Life Writing: Business Letter Write a short business letter to the owner of a local theater. Ask about bringing your class to see a performance or dress rehearsal of a play that this theater is staging. Suggest a time at which you, your teacher, and the owner can meet to work out the details for the class trip. Be sure to use colons correctly in your letter.

Extra Practice

A. **Write each sentence, punctuating each direct quotation correctly.** *pages 390–393*

Example: I can't remember my lines Emily complained.
"I can't remember my lines," Emily complained.

1. You have to remember your lines Jo objected. You have the first speech.
2. I know the lines, but I get scared when I am on stage said Emily.
3. Mr. Brodsky said That's called stage fright, and it's very common.
4. He went on Many actors have had stage fright for their whole careers.
5. How can I get over it? I don't want to ruin the play said Emily.
6. Tell yourself that there's nothing to be scared of Tom suggested. Then you won't be scared.
7. Whenever I had stage fright, I told myself how much fun it was to be an actor said Mr. Brodsky.
8. Ben said When I get scared backstage, I tell jokes.
9. I stretch and exercise to calm down said Jo.
10. Emily said I'll try all those ideas!

B. **Punctuate each divided quotation correctly.**
pages 392–393

11. As you heard in Ben's report Mr. Brodsky said dramas in Asia are different from dramas in the United States.
12. Traditional Asian actors he said must be singers and dancers.
13. That's interesting Trina remarked because I like to do both of those things.
14. In Asian drama Mr. Brodsky told her the costumes are very formal.
15. The colors and designs he continued have special meanings to the audience.

DID YOU KNOW?
The word *drama* comes from ancient Greece, where it meant "deed" or "action." Many plays are about action, or doing. Other plays focus on characters. What stories have you seen acted on stage or in a movie? Which do you like better, those about action or those about characters?

For more activities on punctuating dialogue, visit *The Learning Site:*
www.harcourtschool.com

C. **Write each sentence, using colons correctly. If a sentence needs no changes, write *correct*.** *pages 394–395*

Example: The play will be performed on the following dates
April 9, 10, 16, and 17.
*The play will be performed on the following dates:
April 9, 10, 16, and 17.*

16. "It's 2:30," Mr. Brodsky announced. "Let's talk about the play."

17. Emily said, "The following stores have promised to display our poster: McCloskey's, Hobby Hut, and Lane Flowers."

18. "Great!" exclaimed Tino. "I got the same promise from these stores Burger Barn, The Hattery, and King Jewelers."

19. "Let's try to get those posters up by 5:00 this Friday," Mr. Brodsky suggested.

20. "These are some other places that might display a poster for us card shops, supermarkets, and pizza parlors."

21. "If we're finished here by 4:00," said Luisa, "Jo and I will try a few more stores today."

22. Ben said, "We need to talk about a few important things, printing programs, taking tickets, and providing refreshments."

23. "Right!" replied Mr. Brodsky. "Tickets will be on sale on: Monday."

24. Ben said, "Anyone who wants to talk about programs or refreshments, see me tomorrow at 2:50."

25. He added, "The following students volunteered to take tickets Tino, Tom, and Yasmine."

Writing Connection

Technology With a partner, find a dialogue between two characters in a story or invent your own. Input the dialogue into a computer. Use quotation marks around the words spoken. Start a new paragraph when the speaker changes, and omit speakers' tags. Then use the computer's text-to-speech feature to try out different voices for the characters. How accurately does the feature read? How do the different voices affect your impression of a character?

Chapter Review

Look for mistakes in punctuation in the sentences below. When you find a mistake, write the letter of the part containing the mistake. Some sentences do not have any mistakes at all. If there is no mistake, choose the letter beside *No mistakes*.

STANDARDIZED TEST PREP

TIP Don't forget that in tests like these, some of the examples may be correct as written. For these, choose the letter for *No mistakes*.

For additional test preparation, visit *The Learning Site*:
www.harcourtschool.com

398

1 A "Well," said Mr.
  B Brodsky, I think Ben
  C read that very well."
  D (*No mistakes*)

2 J May I go next?"
  K pleaded Yasmine. "I'm afraid
  L I'll forget my lines!"
  M (*No mistakes*)

3 A "Yes, but then we need to hear
  B from these people Jo, Emily,
  C and Tino," said Mr. Brodsky.
  D (*No mistakes*)

4 J "Once I lived in a castle,
  K Yasmine began,
  L "with beautiful gardens."
  M (*No mistakes*)

5 A "That was just great!" cried
  B Tino. He looked at his watch and
  C saw that the time was 4.10.
  D (*No mistakes*)

6 J "Let's hear Tino next,"
  K said Mr. Brodsky, "since his
  L speech is from the same play."
  M (*No mistakes*)

7 A "Don't applaud," pleaded
  B Tino as he sat down, because
  C I read that terribly!"
  D (*No mistakes*)

8 J "You remembered every
  K word correctly, and that's
  L better than I did, said Ben."
  M (*No mistakes*)

9 A "I think Tino did a great
  B job," agreed Jo. Didn't
  C he, Mr. Brodsky?"
  D (*No mistakes*)

10 J "You did just fine, Mr.
  K Brodsky told Tino. "Much better
  L than I did at your age!"
  M (*No mistakes*)

Words from Many Languages

VOCABULARY

Look at these words: *kimono, sauerkraut, pirouette, wigwam.* Can you guess what they all have in common? Each word is from a language other than English. *Pirouette*, for example, is a French word whose French and English meanings are the same —"a spin or turn." *Kimono* is a Japanese word for a long, loose robe fastened with a sash.

These and many other words have been adopted into the English language, but some of the words have changed. For example, the English word *cypress* (a kind of tree) comes from the Greek name for the same tree, *kyparissos.*

Some people in the United States can trace their family histories to other countries. People who settled in the United States often spoke the languages and cooked the foods of their countries of origin. Many words from other languages are food words. The chart below shows some of these words and the countries from which they came.

China	Greece	Italy	Japan	Mexico	Germany
chow mein	gyro	spaghetti lasagna	sushi	burrito enchilada	sauerbraten

YOUR TURN

RESEARCHING Almost every culture has its own history and traditions of drama. In English there are many words about theater from other languages. Here is a short list:

ballet	kabuki	masque
aria	libretto	opera

Work with a partner to find out about these words. First, define as many as you can from your own knowledge. Then look in a dictionary to learn the meanings of the words you don't know. A good dictionary will give more than a word's definition and pronunciation. It will also tell you from what language the word came. Work with your partner to make a poster illustrating one of the words from the list. The poster should show the meaning of the word and its original language.

TIP You don't have to speak a foreign language to know a foreign word. You can sometimes figure out the meaning by thinking about the sentence in which the word appears. Nearby sentences may give clues, too.

399

Writer's Craft

Word Choice

SHOWING CHARACTER Characters are important in many kinds of **expressive writing**, including plays, stories, and poems. A writer can bring a character to life by describing how the character looks and acts, telling what the character says, and telling what the character thinks.

As you read the following passage from the book *Julie* by Jean Craighead George, notice words and phrases the author uses to describe the character.

LITERATURE MODEL

> Julie did not answer. She studied her father.
> Kapugen was a stocky man with a broad back and powerful arms. His face was burned brown from the Arctic wind and sun, and his hands were blackened by frostbite. His hair was shorter than she remembered, but his chin was still smooth and plucked hairless. A faint mustache darkened his upper lip. He sat with his legs straight out before him.

Analyze THE Model

1. What character is the writer describing?

2. How do words and phrases like *powerful arms* and *blackened by frostbite* help you picture the character?

3. What other words and phrases help give you a mental image of Kapugen?

4. Does the writer intend for the scene to be serious or humorous? How can you tell?

Vocabulary Power

pow·er·ful [pou′ər·fəl]
adj. Having great power, or ability, to do something.

Using effective language means choosing words and phrases that have the effect you intend. To give a good description of a character, you need to use words that give your reader a clear picture of the person you are describing.

To learn more about word choice, study the chart on the next page.

Word Choice Strategies	How to Use Strategies	Examples
Use **vivid verbs** and **specific nouns**.	Choose strong verbs that describe actions in interesting ways.	Use words like **bounces** or **trudges** to tell how a person walks.
	Choose nouns that say exactly what you mean.	Use exact nouns like **cottage** or **skyscraper** instead of a general noun like **building**.
Use **descriptive words and phrases**.	Choose colorful adjectives, adverbs, and phrases to give a clear description.	Use words like **brawny** or **frail, cautiously** or **heedlessly**, and phrases like **hair as soft as velvet**.
Express a **tone** in your writing.	Choose words that express your general feeling or attitude toward your subject.	The overall tone may be humorous, sad, joyful, angry, sympathetic, and so on.

YOUR TURN

ANALYZE WORD CHOICE **Work with a partner. Find descriptions of characters in works of fiction or poetry. Discuss the language the writers use to describe their subjects.**

Answer these questions:

1. Whom is the writer describing?
2. How does the writer show what the character is like?
3. What vivid verbs and specific nouns does the writer use?
4. What descriptive words and phrases help you create a mental image of the character?
5. What is the writer's attitude toward the character? What words and phrases help you identify the tone?

Vivid Verbs
and Specific Nouns

A. Think of a vivid verb or specific noun to replace the underlined word in each sentence. Write the revised sentences on your paper.

Vivid Verbs

1. "What a surprise!" Angie <u>said</u>.
2. I see my uncle <u>going</u> down the road.
3. Mike <u>looked</u> at the dark clouds overhead.
4. Mrs. Lewis <u>says</u> hello to all her neighbors.
5. Alex <u>walked</u> into the room.

Specific Nouns

6. He climbed into his <u>vehicle</u> and drove away.
7. Aunt Mary cooks delicious <u>food</u>.
8. The <u>animal</u> ran around the side of the house.
9. She picked a <u>flower</u>.
10. Let's carry this <u>thing</u> into the other room.

Descriptive Words and Phrases

B. Read the following paragraph. Think of descriptive words and phrases you can add to make the paragraph more interesting and detailed. Write the revised paragraph on your paper.

Mr. Chester lives in a city. He likes to go to the park. He finds a place to sit where he can watch the squirrels and pigeons. When people pass by, Mr. Chester tips his hat and says hello. He enjoys the city and his place in the park.

Tone

C. **Read each paragraph. On your paper, identify the tone of the paragraph, and explain how you identified it.**

11. The old door creaked open slowly. Ted held his breath, waiting to see what would happen next.

12. Rosa didn't have an easy life, but she never let things get her down. She complained sometimes, but she had good reason. Besides, she never complained very loudly or for very long.

13. The wind that night had a lonesome sound, and the rain fell like tears. Marty kept thinking of the look on Papa's face the night he went away.

14. Charlie said his old mule Zeke was about as ornery and stubborn as a creature could be. There were people who thought Charlie himself had Zeke beat by a mile.

15. That boy is not a true friend. He tells you one thing to your face and then says something else behind your back. He doesn't care about anyone's feelings but his own.

Writing and Thinking

Writer's Journal

Write to Record Reflections When you read a description of a character, are you mostly interested in how the character looks or in what kind of person he or she is? Do you think that physical characteristics like twinkling eyes or hands made rough by hard work can tell something about the kind of person someone is? Write your reflections in your Writer's Journal.

Character Study

Jean Craighead George wrote a brief character study of
an Eskimo father named Kapugen. Brandon wrote a
description of a character he planned to use in a short
story. As you read this character study, look for examples
of language that Brandon used to create an image of the
character in your mind.

MODEL

descriptive words
and phrases

vivid verbs

> Marcus's mother, Mrs. Blake, was not a tall
> woman, but she stood straight as a soldier. When
> she walked, her small feet tapped rapidly and
> lightly. Her voice rang out in firm, clear tones,
> leaving no doubt that she expected Marcus to
> listen.

vivid verbs

> Marcus often noticed his mother's large, dark eyes.
> They flashed like lightning when she was angry.
> More often, though, they crinkled with laughter.
> Sometimes she laughed so hard that tears streamed
> down her face.

descriptive words
and phrases

specific nouns

> Mrs. Blake loved to cook. She made crumbly corn
> muffins, steaming hot biscuits, and stew so
> delicious it made Marcus hungry just to smell it.

Analyze THE Model

1. What kind of person is Marcus's mother, and how
   do you know?

2. How does Brandon use effective language to develop
   the description?

3. Does this character study give you a clear picture
   of Marcus's mother? Why or why not?

4. What is the tone of the character study, and how
   did you identify it?

YOUR TURN

WRITING PROMPT Create a character, perhaps one based on someone you know. Choose one of these writing forms in which to present your character: descriptive paragraphs, a diary entry written by the character, a dialogue in which the character speaks to someone, or a poem. Use words that help your readers create a mental image of the character.

STUDY THE PROMPT
Answer these questions:

1. What is your purpose for writing?

2. Who is your subject?

3. Which writing form will you use?

4. Who is your audience?

Prewriting and Drafting

Plan Your Character Study First, think of a character you would like to write about, and give the character a name. Brainstorm details for your character study, and organize them in a web like the one shown here.

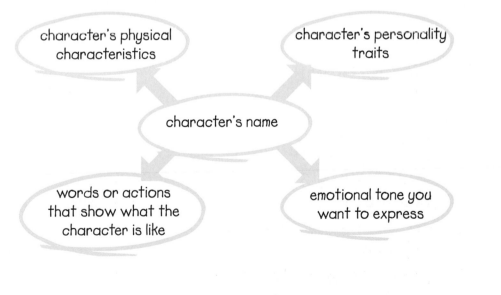

USING YOUR
Handbook
• Use the Writer's Thesaurus to find vivid verbs and descriptive words to use in your character study.

Editing

Reread the draft of your character study. Are there any changes you would like to make? Use this checklist to help you revise your work:

☑ Will your reader be able to create a clear mental image of your character?
☑ Are there any details you might add to further describe your character?
☑ Can you replace ordinary verbs with more vivid ones or general nouns with more specific ones?
☑ Can you add descriptive words and phrases?
☑ Does the language you use express an overall tone?

Use this checklist as you proofread your paragraph:

☑ I have used commas, quotation marks, and colons correctly.
☑ I have avoided sentence fragments, run-on sentences, and comma splices.
☑ I have used a variety of sentences, including compound and complex sentences.
☑ I have used a dictionary to check my spelling.

Editor's Marks

ℐ	delete text
∧	insert text
℧	move text
¶	new paragraph
≡	capitalize
/	lowercase
◯	correct spelling

Sharing and Reflecting

After you have made a final copy of your character study, share it with a partner. Point out examples of effective word choice in your partner's work, and tell why you like them. Share ideas with your partner about how you can improve your use of language. Write your reflections in your Writer's Journal.

Making Word Lines

William has a small dog. Walter has a tiny dog. Whose dog is smaller?

The words *small* and *tiny* have similar meanings, but *tiny* usually suggests that something is even smaller than *small*. Walter's dog is most likely smaller than William's.

You can probably think of many other words that describe small things. Look at the words on the word line below. Someone has arranged them from the least small to the smallest, but you may not agree with the order of the words. For example, you may think that something *little* is smaller than something *small* or that *wee* is smaller than *diminutive*. Talk with classmates about how you would rearrange the words on this word line.

petite	little	small	miniature	tiny	wee	diminutive	minute	microscopic
least small								smallest

YOUR TURN

Work in a small group to create your own word line. Follow these steps:

STEP 1 Choose an adjective for which you can think of five or more synonyms, or words with similar meanings. For example, you might choose a word like *large*, *strong*, *cold*, *hot*, *happy*, or *pretty*.

STEP 2 Brainstorm and list words with meanings similar to the word you chose. If you wish, use a thesaurus to add words to your list.

STEP 3 Draw a word line, and discuss the order in which you want to place your words. If group members have different ideas about placement, you may want to make more than one line to reflect the different points of view. Remember that it is often a matter of opinion rather than a question of who is right or wrong.

Punctuating Titles

Underline the titles of books, movies, plays, and television programs and the names of newspapers and magazines. Use **quotation marks** around the titles of stories, magazine articles, essays, songs, and poems.

When you mention titles in your writing, use quotation marks or underlining. When titles of underlined works appear in print, *italics* take the place of underlining.

Examples:

Does this library have a copy of <u>The Oxford Book of Nursery Rhymes</u>?

"Old King Cole" is a famous nursery rhyme.
<u>Birthday Surprises</u> is an anthology of short stories.

Guided Practice

A. **Identify each title. Tell whether it should be underlined or placed in quotation marks.**

Example: I read a story called What's New in Science? in the Daily Gazette.

I read a story called "What's New in Science?" in the <u>Daily Gazette</u>.

1. Lois Lowry's Number the Stars is my favorite book.
2. The book was reviewed in the Boston Globe.
3. Lewis Carroll is the author of the novel Alice's Adventures in Wonderland.
4. In the novel, the Mad Hatter sings a song called Twinkle, Twinkle, Little Bat.
5. The Gift of the Magi is one of O. Henry's most famous short stories.

Independent Practice

B. Write each sentence. Use quotation marks or underlining to punctuate the title. Some sentences have more than one title.

> **Example:** The book Johnny Tremain was written by Esther Forbes.
> *The book <u>Johnny Tremain</u> was written by Esther Forbes.*

6. Cinderella is my sister's favorite fairy tale.
7. Casey at the Bat is a funny poem about baseball.
8. One of the first picture books was The Tale of Peter Rabbit by Beatrix Potter.
9. Robert Louis Stevenson's books Treasure Island and Kidnapped were made into movies.
10. I love to read Cricket magazine every month!
11. The Monkey's Paw is a short story about the danger of having wishes come true.
12. Chris Van Allsburg's book Jumanji is now a movie.
13. The poems in the book Bronzeville Boys and Girls are about African American children.
14. Gulliver's Travels is Jonathan Swift's most famous novel.
15. The Camelephant is a poem in the book Animal Fare.
16. Laurence Yep includes the writing of many Asian Americans in his anthology American Dragons.
17. The musical play West Side Story is based on Shakespeare's play Romeo and Juliet.
18. The Raven and Annabel Lee are well-known poems by Edgar Allan Poe.
19. The Outlaws of Sherwood is an anthology of stories about Robin Hood.
20. "'Twas the night before Christmas" is the first line of the famous poem A Visit from Saint Nicholas.

> **Remember** to underline the titles of books and other larger works and to use quotation marks around the titles of works published as part of a larger work.

Writing Connection

Art Draw a cartoon that shows two characters talking about their favorite books or stories. Place the characters' words in speech balloons. Be sure to punctuate the titles correctly. Exchange cartoons with a partner to proofread.

Capitalizing Words in Titles

Capitalize the first word, the last word, and all the important words in a title.

You have learned that quotation marks and underlining are used to mark titles. Capital letters are used to mark titles, too. Important words in titles include all nouns, pronouns, verbs, adjectives, and adverbs. Do not capitalize articles *(a, an, the)* or conjunctions *(and, or, but)* unless they begin or end a title. Do not capitalize a preposition unless it has five or more letters *(above, outside)* or unless it is the first or last word in the title.

Examples:	
Incorrect:	"the highwayman" (poem)
Correct:	"The Highwayman"
Incorrect:	Mystery Of The Roman Ransom (book)
Correct:	Mystery of the Roman Ransom

Guided Practice

A. Write each title. Capitalize the important words.

Example: the cat in the hat
The Cat in the Hat

1. "mama is a sunrise" (poem)
2. ajeemah and his son (book)
3. where the wild things are (book)
4. "in search of cinderella" (poem)
5. sarah, plain and tall (book)
6. a child's garden of grammar (book)
7. "america the beautiful" (song)
8. island of the blue dolphins (book)
9. my life as a human hockey puck (book)
10. harriet tubman: conductor on the underground railroad (book)

Independent Practice

B. Write each title. Capitalize the important words.

Example: the sign of the beaver (book)
The Sign of the Beaver

11. beauty and the beast (play)
12. the view from saturday (book)
13. "this is my country" (song)
14. "serious about fun" (magazine article)
15. "under the sunday tree" (poem)

C. Punctuate each title, and correct any mistakes in capitalization.

Example: the Talking Earth (book)
The Talking Earth

16. The kids' mystery hour (TV show)
17. I Can be your Friend (song)
18. James And The Giant Peach (book)
19. some things don't make any sense at all (poem)
20. over the Edge: Flying With the arctic Heroes (book)
21. Kids discover (magazine)
22. The fox and the Grapes (short story)
23. Weekly Reader (newspaper)
24. The Fun they Had (short story)
25. I Want to be an Astronaut (book)

> **Remember**
> that the first word, the last word, and all the important words in a title should be capitalized.

Writing Connection

Real-Life Writing: Magazine Contents Look at the Contents page of a magazine. Write a paragraph telling which items you would most like to read and why. Include the name of the magazine, too. Be sure to capitalize and punctuate titles correctly to make your meaning clear.

USAGE AND MECHANICS

Hyphens

Use a **hyphen** to connect two words to form a compound word. Use a hyphen to join syllables of a word that has been divided at the end of a line.

Many words always contain a hyphen. In addition, compound adjectives need a hyphen when they come before the nouns that they describe.

Words That Always Contain a Hyphen	Compound Adjectives Before Nouns
fifty-five	well-known author
president-elect	two-day trip
mother-in-law	one-story house

Look at these examples. Notice how the hyphen in the compound adjective helps make the sentence clear.

Charles Dickens is a **well-respected** author.

I bought two **three-dollar** tickets.

When you divide a word at the end of a line of writing, the hyphen must come between the syllables of the word. If you are not sure about the syllables, look in a dictionary.

Incorrect: lib-rary　　　**Correct: li-brary**

Guided Practice

A. **Study the words in parentheses. Decide which spelling or word division is correct. If you are not sure about a division, check a dictionary.**

Example: I enjoyed the final (parag-raph, para-graph) of that novel.
para-graph

1. A (well known, well-known) author visited our school.
2. She is an (award-winning, award winning) reporter.
3. She also has written a (wonder-ful, wonderf-ul) series of children's books.
4. The books are (histo-rical, histor-ical) fiction set during the Civil War.
5. The characters of that (long ago, long-ago) time faced many problems.

Independent Practice

B. Rewrite the sentences. Add hyphens where needed.

Example: My sister and brother in law gave me this book.
My sister and brother-in-law gave me this book.

6. A best selling author wrote it.
7. The book is set in present day London.
8. The characters live in a second rate apartment outside of town.
9. One day the main character decides to talk to a short tempered man.
10. They have a heart to heart talk and become good friends.

C. Write the word in parentheses that is correctly divided. Use a dictionary if necessary.

Example: Miguel and I spent summer (vaca-tion, vacat-ion) reading books. *vaca-tion*

11. Some books were (paperb-acks, paper-backs), but many books had hard covers.
12. We read them as part of a program for (summ er, sum-mer) readers.
13. During the summer, I read six (bio-graphies, biog-raphies).
14. We spent almost every (even-ing, eve-ning) reading.
15. How surprised we were to (disc-over, dis-cover) that we tied for first place!

Writing Connection

Writer's Craft: Vivid Adjectives Write a short descriptive poem in which you use at least two compound adjectives. You might form adjectives with color words, such as *blue-black* or *red-eyed*, or you might use action words, as in *slow-falling leaves*. Try making up a compound adjective of your own.

Extra Practice

A. Write the sentences. Use quotation marks or underlining to mark the titles. *pages 408–409*

Example: Mark Twain's The Celebrated Jumping Frog of Calaveras County is my favorite short story.
Mark Twain's "The Celebrated Jumping Frog of Calaveras County" is my favorite short story.

1. Elijah's Violin & Other Jewish Fairy Tales is a book of folktales and fairy tales.
2. I can sing America the Beautiful without forgetting the words.
3. The All-American Slurp is a short story about a Chinese American family.
4. The movie National Velvet tells the story of a girl and her horse.
5. Our class wrote a letter to the editor of the Springfield Journal.
6. Read the poem Paul Revere's Ride to learn about an American hero.
7. The Miracle Worker is a play about a girl who could not see or hear.
8. The children sang Row, Row, Row Your Boat as they sat around the campfire.
9. The Amazing Munson was my favorite television show when I was younger.
10. The title of my essay is Three Funny Novels I Have Enjoyed.

B. Punctuate each title, and capitalize the important words. *pages 410–411*

Example: Little House in the big Woods (book)
Little House in the Big Woods

11. the wonderful wizard of Oz (book)
12. Local Girls' Soccer Team Wins In Overtime (newspaper article)
13. Someone to watch over Me (song)
14. Willy Wonka and the chocolate factory (book/movie)
15. fiddler on the roof (play/movie)

Remember to underline the titles of books, newspapers, and other long or complete works. Use quotation marks around the titles of stories, poems, and other short works. Use a hyphen to connect two words to form compound words or to join syllables of a word that has been divided.

C. The word forms in parentheses show the use of a hyphen. The hyphen may connect the parts of a compound word or divide a word into syllables. Write the correct word form. Use a dictionary to check your answers. *pages 412–413*

DID YOU KNOW? The first known collection of fairy tales was printed in France in 1697. The book's title in English was <u>Stories and Tales of Past Times with Morals; or, Tales of Mother Goose</u>.

Example: There are (forty two, forty-two) chapters in the book.
forty-two

16. The (air conditioned, air-conditioned) library was very comfortable.
17. Look for the book with the (blue-green, blue green) cover.
18. The store sells old, (worn out, worn-out) books for a quarter.
19. Another book is about workers in the (mi-ning, min-ing) industry.
20. Louisa May Alcott's <u>Little Women</u> is a (tou-ching, touch-ing) book about a New England family.

D. Each sentence below has an error in the title or in the use of a hyphen. Rewrite each sentence, correcting the errors. *pages 408–413*

21. Our class recently completed a long reading pr-oject that included novels and stories.
22. "A Christmas Carol" was the first novel we read.
23. Then we read <u>Where the red fern Grows</u>.
24. In addition to these full length novels, we read several short stories.
25. My favorite was <u>The Wheelbarrow Boy</u>.

Writing Connection

Writer's Journal: Plot Plan a story about two students who are preparing for a big test. What problems might the students face? How might they solve their problems? Make a story map to record your ideas.

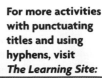

For more activities with punctuating titles and using hyphens, visit *The Learning Site:* www.harcourtschool.com

Chapter Review

Read each sentence. Look at the word or words in brackets [ ]. There may be a mistake in punctuation or capitalization. If you find a mistake, choose the best way to write the section in brackets. If there is no mistake, choose *Correct as is*.

TIP Look for answers that you know are incorrect, and focus on the choices you have left.

1 Our class has read much during the past [eight month] period.

  A eightmonth
  B eight-month
  C Eight Month
  D Correct as is

2 One of my favorite books was a [collec tion] of stories.

  F collec-tion
  G colle-ction
  H collecti-on
  J Correct as is

3 The book was titled [The Silver treasure.]

  A "The Silver treasure."
  B "The Silver Treasure."
  C The Silver Treasure.
  D Correct as is

4 We read poems in the book ["Great American Poetry."]

  F "Great American poetry."
  G Great American Poetry.
  H Great American Poetry.
  J Correct as is

5 My favorite poem is Robert Frost's ["Stopping by Woods on A Snowy Evening."]

  A Stopping by Woods on A Snowy Evening.
  B "Stopping By Woods On A Snowy Evening."
  C "Stopping by Woods on a Snowy Evening."
  D Correct as is

6 Some of us sent our own poems to [the magazine Stone Soup.]

  F the magazine stone soup.
  G the Magazine Stone Soup.
  H the magazine "Stone Soup."
  J Correct as is

For additional test preparation, visit *The Learning Site:* www.harcourtschool.com

Listening and Speaking in a Group

At school, students who work together often come up with creative answers to problems. Listening to what others have to say often gives you new ideas or helps you figure something out.

Brainstorming is one strategy a group may use to share ideas and come up with plans for solving problems. In brainstorming, group members present many ideas quickly.

To begin, state the problem that you need to solve. Use *Why? How?* and *What?* questions to focus on the topic.

> **Brainstorming Rules**
>
> - Think about all ideas, no matter how unusual they sound.
>
> - The more ideas group members express, the better. Share your thoughts.
>
> - Do not interrupt other speakers.
>
> - Ask questions if you don't understand something.
>
> - Record the ideas where everyone can see them.
>
> - Talk over your ideas. Build on other people's ideas.

After brainstorming, the group should talk about and combine ideas. They may want to vote on the idea or ideas that they like best. Choose someone to keep a journal of the group's progress.

YOUR TURN

BRAINSTORMING Work with a small group of classmates to choose and discuss a school-related problem, such as a safety need or a lack of computer time. Brainstorm ideas about the problem, using the rules. Then combine your ideas, and decide what can be done about the problem. Make a plan of action, and report your plan to the class. Finally, tell what you like about working with a group.

TIP The goal of brainstorming is to come up with many different answers to problems. All ideas are helpful, as long as they relate to the topic.

Negatives and Double Negatives

A word or phrase that has *no* or *not* in its meaning is called a **negative**. Use only one negative in a sentence.

Some common negatives are *never, no, not, nobody, none, nothing, nowhere,* and *no one.*

Example:
Nothing is more universal than music.

The negative *not* appears often in contractions with verbs. Here are some common contractions: *aren't, can't, don't, hasn't,* and *won't.* Do not use these contractions with another negative in the same sentence. When two negatives are in the same sentence, they form a **double negative**.

Example:
Incorrect: I **don't** want to listen to **no** music!

Correct: I don't want to listen to any music!

Guided Practice

A. Identify the negative word in each sentence.

Example: Jazz didn't exist before the late 1800s. *didn't*

1. No other art form is as American as jazz.
2. Jazz is not a single type of music but a mixture of forms.
3. Most musicians need training, but many early jazz artists had none.
4. They did not play from written music.
5. The rhythms they used were never boring.
6. Many jazz performers do nothing but improvise.
7. Each performance is one of a kind and cannot be repeated.
8. Nobody knew how popular jazz would become.
9. Jazz isn't enjoyed only in America.
10. Nowhere are there more loyal jazz fans than in Europe.

Vocabulary Power

im·pro·vise
[im′prə·vīz] *n.* To make up at the time of performance and without preparation.

Independent Practice

B. **Write the negative word in each sentence.**

Example: No history of jazz could ignore New Orleans.
No

11. Nowhere was jazz more alive.
12. Soon jazz bands were no longer found just in New Orleans.
13. People who had never heard of jazz began hearing it on the radio.
14. The smooth sound of Chicago jazz bands was like nothing else.
15. Jazz is not always played by a big band, though.

C. **Rewrite each sentence, correcting the double negative.**

Example: Benny Goodman wasn't no ordinary clarinet player.
Benny Goodman wasn't an ordinary clarinet player.
or
Benny Goodman was no ordinary clarinet player.

16. Nobody couldn't play smoother jazz than Benny Goodman.
17. Before 1948, recordings couldn't be no longer than three minutes.
18. Records spread jazz to places where nobody hadn't heard it before.
19. Soon music fans couldn't go nowhere without hearing jazz.
20. Haven't you never listened to jazz?

Remember

to avoid using two negative words to express a negative meaning. To correct a double negative, remove one negative word or replace one with a positive word.

Writing Connection

Writer's Craft: Characterization Think of a character from a popular book, movie, or TV show. Write a riddle about the character. The riddle should have four sentences as clues. Each clue should tell what the character is not. Read your riddle to a classmate, and ask for guesses.

Using *I* and *Me*

Use *I* as the subject of a sentence. Use *me* as an object. When referring to yourself and someone else, refer to yourself last.

First-person subject pronoun	First-person object pronoun
I take piano lessons.	My teacher is patient with **me**.
My sister and **I** play duets.	Our teacher chooses music for her and **me**.

Use a subject pronoun after the word *than*. A good way to remember this rule is to add the missing verb to the sentence. Look at the example below. Read aloud each sentence with the verb in parentheses. The incorrect sentence will sound wrong.

Incorrect: She is quicker to learn than **me** (*am*).

Correct: She is quicker to learn than **I** (*am*).

Guided Practice

A. Identify the first-person pronoun in each sentence. Tell whether it is used as a subject or an object.

Example: I was surprised to learn that the piano is a percussion instrument.
I, subject

1. I know that a piano and a harp have strings.
2. My teacher told me that harps can have up to forty-seven strings.
3. I press the black keys on the piano to make certain tones.
4. The harpist uses a pedal to let me hear the same tones.
5. Someday I will take harp lessons.

Independent Practice

B. Choose the correct pronoun in parentheses. Write the sentence.

Example: My teacher explained rhythm to Ellen and (I, me).
My teacher explained rhythm to Ellen and me.

6. Mr. Neff told Ellen and (I, me) that rhythm is the arrangement of notes in time.
7. (I, Me) learned that each note is a certain length.
8. Ellen and (I, me) found out about regular beats in music.
9. The composer can vary these patterns to make the music more interesting for you and (I, me).
10. Ellen and (I, me) discovered that composers can change the length of notes.
11. Ellen and Julio talked to (I, me) about playing music together.
12. (I, me) wanted to join them.
13. Ellen, Julio, and (I, me) will practice on Saturday.
14. Julio will meet Ellen and (I, me) at noon.
15. You and (I, me) can go to the movie afterward.
16. (I, me) find that written music is similar to written words.
17. Mr. Neff showed (I, me) the clef sign at the left of the staff.
18. The bass notes are lower than Ellen and (I, me) can sing.
19. Ellen and (I, me) sometimes like to improvise instead of playing written music.
20. Music is fun for her and (I, me).

Writing Connection

Writer's Journal: Reflecting Think about a musical instrument that you play or would like to play. Ask yourself the following questions: What made you choose the instrument? Do you like the way it sounds? Do you think it is easy to learn? Write to reflect on your choice. Be sure to use the pronouns *I* and *me* correctly.

USAGE AND MECHANICS

Commonly Confused Words

Some commonly confused words sound alike but are spelled differently and have different meanings. Choose the word that means what you want to say.

Word	Use	Examples
to	"in the direction of" before a verb form	Go **to** the band room. I like **to** sing.
too	"also" or "very"	The song was **too** long.
two	the number 2	I had **two** lessons.
it's	contraction of "it is"	**It's** time to begin.
its	"belonging to it"	**Its** sound is good.
their	"belonging to them"	**Their** music is new.
there	where something is	Leave the drums **there**.
they're	contraction of "they are"	**They're** playing now.
you're	contraction of "you are"	**You're** first in line.
your	"belonging to you"	You'll need **your** book.

Guided Practice

A. **Tell what each underlined word means or how it is used. Look at the chart for help.**

> **Example:** Wind instruments come in two types—woodwinds and brass. *the number 2*

1. You play a recorder, one kind of woodwind, by blowing through its mouthpiece.
2. Flutes and piccolos are woodwinds, too.
3. You play a flute by pressing your bottom lip next to the hole and blowing across it.
4. When you blow through the reeds of an oboe or a bassoon, their vibrations make the sound.
5. By placing fingers over the holes or on the keys, you're changing the size of the column of air.

Independent Practice

B. Tell what each underlined word means or how it is used. Look at the chart for help.

Example: A trombone changes pitch when the player moves its slide.
belonging to it

6. It's the length of the column of air that affects the sound of a brass instrument.
7. The two types of wind instruments, woodwinds and brass, produce sound a little differently.
8. Your lips vibrate as you blow into a trumpet or trombone.
9. When players tighten or relax their lips, they're changing the vibrations.
10. The sound waves travel from the instrument's mouthpiece to the column of air.

C. Choose the correct word in parentheses. Write the sentence.

11. In the back of the orchestra, (there, their, they're) is an important group.
12. (There, Their, They're) called percussionists.
13. (Your, You're) probably most familiar with drums.
14. This section includes any instrument that makes (its, it's) sound by being shaken or struck.
15. Some percussion instruments can make different notes, (to, too, two).

Remember to check for **commonly confused words** in your writing. Be sure you have used the word that means what you want to say.

Writing Connection

Writer's Craft: Words and Sounds Choose one set of commonly confused words. Using the words, write either a humorous song verse or a rhythmic tongue twister.

Extra Practice

A. Rewrite each sentence to correct the double negative. *pages 418–419*

Example: Music doesn't have no hard and fast categories.
Music has no hard and fast categories.

1. You might think that popular music doesn't have nothing in common with classical music.
2. You might also think that one piece of classical music doesn't sound no different from another.
3. Composers don't think nothing of using popular or folk music in their works.
4. Works of composers such as Dvorak and Grieg wouldn't never be the same without the influence of folk music.
5. Haven't you never heard a classical arrangement of a folk tune?

B. Choose the correct pronoun in parentheses. Write the sentence. *pages 420–421*

6. My group and (I, me) have just finished a report on music.
7. On display was a chart written by Nathan and (I, me).
8. Nathan explained it better than (I, me).
9. The class and (I, me) listened to him tell why popular music is not the same as folk music.
10. Work songs are folk songs that may be familiar to you and (I, me).
11. You and (I, me) know folk music that dates back hundreds of years.
12. New music is always being written to entertain you and (I, me).
13. Julie and (I, me) listened to many forms of music, such as bluegrass, country, gospel, and rock.
14. Musical comedy has produced many famous songs for you and (I, me) to sing.
15. My group and (I, me) concluded that music has many important uses.

Remember
to use *I* as the subject in a sentence and *me* as the object of a verb or a preposition.

For more activities with negatives, *I* and *me*, and easily confused words, visit *The Learning Site:*
www.harcourtschool.com

C. Write each sentence, using the correct word or words in parentheses. *pages 422–423*

16. Music is important (two, to, too) people of all cultures.
17. (It's, Its) part of daily life and special occasions.
18. Our marching band went (there, they're, their) to be in the parade.
19. You should never miss (you're, your) band practices.
20. People sing or play music for other important events, (two, to, too).
21. When people do hard work by hand, they sing songs to make (there, they're, their) work seem easier.
22. Music shows (it's, its) power to affect people's feelings.
23. Music may help you relax when (you're, your) nervous.
24. Musicians may be teachers or performers, but (there, they're, their) composers when they write music.
25. (Two, To, Too) of my friends want to be musicians.

D. Write each sentence, correcting the errors. *pages 418–423*

26. Nobody hadn't heard of country music until they heard it on the radio.
27. Bluegrass music had it's influence on country music.
28. Nashville became the center of country music, and me and you can still hear the "Nashville sound."
29. Country music stars were popular, but many of there fans enjoyed other kinds of music, too.
30. Other country music fans didn't want to listen to nothing else.

Writing Connection

Writer's Journal: Writing Idea Think of a story setting inspired by your favorite kind of music. Imagine yourself in the setting, and freewrite about it. Be sure to use *I* as a subject and *me* as an object. When you have finished, check your usage of commonly confused words.

Chapter Review

Read the passage and choose the word or group of words that belongs in each space. Write the letter for your answer.

> Throughout the world __(1)__ many forms of music. In most cultures, music is an important part of other arts as well. In China and Japan, all drama is set __(2)__ music. All around the world, dancers use music to accompany __(3)__ movements. Music is an important part of films and television, __(4)__ . __(5)__ a mood as well as music. Directors of horror movies use music to add suspense for viewers like __(6)__ . The music often keeps you on the edge of __(7)__ seat. __(8)__ hard to imagine a movie without music.

1 A their are
  B there are
  C they're
  D they are

2 F to
  G too
  H tow
  J two

3 A their
  B they
  C they're
  D there

4 F two
  G to
  H too
  J tow

5 A Nothing doesn't create
  B Nothing creates
  C Nothing won't create
  D Anything doesn't create

6 F me and you
  G you and I
  H I and you
  J you and me

7 A you're
  B you are
  C your
  D yours

8 F Its
  G It
  H Isn't
  J It's

Using the Internet and Websites

In some ways, exploring the Internet, or going online, is like going out in public. Many of the same safety rules apply. You and your family may have talked about how to research online safely. Most important, if you ever feel uncomfortable or unsure while you are online, be sure to ask a family member or your teacher for guidance.

- Never give out information about yourself, such as your last name, address, or telephone number, or your parents' work addresses or telephone numbers.
- Don't give out your school's name, address, or telephone number or the name of your teacher without asking an adult for permission first.
- Do not respond if something comes up on the screen that makes you uncomfortable. If this happens, don't look around or explore. Instead, tell an adult right away. Also, tell an adult if you get a mean e-mail message from anyone.
- It is never safe to meet with someone you've talked to online. If someone asks you to meet them or even to call or write to them, tell your parents right away.
- Never send or e-mail pictures of yourself or your family to anyone you meet online.
- Don't do anything online that costs money. Ask your parents for help and permission.

YOUR TURN

IN SMALL GROUPS, search for websites that tell about Internet safety. Using information from those sites, create posters to remind classmates about Internet safety. Display the posters in your classroom or computer lab.

TIP When using the Internet, always keep safety in mind.

LITERATURE MODEL

Writers of short stories often try to create realistic pictures of their characters' experiences. In this story, R. E. Richards tells about a young Pony Express rider's life on the frontier. As you read, notice how Richards makes this picture of life vivid and realistic.

THE LONG RIDE

by R. E. Richards

David Jay arose and stumbled bleary-eyed to the long, wooden-plank breakfast table. A steaming plate of fried eggs was waiting for him. He gobbled down his breakfast, snatched up a water flask and packet of dried beef jerky, and rushed outside.

In the dim morning light David could just barely make out the lanky form of Mr. Thompson, the station keeper. Mr. Thompson stood alongside the log station house, holding the reins of a horse.

From the distance came the thunder of hoofbeats as a rider approached at full gallop. The dusty, buck-skinned rider, a young man of about nineteen, pulled his horse up alongside Mr. Thompson. The rider sprang from the saddle, pulled leather mail pouches from the back of his horse, and slipped them over the saddle of the horse that Mr. Thompson was holding.

In an instant David leaped into the saddle of the fresh horse and was off at full speed. The sun was just peeking above the edge of the Nebraska plains.

David began his daily race against time. He was a Pony Express rider. The Pony Express was a cross-country mail company. Its riders carried pouches of mail between St. Joseph, Missouri, and Sacramento, California. For months David had carried the mail back and forth across the Nebraska territory in this "relay race" on horseback.

After an hour's ride David approached the first swing station. Swing stations were spaced about fifteen miles apart along the Pony Express route. At the station, riders could exchange tired horses for fresh ones. David dismounted and handed the reins of his sweating, exhausted horse to the station keeper, who put the mail onto a new horse. Moments later, David was again flying along the trail.

Late in the day, David pulled up to the Fort Kearny express station, sore and tired from his long ride. Karl, the station keeper, rushed out to meet him.

"David, we've got a problem," explained Karl. "Charlie was attacked by bandits and wounded. I don't have a rider to take the mail to Cold Springs."

David knew that, above all else, the mail must get through.

"I'll make the trip," he replied quickly.

Although he dreaded riding another eighty miles on the trail, David was glad to get a chance to go to Cold Springs. Old Hank Torrens was the Cold Springs station keeper. Hank had been a good friend of David's family. It was Hank who had taught David to ride.

David stayed in Fort Kearny only long enough to eat a hot meal and catch his breath. Back in the saddle, he rode westward toward the setting sun.

Darkness came soon, and David had to slow his pace. But the moon was full, and it was fairly easy to follow the trail. By the time David arrived at the fifth and last relay station, his body ached from seventeen hours in the saddle. He longed to rest, but he knew that if he stopped

even for a short while, he would never be able to get up and finish the ride.

For miles, David rode on through the darkness. Suddenly, he heard the sound of hoofbeats close behind. *Mail bandits!* David dug his spurs into the horse's sides. The horse responded with a burst of speed. With only a thin boy and twenty pounds of mail, David's mount had the lighter load. The sound of riders grew fainter and fainter.

Just about the time David had put a safe cushion of distance between himself and the bandits, his horse stepped into a hole, stumbled, and fell. David was pitched headlong onto the trail. Shaken but unhurt, he ran back to remount and continue his ride. The horse had gotten to its feet but was limping badly. David's heart sank when he realized the injury was too serious for the horse to be ridden.

He led the crippled horse off the trail, listening all the while for hoofbeats. But the cool night air was still and silent. He slid the mail pouches off the horse's back and slung them over his own shoulders. He would come back later for the horse.

Back on the trail, David ran in the direction of Cold Springs with the precious pouches bouncing against his chest. On and on he went. The mail pouches felt like thousand-pound weights dragging him to the ground.

His last ounce of strength was gone, but David's legs kept moving—driven by the desire to complete his mission. Finally, he could go no farther. He collapsed onto the cold ground, totally spent.

In his dazed, weary mind, David thought he was in a cabin, resting comfortably by a warm, crackling fire. Suddenly the sound of approaching hoofbeats quickly snapped him back to reality. Could it be the bandits? The rider stopped. David clutched the mail tightly, dreading what might happen next. At the rider's gentle touch, though, he soon relaxed. When he opened his eyes, he found himself peering into the kind, smiling face of his friend Old Hank.

Analyze THE Model

1. Where do you first learn of the problem in the story? Why does the writer describe other things first?

2. How does the writer tell about the setting and the period of history in the story?

3. What kind of person is David, and how do you know?

4. Find examples of vivid verbs in the story, and tell why the writer uses them.

Vocabulary Power

val·iant
[val′yənt] *adj.*
Having or showing courage; brave.

READING — WRITING CONNECTION

Parts of a Short Story

R. E. Richards made the past come alive in "The Long Ride."
Study this short story written by a student named Dana.
Notice how she uses vivid words to make the story realistic.
Pay attention to the parts of her story.

MODEL

beginning

problem

rising action

On Location

"Schools are closed for the holiday!" screeched
the radio. Shelley groaned and fumbled for the
switch. She had to get going right away. After
wolfing her breakfast, Shelley snatched her guitar
and headed for the car. Her mom dropped her off
at the Community Center just as Tamara, Lucy,
and Roger arrived.

"What are we waiting for?" Roger asked,
starting toward the building. As they got nearer,
they noticed that it looked strangely empty.
The front door was locked. They looked at one
another in dismay.

"How could we forget?" wailed Tamara. "It's a
holiday! Now where will we tape the music video
for tomorrow's class?"

Shelley absentmindedly kicked a pebble and
gazed across the parking lot at the park.
Suddenly she grabbed Tamara's arm.

"Let's do the video in the park! It's a beautiful
day, and we can use the pond and garden as a
backdrop."

Quickly, they set up for taping. As Shelley
strummed the guitar, Roger focused the camera
and zoomed in on Lucy and Tamara. Moving

gracefully, the two dancers acted out the music. When the music ended, they were startled to hear applause! They'd been so busy taping, they hadn't seen a growing crowd of onlookers.

The next day, their classmates watched the finished video. To Shelley's surprise, everyone agreed that the outdoor location was super. Having a live audience helped make the video more realistic, too.

Shelley turned to her friends. "I guess it was really lucky that the Community Center was locked yesterday," she said with a laugh.

problem solved

ending

Analyze THE Model

1. **What is the setting of the story? How does it affect the plot?**

2. **What is the problem in the story? How is it solved?**

3. **Find some vivid verbs that Dana uses. Explain how these make her characters seem more real.**

Summarize THE Model

Use a graphic organizer like the one at the right to fill in the setting, characters, problem, and solution in Dana's short story. Then write a summary of Dana's story.

setting → characters → problem → solution

Writer's Craft

Word Choice Dana chose words carefully for her story. Try replacing some of the vivid words Dana used. Tell whose words sound better—yours or Dana's—and why.

Prewriting

Purpose and Audience

"The Long Ride" and "On Location" both explore ways people deal with problems as they try to complete tasks. In this chapter, you will write about a character who must solve a problem in order to finish a job.

WRITING PROMPT Write a short story about a character who must solve a problem and complete a task. Use details of setting, vivid words, and dialogue to make your story lifelike and interesting.

Begin by thinking about your purpose, audience, and topic. Would you like to write about the character you created in your character study in Chapter 33 or about another character? Would you like to write for your classmates or for younger children?

MODEL

Dana began thinking about tasks that interested her. She decided to write about making a music video. She used this graphic organizer to plan her story:

My purpose and audience:
to entertain my classmates with
a story about making a music video

⬇

Plot idea: main problem—where to tape?
locked out of location

⬇

Characters: Shelley, a
quick-thinking problem solver; her
partners in a class project

⬇

Setting: town like my town,
recent times

Strategies Good Writers Use

- Focus on your purpose for writing: to entertain.
- Think of possible problems familiar to your audience.
- Brainstorm ways to make the story come alive for your audience.

YOUR TURN

Choose a task that interests you. Use a graphic organizer to group your ideas about the story elements.

Drafting

Organization and Elaboration

Use these steps to help you organize your story:

STEP 1 **Introduce the Setting and Characters**
Give a few details about the setting. Introduce the main character or characters.

STEP 2 **Provide the Problem**
Introduce the problem. Include the characters' reactions to it.

STEP 3 **Tell What Happens Next**
Use vivid words and dialogue to tell what the characters do.

STEP 4 **Solve the Problem**
Show how your characters solve the problem.

STEP 5 **Conclude Your Story**
Show how your characters feel about solving the problem.

MODEL

Here is the first paragraph of Dana's story. What details does she use to introduce the characters and setting? How does she create suspense, or make the reader wonder what will happen?

> "Schools are closed for the holiday!" screeched the radio. Shelley groaned and fumbled for the switch. She had to get going right away. After wolfing her breakfast, Shelley snatched her guitar and headed for the car. Her mom dropped her off at the Community Center just as Tamara, Lucy, and Roger arrived.

YOUR TURN

Now draft your short story. Use your notes from prewriting. Include vivid words and details. Use the stories by R. E. Richards and Dana as models.

Strategies Good Writers Use

- Introduce the characters and setting at the beginning.
- Grab the reader's attention with vivid language.
- Create suspense by waiting to tell key plot details later in the story.

 Draft your story on a computer. Use the cut and paste functions to move details around in the story.

Revising

Organization and Elaboration

Reread your draft. Use these questions as a guide.

- How well have I created suspense in the beginning of my story? (Consider moving some details to a later point in the story.)
- How well have I used verbs and descriptive words?
- How often have I used dialogue to show the characters and their actions?
- Have I varied my sentences to keep my writing interesting?

Strategies Good Writers Use

- Replace weak or dull verbs with vivid ones.
- Add details and dialogue for more interest.
- Ask other writers to suggest improvements.

Highlight a weak word, and click on the Thesaurus tool. The thesaurus can help you find a more vivid word.

MODEL

Here is part of Dana's draft. Where in it did she replace weak words with stronger ones? Notice where she put in more dialogue to add interest.

"What are we waiting for?" Roger asked, starting

~~It was time to start taping their~~

~~music video in the Center's auditorium.~~

As they got nearer,

~~They started~~ toward the building. ∧They

noticed that it looked strangely empty.

The front door was locked. They looked

in dismay

at one another ∧ ~~with concern.~~

wailed

"How could we forget?" ~~asked~~ Tamara.

"It's a holiday!" ∧"Now where will we tape the music

∧ video for tomorrow's class?"

absentmindedly   gazed

Shelley ∧ kicked a pebble and ∧ ~~looked~~

across the parking lot at the park.

Suddenly   grabbed

~~Then~~ she ∧ ~~took~~ Tamara's arm.

YOUR TURN

Revise your short story to add vivid words and details. Think about adding dialogue and varying your sentences.

Proofreading

Checking Your Language

You need to check your story for errors in spelling, punctuation, capitalization, and grammar. Such errors confuse the reader and make the story less enjoyable.

MODEL

Here is the ending of Dana's revised draft. See the spelling errors and other mistakes she had to fix when she proofread her draft.

> The next day, ~~there~~ *their* classmates watched the finished video. To Shelley's surprise, everyone agreed⁀That the outdoor location was super. Having a live ~~audiense~~ *audience* help^*ed*se make the video more realistic, ~~to~~ *too*.
>
> Shelley turned to her friends. "I guess it was really lucky that the Community Center was locked yesterday," she said with a laugh.

Strategies Good Writers Use

- Check for correct use of quotation marks in dialogue.
- Look for commonly confused words.

Editor's Marks

✗	delete text
∧	insert text
↻	move text
¶	new paragraph
≡	capitalize
/	lowercase
◯	spelling

YOUR TURN

Proofread your revised story. Then trade papers with a partner and proofread each other's story. Check for
- correct spelling and capitalization.
- correct punctuation and complete sentences.
- correct grammar.

Publishing

Sharing Your Work

Now you are ready to publish your short story. Use these questions to choose the best way to share it with your audience.

1. Who is your audience? Would people enjoy your story more if they heard it read aloud?

2. Should you print your story or write it in cursive? Your classmates can read cursive, but a younger audience might read only printed words. Which type of handwriting would your audience prefer? Is it possible for you to type your story on a computer?

3. Should you act out your short story? To give a performance of your story, use the information on page 439.

Reflecting on Your Writing

 Using Your Portfolio What did you learn about your writing in this chapter? Write your answer to each question below.

1. Did you use vivid language in your writing? Give at least two examples.

2. Do you think your characters are realistic and believable? Why or why not?

3. Does your story capture your reader's attention? Is there suspense to make the reader keep reading?

Add your answers and the short story to your portfolio. Then review your portfolio. Write a few sentences about how your writing has improved since you began your portfolio. Tell what your favorite pieces are and why.

USING YOUR
Handbook

Use the rubric on page 511 to evaluate your short story.

Tips for Performers

Dana decided to perform her short story. This can be an enjoyable way to share your work with your class. Follow these steps to perform your short story:

STEP 1 Decide whether you want to perform the story by yourself or with others. If you perform with others, divide your story into roles, including a narrator and the characters who have dialogue. Write a script for acting out the story.

STEP 2 Make notes on your copy of the story about gestures or expressions to use. You may want to use simple props, if possible.

STEP 3 Practice in front of someone. Try using different voices. Have your listener tell you which ones work best.

STEP 4 Relax before your performance. Close your eyes and count to ten while breathing slowly and deeply.

STEP 5 Speak slowly and clearly. Make your voice loud enough to be heard in the back of the room.

STEP 6 Have fun, and your audience will, too!

Strategies for Listeners

As you listen to your classmates perform their stories, use these strategies to understand the story and enjoy the performance:

- Focus on the speaker.
- Listen for changes in the speaker's voice.
- Notice the speaker's expressions and gestures.

Commas *pages 380–381*

A. Write each sentence. Correct any errors in comma usage. If the sentence is correct, write *correct*.

1. Artists use many different tools materials and methods to do their work.
2. Paint ink and charcoal are common art materials.
3. Many artists paint on canvas but others prefer to paint on more unusual surfaces.
4. Some artists continue to work with these materials, but others use computers to create art.
5. Computers have greatly changed film video and animation production.

More About Commas *pages 382–383*

B. Write each sentence. Add commas where they are needed.

6. Maria did you know that the Art Institute of Chicago has several buildings?
7. Yes I know that it is a very large museum.
8. In fact it has one of the largest spaces for temporary art exhibits in the United States.
9. Believe it or not the museum has over 300,000 works of art.
10. By the way the museum also has its own art school.

Using Commas with Appositives

pages 384–385

C. Write each sentence. Underline the appositive. Add commas where they are needed.

11. Mr. Bernstein my next-door neighbor works at the new art museum.
12. I read an article about the museum in the *Lexington Star* our local newspaper.
13. The director of the museum Ms. Fernandez seems like a very friendly person.
14. Ms. Fernandez an expert on Asian art is planning many programs for students.
15. Our class is going to the first program a presentation about Chinese paintings.

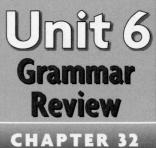
Using Quotation Marks *pages 390–391*

A. Write each sentence. Correct any capitalization and punctuation errors.

1. Our class will present a play at the assembly next month announced Mr. Hawkins.
2. Can I be in the play asked Charlotte.
3. Everybody will have a part replied Mr. Hawkins.
4. Toshi asked what play are we going to do.
5. Let's write an original play. one of the girls suggested.
6. Then she asked will there be enough time.
7. I think so Mr. Hawkins said.
8. Ann added I'd like to help with the sound and lighting.
9. Everyone will have a job to do our teacher said.
10. This is going to be so much fun Charlotte said with a grin.

More About Quotation Marks

pages 392–393

B. Write each sentence using correct punctuation.

11. When we go to New York my father said we will try to see a Broadway show.
12. I can hardly wait I said. I love musical theater.
13. Not every show on Broadway said my mother is a musical.
14. I know I replied but musicals are my favorite.
15. I do not care what we see I added as long as it is a musical.

Colons *pages 394–395*

C. Write each sentence. Use a colon where it is needed.

16. The following people signed up for the theater workshop Maria, Paul, and Eva.
17. Our parents will pick us up at 745.
18. The skills we will be learning include the following singing, dancing, and set design.
19. We do voice exercises from 700 to 715.
20. My three favorite Broadway shows are these *Cats*, *Beauty and the Beast*, and *The Lion King*.

Punctuating Titles *pages 408–409*

A. Write each sentence. Use quotation marks or underlining to punctuate the titles.

1. The library has the book called Stories About the Future.
2. My favorite story is Tones and Tears, a story about rock music in the future.
3. Steve called his poem A Winning Team.
4. Sara's favorite song is This Land Is Your Land.
5. I have never read the magazine called Science Fiction for Kids.
6. I did enjoy the article Is Time Travel Possible? in the magazine Let's Explore Science.
7. Geraldo always reads the sports section of the Daily News.
8. High Adventure is a movie about mountain climbing.
9. The essay Don't Forget to Vote won the contest.
10. A story called A Green Future is about a farm in the year 2040.

Capitalizing Words in Titles

pages 410–411

B. Punctuate each title and capitalize the important words.

11. the variety of life (article)
12. up a winding road (book)
13. the highwayman (poem)
14. east of the sun, west of the moon (story)
15. the tale of the summer cat (book)

Hyphens *pages 412–413*

C. Write each sentence. Add hyphens where they are needed. Check your answers in a dictionary.

16. The library had an end of year sale.
17. My sister in law took me to buy books.
18. This was a ten dollar book.
19. We bought it for sixty five cents.
20. Many people come to this well known sale.

Negatives and Double Negatives

pages 418–419

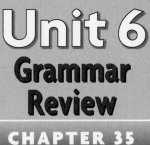

A. Rewrite each sentence, correcting the double negative.

1. Some people say a marching band doesn't add nothing to a football game.
2. I think people who say this don't know nothing.
3. No half-time show isn't a waste of time.
4. No one can say nothing against half-time shows to me!
5. Hasn't nobody ever thought that marching bands work as hard as the football players?

Using *I* and *Me* *pages 420–421*

B. Write each sentence, choosing the correct pronoun in parentheses.

6. Jonathan and (I, me) like to study to music.
7. Jonathan likes to study to rock music, but that's not for (I, me).
8. Mozart's music helps (I, me) study.
9. (I, Me) study hard when I listen to Mozart.
10. Rock music works differently for him and (I, me).

Commonly Confused Words

pages 422–423

C. Write each sentence, choosing the correct word in parentheses.

11. The school band is going (to, two, too) the band contest next week.
12. The teacher, Mr. Pitt, said that (too, to, two) flutes would play a duet.
13. Fiona and Karl will play a duet, (to, two, too).
14. (They're, Their, There) in the brass section.
15. They must remember to bring (they're, their, there) music to the contest.
16. I will go (there, their, they're) to watch my friends play.
17. The contest will last for (to, two, too) hours.
18. (Its, It's) important that the band does well.
19. "(Your, You're) all first-rate musicians," Mr. Pitt told the band.
20. "The outcome is in (your, you're) hands," he added.

Stories on the Stage

Some stories make great plays. With a group, select a story and adapt it into a script. Make or find props and scenery. Then perform it for your class.

Choose a Story

- Pick a short story with your group. Make sure the story you pick has several characters so that each of you can play a part.

Plan and Write a Script

- Read the story. Underline all the dialogue.

- Find the part of the story that gives background information. Think about how you can fit it into the play.

- How do characters feel and move in different scenes?

- Retell the story using dialogue only. Write stage directions to indicate how characters feel or move.

- Make a list of the props and simple sets you need. Have group members with strong abilities in art help create props and scenery.

Rehearse

- Make enough copies of the script for your group.

- Decide which roles the members of your group will play. Then read the script together. Make notes in your script to help you remember where to move and when.

- Get familiar with your character. What is he or she like? What does he or she feel? Try to speak and act the way your character would.

Show Time!

- Plan with your teacher an appropriate time to perform your play.

- Make and distribute to the audience a list, or program, of characters and performers in your play.

- Perform your play for your class.

Live Writing: Breathing Life into Your Words
by Ralph Fletcher
NONFICTION
Make your script more entertaining and believable with hints from well-known authors.
Award-Winning Author

Alvin Ailey
by Andrea Davis Pinkney
BIOGRAPHY
Alvin Ailey invented his own style of dance as a way to express the songs and stories he heard as a child.
Award-Winning Author

Four Types of Sentences   pages 24–29

Write each sentence, and add the correct end punctuation. Then write *declarative*, *interrogative*, *imperative*, or *exclamatory*.

1. Please tell me about the Feather Dance
2. The Feather Dance is a custom of Native Americans in Mexico
3. What do the performers wear
4. The dancers wear costumes decorated with colorful bird feathers
5. What an interesting custom

Subjects and Predicates   pages 34–39, 52–57

Write each sentence. Use commas to separate three or more subjects and three or more predicates. Then draw one line under the complete subject and two lines under the complete predicate.

6. Nora visited a folk festival last Saturday.
7. Pepe and Carmen went with her.
8. Pepe Carmen and Nora had a wonderful time.
9. Men women and children crowded onto the fairgrounds.
10. People drove cars rode bikes and walked to the event.
11. Dancers in colorful costumes danced to the folk music.
12. Musicians strummed and plucked the strings of their instruments.
13. People in the audience cheered clapped and waved their arms above their heads.
14. The three young friends sang danced and laughed.
15. Nora Pepe and Carmen left after the last performance.

Simple and Compound Sentences

pages 62–67

Use a conjunction or semicolon to combine each pair of sentences into one compound sentence. Choose the method that you think combines the sentences in the best way.

16. Mark likes stories. He also likes books about science.
17. Hardback books are sturdy. Paperback books are less expensive.
18. Should Claudia buy that book? Should she borrow it from the library?
19. You can keep books you buy. You must return library books.
20. Ricardo has read that book. He enjoyed it.

Nouns and Abbreviations *pages 94–99*

Write each sentence. Use the correct form of the noun or the abbreviation in parentheses.

1. The colonist's son played with his two pet (gooses, geese).
2. (Tomatos, Tomatoes) were first grown in the Americas.
3. Huge (forests, forestes) once covered much of North America.
4. (Mrs., MRS) Diaz and her daughter wore colonial (dress's, dresses) to the costume party.
5. Colonists in New England often caught (fish, fishies).
6. The fate of the colonists on Roanoke Island is one of history's great (mysterys, mysteries).
7. Early settlers in the Southwest sometimes traveled on (donkeys, donkies).
8. Karen saw a set of colonial (dishs, dishes) in a museum.
9. The collection included (knives, knifes) and forks.
10. (Dr, Dr.) Bohune may have treated the (childs, children) of the colonists at Jamestown.

Possessive Nouns *pages 104–109*

If each possessive noun in a sentence is used correctly, write *correct*. If a possessive noun is incorrect, write the sentence, using the correct form.

11. Colonists's animals were more than just childrens' pets.
12. The dog's bark scared foxes away from the henhouse.
13. The familys' horse could pull a wagon or a plow.
14. A gooses' feathers might stuff a pillow.
15. The rooster's loud morning call was like an alarm clock.

Verbs *pages 122–127, 132–137*

Write each sentence. Underline each main verb once and each helping verb twice. Write *action* or *linking* to tell what kind of verb phrase the sentence has.

16. Carpenters and plumbers are working on the house.
17. A carpenter can build wooden objects.
18. Hammers and saws have become tools of the carpenter's trade.
19. Plumbers will repair the water pipes.
20. These plumbers do seem very busy.

Verb Tenses *pages 166–169, 176–177, 204–207*

Write each sentence. Underline each verb or verb phrase. Then write the tense of the verb: *present, past, future, present perfect, past perfect,* or *future perfect.*

1. Lucia had asked her mom and dad for a dog.
2. Her parents bought their daughter a black-and-white puppy.
3. Lucia has played with her new pet for hours.
4. Tomorrow Lucia will have fed her puppy three times.
5. Her mom and dad are proud of their daughter.

Subject-Verb Agreement *pages 170–171*

Write whether the subject in each sentence is singular or plural. Then write the correct form of the verb.

6. Visitors to the zoo (enjoy, enjoys) the parrots.
7. That parrot (know, knows) a number of words.
8. Brendan and Michael (laugh, laughs) at its funny behavior.
9. The bird (squawk, squawks) at them when they laugh.
10. Other visitors also (find, finds) the bird amusing.

Regular and Irregular Verbs *pages 194–197*

Write each sentence. Use the correct form of the verb in parentheses. Write whether each verb is regular or irregular.

11. Leon and his classmates (visited, visit) the zoo last Thursday.
12. Have the children (went, gone) to the rare-animal house?
13. The class (saw, seen) a koala and a parrot.
14. The zookeeper (brang, brought) the koala some food.
15. I (done, did) some research about koalas before I (goed, went) to the zoo.

Sequence of Tenses *pages 208–209*

Write each sentence. Use the verb tense in parentheses that shows the correct sequence of tenses.

16. A steady rain had fallen all morning as the meteorologist (predicts, predicted).
17. The coaches will cancel the game if the rain (continues, has continued).
18. I watched as the sun (peeks, peeked) through the clouds.
19. The rain (has stopped, had stopped) by the time the game started.
20. I have worked a long time, and I (am, was) tired.

Possessive and Reflexive Pronouns *pages 244–245, 246–247*

Write each sentence. Fill in the blank with a correct possessive or reflexive pronoun.

1. Rosa eats brown rice because of _____ nutrients.
2. Dad and I include rice in _____ diets regularly.
3. Farmers in many countries grow rice in _____ fields.
4. My brother pours milk on _____ cereal before he eats it.
5. We should keep _____ in good physical condition.
6. Linda keeps _____ fit by walking every day.
7. Robert joined the track team to get _____ in shape.
8. My friends are teaching _____ about physical fitness.
9. I am going to buy _____ a good pair of hiking boots.
10. Robert, are these shoes _____?

Comparing with Adjectives and Adverbs *pages 274–277*

Write each sentence. Use the correct comparing form of the adjective or adverb in parentheses.

11. Which do you like (well)—apples or oranges?
12. This is the (good) peach I have ever tasted.
13. A pink grapefruit is (nutritious) than a white grapefruit.
14. Doughnuts are one of the (bad) foods you can eat.
15. Cats can move (quickly) than people can.
16. Of all the cats, the cheetah runs short distances (fast).
17. I think a cardinal is the (beautiful) bird in the world.
18. My sister believes that a blue jay is (pretty) than a cardinal.
19. The (playful) animal of all may be the dolphin.
20. I did (badly) than you on the test.

Prepositional Phrases *pages 310–315*

Write each sentence. Underline each prepositional phrase. Circle each object of a preposition.

1. Native Americans have lived here for thousands of years.
2. Have you ever ridden in a kayak?
3. A kayak is a small boat with a wooden frame.
4. Doug has learned many interesting facts about different Native American groups.
5. He has borrowed books on the subject from the library.

Compound and Complex Sentences

pages 324–325, 338–343

Write whether each sentence is compound or complex. Write each complex sentence. Underline the dependent clause.

6. Lisa was walking in a field when she found an arrowhead.
7. If she had not been looking down, she would not have seen the arrowhead.
8. After she found the arrowhead, she searched and found another one.
9. One arrowhead was gray, and the other was brown.
10. Because Lisa's story interested me, I started reading books about Native Americans.
11. Sara read a book about pioneers moving west, and she told me about it.
12. Although it was a long trip in a wagon, most people did not give up.
13. Because the oxen pulled heavy loads, people walked beside their wagons.
14. Some pioneers went to Oregon, but others did not go as far.
15. Today we can travel long distances easily whenever we wish.

Sentence Fragments *pages 348–351*

Write whether each group of words is a sentence or a fragment. If it is a fragment, write *S* if it needs a subject. Write *P* if it needs a predicate. Write *IC* if it needs an independent clause.

16. Built large dwellings on cliff walls.
17. Some Native American groups moved from place to place.
18. The Apaches, the Navajo, and the Iroquois.
19. Because they fished for salmon.
20. Native Americans living on the plains.

Commas, Quotation Marks, and Colons *pages 380–385, 390–395*

Write each sentence. Add commas, quotation marks, or colons where they are needed.

1. William Shakespeare wrote three kinds of plays histories comedies and tragedies.
2. The actors the director and the stage crew all play a part in the success of a play.
3. My friend has written directed and acted in a play.
4. I have seen a play but I have never acted on stage.
5. Vince please meet me outside the theater Jean said.
6. I'll be there on time Vince replied.
7. Mr. Ramirez our principal directs the school play.
8. The play starts at 800 tonight.
9. The following groups all came to see the play parents teachers and friends of the actors.
10. Yes said Mr. Ramirez, the play was a huge success.

Punctuation and Capitalization in Titles *pages 408–411*

Write each sentence, adding your personal favorite to complete the thought. Underline titles, place titles in quotation marks, and capitalize words in titles, as needed.

11. My favorite book is _____.
12. My favorite song is _____.
13. My favorite magazine is _____.
14. My favorite story is _____.
15. My favorite movie is _____.

Common Usage Problems *pages 418–423*

Write the sentence, correcting each error.

16. I never heard no other song like that one.
17. Me and my friend are going to the music store.
18. I like too listen to there music.
19. Its a beautiful tune, and the words are nice, to.
20. Your going to play the guitar, and I can't hardly wait to hear you.

Language Use

Read each sentence. Look at the underlined words in each one. There may be a mistake in punctuation, capitalization, or word usage. If you find a mistake, choose the answer that is the best way to write the underlined section of the sentence. If there is no mistake, choose *Correct as is*.

1 What did you learn about jupiter.

  A about Jupiter.

  B about jupiter?

  C about Jupiter?

  D Correct as is

2 Jupiter is the most largest planet.

  F the more largest

  G the largest

  H the more larger

  J Correct as is

3 Jupiter is the largest planet Pluto is the smallest.

  A planet. Pluto

  B planet, Pluto

  C planet. pluto

  D Correct as is

4 Titan Rhea and Pan are three of Saturn's moons.

  F Titan, Rhea and Pan

  G Titan, Rhea, and Pan

  H Titan, Rhea, and Pan,

  J Correct as is

5 Ms. Lee, our science teacher, has a telescope.

  A Ms. Lee, our science teacher

  B Ms. Lee our science teacher

  C Ms. Lee our science teacher,

  D Correct as is

6 Tell me more about Pluto, said Ken.

  F "Tell me more about Pluto," said Ken.

  G "Tell me more about Pluto, said Ken."

  H "Tell me more about Pluto" said Ken.

  J Correct as is

7 Mercury doesn't have no moons.

  A does'nt have any

  B doesn't have any

  C does not have no

  D Correct as is

8 Can you come with my parents and I to the science fair?

  F me and my parents

  G I and my parents

  H my parents and me

  J Correct as is

Written Expression

Read the paragraph. Then use it to answer the questions that follow. Write the letter of each answer you choose.

---

    (1) Red, blue, yellow, and white wildflowers are blooming. (2) A gentle breeze dances through the <u>trees, but it</u> cools my face. (3) The breeze also carries the smell of mowed grass. (4) Their colors are a treat for the eyes. (5) Farm animals <u>watched lazy</u> from behind fences. (6) Their moos, cackles, and baas sound like an orchestra to me. (7) A bicycle ride is nice, too.

---

1 Choose the best opening sentence to add to this paragraph.

  A I have lived in the country for a long time now.

  B A country walk is a wonderful way to spend a spring afternoon.

  C Country life is very different from life in the city.

  D A country walk isn't a bad idea if you have nothing else to do.

2 Which sentence should be left out of this paragraph?

  J Sentence 2

  K Sentence 3

  L Sentence 6

  M Sentence 7

3 Where is the best place for sentence 4?

  A Where it is now

  B Between sentences 1 and 2

  C Between sentences 2 and 3

  D Between sentences 6 and 7

4 What is the best way to write the underlined part of sentence 2?

  J trees, and

  K trees. But it

  L trees, or it

  M (*No change*)

5 What is the best way to write the underlined part of sentence 5?

  A will watch lazily

  B watch lazy

  C watch lazily

  D (*No change*)

6 Choose the best concluding sentence to add to this paragraph.

  J You can go faster on a bicycle.

  K There are many things to enjoy on a walk in the country.

  L Of course, you may not agree with what I have written.

  M Farm animals have always amused me.

Extra Practice

A. Write whether each group of words is a sentence or not a sentence. *pages 24–25*

1. Our class went to a piano concert yesterday.
2. Learned to play at a young age.
3. Different kinds of piano music.
4. All of the pianists performed very well.
5. The piano for the different performers.

B. Write whether each sentence is declarative, interrogative, imperative, or exclamatory. *pages 26–27*

6. What is the best way to get to the theater?
7. Most people take Franklin Avenue to get there.
8. The concert hall can't be on Franklin Avenue!
9. It is on Derby Street.
10. Give me exact directions.

C. Write each sentence. Add the correct end punctuation. *pages 28–29*

11. My brother takes guitar lessons and also writes songs
12. Does he write many songs
13. He won a prize for one of his songs
14. That's wonderful
15. Tell me about the song
16. Come with me to hear him play it
17. Did you know that the school chorus will perform the song
18. How exciting that will be
19. Your brother must be very happy
20. Our family will attend the performance

Extra Practice

A. Write each sentence. Underline the complete subject. Circle the simple subject. *pages 34–35*

1. We live in a very large country.
2. It is located south of Canada and north of Mexico.
3. High, snowy mountains are found in the western United States.
4. Lower mountains with forests are found in the eastern United States.
5. Many long rivers flow throughout this land.
6. The national capital is Washington, D.C.
7. The country's population grows every year.
8. The natural resources include oil, minerals, and forests.
9. Some people work as farmers and ranchers.
10. Other workers have jobs in factories and offices.

B. Write each sentence. Underline each noun. Circle the noun that is the simple subject. *pages 36–37*

11. Some mountains in the world are very high.
12. Snow stays on these mountains all through the year.
13. Tourists often go to the mountains to ski.
14. Some people climb mountains.
15. My brother enjoys challenge and adventure.

C. Combine each pair of sentences to form one sentence with a compound subject. *pages 38–39*

16. My older sisters cook sometimes. My older brothers cook sometimes.
17. Stir-fried vegetables are delicious. Egg rolls are also delicious.
18. Soups are cooked in a pot. Stews are cooked in a pot.
19. Cereals are good for breakfast. Fruits are good for breakfast.
20. Barbecues are outdoor meals. Picnics are also outdoor meals.

Extra Practice

A. Write each sentence. Draw a line between the complete subject and the complete predicate. Underline the simple predicate. *pages 52–53*

1. Badminton is a game similar to tennis.
2. Players of both sports use rackets to hit an object.
3. The game is popular in England.
4. Miles and Carrie like to play badminton.
5. They know how to play tennis also.

B. Write the sentence. Underline each verb. *pages 54–55*

6. Birds, squirrels, and deer are common animals in a forest.
7. People have hiked through forests for centuries.
8. Hiking is a favorite American activity.
9. Hikers enjoy the beauty of our national parks.
10. My family had an interesting hiking adventure.

C. Combine each group of sentences to form one sentence with a compound predicate. *pages 56–57*

11. Carlos sketched an action hero. He created an exciting story for him.
12. His aunt writes children's stories. She illustrates them.
13. I wrote a short story. I drew pictures for it. I sent it to Carlos.
14. Carlos and his aunt read my story. They liked it. They thanked me.
15. My next story is about space travel. It happens in the future.

D. Write each sentence, correcting the errors in punctuation. *pages 52–57*

16. Maria plays the piano, and practices daily.
17. Her sister plays the clarinet, but prefers to play the trumpet.
18. Maria and her dad often write music practice and perform together.
19. We will go to the school, and watch them perform a duet.
20. After school I practice the piano do my homework and play computer games.

Extra Practice

A. Write each sentence. Draw one line under each complete subject and two lines under each complete predicate. Then write whether the sentence is simple or compound. *pages 62–63*

    I. Some cities have many historic buildings.

    2. My uncle traveled to many countries and took photographs.

    3. One old city had a stone wall around it, but the other city had no wall.

    4. He usually rode trains, but he sometimes took a bus.

    5. Trains and buses let him see the country.

B. Write each sentence. Choose the conjunction in parentheses that best fits each sentence. Add commas as needed. *pages 64–65*

    6. Mr. Wilson takes many trips, (and, but) he stays home on holidays.

    7. My mom lived in France, (or, and) she learned to speak French.

    8. People who travel learn a lot, (and, but) they have interesting stories to tell.

    9. I could visit France some day, (but, or) I could live there.

    10. Some people travel for a living, (and, or) they write about their travels.

C. Use a conjunction or a semicolon to combine each pair of sentences. Write one compound sentence.
pages 66–67

    11. Some travel writers write about famous buildings. They may write about food.

    12. Buildings are important. They can tell a lot about the history of a country.

    13. Food from other countries is different. It tastes good.

    14. I ate Irish stew once. It was wonderful.

    15. My dad makes good chili. My aunt does, too.

Extra Practice

A. **Write each sentence, capitalizing any proper nouns you find. Then underline each noun in the sentence.** *pages 94–95*

1. When did texas become part of the united states?
2. The capital of texas is austin.
3. Two rivers that run through parts of texas are the rio grande and the red river.
4. The alamo in san antonio is a famous attraction.
5. The land in texas includes grassy plains and pine forests.

B. **Write each sentence. Change each underlined singular noun to the correct plural form.** *pages 96–97*

6. I love dancing to <u>waltz</u>.
7. In some <u>dance</u>, the <u>foot</u> move quickly.
8. In some countries <u>man</u> and <u>woman</u> sing while dancing.
9. <u>Child</u> of all ages enjoy lively <u>song</u>.
10. I once saw <u>monkey</u> trained to dance.

C. **Rewrite the items below, using abbreviations.** *pages 98–99*

11. Mister Harrison, Junior
12. Rodriguez Street
13. Thursday
14. one second
15. 50 pounds

D. **Write each sentence, correcting the errors.** *pages 94–99*

16. My ancestors came from scotland.
17. They traveled across the atlantic ocean and settled in new york.
18. We are going to a family reunion this friday at 1:00 P.M.
19. My grandmother, Mrs elliot, is giving a real Scottish party.
20. Her address is 100 maple avenue.

Extra Practice

A. Write each sentence. Underline the possessive nouns. Write whether each possessive noun is singular or plural. *pages 104–107*

1. Our school principal's personality is warm and friendly.
2. The students' and the teachers' faces brighten when the principal is around.
3. Mrs. Thomas's personality is also cheerful.
4. My friends' comments about her are positive.
5. A teacher's job is to help students learn.

B. If the possessive noun in a sentence is used correctly, write *correct*. If it is not used correctly, rewrite the sentence, using the correct form.

pages 104–107

6. Jacks clothes were wrinkled.
7. Marilyns' clothes are always neat.
8. The dry cleaner's clothes press broke last week.
9. Elenas' and Kristens' sewing skills are well known.
10. They repaired the huge tear in Mrs. Wilsons quilt.

C. If the nouns in a sentence are written correctly, write *correct*. If any noun is incorrect, rewrite the sentence correctly. *pages 104–109*

11. The citys streets were filled with colorful lights.
12. At night, the lights red, white, and blue colors shone brightly.
13. The communitys' annual Fourth of July celebration was about to begin.
14. The peoples' excitement was easy to see.
15. Everyone enjoyed the fireworks' beautiful colors.

D. Write each sentence. Choose the correct noun form of the two in parentheses. *pages 104–109*

16. The (Taylor's, Taylors) repainted their house.
17. The (house's, houses) doors are still white.
18. Their (neighbors', neighbors) houses are different colors.
19. The (childrens', children's) bedrooms are now blue.
20. The (painters, painters') did a good job.

Extra Practice

A. **Write the sentence. Underline each action verb and circle each direct object.** *pages 122–123*

  1. Mrs. Elliott studied science in college.
  2. She graduated and now teaches school.
  3. Some people attend college at night.
  4. My sister takes art classes in college.
  5. She likes her art teacher.

B. **Write the verb in each sentence. Then write *action* or *linking* to identify the kind of verb.** *pages 122–125*

  6. Our neighbor plants a large garden each year.
  7. Her tomatoes and peppers grow tall and large.
  8. They taste delicious right from the garden.
  9. I smell the flowers in her garden.
  10. All of the flowers smell sweet.

C. **Write each sentence. Underline each linking verb. Draw an arrow from each subject to the word in the predicate that renames or describes it.**
pages 124–127

  11. Astronomy is the study of stars and planets.
  12. People became more interested in space after the moon landing.
  13. From the Earth, the moon seems larger than the sun.
  14. I feel excited about our visit to the observatory.
  15. The observatory's telescope is gigantic.

D. **Write each sentence. Choose a form of *be* from the box to complete each sentence. Use each verb once.**
pages 126–127

am	is	are	was	were

  16. My sister and I _____ in the chorus last year.
  17. My voice _____ tired at the end of the concert.
  18. Voice exercises _____ good for singers.
  19. I _____ glad that I did the exercises.
  20. Friday _____ the day we practice.

Extra Practice

A. Write the verb phrase in each sentence. *pages 132–133*

1. Devin is writing his research report.
2. He has worked at the library on Saturdays.
3. The librarian will help students find books about their topics.
4. Devin could become a good researcher.
5. He should feel good about his finished report.

B. Write each sentence. Underline each verb phrase. Circle each main verb. *pages 134–135*

6. Are you coming to the game tonight?
7. Erin has played soccer for six years.
8. Erin has trained hard to become a good athlete.
9. She has practiced every day.
10. She will enter a soccer tournament next spring.

C. Write each sentence. Use the contraction that is formed from the words in parentheses. *pages 136–137*

11. She (does not) know how to swim.
12. They (would not) have known without lessons.
13. I (could not) teach her because I (did not) know how to swim either.
14. We (have not) taken swimming lessons yet.
15. The lessons (are not) too hard.

D. Write each sentence, correcting the errors in contractions. *pages 136–137*

16. I cant remember where I left my glasses.
17. It hasnt' been long since I last used them.
18. You do'nt know where I left them, do you?
19. I wont' be able to read the book without them.
20. This isnt the first time I have lost them.

Extra Practice

A. Write each sentence. Underline the verb. Then write whether the verb is in the present tense, the past tense, or the future tense. *pages 166–167*

1. Our school started a recycling program.
2. Many students helped collect newspapers.
3. We also recycle aluminum cans.
4. Some other schools in our area will start recycling programs.
5. We collect only aluminum cans.
6. We will collect glass bottles next month.
7. There is also a recycling center in town.
8. It takes different kinds of plastic.
9. The center started five years ago.
10. Soon it will move to a larger building.

B. Write each sentence. Use the correct form of the present tense verb in parentheses. *pages 168–169*

11. Frances _____ going to the park. (like)
12. She _____ there almost every day. (play)
13. Sometimes her friends _____ her there. (meet)
14. A squirrel _____ its tail back and forth as it watches them play. (swish)
15. It _____ to get their attention by running up and down a tree. (try)

C. Write whether the subject in each sentence is singular or plural. Then write the form of the verb in parentheses that agrees with the subject.

pages 170–171

16. My favorite sport _____ ice-skating. (be)
17. My mom _____ ice-skating. (enjoy)
18. She and I _____ across the ice together. (skate)
19. We always _____ to the rink on Saturdays. (go)
20. The ice _____ brightly in the sun. (shine)

Extra Practice

A. Write each sentence. Use the verb and the tense in parentheses. *pages 176–177*

1. Emily _____ a different color for her room. (*want*, past)
2. Tomorrow she _____ her mom paint the room. (*help*, future)
3. Together they _____ on a new color. (*decide*, past)
4. First, Emily _____ her furniture. (*move*, future)
5. Emily _____ very happy about the change. (*feel*, present)

B. Write each sentence. Underline the verb or verb phrase. Then write the kind of principal part used in the verb (present, present participle, past, or past participle). *pages 178–179*

6. Yesterday I watched our six puppies.
7. They look very cute and cuddly.
8. They have grown a lot in the past few weeks.
9. They are beginning to explore the yard.
10. I play with them every day.

C. Write each sentence, correcting the verb. *pages 176–179*

11. The travelers have visiting many countries.
12. They were planned to go to Mexico next summer.
13. They change their plans last week.
14. They are gone to Florida instead.
15. Next summer we will going swimming at the lake.

D. Write a sentence using each verb form. *pages 180–181*

16. see
17. seen
18. do
19. done
20. seeing

4

Extra Practice

A. Write each sentence. Underline each verb. Then write whether the verb is a regular verb or an irregular verb. *pages 194–197*

1. I watched a film about volcanoes last night.
2. It showed many active volcanoes.
3. I wrote a report about lava.
4. The lava cooled into many different shapes.
5. My science teacher has taught us more about volcanoes this year.

B. Write each sentence. Use the correct past or past-participle form of the verb in parentheses.

pages 194–197

6. Nicole (write) words for a new song last week.
7. She has (begin) creating music also.
8. I have (take) music lessons before.
9. Last week, my teacher (say) I had natural talent.
10. Nicole and I (go) to a musical play once.
11. We (bring) our cameras with us.
12. We (make) it to the theater just in time for the opening.
13. The musical (begin) that night at 8:00.
14. The performers had (fly) in from Seattle.
15. At the end of the show, they all (take) bows.

C. Write each sentence, using the correct verb or verb form in parentheses. *pages 198–199*

16. Where did I (lie, lay) my favorite pen?
17. I thought Mom (set, sit) it on the kitchen counter.
18. I hope I (can, may) find it.
19. Did I (let, leave) my sister borrow it?
20. Losing my favorite pen will (learn, teach) me to put my things away.

Extra Practice

A. Write each sentence, and underline each perfect tense verb. Write whether the tense of the verb is past perfect, present perfect, or future perfect. *pages 204–207*

1. This year has been an excellent year for cotton.
2. Many farmers have planted thousands of acres of cotton.
3. The farmers told us that heavy rains had damaged last year's crops.
4. By August, the farmers will have harvested most of their cotton.
5. Farmers had hoped for a good harvest this year.

B. Write each sentence, and underline each verb. Write whether the verb is in the future or future perfect tense. *pages 206–207*

6. We will be at the zoo in the morning.
7. Many of the animals will have come out to play.
8. Forecasters say the sun will shine tomorrow.
9. My little sister will want to see the monkeys first.
10. By the end of the day, we will have seen every animal in the zoo.

C. Write the sentence, using the correct verb tense in parentheses. *pages 208–209*

11. Jacob (will read, had read) many books before he started fifth grade.
12. His little brother (began, will have begun) to read when he started kindergarten.
13. By the time the game was over, it (started, had started) to rain.
14. I (have read, had read) many books about the rainforest, but this one is the best.
15. We (have learned, will have learned) a lot about recycling by the time we finish this project.

Extra Practice

A. Write each pronoun in the sentence. Then write whether it is a subject pronoun or an object pronoun. One sentence has two pronouns. *pages 234–237*

1. Uncle Ed and Aunt Marcy sent me a letter this week.
2. They moved to Miami last summer.
3. We miss them very much.
4. Uncle Ed told us about Miami's summer heat.
5. My sister and I would like to travel there next year.

B. Write each sentence. Underline the pronoun. Draw an arrow from the pronoun to the antecedent. *pages 238–239*

6. When cats play, they run and pounce.
7. Mrs. Parker raises Persian cats and sells them.
8. Persians have long hair, and they have a special look.
9. Dad avoids cats because he is allergic to cat hair.
10. Mom, however, likes cats because they are so playful.

C. Write the sentence using the correct pronoun in parentheses. *pages 234–239*

11. Our class wrote a play and will perform (them, it) soon.
12. Don and (I, me) have the leading roles.
13. Family members helped (we, us) find props to use.
14. After the performance, we will thank (they, them) for their help.
15. (They, Them) will all be in the audience.
16. Ms. Davis has worked hard with my classmates and (I, me).
17. (We, Us) have been rehearsing the play for weeks.
18. Some of my classmates say that (they, them) have memorized all their lines.
19. (Us, We) are getting ready for our first performance.
20. (I, me) am sure the audience will enjoy the play.

Extra Practice

A. Write each sentence. Replace the possessive noun in parentheses with a possessive pronoun.
pages 244–245

1. Elena walks (Elena's) dog, Rex, every day.
2. Alfie is my dog, and Rex is (Elena's).
3. People in our neighborhood are always walking (people's) dogs.
4. Elena's dog loves to wag (dog's) tail.
5. Elena says, "Rex is (Elena's) best friend."

B. Choose a reflexive pronoun to complete each sentence. Then write the sentence. *pages 246–247*

6. I am teaching _____ how to do tricks with a yo-yo.
7. We can all teach _____ new skills if we try.
8. Kim and Juan make _____ practice daily.
9. Would you like to teach _____ a new sport?
10. Anita surprised _____ by learning to skateboard.

C. Write each sentence. Replace the words in parentheses with a contraction. *pages 248–249*

11. (We have) drawn pictures on the computer.
12. (It is) fairly easy to do.
13. The pictures are simple, but (they are) pretty.
14. (We are) going to print them later.
15. (You will) be surprised when you see them.

D. Write each sentence, using the correct word in parentheses. *pages 246–249*

16. Because you studied, (your, you're) ready for the test.
17. Some students study together; others study by (theirselves, themselves).
18. Students study the information in (they're, their) notes and textbooks.
19. (It's, Its) important to eat a good breakfast before a test.
20. (Your, You're) energy will increase.

Extra Practice

A. Write each sentence. Underline the adjectives. Draw two lines under the articles. *pages 262–263*

1. The bright sun rose in the eastern sky.
2. A soft glow painted the high mountains a pale yellow.
3. Morning dew sparkled on the green trees.
4. A few small birds flew gracefully across the Colorado sky.
5. It was going to be a beautiful day.

B. Write each sentence. Underline each adverb. Draw two lines under the verb or verb phrase the adverb describes. *pages 264–265*

6. Pine trees cover the mountains completely.
7. Eagles often fly over those mountains.
8. Animals travel easily through the forest.
9. Winter arrives quickly in the mountains.
10. The animals will gather food constantly.

C. Write each sentence. Draw an arrow from each underlined word to the word it describes. Write whether the underlined word is an adjective or an adverb. *pages 266–267*

11. The baby sleeps <u>peacefully</u> in his crib.
12. He is a <u>good</u> sleeper.
13. When he eats, he makes <u>funny</u> faces.
14. His parents play <u>happily</u> with him.
15. The baby laughs <u>excitedly</u> at their antics.

D. Write each sentence, using the correct word in parentheses. *pages 262–267*

16. The boat sails near the (Alaska, alaska) coast.
17. Its crew works (hard, hardly) in the cold weather.
18. After a voyage, they are (happy, happily) to go home.
19. The boat's captain (careful, carefully) plans their next voyage.
20. For him, sailing is always (a, an) adventure.

Extra Practice

A. **Write each sentence, and underline each adverb. Draw an arrow from each adverb to the word that it describes.** *pages 272–273*

1. The students worked long and hard on their project.
2. They were extremely careful with every detail.
3. The project is certainly a success.
4. The group is quite pleased with their results.
5. The teacher was very impressed.

B. **Write each sentence, using the correct comparing form of the adjective or adverb in parentheses.**
pages 274–275

6. Chen finished his essay (soon) than Roger did.
7. Roger completed his math homework the (quick) of all the students.
8. Nancy's grades are the (high) of all the students' grades.
9. Of all the students, who is (excited) about next week's field trip?
10. The teacher is (worried) than the students.

C. **Write each sentence, using the correct word in parentheses. Then write the word that your answer describes.** *pages 276–277*

11. The actors performed (good, well).
12. It was a (good, well) play.
13. This play was (better, best) than the last play we saw.
14. The lead actor had been sick, but he was (good, well) on opening night.
15. No one performed (bad, badly) that night.

D. **Write each sentence, correcting the errors.**
pages 272–277

16. Gino plays basketball very good.
17. He is best at lay-up shots than Karl.
18. The championship game will be the more difficult game of the season.
19. Gino and Karl are the better players on the entire team.
20. Karl felt badly about losing the game.

Extra Practice

A. Write the prepositions that appear in these sentences. *pages 310–311*

1. Our apartment is across the street from a city park.
2. After school, my friends and I go to the park.
3. We shoot baskets at the basketball court.
4. We play with Julio's basketball.
5. Later we walk up the street to the ice-cream shop.

B. Write each sentence. Underline each prepositional phrase. Circle each object of a preposition. Some sentences have two prepositional phrases.

pages 312–313

6. The treehouse is made of old wood.
7. We built a ladder of small boards nailed to the tree.
8. We climb from the ladder into the treehouse.
9. The treehouse is a lot of fun.
10. We play in it during most weekends.
11. Tanya started skating at a young age.
12. Tanya's teacher once skated in the Olympics.
13. Tanya practices after school and on weekends.
14. She has learned patterns of leaps and turns.
15. Her skating for this performance was especially good.

C. Expand each sentence. Add one or more prepositional phrases that answer the questions in parentheses. *pages 314–315*

16. We moved. (Where?)
17. We saw a movie. (What kind?)
18. It is hot. (Where? When?)
19. I did not know anyone. (When?)
20. The students are friendly. (Which ones?)

Extra Practice

A. Write whether each group of words is a prepositional phrase or a clause. *pages 320–321*

1. the museum is open
2. at the museum
3. across from Seventh Avenue
4. when they arrive
5. throughout the day

B. Write each sentence. Underline the independent clause. *pages 322–323*

6. I had fun when I cleaned up the attic.
7. When I looked through an old trunk, I found a treasure map.
8. As I studied the map, I recognized the streets of my town.
9. The map showed a spot where treasure was buried.
10. Although I searched hard, I never discovered the treasure.

C. For each item, connect the two clauses to form an expanded sentence. Add a connecting word that shows the kind of information named in parentheses. *pages 324–325*

11. Soccer teams practice (when) they play a game.
12. Team members talk about their performance (when) the game is over.
13. (Condition) players want to win, they must practice.
14. Professional teams have fields (where) games are held.
15. I would like to be on a team (why) I like to play soccer.

D. Add a dependent clause to each sentence. You may want to give the kind of information named in parentheses, using commas where necessary.
pages 324–325

16. Cindi built a model of a volcano. (why)
17. She worked on the model. (when)
18. She will set up the model. (where)
19. The model will be finished. (when)
20. She may make another model. (condition)

Extra Practice

A. Write whether each sentence is a simple sentence, a compound sentence, or a complex sentence. If it is a complex sentence, write each dependent clause. *pages 338–343*

1. We lived in Vermont for many years.
2. We loved Vermont, but Mom found a better job in Ohio.
3. Before we moved, we said good-bye to all of our friends.
4. Mom started her new job, and Dad set up his home office.
5. The move has worked out well because we are all still together.

B. Write the sentences, and underline the dependent clauses. *pages 340–341*

6. Thomas has grown a few inches since I last saw him.
7. He will probably be tall because his parents are tall.
8. Whenever Thomas plays basketball, he makes a lot of baskets.
9. I didn't play very well until I joined a team.
10. If I practice regularly, I can improve my skills.

C. Write each set of sentences as a single sentence of the type given in parentheses. You may vary the order of words or clauses to make the new sentences effective. Add commas where needed. *pages 342–343*

11. I have loved to swim. I was a small child. (complex sentence)
12. I may be an Olympic swimmer. I could be an Olympic diver. (compound sentence)
13. I would swim every day. My parents would let me go to the pool. (complex sentence)
14. I cannot ride my bike to the pool. It is too far away. (complex sentence)
15. I read the biographies of great swimmers. I collect their pictures. (compound sentence)

Extra Practice

A. Identify each group of words as a complete sentence or a sentence fragment. For each fragment, write _S_ if the sentence needs a subject, _P_ if it needs a predicate, and _IC_ if it needs an independent clause. *pages 348–349*

1. Took us five hours to get there.
2. The plane had a two-hour delay.
3. When we finally took off.
4. The trip, usually a three-hour flight.
5. Was midnight when we arrived.
6. Because we arrived late.
7. We still have time to see the sights.
8. A large zoo with trees and ponds.
9. Will have fun at the beach.
10. Until we go back home.

B. Write _RO_ if the group of words is a run-on sentence. Write _CS_ if it is a comma splice. Write _correct_ if it is correct. *pages 350–351*

11. I used the Internet to do research, and I found information.
12. The Internet can be a useful tool, it contains many interesting websites.
13. Mrs. Tam gave me a list of websites several were helpful.
14. Our town has a website, it has colorful graphics.
15. Although the Internet is interesting, libraries are still very useful.

C. Rewrite each incorrect sentence correctly. If the sentence is correct, write _correct_. *pages 352–353*

16. More people began to recycle, we saw that we were not prepared.
17. We needed more recycling bins, the ones we had were overflowing.
18. Mr. Marino went to the recycling center he brought back four more bins.
19. The extra bins helped, they were not enough.
20. We'll have to get two more bins that will take a few days.

Extra Practice

A. Write each sentence. Add commas where they are needed. *pages 380–381*

1. They used wood nails hammers and a saw to build the fort.
2. Joey wanted to help but he was too little.
3. They drew their design measured the wood and cut it with a saw.
4. Erik Elizabeth and Mario took turns cutting and carrying the wood.
5. Joey did help by bringing food drinks and napkins.

B. Write each sentence. Add commas where they are needed. *pages 382–383*

6. To hit the ball Daryl you must keep your eye on it.
7. Yes it is harder than it seems.
8. Tracey see if you can hit the ball.
9. He pitched the ball too fast Mitchell.
10. Well let's try again.

C. Write each sentence. Add commas where they are needed. *pages 384–385*

11. Nathaniel Hawthorne an American author wrote novels and stories.
12. Edgar Allan Poe another American writer is known for his stories and poems.
13. The works of these writers Hawthorne and Poe are still popular today.
14. Have you read "The Raven" one of Poe's most famous poems?
15. Mr. Lewis our teacher thinks <u>The House of the Seven Gables</u> is Hawthorne's best book.

D. Write each sentence. Add commas where they are needed. *pages 380–385*

16. What kinds of books do you like to read Margaret?
17. No I don't like scary stories either.
18. We have read poems short stories and plays.
19. Plays stories meant to be acted out can be long.
20. Yes but they are fun to watch.

Extra Practice

A. Write each sentence, punctuating each direct quotation correctly. *pages 390–391*

1. What should we do this weekend? asked José.
2. Rusty answered I don't know, but Lupe probably has an idea.
3. Lupe said I certainly do.
4. It's probably basketball groaned José.
5. Not this time. I'm ready to try something different Lupe said to her surprised friends.

B. Write each sentence, punctuating each divided quotation correctly. *pages 392–393*

6. Have I told you Mrs. Sneve asked that Joseph Haydn was born in Austria?
7. I have heard of him said Ernesto Didn't he write music?
8. Yes she answered He composed classical music.
9. Is it true asked Marisa that he and Beethoven knew each other?
10. As a matter of fact said Mrs. Sneve Beethoven was one of Haydn's students.

C. Write each sentence, using colons correctly.
pages 394–395

11. The orchestra will perform on the following dates, May 3, May 10, and May 17.
12. Mr. Rawls said that the performances will begin at 330.
13. You can pick up tickets at these locations The Salad Kitchen, Tim's Toys, and Barry's Book Shop.
14. "Hey, Sarah," called Julia. "You're going to: the first performance. Right?"
15. Julia replied, "My mom said I have to finish the following chores first clean my room, sweep the kitchen, and do the dishes."

Extra Practice

A. Write the sentences. Use quotation marks or underlining to mark the titles. *pages 408–409*

1. I am looking for a book called The Collected Poems of Robert Frost.
2. Have you ever read the poem Stopping by Woods on a Snowy Evening?
3. There was an article about Robert Frost in Poetry Gazette.
4. The article was called Poets, Trees, and Nature.
5. I will have to see if Frost's poetry is included in my copy of Major Poets of the Twentieth Century.

B. Punctuate each title, and capitalize the important words. *pages 410–411*

6. the mighty (movie)
7. the golden compass (book)
8. what students are reading (magazine article)
9. home on the range (song)
10. a smart cookie (short story)

C. The word forms in parentheses show the use of a hyphen. The hyphen may connect the parts of a compound word or divide a word into syllables. Write the correct word form. *pages 412–413*

11. The (four story, four-story) building was without electricity.
12. Its (thirty-seven, thirty seven) offices had to close temporarily.
13. The city's power crews are (well known, well-known) for fixing problems such as this one.
14. People who work in the building were able to return to their offices after a (one-hour, one hour) wait.
15. The power crews did a (fantas-tic, fantast-ic) job.
16. I just finished (rea-ding, read-ing) a story by Jack London called "To Build a Fire."
17. It is not a (fast paced, fast-paced) story, but it builds suspense.
18. Jack London has written many (advent-ure, adven-ture) stories.
19. London is a (well respected, well-respected) author.
20. He is also very (well-known, well known).

Extra Practice

A. Rewrite each sentence to correct the double negative. *pages 418–419*

1. That pocket watch doesn't have no numbers.
2. Mr. Floyd can't find no one to repair the watch.
3. Nowhere have I never seen a watch without numbers.
4. Mr. Floyd couldn't not figure out how to put the numbers back on.
5. You can't easily use no watch with no numbers.

B. Write the sentence, using the correct pronoun in parentheses. *pages 420–421*

6. Mom hung pictures of Lita and (I, me) on the wall.
7. Lita and (I, me) helped Mom hang them.
8. As we worked, Mom told Lita and (I, me) the story behind each picture.
9. The stories were very familiar to (I, me).
10. Mom, Lita, and (I, me) knew them all by heart.

C. Write each sentence, using the correct word in parentheses. *pages 422–423*

11. I have (two, to, too) cousins who are talented artists.
12. (There, They're, Their) work is well known in the community.
13. One of the local stores displays my cousins' paintings in (it's, its) front window.
14. Some of (there, they're, their) work also hangs in the bank.
15. The paintings are (two, to, too) beautiful to describe.

D. Write each sentence, correcting the errors.
pages 418–423

16. They were to tired to run anymore.
17. The coach didn't never expect them to run so far.
18. There legs were about to give out.
19. Coach told the to of them too rest.
20. They never thought nothing about it.

Handbook

Contents

Sentence Diagramming

A **sentence diagram** shows how the parts of a sentence work together.

- The **simple subject** is the main word or words in the complete subject of a sentence. The **simple predicate** is the verb in the complete predicate.

- These diagrams show the **simple subject** and **simple predicate** in each kind of sentence. Notice that in the interrogative sentence, part of the verb comes before the subject.

Declarative: **Ellen paints.**

| Ellen | paints |

Interrogative: **Does Ellen paint?**

| Ellen | Does paint |

Imperative: **Paint a picture.**

| *you* (understood) | Paint |

Exclamatory:
How well Ellen paints!

| Ellen | paints |

- A **compound subject** is two or more subjects joined by the conjunction *and* or *or*. These subjects have the same predicate.

Bob and he sang.

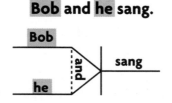

- A **compound predicate** is two or more verbs that have the same subject. The predicates are joined by a conjunction.

Kelly sings and dances.

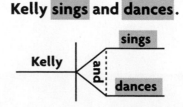

- A **direct object** receives the action of the verb and answers the question *What?* or *Whom?*

Jen likes soccer.

- An **adjective** is a word that describes a noun or a pronoun. Adjectives can tell *what kind, how many,* or *which one.* The articles *a, an,* and *the* are special adjectives that always signal a noun.

The tortoise has a strong shell.

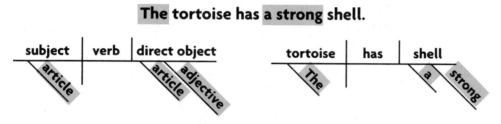

- A **possessive noun** shows ownership and usually precedes a noun. **Possessive pronouns** such as *my, her,* and *our* also precede a noun.

Cyndi's brother is riding my bike.

- A **linking verb** is followed by an adjective that describes the subject or by a noun that renames it. A slanted line is used to show that the word refers back to the subject.

My cat is black.

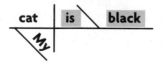

- An **adverb** modifies, or describes, a verb, an adjective, or another adverb. In a diagram, the adverb is connected to the word it modifies.

Maria walks very quickly.

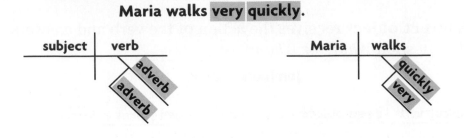

- A **prepositional phrase** is made up of a preposition, the object of that preposition, and any words in between. The object of a preposition is the noun or the pronoun that follows the preposition.

The elephant in the circus stood on its hind legs.

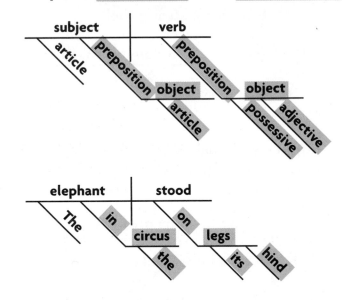

- The **complete subject** includes all the words that help name the person or thing the sentence is about.

The dog in the yard is a golden retriever.

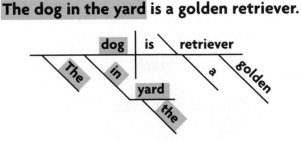

- A **complete predicate** includes all the words that tell what the subject of the sentence is or does.

Jan likes Mike's pet turtle.

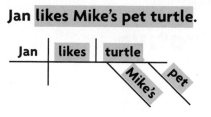

- A **compound sentence** contains two or more simple sentences joined by a comma and a conjunction or by a semicolon.

I saved my money, and I bought a bird.

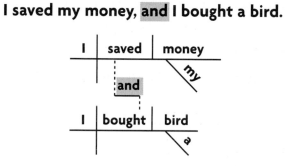

- A **complex sentence** is made up of an independent clause and at least one dependent clause. The position of a dependent clause in a diagram depends on whether it works as an adjective or as an adverb. In the diagram below, the dependent clause tells *when*, like an adverb. Therefore, it is connected to the verb of the independent clause.

After the students cleaned the playground, they received T-shirts.

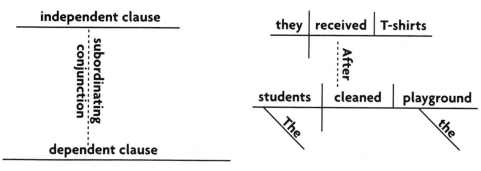

Writing Models

Personal Narrative

A **personal narrative** is a true story about yourself. What is the funniest or most interesting thing that ever happened to you? If you wrote a story about it, you would be writing a personal narrative. In a personal narrative, you tell about an event that happened to you.

How to Write a Personal Narrative

- Answer the 5 W's: who, what, when, where, and why.
- Tell the story in order: what happened first? next? last?
- Add colorful details.
- Include your thoughts and feelings.
- Add dialogue that tells what people say.

Narrator tells who, what, when, where, and why.

The Summer I Was Captured by Sea Monsters

I have always been a little nervous about being in a boat. I am not sure why, but I worry about sharks and whales. As a result, I never used to go canoeing when I went camping with my cousins. Last summer, though, my older cousin Eloise made me face my fears.

As she got the canoe ready, she told me I had nothing to worry about. At our end of Lake Kincaid, the water was only ten feet deep. I strapped on a life vest, sprayed myself with bug spray, and stepped into the canoe.

Seeing that I was calm, Eloise suggested we paddle around a nearby island. I agreed happily. When we were near the island, we decided to stop and rest. We were sitting in the boat enjoying the peace and quiet when we saw them—strange creatures in the water!

What were they? They seemed to have long swimming fins and black noses. For a few minutes, we didn't see them. Then, burbling sounds were all around us. Suddenly, a green and orange and purple head popped out of the water about twenty feet from our boat. Eloise and I screamed and began to paddle furiously. Then the sea monster yelled, "Hey, where are you going? We want to capture you!"

Could sea monsters talk? Our fears melted to embarrassment as we realized the sea monsters were little boys from a summer camp on the island. It was Sea Monster Day at the camp, and they were trying to capture little plastic boats. The team we met had to capture only one more boat to win. The boys thought it would be funny if they brought us back as prisoners, so we went with them. The boys won the competition, and they invited us to stay for the celebration dinner!

Events unfold in order in which they occur.

Colorful details

Dialogue

Narrator's thoughts and feelings

How-to Essay

In a **how-to essay,** a writer explains how to do a particular job. This kind of essay is like a set of directions. Step by step, the writer teaches the reader what to do to get the job done.

How to Write a How-to Essay

- At the beginning, identify the task. Encourage the reader to try the task, using your directions.
- Name any supplies that the reader will need for the task.
- Give the steps in time order, from first to last.
- Include helpful details—for example, possible trouble spots and the way the project should look as the work continues.

How to Cut a Rose

Task → A single rose is a thoughtful gift. Buying a rose from a local florist or market, however, can put a big dent in your allowance. Consider this idea: If you, or a friendly neighbor, have a rosebush in the garden, you can cut the flower on your own.

Supplies → You will need cutting shears and a tall but narrow vase.

Step-by-step directions → First, you must choose a suitable rose. Ignore the roses that are in full bloom. Instead, find a partly opened rosebud. Buds flower longer once they are cut. Look for a bud that does not have dark spots, brown tips, or tiny bugs called aphids. Next, cut the stem at an angle, right above a leaf. Trim the lower leaves, and carefully remove any thorns. Then place the rose in the vase, and fill the vase with cool water. Store the flower in a cool, dark spot for several hours. You might keep it overnight in the refrigerator.

A single rose is a beautiful gift. However, you might wish to arrange the flower with pieces of decorative plants, such as fern or ivy. To be fancier, tie a bright bow around the vase. If you want to give the rose without a container, just moisten its stem, wrap it in a damp paper towel and foil, and tie it with colorful ribbon or yarn.

Helpful details

Persuasive Essay

A **persuasive essay** expresses an opinion about something and shows why that opinion makes sense. The writer tries to get the reader to agree with that opinion.

How to Write a Persuasive Essay

- Begin by getting your audience's attention and by stating your opinion.
- Offer three reasons for your view. Give each reason its own paragraph, and use facts and details to support it.
- Use emotional words to persuade your reader.
- Give the strongest reason last.
- Write a conclusion. Restate your opinion, and then call upon the reader to take action.

What, Me Help?

Attention-getting opening and opinion

Do you ever think about people in your community who need help? "What can I do?" you might ask. "I don't have any money. I'm just a kid." There are many ways you can help others—if you're willing to volunteer.

First reason and support

Volunteering doesn't cost anything but time. Take a look at the way you spend your time. If you add up the time you waste, you may find several hours a week that you could use to help someone. The help can be something simple. For example, you might give an elderly neighbor a hand with gardening jobs. You might form a classroom "clean team" to straighten things up once or twice a week. You might read to a younger sister or brother. There are all kinds of things that you could do!

Volunteering can also be educational. Depending on your volunteer job, you might get to know new people. These people might have interesting stories to tell you about themselves and their families. You also might learn new skills—skills that could be useful to you in the future.

Most important, volunteering helps you personally. I know, because it has happened to me. By volunteering, I learned to care more about other people and to be more understanding. I like and value myself more because I help others.

By volunteering, you can make a difference, help others, and help yourself. Why not look around, find a job that needs to be done, and then volunteer to do it?

Second reason and support

Most important reason and support

Restated opinion and call to action

Comparison/Contrast Essay

A **comparison/contrast essay** is one kind of informative essay. The writer explains how two things are similar and different.

How to Write a Comparison/Contrast Essay
• Write an interesting introduction. End the introductory paragraph by stating the main idea of the essay.
• Present your main points in a logical order. Group similarities and differences together.
• Use transition words and phrases to help make similarities and differences clear.
• Write an interesting conclusion.

Cats or Dogs?

Interesting introduction

Main idea

Describe the ways in which the subjects are alike.

Picture this: Your parents finally have agreed to bring a pet into the family. Your sister wants a cat, but you want a dog. Your mom says that it has to be a family decision. Dogs and cats are alike in some ways and different in others. Here are some facts that may help you make the choice.

Both cats and dogs require special care. They must be fed twice a day with healthful pet food from a supermarket or pet supply store. Both kinds of pets also need checkups with a veterinarian. Cats and dogs should be groomed regularly, especially if they have long hair. Exercise is important for pets, too. Before choosing a pet, remember that you will need to spend time and money on either a cat or a dog.

Choosing between a cat and a dog may depend on the differences between these kinds of animals. Many dogs are playful and friendly, so they make good pals. They often love to romp in the park or wrestle with their owners. Cats, on the other hand, are more independent. They enjoy and return affection in a quieter way. Dogs can be taught to stay, sit, and roll over. Cats are more difficult to train. A dog will stay in a fenced yard, while a cat would climb over the fence. Both animals, however, can live peacefully in the house, and some people prefer to keep their animals indoors most of the time.

Whether your new pet barks or meows, it will be an important part of your family. Treat your pet well, and it will give you many happy times.

Describe the ways in which the subjects are different.

Transition

Interesting ending

Research Report

The purpose of a **research report** is to inform readers. To write a research report, the writer gathers information about a topic, using several sources. The writer takes notes and makes an outline before drafting the report.

How to Write a Research Report

- Choose an interesting topic and title.
- Write a paragraph that introduces the topic and gives the main idea of the report.
- Write one paragraph about each subtopic in your outline.
- Focus on facts, but put information in your own words.
- Give credit for facts, ideas, and quotations. Page 533 of your Handbook shows how to cite sources at the end of a report.

Interesting title →

Attention-getting introduction →

Topic and main idea →

Those Amazing Chameleons!

What looks like a little dinosaur, has a very long tongue, and can change color? It's an amazing reptile called the chameleon. There are about eighty species of chameleons in the world. Chameleons like warm places. In fact, most chameleons live in trees in southern Africa and Madagascar. A chameleon has many unique ways of catching food and of staying safe.

Most chameleons range from seven to ten inches long, but some grow to two feet in size. Their bodies are flattened from side to side. The eyes bulge out and can move in separate directions. The males of some kinds of chameleons have spines or crests decorating their heads. Others have as many as three long horns popping out from the top.

The chameleon catches food with its sticky tongue, which can be almost as long as its body. It keeps this tongue curled up in its mouth until a bug passes by. Then the chameleon flicks its tongue out to capture the insect.

When many people think of the chameleon, they think of its ability to change color. This lizard does not change to blend in with its environment. The color change is a reaction to light, temperature, and the chameleon's emotions. When the chameleon senses danger, its nervous system signals skin cells to change color. Some chameleons become green, yellow, or brown. Others become more red.

Chameleons also can change their shape. If faced by an enemy, they try to look larger. They may puff out their throats or wave their head flaps. If this doesn't work, they may charge the enemy, hissing like a snake and snapping their jaws.

Chameleons are interesting lizards with unique ways of getting food and of staying safe. If you saw a chameleon, you might think it looked like a small dinosaur. However, you could look right at a chameleon and never even see it.

Each subtopic is discussed in its own paragraph.

Information from sources is expressed in the writer's own words.

Interesting conclusion

Story

In a **story,** a writer describes made-up characters and events. A story has characters, plot, and a setting.

> ### How to Write a Story
>
> - Write a beginning that will interest the reader.
> - Write the middle of the story. Show a problem that the characters must solve.
> - Give the events in time order, from first to last.
> - At the end, show how the characters solve the problem.
> - Include dialogue to help make the story lifelike.

An Open-and-Shut Case

Interesting beginning →

Last May, Sonia and I chose the perfect Mother's Day gift. We decided to wash Mom's car. She would be going to an important business meeting the next day, and we wanted the car to look its best. Our little sister Ella asked to help, but she always causes disasters when she helps. We told her that we would do it on our own, and Ella stomped off.

Show the problem. →

Events in time order →

When Ella was busy inside, we began our job. First, I made sure all the car windows were shut. Sonia went to the side of the house to hook up the hose. After Sonia filled the pail with soap and water, she began hosing the car down. I moved to the opposite side of the car and bent down to soap the front fender. Zap! I felt a blast of water part my hair. "Yeow!" I yelled, jumping up. "You did that on purpose!" I flung a sponge in her direction, and it skidded over the hood. It left a beautiful clean streak. Sonia picked up the sponge and slid it back, leaving another clean streak. "Wow!" I said. "This is pretty easy. I thought washing Mom's car would be harder than this." We played with the sponge in this way for several minutes, but then it disappeared. We looked underneath the car, on top of the car, and in the bushes. Then we found it.

Dialogue

"Oh, no!" Sonia cried. "Lili, how could you have forgotten to check the windows?" The wet, soapy, filthy sponge lay in a brown pool of water on the white car seat. Mom had a blanket and boxes of papers on the back seat, too. They were now drenched. I knew I'd checked the windows. Sonia and I looked at each other, feeling sick.

Mom came home just then and walked up to us, smiling. Then she saw what had happened. We thought she would be very upset, but we apologized, and Mom seemed to understand. Just as she began to ask "Where's Ella?" we all heard giggling from the back seat.

Use the ending to solve the problem.

Ella slid out from under the blanket, her hair soaking wet. We all laughed as she yelled, "Happy Mother's Day!"

News Story

A **news story** tells the facts about something that has happened recently.

How to Write a News Story

- Start with a headline, or title, that gets the reader's attention.
- Tell about a recent event that is interesting and important.
- Answer the questions *Who? What? When? Where? Why?* and *How?* in the first paragraph.
- Write detail sentences that give more information about the event.
- Add a concluding sentence.

Important event →

Who? What? When? Where? Why? and How? →

Details about the topic →

Fifth Graders Help Flood Victims

Students at Lyndon B. Johnson Elementary School are collecting bottles and cans to raise money for the Red Cross Flood Relief Fund. Beginning this Friday, March 5, the school custodian, Mr. Victor Bates, will accept plastic bags containing clean bottles and cans that can be returned for a deposit. The collection will continue each Friday morning from 8 to 9 a.m. until the end of April.

This project began in Mrs. Lalo's fifth-grade class. The students were talking about the recent floods in Louisiana. Hector

Gonzalez was upset that many people lost all their belongings when their homes were flooded. He suggested that the class find a way to raise money to help these people.

The project now involves the whole school. Everyone is busy making posters and fliers. Hector and Lisa Trang, another fifth grader, are the leaders. They have spoken on radio station WKVE on the "Good Morning" show about their project. The students hope everyone in Greenville will contribute to the collection.

Details about the topic

Conclusion

Play

The purpose of a **play** is to entertain an audience. In a play a writer tells a story through *dialogue*, the words that the characters say. The actors use movements and gestures as well as their voices to help make the story clear. *Stage directions* tell what the stage should look like and how the actors should move and speak.

How to Write a Play

- Choose an interesting story idea.
- Write dialogue that sounds like real people talking.
- Write the name of the character in front of his or her words. Start a new line for each new speaker.
- Include stage directions to set the scene and to tell the actors how to move and speak.

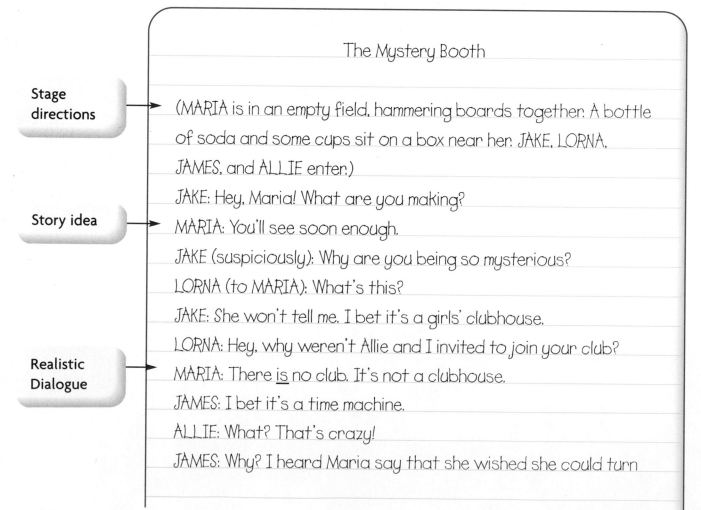

Stage directions →

The Mystery Booth

(MARIA is in an empty field, hammering boards together. A bottle of soda and some cups sit on a box near her. JAKE, LORNA, JAMES, and ALLIE enter.)

JAKE: Hey, Maria! What are you making?

Story idea →

MARIA: You'll see soon enough.

JAKE (suspiciously): Why are you being so mysterious?

LORNA (to MARIA): What's this?

JAKE: She won't tell me. I bet it's a girls' clubhouse.

LORNA: Hey, why weren't Allie and I invited to join your club?

Realistic Dialogue →

MARIA: There is no club. It's not a clubhouse.

JAMES: I bet it's a time machine.

ALLIE: What? That's crazy!

JAMES: Why? I heard Maria say that she wished she could turn back time and study harder for that math test we had yesterday.

JAKE: You both sound silly. It must be a doghouse.

ALLIE: We sound silly? As far as I know, dogs don't grow to be six feet tall.

MARIA (laughing): It's not a clubhouse, time machine, or doghouse. Your guesses are all ridiculous! It's a talking booth.

JAMES: How can a booth talk? That's silly!

LORNA, ALLIE, and JAKE: Yeah!

MARIA: The booth doesn't talk—we do. My talking booth will be a place for people to meet and talk.

JAKE: That's the silliest idea yet! Why would anyone want to meet and talk in the middle of nowhere?

MARIA: Well, it's not even finished, and already five of us are here talking about six-foot-tall dogs, time machines, and clubs that don't exist. (Everyone nods and smiles.) It may be silly, but I guess it works. Soda, anyone?

Stage directions

Business Letter

In a **business letter** a writer may request information, order something, apply for a job, or express an opinion.

How to Write a Business Letter

- The heading contains your address and the date.
- The inside address contains the name, title, and address of the person to whom you're writing.
- The greeting is followed by a colon (:).
- Write the message in the body of the letter.
- Write a closing, followed by a comma (,).
- Under your signature, type your name.

Heading →

7343 Eileen Street
Stanton, CA 92871
June 21, 20—

Inside Address →

Mr. Jason Williams
Recreational Director
Oak Crest Park
28 Blazer Way
Westminster, CA 92683

Greeting →

Dear Mr. Williams:

Body →

Please consider keeping the recreational center at Oak Crest Park open longer. During the past school year, my friends and I have visited the center often. We do crafts, play basketball, and study nature there.

Message is direct, formal, and polite. →

Now that it is summertime, could you keep the doors open from 9 A.M. to 9 P.M.? Most of us stay outside on summer evenings because it doesn't get dark as soon.

I'm sure that everyone who uses the park would appreciate such a summer schedule. Thank you for your time.

Closing →

Sincerely,

Signature →

Lakisha Hilton
Lakisha Hilton

Friendly Letter with Envelope

In a **friendly letter** a writer shares personal thoughts and feelings with a friend. Look at the model below to see how a friendly letter differs from a business letter.

3467 Sycamore Street
Atlanta, GA 30300
October 14, 20—

← Heading

Dear Andy,

← Greeting, followed by a comma

I was happy to get your letter! The kids here are nice, but I miss you and Kathy. Does she still play those goofy tunes on her flute during breaks in band? I've joined the band here at Franklin Elementary. Luckily, the director, Mr. Ramirez, is as nice as Mrs. Choi was last year. He has us practice a lot so that we feel more confident playing at our school assemblies.

← Body

← Language is conversational and friendly.

Write back soon, Andy.

← Closing

Your friend,
José

← Signature

Mail your letter in an envelope like this one:

José Moreno
3467 Sycamore Street
Atlanta, GA 30300

← Your address

← A stamp

USA

Andy DeForest
45 Winslet Avenue
Seattle, WA 98100

← Your friend's address

Poems: Rhymed and Unrhymed

Creating a **poem** is one way a writer might choose to describe something or to express feelings about a subject. Word choice is very important, especially if the poem is to have rhythm and rhyme. Poets often use **figures of speech** such as similes, metaphors, and personification to create interesting images.

Examples:

Simile: Your eyes are <u>as blue as the ocean</u>.
Metaphor: Every turn on our path <u>was a surprise package waiting to be opened</u>.
Personification: The flowers <u>lifted their faces</u> toward the sun.

How to Write a Poem

- Choose a form for your poem.
- Use strong, specific words and sensory details.
- To help describe your subject or feelings, use figures of speech.

In a **rhyming poem**, the ends of some or all of the lines rhyme. This rhyming poem has a regular rhythm as well.

First Snow

At bedtime it began to snow.
We peered into the night.
Our faces to the windowpane,
We shivered with delight.

When morning came, the world was new.
The snow lay like whipped cream.
The sky was an amazing blue.
We stepped into a dream.

Sensory details

Simile

Metaphor

A **limerick** is a funny verse with five lines. Notice the rhyme and rhythm pattern.

> There once was a young cow named Sue,
> Who forgot how to say the word <u>moo</u>!
> She said, "Golly gee,
> This is awful for me!
> I'll have to make up something new!"

Not all poems rhyme. There are many kinds of **unrhymed poems**. Here are two of them:

A **haiku** is a short, three-line poem. Lines 1 and 3 usually have five syllables. Line 2 usually has seven syllables.

> The snow turns to rain.
> Deep down, the tulip bulbs sprout.
> Soon it will be spring.

Free verse does not follow a set pattern.

> ### Concert in the Park
>
> I sit on the bench.
> The sun warms me like a blanket.   ← Simile
> Throwing crumbs to the noisy pigeons,
> I am a conductor.
> They are the orchestra.   ← Metaphor

503

Invitation and Thank-You Note

Two specific kinds of friendly letters are an **invitation** and a **thank-you note**. Here is an example of an invitation.

Heading

Greeting

Body tells *what, when,* and *where.*

Closing

Signature

> 225 Main Street
> Boulder, Colorado 80300
> April 16, 20—
>
> Dear Ali,
>
>   Please come to my birthday party on Saturday, April 30. The party will be at my house at 12:30. We will have pizza and play games.
>
>   Please let me know if you can come. My phone number is 555-3602.
>
>   Your friend,
>   Felicia

A thank-you note should tell specifically what the writer is thanking the person for. Here is an example of the body of a thank-you note. The other parts of a thank-you note are the same as those of a friendly letter.

Body tells *what, why,* and *how.*

>   Thank you very much for the birthday gift. The colored sparkle pens are great! I have already used them to decorate several cards. I love the watercolor paints and paper, too.

Telephone Message and Form

When you take a **telephone message**, first write the name of the person the message is for. Then write down the name of the caller, the date and time of the call, any message, and a phone number.

Telephone Message

For _Lucy_ — Name of recipient

From _Devon_ — Name of caller

Date _10/4/20—_ Time _5:00 p.m._ — Time

He wants to know if you will be going to Anna's play. He can get you a ticket. His dad will drive you, but they're leaving around 6:00 p.m. Call him tonight at (718)555-6044.

Nadine — Person who took message

— Date

— Message

A **form** is a document that requires a person to write information in blanks. Read the entire form before filling in the blanks. Check over your form when you have finished. Make sure you have filled it out completely.

Dimmit County Public Library

Please print. — Note whether you should print your information.

Isabella	E.	Alvarez
First Name	**Middle Initial**	**Last Name**
3/27/1993		(830) 555-2218
Date of Birth		**Daytime Phone Number**
16432 Pena Street		
Street Address		
Carizzo Springs	Texas	78834
City	**State**	**Zip Code**

Provide the information requested.

Have you ever had a Dimmit County Library Card?   Yes ☐   No ☒

Writing Rubrics

Expressive Writing: *Personal Narrative*

The best personal narratives show all the points on the checklist below. Here is how you can use it:

Before writing Look at the checklist to remind yourself of how to make your personal narrative the best it can be.

During writing Check your draft against the list to see how you can make your personal narrative better.

After writing Check your finished work against the list to see if it shows all the points of the best personal narratives.

SCORE OF 4 ★★★★

★ The narrative fits the purpose for writing. The audience it was written for would enjoy it.

★ The narrative has a clear beginning that introduces the topic, a middle that tells events in order, and a logical ending.

★ The narrative uses the first-person point of view and reveals how the writer feels about the events.

★ The narrative has description and rich details that help the reader visualize the events. The ideas are interesting.

★ The narrative has interesting words and phrases, such as specific nouns, vivid verbs, sensory words, and figurative language.

★ The sentences are written in a variety of ways to make the writing interesting to read.

★ The narrative has few errors in spelling, grammar, and punctuation.

What other points do you think are important in a personal narrative?

Informative Writing: *How-to Essay*

The best how-to essays show all the points on the checklist below. Here is how you can use it:

Before writing Look at the checklist to remind yourself of how to make your how-to essay the best it can be.

During writing Check your draft against the list to see how you can make your how-to essay better.

After writing Check your finished work against the list to see if it shows all the points of the best how-to essays.

SCORE OF 4 ★★★★

* The essay fits the purpose for writing. The audience it was written for would understand it.

* The essay has a clear beginning that introduces the topic, a middle that gives directions about the topic in a logical order, and an ending that summarizes or draws a conclusion.

* The essay uses transitions and signal words to help make the sequence of steps clear.

* The essay has description and details that add information about the directions. The ideas are interesting.

* The essay has interesting words and phrases, especially specific nouns.

* The sentences are written in a variety of ways to make the writing interesting to read.

* The essay has few errors in spelling, grammar, and punctuation.

What other points do you think are important in a how-to essay?

Writing Rubrics

Persuasive Writing: *Persuasive Essay*

The best persuasive essays show all the points on the checklist below. Here is how you can use it:

Before writing Look at the checklist to remind yourself of how to make your persuasive essay the best it can be.

During writing Check your draft against the list to see how you can make your persuasive essay better.

After writing Check your finished work against the list to see if it shows all the points of the best persuasive essays.

SCORE OF 4 ★★★★

★ The essay fits the purpose for writing. It was written to persuade a particular audience. The writer cares about the topic.

★ The essay has a clear statement of opinion at the beginning, a middle that gives logical reasons that support the opinion, and an ending that restates the opinion and calls for action.

★ The essay has details, description, or examples that give more information about the reasons.

★ The essay has interesting words and phrases, such as specific nouns, vivid verbs, and emotional language.

★ The sentences are written in a variety of ways to make the writing interesting.

★ The essay has few errors in spelling, grammar, and punctuation.

What other points do you think are important in a persuasive essay?

Informative Writing:
Comparison/Contrast Essay

The best comparison/contrast essays show all the points on the checklist below. Here is how you can use it:

Before writing Look at the checklist to remind yourself of how to make your essay the best it can be.

During writing Check your draft against the list to see how you can make your essay better.

After writing Check your finished work against the list to see if it shows all the points of the best comparison/contrast essays.

SCORE OF 4 ★★★★

★ The essay fits the purpose for writing. The audience it was written for would understand it.

★ The essay has a clear beginning that introduces the topic, a middle that logically classifies similarities and differences, and an ending that summarizes or draws a conclusion.

★ The essay has description and rich details that add information about the topic. The ideas are interesting.

★ The essay has transition words and phrases that help the reader understand how the ideas are related.

★ The sentences are written in a variety of ways to make the writing interesting to read.

★ The essay has few errors in spelling, grammar, and punctuation.

What other points do you think are important in a comparison/ contrast essay?

Writing Rubrics

Informative Writing: *Research Report*

The best research reports show all the points on the checklist below. Here is how you can use it:

Before writing Look at the checklist to remind yourself of how to make your research report the best it can be.

During writing Check your draft against the list to see how you can make your research report better.

After writing Check your finished work against the list to see if it shows all the points of the best research reports.

SCORE OF 4 ★★★★

★ The research report fits the purpose for writing. The audience it was written for would understand it.

★ The report has a clear beginning that introduces the topic. The middle sections give logically organized information and ideas about the topic. The ending summarizes or draws a conclusion.

★ The report presents ideas and information from a variety of sources. The writer uses his or her own words.

★ The report has description, rich details, or narrative parts that add information about the topic. The ideas are interesting.

★ The report has transition words and phrases that help the reader understand how the ideas are related.

★ The sentences are written in a variety of ways to make the writing interesting to read.

★ The report has few errors in spelling, grammar, and punctuation.

What other points do you think are important in a research report?

Expressive Writing: *Story*

The best stories show all the points on the checklist below. Here is how you can use it:

Before writing Look at the checklist to remind yourself of how to make your story the best it can be.

During writing Check your draft against the list to see how you can make your story better.

After writing Check your finished work against the list to see if it shows all the points of the best stories.

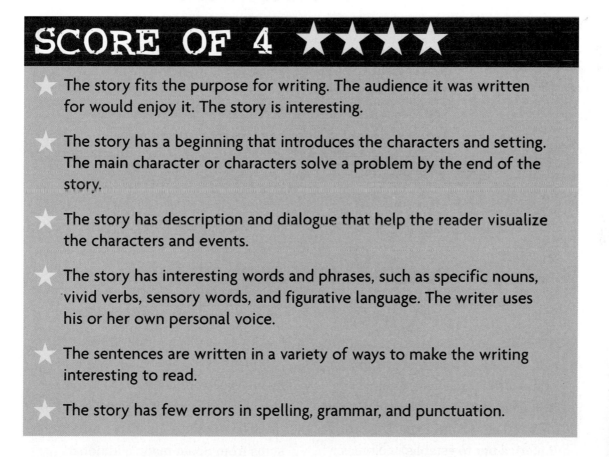

SCORE OF 4 ★★★★

★ The story fits the purpose for writing. The audience it was written for would enjoy it. The story is interesting.

★ The story has a beginning that introduces the characters and setting. The main character or characters solve a problem by the end of the story.

★ The story has description and dialogue that help the reader visualize the characters and events.

★ The story has interesting words and phrases, such as specific nouns, vivid verbs, sensory words, and figurative language. The writer uses his or her own personal voice.

★ The sentences are written in a variety of ways to make the writing interesting to read.

★ The story has few errors in spelling, grammar, and punctuation.

What other points do you think are important in a story?

Study Skills and Strategies

Skimming

Skimming is a high-speed reading strategy. When skimming, a reader reads quickly to gain an idea of the subject of the selection. This helps a reader see whether the information he or she is looking for is in the selection. This selection is from a history book.

UNIT 2

European Exploration in the Americas

Many European countries explored the New World, which later became known as North and South America. Portugal, Spain, France, the Netherlands, and Britain originally were looking for a short water route to the riches of Asia—spices and silks. Later, though, these countries established colonies, or settlements, in the newly explored areas.

> Unit 2 is about the establishment of European colonies in North and South America.

Chapter 1

Exploring North America

> Chapter 1 is about which European countries claimed land in North America, and why.

In this chapter, you will learn which European countries claimed land in North America, especially lands that now are part of the United States. You will see where those claims were and why more than one country often wanted the same land. Finally, you will discover why European nations decided not just to explore North America but to establish colonies.

> Section 1 is about Spain's claim to land and Spain's explorers.

➤ Section 1

Spain Is First

Eventually Sweden, France, the Netherlands, Britain, and Russia all claimed lands in what is now the United States. (See the map on page 5 for the locations of those claims.) Spain, however, was the first European nation to do so.

On his first voyage across the Atlantic Ocean in 1492, Christopher Columbus (who was Italian but was supported by the king and queen of Spain) discovered islands in the Caribbean. On his third voyage, he discovered South America. Other ships from Spain made additional voyages of exploration—and additional discoveries. For example, while searching for the legendary Fountain of Youth, Juan Ponce de León discovered Florida in 1513.

Scanning

Scanning is another high-speed reading strategy. Readers scan a selection to locate specific information.

What is the first step in preparing for a good shoot?

Preparing for an Adventure

You want to know how filmmakers prepare for work in the African bush.

Janice and Juanita Estes are sisters. They are also wildlife photographers. They make films in the African bush, or wild. They usually film animals, such as elephants and lions. Planning is critical for the success of a shoot. Not only are their assignments far from any source of supplies, but they usually stay in the African bush for months at a time while they film. If they forget or break something, a replacement is either hours away or not available at all.

Long before they start shooting, the Estes sisters make a list of everything they think they will need. They read over their list regularly and add to it as they think of other things. The Estes sisters have to be prepared for unexpected situations that may leave them stranded far from help. During a shoot, therefore, they carry extra food. They also have equipment, such as shovels, jacks, and winches, in case their vehicle gets stuck. Extra tires and tools for repairs are necessities, too.

Once they have everything they will need, they sort through it. In order to have enough room for water, they are only able to take seventy pounds of supplies each. This includes film equipment, tools, camping gear, clothes, food, and anything else they might need while they are in the bush. It is difficult to make decisions to leave things behind. Fortunately, their experience with previous trips makes choosing the right equipment easier. Finally, after months of careful planning, they are ready to go!

How do filmmakers decide what they will take?

How do filmmakers decide what they will need?

Using Book Parts

The pages in the front of a book that have small Roman numerals are called the **front matter**. Usually the front matter includes a **title page**, a **copyright page**, and a **table of contents**.

The **title page** shows the title, the author, the publisher, and the city or cities where the publisher has offices.

This is the title of the book.

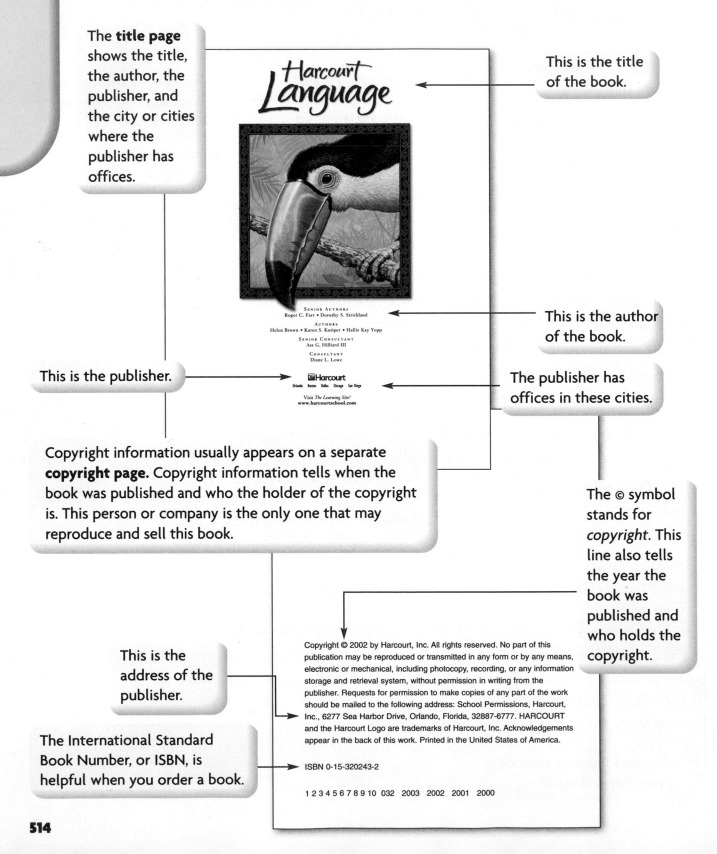

This is the author of the book.

This is the publisher.

The publisher has offices in these cities.

Copyright information usually appears on a separate **copyright page**. Copyright information tells when the book was published and who the holder of the copyright is. This person or company is the only one that may reproduce and sell this book.

The © symbol stands for *copyright*. This line also tells the year the book was published and who holds the copyright.

This is the address of the publisher.

The International Standard Book Number, or ISBN, is helpful when you order a book.

The **table of contents** tells what is in the book. It may list chapters, units, maps, and illustrations, as well as the glossary and index.

Contents

Illustrations

This book is divided into chapters. The first chapter begins on page 1.

This section lists the major **illustrations**, or pictures, in the book and the pages on which they are found.

Publishers often include a glossary and an index in the back of the book.

The **glossary** defines special words in the text that the reader might not understand. The words are listed in alphabetical order, and most words are followed by a phonetic spelling that shows the **pronunciation** of the word.

pronunciation

glossary entry

definition

cell [sel] The tiny basic structural unit of all living matter.

cerebellum [ser′ə·bel′əm] The part of the brain that is at the back of the head and that controls coordination of the muscles.

cerebrum [sər′ē′brəm] The largest and most highly developed part of the brain. It controls voluntary movement and all conscious mental activities.

The **index** lists the information in the book in alphabetical order. The page numbers show where you can find the information.

entry words

page numbers where you can find information

Using a Dictionary

A **dictionary** is a reference book that lists the words in a language and gives information about them. A dictionary tells what the words mean and how they are pronounced.

How a Dictionary Works

Words in a dictionary are arranged in alphabetical order.

There are two words at the top of the page called **guide words**. The guide words name the first word and the last word on the page. All the words listed on that page will come alphabetically between the two guide words.

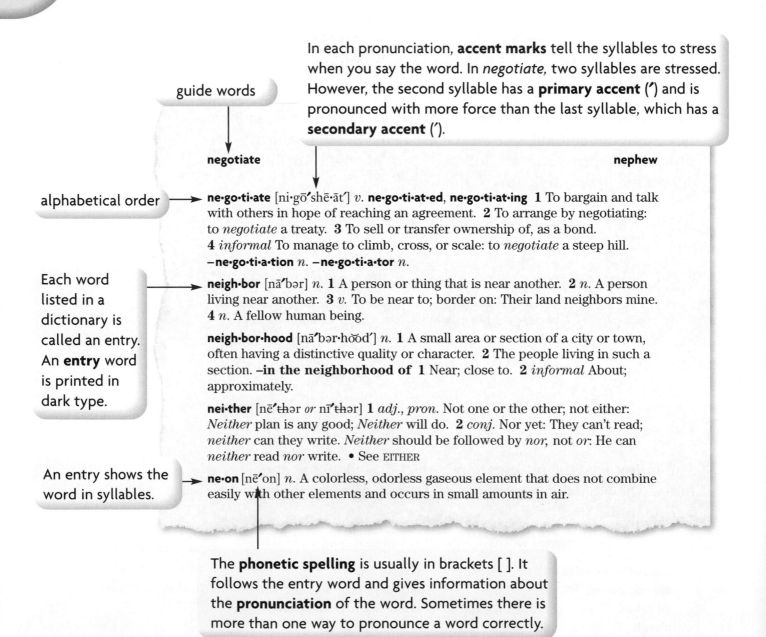

In each pronunciation, **accent marks** tell the syllables to stress when you say the word. In *negotiate,* two syllables are stressed. However, the second syllable has a **primary accent** (′) and is pronounced with more force than the last syllable, which has a **secondary accent** (′).

guide words

negotiate   **nephew**

alphabetical order → **ne·go·ti·ate** [ni·gō′shē·āt′] *v.* **ne·go·ti·at·ed, ne·go·ti·at·ing** **1** To bargain and talk with others in hope of reaching an agreement. **2** To arrange by negotiating: to *negotiate* a treaty. **3** To sell or transfer ownership of, as a bond. **4** *informal* To manage to climb, cross, or scale: to *negotiate* a steep hill. **–ne·go·ti·a·tion** *n.* **–ne·go·ti·a·tor** *n.*

Each word listed in a dictionary is called an entry. An **entry** word is printed in dark type.

→ **neigh·bor** [nā′bər] *n.* **1** A person or thing that is near another. **2** *n.* A person living near another. **3** *v.* To be near to; border on: Their land neighbors mine. **4** *n.* A fellow human being.

neigh·bor·hood [nā′bər·hŏŏd′] *n.* **1** A small area or section of a city or town, often having a distinctive quality or character. **2** The people living in such a section. **–in the neighborhood of** **1** Near; close to. **2** *informal* About; approximately.

nei·ther [nē′thər *or* nī′thər] **1** *adj., pron.* Not one or the other; not either: *Neither* plan is any good; *Neither* will do. **2** *conj.* Nor yet: They can't read; *neither* can they write. *Neither* should be followed by *nor,* not *or:* He can *neither* read *nor* write. • See EITHER

An entry shows the word in syllables. → **ne·on** [nē′on] *n.* A colorless, odorless gaseous element that does not combine easily with other elements and occurs in small amounts in air.

The **phonetic spelling** is usually in brackets [ ]. It follows the entry word and gives information about the **pronunciation** of the word. Sometimes there is more than one way to pronounce a word correctly.

The abbreviation following the pronunciation tells the **part of speech.** Most dictionaries use these abbreviations:

n.	noun	*pron.*	pronoun
v.	verb	*prep.*	preposition
adj.	adjective	*conj.*	conjunction
adv.	adverb	*interj.*	interjection

The **definitions,** or meanings, follow the part of speech. A word often has more than one definition. Each definition is numbered. The first meaning is usually the one that is used most often.

painting [pān′ting] *n.* **1.** The act, art, or occupation of a person who paints. **2.** A picture made with paint.

a	add	i	it	o͝o	took	oi	oil
ā	ace	ī	ice	o͞o	pool	ou	pout
â	care	o	odd	u	up	ng	ring
ä	palm	ō	open	û	burn	th	thin
e	end	ô	order	yo͞o	fuse	th	this
ē	equal					zh	vision

ə = { a in *above*   e in *sicken*   i in *possible*
       o in *melon*   u in *circus*

763

A **pronunciation key** appears on every other page. It uses familiar words to show the sounds that the pronunciation symbols represent.

Using the Internet

You hear about it in movies, on television, and from your friends. Website addresses are on most of the commercials you see. Everyone seems to be **online**. What exactly is the **Internet**? The Internet—often called the Net—is the largest computer network in the world.

A **network** is a group of computers that are hooked together. The Internet is the "network of networks," with about 150 million people using it. In fact, every continent on Earth, and almost every country, is connected to the Internet.

E-mail

Once you are online, there are many services you can use. The most used service on the Internet is **electronic mail (e-mail)**. E-mail lets people send messages in a much faster and more convenient way than regular mail. People use e-mail for both business and personal mail.

E-mail Addresses

When you subscribe to an Internet server, you get an e-mail address. This address allows you to send and receive mail. In order to send someone e-mail, you must have his or her e-mail address.

Internet addresses have two parts that are separated by an @, which means "at." The first part of the address

From: Jane Doe
To: Johndoe55@provider.com
Subject:

an e-mail address

is called the **mailbox** and is often your personal or **user** name. The part after the @ is the **domain**. This is generally the name of your Internet service provider. The last three letters of the domain are called the zone. The **zone** is like a ZIP code or an area code. The zone tells you what kind of site you are visiting. There are many different zones, but here are a few of the most common:

- .com–Commercial company
- .edu–Educational site
- .net–Networking company

Online Communication

Online chat lets you communicate immediately with anyone on the Net. You can "chat" with several people at the same time or with just one person. When you chat, you can read what other people are writing and then respond immediately. The online area where you chat is called a **chat room**.

Search Engines

The Internet is a great source of information. You can download, or copy onto your computer, books, newspaper stories, games, and much more. For a detailed search of the Net, you will want to use a **search engine**. Your choice of a search engine will depend on what you are looking for. You may wish to use more than one. You type **keywords** into the search box to find information.

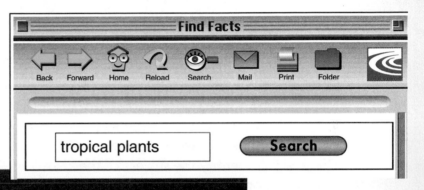

Internet Safety

- It is important to protect your privacy when surfing the Net. Do not provide anyone online with information about yourself or your family.
- Remember that you do not really know the people you "meet" in chat rooms or through e-mail. Do not agree to meet with someone you have met online without talking with your parents or guardians about it.
- Make sure your parents or guardians know your password so that they can get into your account if you need help. Do not give out your password to anyone else.
- If you get a scary or upsetting e-mail from someone, do not respond to it. Report it to your parents, guardians, or teacher.

Using an Encyclopedia

An **encyclopedia** contains information about many topics. Most encyclopedias come in a **set,** or group, of books. Each book in the set is called a **volume.** The volumes are numbered and arranged in alphabetical order by subject.

A-B 1 C-D 2 E-F 3 G-H 4 I-J 5 K-L 6 M-N 7 O-P 8 Q-R 9 S-T 10 U-W 11 X-Z 12

At the top of every page are **guide words.** Guide words identify the subject of the first article on a left-hand page and of the last article on a right-hand page.

Stained glass   821

Entry words may be printed in **boldface** or *italics*.

Information about a subject is given in an **article**.

Stagecoach, a horse-drawn coach used to carry passengers and mail on a regular route. Sometimes it also carried freight. The first long stage line was established about 1670 between London and Edinburgh, Scotland, a distance of 392 miles (631 kilometers).

Using an Encyclopedia Index

Most encyclopedias include an **index**, or alphabetical list of subjects. The index usually appears at the end of the final volume in the set. The purpose of the index is to help readers locate information quickly. A typical encyclopedia index contains the following kinds of entries:

Subjects are the titles of articles in the encyclopedia. Encyclopedia articles can be between one paragraph and several pages long.

Index

Topics name the kinds of information in a longer article.

Subtopics name more specific kinds of information given in each topic. In the index, subtopics usually appear in an indented list beneath the topics.

Texas 18-127 *with pictures and maps*
    cattle trails **4**-285
    cowboys **5**-306
    disasters **6**-15, 17
  Economic Activities 18-128
    oil production **14**-569
    ranching **15**-508
    wool **19**-543
  Geography 18-130
    Great Plains **8**-227
    Red River **15**-42
    Rio Grande River **16**-60
    See also **South Central States.**

History 18-141
  Alamo, the **1**-289
  Austin, Stephen Fuller **2**-385
  Houston, Samuel **9**-111
  Mexican War **12**-156
  Santa Anna, Antonio
    López de **16**-340
National Park System 18-141
  Big Bend National Park **3**-135
  Padre Island National
    Seashore **14**-235
  San José Mission National
    Historic Site **16**-333

The **volume** and **page number** tell where you can find the information about a subject, a topic, or a subtopic.

Cross-references name other articles with information related to the topic. The expression *See also* often appears before a cross-reference.

Using Periodicals and Newspapers

A **periodical** is a work that is published at regular times. **Magazines** and **newspapers** are two kinds of periodicals. A periodical may come out every day, week, or month. Others are printed quarterly, or four times a year. Each publication of a periodical is a new **issue**. A monthly magazine, for example, has a June issue, a July issue, and so on.

Pieces of writing in a magazine are called **articles**. For instance, a report on a new type of medicine is an article. Each article focuses on one topic. Writers usually present facts in articles. At times, however, writers may entertain readers or state what they think about topics. Some magazines have articles on only one topic, such as news, sports, or science. Other magazines have articles on many kinds of topics.

The main parts of a magazine are the **cover page**, the **table of contents**, and the **articles**. The **cover page** is the front cover.

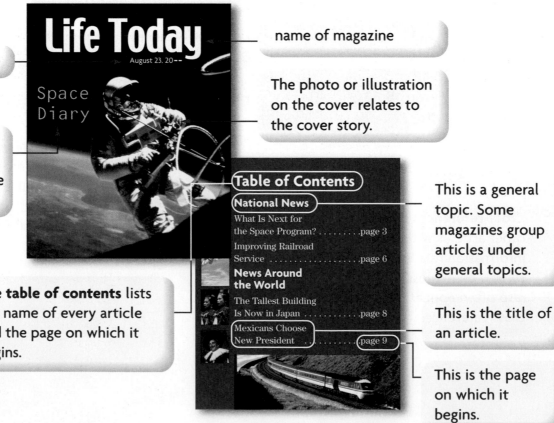

date of the issue

The **cover story** is the most important article in the issue.

The **table of contents** lists the name of every article and the page on which it begins.

name of magazine

The photo or illustration on the cover relates to the cover story.

This is a general topic. Some magazines group articles under general topics.

This is the title of an article.

This is the page on which it begins.

Life Today
August 23, 20--

Space Diary

Table of Contents

National News
What Is Next for
the Space Program? . . . . page 3
Improving Railroad
Service . . . . page 6
**News Around
the World**
The Tallest Building
Is Now in Japan . . . . page 8
Mexicans Choose
New President . . . . page 9

Periodicals are often more up-to-date than books, so when you are writing a report, you may want to use magazines. You can find the locations of articles in the *Readers' Guide to Periodical Literature*. First, look up the topic. Topics are in alphabetical order. Articles and their locations are listed under topics. Your library may also have such a guide on a computer.

Most **newspapers** are printed every day. In general, they tell about, or report, events that have just happened. Some newspapers, however, come out once a week. These papers often focus on local news and information.

The main parts of a newspaper are the **front page**, the **editorial page**, and the **features**. The most important articles are on the **front page**. They may be continued on pages inside the paper. Less important articles are also on inside pages.

People who run a newspaper write **editorials** about important topics in the news. An editorial tries to convince readers to support an opinion. Readers, too, can state their opinions by writing letters to the editor.

name of newspaper

date of the issue

This **banner headline** names the most important story of the issue. It is in the largest type on the page.

A **headline** appears in large type above an article. A **subhead** tells more about the article.

This story is not as important, so the headline is in smaller type.

This list names the major sections in a paper and tells the page on which each begins.

DAILY BULLETIN

May 16, 20--

Space Station Almost Completed

Last Materials Headed to Station

New School Okayed for Elm Street

U.S. Wins Gold at Olympics

Contents:
Editorials 12
TV and Entertainment 16
Comics 18
Crossword 19
Sports 22
Classified Ads 36

Using an Atlas

An **atlas** is a book of maps. Most atlases have different kinds of maps. **Political maps** show countries, regions, or states. They also show capitals, major cities, towns, and roads. **Physical maps** highlight natural features such as mountains, lakes, and rivers. **Population maps** use symbols to show how many people live in an area.

The **index** in the back of the book tells you the page or pages on which you can find places shown on the maps. The index may also list the meanings of abbreviations and symbols used in the atlas.

> Colors are used to show the height of different features on this physical map.

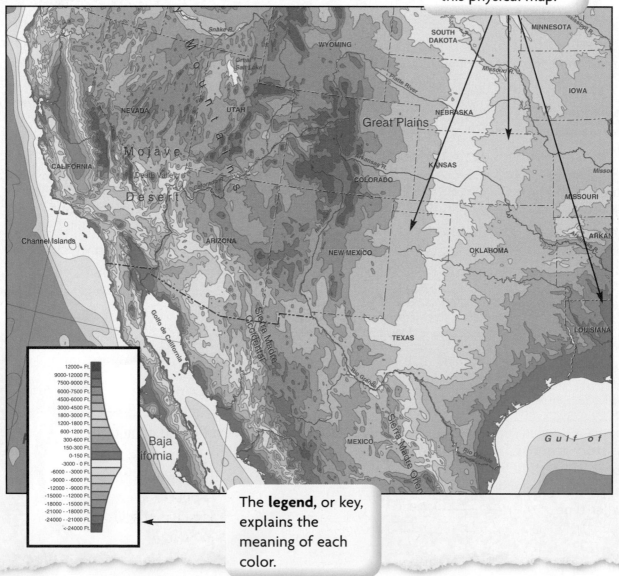

> The **legend,** or key, explains the meaning of each color.

Using an Almanac

An **almanac** is a book that contains basic facts about many subjects. In an almanac you can find facts about subjects such as population statistics, key information about the countries of the world, and information about famous people. Much of the information in an almanac appears in charts, tables, graphs, maps, or lists. Almanacs usually are updated and published yearly.

Almanacs contain a section on **Countries of the World**. The countries are listed in alphabetical order. A brief article describes each one. The article includes facts about that nation's people, government, economy, geography, and history.

Spain

Kingdom of Spain

People: Population: 39,133,996. **Age distrib.** (%):<15: 15.2; 65+: 16.3. **Pop. density:** 200 per sq. mi. **Urban:** 77%. **Ethnic groups:** Mix of Mediterranean and Nordic types. **Principal languages:** Castilian Spanish (official), Catalan, Galician, Basque. **Chief religion:** Roman Catholic 99%.

Geography: Area: 195,364 sq. mi. **Location:** in SW Europe. **Neighbors:** Portugal on W, France on N. **Topography:** The interior is a high, arid plateau broken by mountain ranges and river valleys. The NW is heavily watered; the S has lowlands and a Mediterranean climate. **Capital:** Madrid. **Cities:** Madrid 4,072,000; Barcelona 2,819,000; Valencia 751,000*.

Almanacs also have a section on **Business and the Economy**. This section usually tells about the United States. It has brief articles on important money-related matters. You can also find facts and figures about topics such as jobs, farm products, and businesses.

Fastest Growing Occupations, 1994–2005

Occupation	Growth, %
Personal and home care aides	119
Home health aides	102
Systems analysts	92
Computer engineers	90
Physical and corrective therapy assistants and aides	83
Electronic pagination systems workers	83
Occupational therapy assistants and aides	82
Physical therapists	80
Residential counselors	76
Human services workers	75
Manicurists	72
Medical assistants	69
Paralegals	59
Medical records technicians	56
Teachers, special education	53
Amusement and recreation attendants	52

Postal Abbreviations

Alabama AL	Idaho ID	Missouri MO	Pennsylvania PA
Alaska AK	Illinois IL	Montana MT	Rhode Island RI
Arizona AZ	Indiana IN	Nebraska NE	S. Carolina SC
Arkansas AR	Iowa IA	Nevada NV	S. Dakota SD
California CA	Kansas KS	New Hampshire NH	Tennessee TN
Colorado CO	Kentucky KY	New Jersey NJ	Texas TX
Connecticut CT	Louisiana LA	New Mexico NM	Utah UT
Delaware DE	Maine ME	New York NY	Vermont VT
District of	Maryland MD	North Carolina NC	Virginia VA
Columbia DC	Massachusetts MA	North Dakota ND	Washington WA
Florida FL	Michigan MI	Ohio OH	W. Virginia WV
Georgia GA	Minnesota MN	Oklahoma OK	Wisconsin WI
Hawaii HI	Mississippi MS	Oregon OR	Wyoming WY

Some almanacs include a section on **Postal Information**. This section gives postal rates and state abbreviations used in addresses.

Using a Map

A **map** is a drawing of a geographical area. All maps include **guides** that help a person understand the information that they contain. The map shown here is of California.

A **legend**, or key, explains what each symbol means.

Symbols, or special marks, identify places on the map. The shape of this symbol, for example, identifies Sacramento as the capital of California.

This symbol points out national parks.

The **compass rose** shows the directions *north*, *south*, *east*, and *west* on the map.

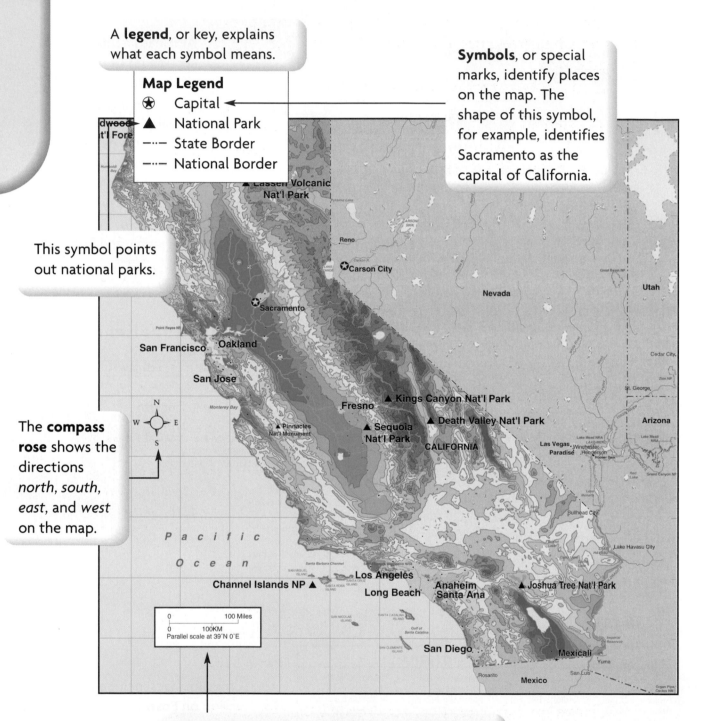

Map Legend
- ⊛ Capital
- ▲ National Park
- –··– State Border
- –·– National Border

The **distance scale** tells you how far apart places on the map really are. The spaces between the numbers on the line represent set distances on the map. For example, 3/4 inch on the map equals 100 miles in the real world.

Using Graphs

A **graph** is a special kind of chart. We use graphs to compare information about numbers. Two useful kinds of graphs are **bar graphs** and **line graphs**.

A bar graph uses bars, or rectangles, to represent numbers. The bars on a bar graph can run from side to side, or they can run up and down.

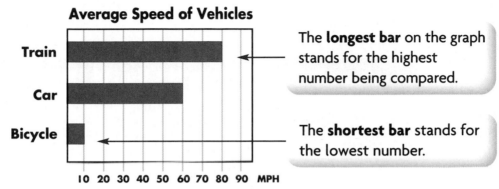

Average Speed of Vehicles

Train · Car · Bicycle

10 20 30 40 50 60 70 80 90 MPH

The **longest bar** on the graph stands for the highest number being compared.

The **shortest bar** stands for the lowest number.

A line graph uses points on a line to represent numbers.

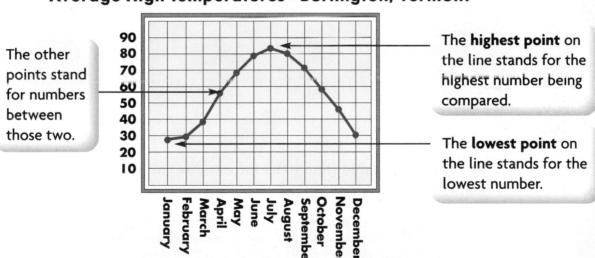

Average High Temperatures—Burlington, Vermont

The other points stand for numbers between those two.

The **highest point** on the line stands for the highest number being compared.

The **lowest point** on the line stands for the lowest number.

Follow these steps to read a graph.

1. Read the title at the top. This tells you what group of things is being compared.
2. Next, read the words or numbers on the side and at the bottom of the graph.
3. For bar graphs, find the number where each bar stops. That location tells you what number each bar represents.
4. For line graphs, find the height of each point on the line.

Using Tables

Tables are one way to show information visually. We call information arranged in columns and rows a table. *Columns* run up and down on a page. *Rows* run across a page. We often use tables to compare information about numbers.

This table shows distances between five cities.

Column

Row

Chicago is 936 miles from Dallas.

Traveling Across the United States					
	Boston, MA	Chicago, IL	Dallas, TX	Miami, FL	Seattle, WA
Boston, MA		976 miles	1,868 miles	1,547 miles	3,163 miles
Chicago, IL	976 miles		936 miles	1,386 miles	2,184 miles
Dallas, TX	1,868 miles	936 miles		1,394 miles	2,222 miles
Miami, FL	1,547 miles	1,386 miles	1,394 miles		3,469 miles
Seattle, WA	3,163 miles	2,184 miles	2,222 miles	3,469 miles	

This is part of a table that gives information about the Presidents of the United States.

Presidents of the United States			
No.	Name	Born	In
1	George Washington	1732, Feb. 22	VA
2	John Adams	1735, Oct. 30	MA
3	Thomas Jefferson	1743, Apr. 13	VA
4	James Madison	1751, Mar. 16	VA
5	James Monroe	1758, Apr. 28	VA
6	John Quincy Adams	1767, July 11	MA
7	Andrew Jackson	1767, Mar. 15	SC
8	Martin Van Buren	1782, Dec. 5	NY
9	William Henry Harrison	1773, Feb. 9	VA
10	John Tyler	1790, Mar. 29	VA

Using Charts and Diagrams

A **chart** shows information arranged according to a plan. Maps, tables, diagrams, lists, and graphs are some of the many kinds of charts.

A **diagram** explains something by showing its parts. This diagram shows the parts of the human eye.

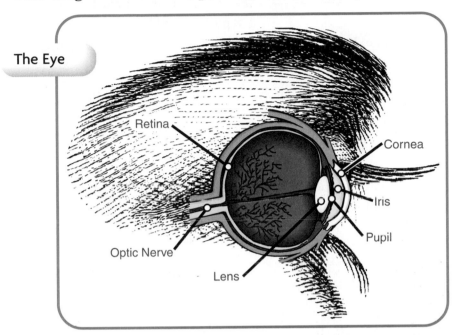

The Eye

Retina

Cornea

Iris

Pupil

Optic Nerve

Lens

A **pie chart** is another name for a circle graph. Pie charts are useful for showing parts of a whole. Each part of the circle graph is like one piece of a pie. The entire pie chart represents 100 percent. The pie chart below shows the results of a survey. Students were asked to choose their favorite from a list of three sandwiches.

Favorite Sandwiches

Ham and Cheese 15%

Tuna 25%

Peanut Butter and Jelly 60%

Note Taking

Taking notes is a way of keeping information for later use. Taking good notes can save time when you write a paper or study for a test. This page shows a passage from a book on blue whales and the notes a student might take for a report.

The Blue Whale

The blue whale is the largest animal in the world. Blue whales can grow to 100 feet in length. They may weigh more than 100 tons. Blue whales live in the ocean. However, they are not fish; they are mammals. Unlike fish, mammals breathe through lungs. Mammals also give birth to live young, while fish spawn eggs. Blue whales do not live in one place. They migrate, or travel, as the seasons change. They move to locations where food is plentiful. Their migration may take them from far northern to far southern waters and back again.

Take notes on index cards. Use a separate card for each topic.

Topic: Size
largest animal–100 feet; 100 tons
Source: <u>Wonders of the Ocean</u>, J. Kofi, 1999, p. 15

Write the name of the **topic** in the upper left corner of the card.

Jot down **key words**.

Try to **paraphrase**, or restate, the information in your own words.

Topic: (Migration)
(migrate)–move about as seasons change
migrates to find food
may travel the length of the earth
Source: <u>Wonders of the Ocean</u>, J. Kofi, 1999, p. 15

At the bottom of the card, write source information: the **name of the book** in which you read about the topic, the **author**, the **year** it was published, and the **page number(s)** on which the information appears.

Topic: Mammal
mammal–breathes through lungs
gives birth to live young
Source: <u>Wonders of the Ocean</u>, J. Kofi, 1999, p. 15

When you have finished taking notes, review them. If you have trouble remembering important facts, read the original information again. Add more details to your notes, as needed.

Arranging your notes in a pattern can help you see how pieces of information fit together. Graphic organizers are useful tools for this purpose. There are several types of graphic organizers, including flowcharts, webs, and Venn diagrams. Choose the organizer that does the best job of helping you see how certain facts are related.

Sending an E-mail Letter

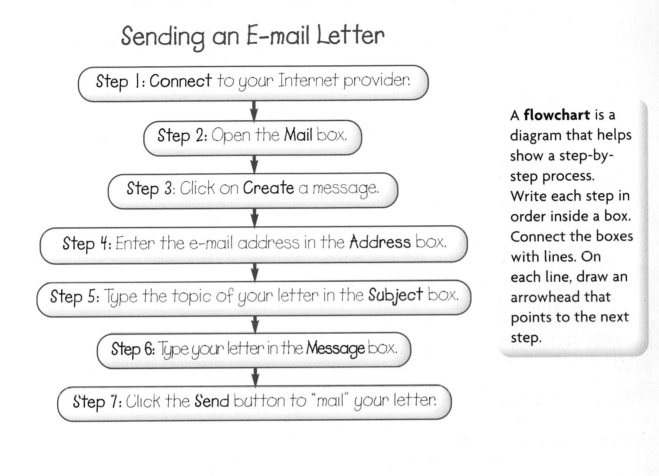

A **flowchart** is a diagram that helps show a step-by-step process. Write each step in order inside a box. Connect the boxes with lines. On each line, draw an arrowhead that points to the next step.

Twister: A Violent Storm

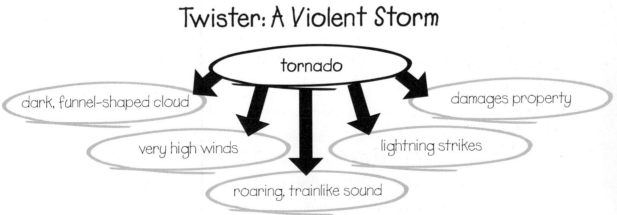

A **web** is a good way to arrange a main idea and supporting details. Write the main idea inside a circle at the center of the web. Write supporting details around the center circle.

Summarizing Information

When you give a **summary**, you briefly explain something. A summary includes

- the main idea or ideas.
- the most important facts that support the main idea.

When you write a summary, you use your own words. To do this, you must understand the facts or the story. Summarizing information helps you understand and remember it better.

Read the paragraph on the left. Look for the main idea. Next, reread the paragraph. Find the most important supporting ideas. Then read the column on the right, which shows two ways to summarize the paragraph.

The first summary states the main idea, summarizes *how* caves are formed, and briefly explains *why* certain shapes are found in them. The second summary states the main idea of the passage in a sentence.

Underground caves are usually found in areas made of limestone, a type of soft rock. Caves are formed when water wears away, or erodes, the surrounding rock. This erosion takes place over thousands of years. The shape of a cave depends on how soft the layers of limestone are. Sometimes erosion carves narrow, deep caves called sinkholes. Water flowing through such a cave would look like an underground waterfall! At other times, erosion makes caves whose floors are horizontal, or mostly on one level. Water can also create different shapes inside a cave. Limestone contains a mineral called calcite. When water seeps down from the outside, through the cave's roof, the calcite dissolves. As the water evaporates, the calcite is left behind. Drop by drop the calcite builds on top of itself. Over thousands of years, it forms cone-shaped stalactites that hang from the ceiling. Sometimes the water drips onto the cave's floor. The cone-shaped forms that grow up from the floor are called stalagmites.

Water erosion creates underground caves. They are usually in places made of limestone because it is a soft rock. Erosion of the limestone sometimes makes caves that go up and down. At other times, it makes horizontal caves. The different shapes inside a cave are created by the calcite in the water. Dripping water gradually makes cone shapes. Stalactites hang down and stalagmites stick up.

One-sentence summary: Water erosion of limestone creates underground caves and the cone shapes inside them.

Bibliographic Citations

A research report ends with a **bibliography**, a list of the sources used by the writer. A **bibliographic citation** tells the reader where to find more information on the subject. It also shows how much research the writer did and what kinds of sources he or she used. The items in a bibliography are alphabetized by the author's last name. Follow these examples for writing a bibliographic citation:

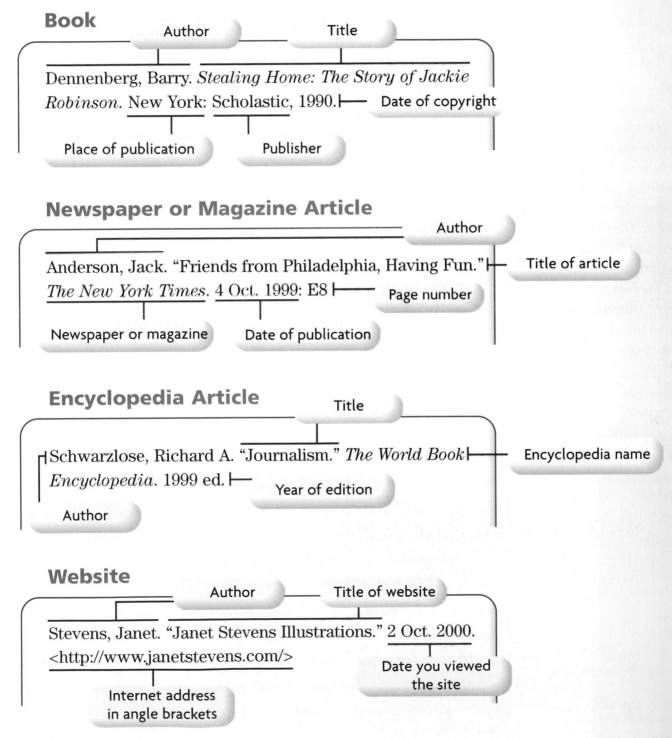

Book

Author · Title

Dennenberg, Barry. *Stealing Home: The Story of Jackie Robinson*. New York: Scholastic, 1990. — Date of copyright

Place of publication · Publisher

Newspaper or Magazine Article

Author

Anderson, Jack. "Friends from Philadelphia, Having Fun." — Title of article
The New York Times. 4 Oct. 1999: E8 — Page number

Newspaper or magazine · Date of publication

Encyclopedia Article

Title

Schwarzlose, Richard A. "Journalism." *The World Book* — Encyclopedia name
Encyclopedia. 1999 ed. — Year of edition

Author

Website

Author · Title of website

Stevens, Janet. "Janet Stevens Illustrations." 2 Oct. 2000.
<http://www.janetstevens.com/>

Internet address in angle brackets · Date you viewed the site

Outlining

An **outline** helps writers organize their writing. It is like a skeleton on which writers can build their compositions.

This is the title of the outline and of the piece of writing.

Fascinating Hieroglyphs

I. What hieroglyphs are
    A. Meaning of the word
    B. Where hieroglyphs appear
    C. What hieroglyphs were used for
    D. The importance of papyrus
II. How to read hieroglyphs
    A. What the symbols meant
    B. Reading and writing hieroglyphs
    C. Why scribes were needed
III. The Rosetta Stone
    A. Knowledge of how to read hieroglyphs is lost
    B. Knowledge of how to read hieroglyphs is learned again

Use a capital letter and a period for each important detail in a main section. Indent the details under the name of the section, and keep them short. Do not use an *A* unless there is a *B*. This section has three important details: A, B, and C.

Use a Roman numeral for each main section, and write a period after the number. Keep the name of a main section short. Do not use a *I* unless there is a *II*. This outline has three main sections.

This is the first paragraph of the essay written by using the outline above.

The first paragraph goes with the first Roman numeral on the outline.

Detail A

Detail B

Detail C

Detail D

Fascinating Hieroglyphs

The ancient Egyptians did not use letters to write their words. Instead, they used pictures, or hieroglyphs. This word comes from the Greek word for sacred, or holy, writing. Hieroglyphic writing is often found on temple walls. The government also had hieroglyphs carved on columns and buildings to record important events. Records of daily life, such as those for business, were written on scrolls. These long, rolled sheets of paper were made from papyrus, a plant.

Test-Taking Strategies

The best way to study for a test is to keep up with your schoolwork. Doing a little each day makes it easier to remember facts and understand ideas. The guidelines below can help you develop good study habits.

Tips for Developing Good Study Habits

In Class

- Pay attention. Think about what the teacher is saying.

- If you do not understand something, ask questions.

- Join in class discussions. Listen carefully to what other students say. Express your own thoughts, too.

Outside Class

- Study in an area that is quiet and comfortable. Make sure that the lighting is good.

- Read a little about each subject every day.

- Take notes on what you read.

- Every now and then, pause and think about what you have just read.

- At the end of each study session, review what you have learned. Summarize the information in your own words.

Tips for Taking Multiple-Choice Tests

1. Read each question carefully. Be sure you know what is being asked.
2. Read every choice before you decide on an answer.
3. If you know which choice is correct, answer the question.
4. If you are not certain which choice is correct, go on to the next question.
5. When you reach the end of the test, go back over the questions that you did not answer.
6. Use the process of elimination to improve your chances of making the right choice. The following model shows you how to use the process of elimination:

George Washington was a President, but he was the first President. A is not the correct answer.

Sample Question: Who was the third President of the United States?

(A) George Washington
(B) Abraham Lincoln
(C) Thomas Jefferson ◄— Choose the best answer: C. Thomas Jefferson is correct.
(D) Benjamin Franklin

Benjamin Franklin was not a President. D is not the correct answer.

The correct answer must be either B or C. Ask yourself: "What do I know about Abraham Lincoln? What do I know about Thomas Jefferson? How can this information help me decide between these two choices?"

Make a decision based on what you know. "Lincoln was President during the Civil War, and that wasn't until 1861. Jefferson wrote the Declaration of Independence, so he lived during the late 1700s and early 1800s, which is the right time period."

Tips for Taking Essay Tests

Taking an essay test is like writing several very short reports. The following tips can help you plan and write each answer.

> 1. Read each question carefully.
> 2. Look for key words such as *explain, contrast,* or *describe.* They can help you identify your purpose.
> 3. Decide how to organize your main idea and supporting details.
> 4. Write your answer.
> 5. Read the question again, and review your answer. Make sure that you have answered the question as completely as you can.
> 6. Make any changes or additions that you think will improve your essay.

Study these examples. They show how you can use **key words** to help you identify your purpose.

When you **explain**, your purpose is to tell *why* and *how*.

> **Essay question:** Explain the importance of the Bill of Rights in the United States Constitution.
>
> **Response:** The Bill of Rights protects basic rights that all people should have. The Bill of Rights protects people by stating that the government cannot take away certain rights. Two of these rights are freedom of speech and freedom of religion.

When you **contrast**, your purpose is to tell ways in which things are different.

> **Essay question:** Contrast Earth and Mars.
>
> **Response:** Earth and Mars are quite different. One moon circles Earth, but two moons circle Mars. Earth's atmosphere can support human life; the atmosphere of Mars cannot. Water covers a large part of Earth's surface. We have found no water on Mars.

Study Steps to Learn a Word

STEP 1 **Say** the word. Remember how you have heard the word used. Think about what it means.

STEP 2 **Look** at the word. Look for prefixes, suffixes, or other word parts you know. Think about other words that are related in meaning and spelling. Try to picture the word in your mind.

STEP 3 **Spell** the word to yourself. Think about the way each sound is spelled. Notice any unusual spelling.

STEP 4 **Write** the word while looking at it. Check the way you have formed the letters. If you have not written the word clearly or correctly, write it again.

STEP 5 **Check** your learning. Cover the word and write it. If you did not spell the word correctly, practice these steps until the word becomes familiar to you.

Making Your Own Spelling List

You may want to keep your own spelling word list in a notebook. You can organize your spelling word list alphabetically, by subject areas, by parts of speech, or by other categories. Follow these guidelines.

1 **Check** your writing for words you have misspelled. Circle each misspelled word.

an (invisable) mark

2 **Find** out how to spell the word correctly.
- Look up the word in a dictionary or a thesaurus.
- Ask a teacher or a classmate.

invisible
an (invisable) mark

3 **Write** the word in your notebook.
- Spell the word correctly.
- Write a definition, a synonym, or an antonym to help you understand the meaning of the word.
- Use the word in a sentence.

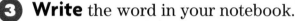
Writer's Journal

invisible — unable to be seen
Air is invisible.

4 **When** you write, look at your spelling word list to check your spelling.

The green insect was invisible on the leaf.

Spelling

Commonly Misspelled Words

accident	championship	everything
against	circles	except
allowed	classroom	excited
a lot	clothes	exclaimed
answer	clumsy	fault
anymore	concentrate	field
anyway	congratulated	finally
assignment	connected	forever
attention	covered	goal
audience	degrees	happened
backward	describe	herself
balloon	description	himself
beginning	different	hungry
believe	disappointed	important
break	doesn't	invited
business	elevator	it's
catching	especially	kitchen
caught	everybody	ladder
celebrate	everyday	language
central	everyone	leaving

let's	recess	themselves
library	remember	thermometer
losing	signed	they're
maybe	sincerely	title
metal	smiling	tomorrow
month	social	too
myself	someone	touched
nervous	square	unknown
opposite	staircase	unusual
outside	stairway	usual
overtime	steal	weird
paid	straight	we're
pictures	struck	what's
popped	studying	where
position	supposed	winner
principal	surprise	without
probably	telephone	wondering
question	television	won't
realized	temperature	written
reason	that's	young

Handwriting Models

Cursive Alphabet

A B C D E F G H
I J K L M N O P
Q R S T U V W
X Y Z

a b c d e f g h
i j k l m n o p
q r s t u v w
x y z

D'Nealian Cursive Alphabet

A B C D E F G H
I J K L M N O P
Q R S T U V W
X Y Z

a b c d e f g h
i j k l m n o p
q r s t u v w
x y z

Thesaurus

What Is a Thesaurus?

A *thesaurus* lists words with their definitions and synonyms. *Synonyms* are words whose meanings are the same or similar. The words listed in a thesaurus are called *entry words*, and they appear in alphabetical order. Following each entry word is a list of synonyms for the word. Sometimes a thesaurus also lists *antonyms*, or words with opposite or nearly opposite meanings.

Look at this sample thesaurus entry for the word *leave*.

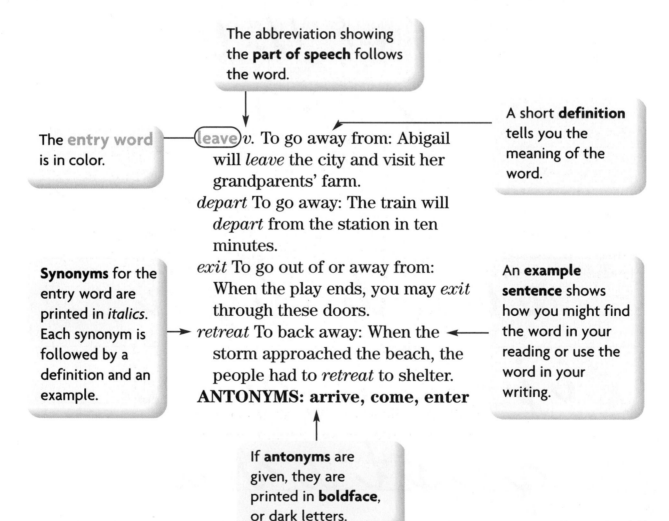

The abbreviation showing the **part of speech** follows the word.

A short **definition** tells you the meaning of the word.

The **entry word** is in color.

leave *v.* To go away from: Abigail will *leave* the city and visit her grandparents' farm.
depart To go away: The train will *depart* from the station in ten minutes.
exit To go out of or away from: When the play ends, you may *exit* through these doors.
retreat To back away: When the storm approached the beach, the people had to *retreat* to shelter.
ANTONYMS: arrive, come, enter

Synonyms for the entry word are printed in *italics*. Each synonym is followed by a definition and an example.

An **example sentence** shows how you might find the word in your reading or use the word in your writing.

If **antonyms** are given, they are printed in **boldface**, or dark letters.

How to Use Your Writer's Thesaurus

A **thesaurus** is an important tool for writers. Suppose that you are writing a story about a sporting event that you attended, and you want to use a word that means "crowd." A look in your thesaurus can help you find a synonym for *crowd* that expresses the exact meaning you have in mind. In fact, you can use a thesaurus to find

- a more interesting or colorful word.
- a more specific or exact word.
- a word that could replace an overused word.

Use the **Writer's Thesaurus** to help you find a better word. The *index* lists all of the entry words, synonyms, and antonyms in the thesaurus.

Courage is listed as an entry word. Entry words are shown in color. These words are listed alphabetically in the thesaurus. You can find a definition for this word as well as synonyms and antonyms in the thesaurus.

(courage)*n.*
cravenness courage *n.*
credit **honor** *v.*
criticize honor *n.*
crowd **audience** *n.* ←
curious **strange** *adj.*
current new *adj.*
current old *adj.*

Crowd is listed as a synonym. Synonyms are written in *italic* letters. You will find *crowd* listed as a synonym with the entry word *audience*. Read all of the definitions to find the right word.

Current is listed as an antonym. Antonyms are written in **bold** letters. You will find *current* listed as an antonym with the entry word *old*.

A

afraid *adj.* State of fear or being frightened: Terribly *afraid*, the child hid under the blanket.

alarmed Startled by something dangerous or scary: The *alarmed* baby-sitter jumped from her chair when the child suddenly burst into tears.

fearful Filled with fright or fear: The *fearful* passengers quickly got out of the smoke-filled car.

frightened Full of fear or terror: Lost and *frightened*, the child began to cry.

timid Easily frightened; shy; lacking self-confidence: With a *timid* smile, Eddie asked Marissa to dance.

ANTONYMS: bold, brave, calm, confident, courageous

angry *adj.* Feeling displeased or upset: Jake held back his *angry* words when Bethany broke his toy truck.

annoyed Feeling or showing mild anger; bothered: When she saw my muddy shoes, Mom gave me an *annoyed* look.

furious Feeling fury or great anger: Kurt let loose a *furious* shout after the dog trampled his garden.

upset Feeling bothered and in a bad mood: An *upset* Dr. Evans left because the store didn't have the shoes in her size.

ANTONYMS: calm, content, pleased, serene, unruffled

argue *v.* To give reasons for or against something; to disagree; to dispute: Mr. and Mrs. Cisneros always *argue* when they talk about politics.

debate To discuss or argue formally: Candidates for political office often *debate* issues.

dispute To challenge an argument or idea: Although Mario thought he was safe, he decided not to *dispute* the umpire's call.

oppose To argue or fight against: We will continue to *oppose* the construction of a six-lane highway in our neighborhood.

quarrel To dispute; to argue angrily or violently: The coach and the umpire often *quarrel* when a play is close.

ANTONYMS: accord, agree, concur, consent, reconcile

audience *n.* A group of people who see, hear, or read something together but not always at the same time: The author wrote for an *audience* of young adults.

assembly A group of people gathered together, often for a serious purpose: As the mayor dedicated the statue, the *assembly* listened in respectful silence.

crowd A large group of people gathered closely together in one place: A noisy *crowd* quickly surrounded the man who was giving away tickets.

fans People who are enthusiastic in their support of a sports team, a celebrity, or an activity: When the batter scored a home run, baseball *fans* rose to their feet and cheered.

listeners An audience that hears but does not see: Some radio programs invite *listeners* to call in requests for certain songs.

onlookers People who watch something; observers: The many *onlookers* in front of the burning building nearly blocked the path of the fire trucks.

spectators A group of people who watch something but do not participate in it; onlookers: The stadium was crowded with *spectators*.

B

bad *adj.* Not good; disobedient; unpleasant; harmful or unsafe: We called an electrician to repair the *bad* wiring in the house.

awful Very unpleasant or unwelcome: The announcement that our field trip had been canceled was *awful* news.

dreadful Unpleasant in a shocking or frightening way: News crews showed the *dreadful* conditions at the refugee camp.

faulty Imperfect or defective: Using *I* when you mean *me* is an example of *faulty* grammar.

horrible Unpleasant in a disgusting or frightening way: Is the *horrible* smell coming from that pile of trash?

unpleasant Objectionable; disagreeable: Cleaning the bathroom is the most *unpleasant* chore at home.

ANTONYMS: appropriate, benevolent, superb, virtuous

beautiful *adj.* Very pleasing to the senses or the mind: The Grand Canyon is the most *beautiful* sight I've ever seen.

breathtaking Causing great excitement; awe: There was a *breathtaking* view of the ocean from the cliffs.

gorgeous Stunning to look at: The *gorgeous* diamond necklace glittered like a string of lights.

lovely Highly pleasing; delightful: The *lovely* room was bright and well furnished.

picturesque Visually charming: We saw many *picturesque* towns on our trip to the ocean.

ANTONYMS: hideous, homely, ugly, unattractive, unsightly

believe *v.* To accept as true or real: Some scientists *believe* that the universe is expanding.

accept To take as true or important: I *accept* her explanation for what happened last night.

conclude To come to a decision by reasoning: I *conclude* that the sink will not drain because something is stuck in the pipe.

suppose To assume: If that shopping mall is built, I *suppose* those shops in town will suffer.

think To have in mind, especially as an opinion or a plan: I *think* that we should rent a movie to show at the party.

understand To grasp the meaning or importance of something: All of us students *understand* that we must study to pass the test.

ANTONYMS: deny, disbelieve, doubt, question, reject

change *v.* To make different: I will *change* my clothes before I go on the field trip.

alter To make something somewhat different: The tailor will *alter* the jacket by making the sleeves shorter.

modify To change something slightly: If we *modify* the recipe by using applesauce instead of oil, the cake will be more healthful.

replace To substitute one thing for another: In this recipe Matthew will *replace* the apples with pears.

ANTONYMS: continue, endure, remain, sustain

child *n.* A very young person; parents' offspring: Brianna, my teacher's *child*, is celebrating her fifth birthday today.

kid Slang for a child or youth: My best friend is the *kid* who lives next door.

youngster A child of any age: Every *youngster* in the neighborhood was playing in the park this afternoon.

youth A young, energetic, and sometimes impulsive person, usually a boy: Even as a *youth*, Coach Jackson loved to play basketball.

ANTONYMS: adult, grown-up

close *adj.* Next to or near something; carefully guarded: At the playground, Mom kept a *close* eye on little Maria.

adjacent Near or close; next to: The gameroom is operated by the owners of the *adjacent* restaurant.

bordering Next to; on the edge of: We will use the *bordering* parking lot behind my school.

neighboring In the same general area; nearby: The *neighboring* town has a swimming pool.

ANTONYMS: distant, far, outlying, remote

clothes *n.* Items made of fabric or other material that people wear on their bodies: Scott is growing so quickly that he will need new *clothes* to wear this winter.

apparel What people wear to protect or adorn their bodies: There are several stores at the mall that sell women's *apparel*.

dress Clothing in general, or an article of women's outer clothing made up of a skirt and top; gown: Their *dress* is formal when they go out to dinner.

garments Articles of clothing: The *garments* in Grandma's wardrobe include dresses, skirts, blouses, and pants.

wardrobe A collection of one's garments: I bought my entire *wardrobe* from one store.

cold *adj.* Having a low temperature: After a morning of softball practice, I enjoyed a glass of *cold* milk and a sandwich.

arctic Very cold; as cold as at the North Pole: The strong, *arctic* winds made the day seem colder than it really was.

chilly Unpleasantly cool: I'll need my sweater in that *chilly* theater.

frigid Very cold in temperature: The *frigid* temperatures kept everyone indoors.

frosty Cold enough to make frost: As he talked in the *frosty* air, he could see his breath.

icy Seeming as cold as ice: When I set foot in the *icy* water, I knew that there would be no swimming today.

ANTONYMS: burning, hot, roasting, scorching

combined *adj.* Joined or united to a whole: It took a *combined* effort to complete the project.

allied Joined for a specific purpose: The *allied* armies worked hard to win the war.

joint Shared or owned by more than one person; combined: The *joint* efforts of the entire team led to victory.

linked Chained or joined together: Three *linked* sausages were hanging from the dog's mouth.

ANTONYMS: disconnected, isolated, separate, unrelated

courage *n.* Emotional strength in unwelcome or dangerous situations: Kyesha found the *courage* to jump into the water and save the drowning dog.

bravery Confidence in the face of danger or difficulty: Because of the firefighters' *bravery*, the child was saved from the burning house.

daring Willingness to take risks: The trapeze artist showed great *daring* on the high wire.

heart Emotional strength or energy: I don't have the *heart* to tell him that he didn't make the team.

valor Strength of mind or spirit; personal bravery: Many soldiers show great *valor* when they risk their lives in battle.

ANTONYMS: cowardice, cravenness, faintheartedness, timidity

D

discover *v.* To find out about, to see, or to know something, especially for the first time: Isaac Newton was the first scientist to *discover* and to write about the force of gravity.

detect To see or know something not easily noticed: The mother could *detect* sleepiness in her child's behavior.

find To come to understand; to realize; to come upon; to search successfully: You will *find* that to do well in school, you must study.

invent Produce from one's own imagination: The necessity for special reading glasses led Benjamin Franklin to *invent* bifocals.

reveal To show; to make known; to disclose: After the show, the magician will *reveal* some of the ways in which he performs his tricks.

uncover To find something previously hidden; to reveal: The detectives will *uncover* the motives for the crime.

ANTONYMS: conceal, cover, hide

eat *v.* To take food into the body: If you *eat* now, you won't be hungry at dinner.

bolt To eat quickly by swallowing in large bites, with little chewing: You run the risk of choking if you *bolt* your food.

consume To eat something until it is gone: Did the team really *consume* all that pizza?

dine To eat a meal: Every year we *dine* at a nice restaurant on my mother's birthday.

gobble To eat quickly and greedily: My dogs *gobble* their food and leave their bowls clean in about two minutes.

gulp To eat or drink in large swallows: During their breaks, the thirsty players sit down and *gulp* water.

munch To eat with a chewing action (often related to snacking): The guests *munch* on raw vegetables as they wait for dinner.

nibble To take small bites: The birds *nibble* on the sunflower and then fly away.

ANTONYMS: fast, hunger, starve

excited *adj.* Stirred up emotionally: Joelle was *excited* all day, preparing for the party.

anxious Nervous and uncertain: Meredith had an *anxious* look on her face when the teacher announced a quiz.

eager Looking forward to something: There is a busload of *eager* students waiting to see the camels.

enthusiastic Having intense interest in or admiration for something: Derek was an *enthusiastic* student of the guitar.

thrilled Very glad and full of excitement: The *thrilled* pitcher celebrated his first win.
ANTONYMS: bored, calm, disappointed, unenthusiastic, uninterested

fake *adj.* Not genuine: Do not let him fool you with that *fake* spider.
false Not true or genuine: The actress wore *false* eyelashes to make her eyes look larger.
fictitious Created and assumed as truth: The double agent used *fictitious* names to complete his mission.
imitation A substitute that is like the original: Margarine was invented as a type of *imitation* butter.
ANTONYMS: authentic, genuine, true

famous *adj.* Well-known: Have you ever met a *famous* author?
celebrated Honored; well spoken of: William Shakespeare is a *celebrated* playwright.
distinguished Well-known because of a particular quality or achievement: The *distinguished* violinist drew a large audience for the concert.
noted Talked about for being exceptional; having a good reputation: The *noted* author has won the Pulitzer Prize for her latest novel.
renowned Widely known and praised: The *renowned* scientist won the Nobel Prize for her discovery.
well-known Recognized or known by many people: It is a *well-known* fact that too much sugar is not good for your health.
ANTONYMS: obscure, unheard of, unknown

fancy *adj.* Decorative or elaborate: Jessica wore a *fancy* dress to the party.
elaborate Complex or intricate: Walter's sweater had an *elaborate* design of many colors.
elegant Richly dignified; stylish: The men in the movie dressed in *elegant* tuxedos.
gaudy Excessively showy: Theresa wears such *gaudy* earrings.
luxurious Fancy in a way that promises comfort: I sat on a sofa covered in *luxurious* red velvet.

ornate Highly decorated, often with bright colors, in an elaborate style: The *ornate* box was made of gold and encrusted with jewels.
ANTONYMS: plain, simple, unadorned, untrimmed

fast *adj.* Speedy; taking little time: Our *fast* runners will win this race.
hasty Done in a hurry, often impatiently: When I heard the car honk, I took a *hasty* look inside my suitcase, slammed it shut, and ran.
rapid Moving or acting with great speed: Part of his success is that he works at a *rapid* pace.
swift Moving easily and with speed: Tina picked up the ball and threw it to first base with one *swift* move.
ANTONYMS: leisurely, lengthy, slow, sluggish

funny *adj.* Causing others to laugh or smile; comical: How I laughed at Cassie's *funny* joke!
amusing Funny in a quiet way: The *amusing* story made Dad smile.
hilarious Extremely funny; causing loud laughter: Martin did a *hilarious* impression of a frog with hiccups.
ridiculous Causing laughter or ridicule because of silliness: The clown's *ridiculous* pants were much too big.
silly Funny in a foolish way: That *silly* squirrel is trying to carry an apple by itself.
witty Funny but clever: Kaye has a *witty* answer to every question.
ANTONYMS: serious, solemn

gentle *adj.* Not harsh; softhearted: This *gentle* soap keeps your skin smooth.
mild Not harsh; even-tempered: Cindy's *mild* answer ended the disagreement.
peaceful Not excited; serene; free from disturbance; not fighting: The generals wanted to meet in a *peaceful* place to discuss their agreement.
sensitive Aware of the feelings of others: The *sensitive* father knew when his son needed encouragement.

sympathetic Understanding and sharing the feelings of others: When my dog died, my *sympathetic* friend cried with me.

tender Expressing care and affection: With a *tender* smile, my teacher asked if I was feeling better.

ANTONYMS: harsh, inconsiderate, mean, rough, uncaring, violent

good *adj.* Correct in thought and action; obedient; pleasant; enjoyable: Eric is a *good* little boy.

appropriate Suitable: This is an *appropriate* time for us to talk.

excellent Extremely good; of very high quality: When we went to Italy, we ate *excellent* bread and pasta.

honest Truthful: Tom made an *honest* admission that he broke the window.

marvelous Pleasant enough to create surprise: We had a *marvelous* time at Brian's party.

superb Of very high quality: Danielle has a *superb* voice, doesn't she?

truthful Honest; faithful to the truth or to facts: Her diary is a *truthful* account of the years she spent in Africa.

virtuous Having excellent qualities, especially of honesty and goodness: Dr. Stein's kind heart and *virtuous* behavior were known to everyone in town.

well-behaved Showing control of one's actions: For someone so young, Jenny is a surprisingly *well-behaved* child.

worthy Deserving respect; valuable: Both Ben and Karin are *worthy* candidates for class president.

ANTONYMS: awful, bad, disappointing, dishonest, nasty, unpleasant

guard *v.* To keep from escaping; to keep from harm: The officer will *guard* the criminal until he is safely behind bars.

defend To fight off a threat or an attack: The Tigers will *defend* their title at the game Saturday.

protect To keep from harm: If you're going to be outside for very long, wear a sunscreen to *protect* your skin against burning.

shelter To provide a safe or covered place: Uncle Mark offered to *shelter* the stray dog in his garage.

shield To protect or hide, as if behind or under something: This umbrella will *shield* you from the rain.

ANTONYMS: abandon, endanger, jeopardize

happen *v.* To take place: What will *happen* in our town if the factory closes?

befall To happen or take place: We cannot wait here for something to *befall* us.

occur To come about: The football playoffs will *occur* in December or January.

happy *adj.* Full of joy; pleasant: The *happy* little girl giggled when her parents hugged her.

cheerful Having or creating a good attitude: Yellow walls and colorful posters make the classroom *cheerful*.

contented Satisfied with things as they are: Peter spent a *contented* afternoon with his microscope.

delighted Feeling great joy or pleasure: Linda looked over to see her *delighted* grandparents.

jolly Full of cheer; merry: The *jolly* singers entertained holiday shoppers at the mall.

joyful Showing much happiness: On the first day of school, the students greeted each other with *joyful* shouts.

merry Full of fun and laughter; festive: What a *merry* time we had at the party!

overjoyed Feeling great happiness (especially about an event that could have been disappointing): Marianne was *overjoyed* when she heard that she had won the contest.

pleased Having good feelings about something: The teacher seems *pleased* that everyone passed the test.

ANTONYMS: gloomy, glum, grim, heartsick, sad, sorrowful, unhappy, wretched

honor *v.* To treat with respect; to praise: The city will *honor* the returning soldiers with a parade.

credit To give praise or respect to those who deserve it: I *credit* my best friend with the idea for this story.

praise To express approval: Good teachers *praise* pupils who try their best.

respect To think highly of someone or something: The players *respect* their coach very much.
ANTONYMS: attack, criticize, ridicule, scorn

hot *adj.* Having a high temperature: I could not pick up the *hot* pan without a potholder.

boiling Hot enough to make liquid bubble: We dropped the spaghetti into the *boiling* water to cook.

burning Hot enough to seem or to be covered by fire: The *burning* marshmallows had been in the campfire too long.

scorching Hot enough to cause burn marks: Even the bravest beachgoers had to find shelter from the *scorching* August sun.

sizzling Having such a high temperature that a hissing or crackling sound is made: The smell of *sizzling* bacon woke me up.

steaming Hot enough to make water turn to gas: When I saw the *steaming* cup, I knew that the hot chocolate was not yet ready to drink.
ANTONYMS: cold, cool, freezing, frosty, frozen, icy

however *adv.* Nevertheless; on the other hand: My father wanted to go to the concert; *however*, he had to work.

conversely In the opposite way: We are late, and *conversely*, they are early.

nevertheless In spite of: The first three experiments have failed; *nevertheless*, the scientist plans to try again.

though In spite of the fact or chance: The Eagles probably will win, *though* most spectators are rooting for the other team.

important *adj.* Having worth, value, or influence: The governor will visit our city to give an *important* speech.

necessary Needed, without question: Math is a *necessary* subject for all students.

noteworthy Attracting attention because of its importance: When our band earned a blue ribbon in the state competition, it was a *noteworthy* event.

pressing Urgently important: Our most *pressing* need for the party is finding a place to have it.

prominent Standing out because of importance: Is the mayor the most *prominent* citizen of our town?

vital Absolutely necessary to the life of something: This is a *vital* project, and the purity of our drinking water depends on it.

weighty Having important, serious effects: Whether or not to have a dog as a pet is a *weighty* decision.
ANTONYMS: needless, trivial, unimportant, unnecessary, useless, worthless

interesting *adj.* Holding someone's attention: I spent all afternoon reading this *interesting* book.

absorbing Interesting enough to firmly hold a person's attention: She told such an *absorbing* story that I never noticed the storm outside.

fascinating Intensely holding someone's attention: My grandmother tells *fascinating* stories about her childhood.

intriguing Interesting because it challenges the mind: I'll keep working on this *intriguing* puzzle until I solve it.

riveting Holding someone's attention as if bolting that person in place: We held our breaths as we watched the *riveting* flood scene that ended the movie.
ANTONYMS: boring, dull, uninteresting

large *adj.* Big, as in size, amount, or extent: I'll need help to move that *large* box.

colossal Astonishingly large: Visitors at the fair couldn't stop talking about the *colossal* pumpkin that won first prize.

enormous Much larger in size or number than usual: Because she assigned so much homework this week, Ms. Kim has an *enormous* number of papers to grade before Monday.

gigantic Unusually large, powerful, or important; like a giant: With a *gigantic* roar, the rocket rose into the sky.

grand Large and impressive: The new gymnasium is a *grand* addition to our school.

great Large and important: The *great* oak was the tallest and oldest tree in town.

huge Very large in size or area: What a *huge* stadium this is!

immense Of very great size: The *immense* living room held four sofas and fifteen chairs.

ANTONYMS: little, small, tiny, undersized, unimportant

leave *v.* To go away from: Abigail will *leave* the city and visit her grandparents' farm.

abandon To quit or give up completely: The car is in such poor shape that Dad will *abandon* all efforts to repair it.

depart To go away: The train will *depart* from the station in ten minutes.

exit To go out of or away from: When the play ends, you may *exit* through these doors.

retreat To back off or away: When the storm approached the beach, the people had to *retreat* to shelter.

ANTONYMS: arrive, come, progress

let *v.* To give permission for an activity: The teacher *let* the children play in the schoolyard.

allow To permit; to make no objection: My parents *allow* me to stay up until 10:00 on Saturday nights.

authorize To allow, with permission granted by a person in command: Principal Davis will *authorize* this announcement.

consent To give approval for something: I hope my parents will *consent* to my idea of having a TV in my room.

permit To allow to do something: The teacher would not *permit* Rachel to leave the room.

ANTONYMS: decline, deny, refuse

love *v.* To like very much; to have strong affection or enthusiasm for someone or something: I *love* the smell of October mornings.

admire To hold in high regard; to respect: I *admire* him for his patience.

adore To hold in high esteem; to love: I *adore* strawberries.

cherish To hold dear to one's heart: Juan always will *cherish* the memory of his family's visit to Mexico.

revere To regard with respect and awe: You just have to like him, not *revere* him.

treasure To prize or value anyone or anything: Tara and Michelle *treasure* their memories of summer vacation.

ANTONYMS: abhor, detest, dislike, hate, loathe

major *adj.* Having greater importance than others of its kind: The *major* reason for the building's collapse was its poor construction.

chief Greatest and most important: Oil is Texas's *chief* export.

essential Absolutely necessary: The *essential* need when exercising is to get enough oxygen.

important Significant; valuable; deserving special attention: Make sure you slow down and take notes when you read the most *important* parts of the chapter.

leading First among many: That was the *leading* reason for not eating there.

primary First and most important: Mother's *primary* concern is that her children be happy.

ANTONYMS: insignificant, least, minor, trivial, unimportant

neat *adj.* In good order: Kelly's room looks *neat* when she puts away her books and clothes.

manageable That can be managed; accomplished: Mr. Ramirez keeps a *manageable* variety of plants in his yard.

orderly With everything in its place: Books in the library are kept in a very *orderly* way.

organized Structured; well-planned: The newly *organized* committee has a president and a vice president.

tidy Trim and in good order: After we made the beds, the room appeared *tidy* again.

ANTONYMS: cluttered, dirty, disorganized, messy, sloppy

new *adj.* Just made, started, or arrived: What do you think of that *new* cartoon show?

current Taking place now: Bring in the *current* edition of your favorite magazine.

fresh New or clean; not spoiled: Jamal turned to a *fresh* page in his notebook and began to write.

latest Most recent: This is the *latest* book in my favorite mystery series.

modern In the present time; up-to-date: Automobiles are a *modern* invention.

original Earliest or first: The *original* recipe calls for two cans of tomatoes.

unfamiliar Not well known: This is an *unfamiliar* road, but we are going in the right direction.

ANTONYMS: ancient, experienced, old, used, worn

normal adj. Following the standard; usual: Wanting to have friends is a *normal* wish.

common Shared by many or all: The students' *common* concern was doing well on the test.

ordinary Everyday: Janetta wore *ordinary* school clothes, as everyone else did.

quotidian Something recurring daily: Some of her *quotidian* activities include walking the dog and watering the plants.

routine Done out of habit: Mr. Kresge's *routine* morning tasks begin with shaving, followed by breakfast.

typical Expected; usual: Our *typical* school day begins at 8:30 in the morning.

usual Standard; customary: Chloe's *usual* breakfast is oatmeal and apples.

ANTONYMS: extraordinary, rare, uncommon, unusual

number n. A quantity or an amount; a group of units (as in counting): The *number* of children in the class was twenty-five.

amount The sum: What is the *amount* of money you will need for the trip?

quantity An estimated or indefinite amount: Uncle Ray bought an enormous *quantity* of corn to cook for the barbecue.

sum The added total: The *sum* of two plus two is four.

total The complete quantity or amount: After the fair, I added up the money from the various booths and was surprised at the *total*.

old adj. Having lived or existed for a long time: The *old* clay pot is painted with a lively scene.

aged Very old: The *aged* man walked with a cane.

ancient Extremely old; from very long ago: Built over four thousand years ago, the *ancient* pyramids of Egypt are a popular tourist attraction.

antique Dating from an earlier period: The *antique* necklace had an intricate design.

bygone Belonging to a past time and not part of today; out-of-date: The horse and buggy represent a *bygone* time.

familiar Well-known: "Better safe than sorry" is a *familiar* saying.

mature Completely developed; full-grown: The *mature* oak was a perfect place to build a treehouse.

used Previously owned or worn; not new: Miguel bought a *used* bike for twenty dollars.

worn Damaged by use over time: Yoko's *worn* jeans were badly stained.

ANTONYMS: contemporary, current, fresh, modern, new, young

outside n. The outer area of something: Colorful stickers covered the *outside* of the gift box.

cover A wrapping or outer protection: I put a *cover* on my textbook to keep it clean.

exterior The outer part of something: The *exterior* of the house was covered with yellow aluminum siding.

skin The outer covering: Peel the *skin* off a banana before you eat it.

surface The top or outer layer of something: Oceans cover 70 percent of Earth's *surface*.

ANTONYMS: inside, interior

P

piece n. Part of a whole: For a special treat, Mom gave me a big *piece* of cake.

chunk A thick, rough, lumpish piece: Chris tripped over a *chunk* of brick.

fraction One of several or many parts of a whole; a little bit: Five minutes is just a *fraction* of the time I'll need to do this job.

portion A share of something divided among many people: Doug's *portion* of the turkey was the drumstick.

scrap A fragment; a leftover: Look, there's something written on this *scrap* of paper!

section A part made by cutting or other form of division: Is there a children's *section* in the movie theater?

slice A thin or wedge-shaped piece, often made by cutting with a knife: I'll have a *slice* of pie and a glass of milk.

ANTONYMS: entirety, total, whole

probably *adv.* With little doubt: Andy studies every day and *probably* will do well on the test.

likely Having strong possibilities: Mrs. Reyes is *likely* to change her mind and let us go to the game.

reasonably With assurance that comes from thoughtful consideration: Joyce is *reasonably* sure that the story she is writing will be a good one.

ANTONYMS: doubtfully, dubiously, questionably

quite *adv.* Completely; to a considerable degree; very: Nikki is *quite* skillful for such a young musician.

completely Totally: Mr. Ortega was *completely* satisfied with his new lawnmower.

entirely Absolutely: I am *entirely* sure that I can run a mile.

really Truly; without question; very: The trumpet player had a *really* impressive solo.

wholly To the whole and complete amount: I *wholly* agree with your decision.

ANTONYMS: barely, hardly, partially

receive *v.* To take possession of something that has been given: Did you *receive* the CDs that you had wanted for your birthday?

accept To receive something willingly: Quentin was there to *accept* the position as team captain.

adopt To accept formally: The class will *adopt* new rules for conduct.

assume To take over the responsibilities of: Giacomo will *assume* the role of organizing class parties.

earn To receive as the result of effort: If I study hard, I will *earn* an A on the spelling test.

inherit To obtain in turn from an ancestor: Someday, Dan will *inherit* his great-grandfather's pocket watch.

ANTONYMS: give, reject, turn away

report *v.* To give an account: As its leading story, the program will *report* the news about the terrible earthquake.

describe To give a picture in words: A good writer can *describe* a scene with a few well-chosen words.

inform To present the facts to someone: The train conductor will *inform* passengers about the delay.

narrate To tell or recount: Diana will *narrate* the story of *Peter Pan*.

notify To tell about an occurrence; to inform: Some teachers will *notify* parents when a student performs poorly.

summarize To present a brief report of a longer account: If you want to know about that movie, I can *summarize* its plot for you.

sad *adj.* Feeling unhappy or low; unfortunate; troubling: I have a *sad* feeling when it is raining.

distressed Worried and upset: They said I had a *distressed* look on my face when I noticed that my bicycle had been stolen.

glum Filled with gloomy thoughts: With a *glum* look, Jeremy told Anna that he had lost his report.

heartbroken Overcome by sadness: Kristen was *heartbroken* when she could not find her cat.

sorrowful Feeling or inspiring sorrow; sad: That movie had such *sorrowful* music.

sorry Feeling sadness for someone or something; feeling regret for something done: I am *sorry* that the baseball season has come to an end.

unhappy Without joy: The team was *unhappy* when the game was rained out.

wistful Sadly wishing: I get a *wistful* feeling whenever I remember the friends in my old neighborhood.

ANTONYMS: glad, happy, joyful, joyous, overjoyed, pleased

say v. To express in words: "Don't be shy; *say* what's on your mind!" exclaimed Marta.

announce To make known to the public: We are waiting for the newscaster to *announce* the winner of the election.

answer To respond to a question: When my sister asks me what my favorite meal is, I *answer,* "I don't know."

express To tell in words or to show in actions: Sometimes it can be hard to *express* one's feelings.

mention To say something briefly in passing: Did you *mention* this project to Vicki?

remark To express a comment, especially about something that one has seen: People will *remark* about last night's storm for days to come.

speak To talk; to give a speech: The two candidates will *speak* to the students next week.

state To declare; to say: Please stand and *state* your name.

utter To make a sound: My throat is so sore that I barely can *utter* a croak.

see v. To process images of things through the eyes: Mrs. Haynes could *see* the storm clouds approaching quickly.

behold To look on with respect or appreciation: Come and *behold* the beautiful paintings of this artist.

examine To look at closely; to study: Dr. Meyer will *examine* these bones in his laboratory.

gaze To look at steadily and with great interest: If you *gaze* at the clouds long enough, you can see them change shape.

notice To take note of; to glance at or perceive: I *notice* that you are wearing your best shoes today.

observe To watch closely: Class, *observe* what happens when we combine these two chemicals.

view To see or observe: From the mountaintop you can *view* the entire valley.

silent adj. With no noise: *Silent* movies showed pictures and action but had no sound.

hushed Purposely kept quiet: We spoke in *hushed* voices as we waited for the concert to start.

muted Silent; not producing sound: Maria's cry was *muted* as the snake slithered in front of her.

noiseless Without noise, silent: The *noiseless* insects worked hard and steadily.

soundless Making no sound: Our *soundless* steps kept the birds from flying away too quickly.

ANTONYMS: boisterous, clamorous, tumultuous, uproarious

small adj. Little or undersized; of little importance: I'm not very hungry, so I'll just have a *small* piece of fruit.

diminutive Small; tiny: My grandmother is a sweet, *diminutive* woman.

lilliputian Very small; tiny: It is hard to believe she can carry so much with those *lilliputian* hands.

miniature A smaller-size version of something: The dollhouse was filled with *miniature* furniture.

petite Delicate and trim or small: The *petite* woman looked almost like a child.

undersized Smaller than normal: I'm not very hungry, so an *undersized* portion would be best.

ANTONYMS: big, enormous, gigantic, huge, immense, large

smart adj. Having or showing a keen mind or a good education; intelligent: *Smart* plays and a little luck will win the game.

brilliant Marked by extraordinary intelligence or cleverness: Elaine made a *brilliant* move and won the chess match.

clever Having a skillful and quick mind: The *clever* girl put the puzzle together quickly.

crafty Clever, often in a sly way: In folktales, Coyote is a *crafty* character who tries to get what he wants by fooling others.

resourceful Skillful in figuring out solutions to problems: Amy, who is a *resourceful* student, found some great information on Thomas Jefferson.

sharp Having or showing a quick, keen mind: Adam has a *sharp* wit.

wise Showing good sense: Not turning your back on that dog was a *wise* decision.
ANTONYMS: foolish, silly, stupid, unwise

special *adj.* Distinctive; not ordinary: I gave my parents a *special* gift for their twentieth anniversary.

distinctive Standing out because of a special quality: Our school buses were painted a *distinctive* new color last week.

extraordinary Beyond what normally would be expected: Joe DiMaggio had *extraordinary* athletic talent.

rare Hard to find or to duplicate; happening only from time to time: This peach ice cream is a *rare* treat.

uncommon Unusual; rare: Is rain in the desert an *uncommon* event?

unique One of a kind: The chef created a *unique* sauce recipe.
ANTONYMS: common, ordinary, usual

strange *adj.* Unusual; weird: Our hero's nemesis wore a *strange*, lopsided hat.

bizarre Very unusual or strange; odd: No one could explain the *bizarre* happenings at the library.

curious Drawing attention because of an unexpected quality: The *curious* old shop attracted people from all over the town.

mysterious Unexplained or unknown: The walls of the ancient cave were covered with *mysterious* paintings.

novel Original and new: What a *novel* idea that is!

peculiar Strangely different: Hallie's new perfume had a *peculiar* but pleasant scent.
ANTONYMS: common, everyday, familiar, ordinary, usual

tired *adj.* Sleepy or weary; bored with something: After a hard-fought win, the *tired* but happy players went out for pizza.

enervated Deprived of strength and vigor: You should have seen those *enervated* children after our day at the aquarium.

exhausted Having lost all one's energy: They were *exhausted* from looking for Michelle's dog all night.

fatigued Feeling sleepy or without energy: After the double-header, the *fatigued* players were happy to go home.

weary Having no energy; fatigued: The *weary* hiker stopped for lunch and then continued on the mountain trail.
ANTONYMS: energetic, lively

turn *v.* To move in a circular motion: When I have a stiff neck, it hurts to *turn* my head.

circle To move completely around something: We watched the elephants *circle* their young when the lions came near.

revolve To orbit; to move in a circle: Until the tournament is over, their lives will *revolve* around studying and soccer practice.

rotate To spin on an axis (around a central part): As long as Earth continues to *rotate*, we'll always have day and night.

spin To whirl or cause to whirl around and around: The child likes to *spin* the top and watch its swirling colors.

twist To wring or wind: The label reads, "*Twist* to open."

useful *adj.* Serving a purpose: This is a *useful* book because it explains the process step by step.

handy Convenient and easy to use: I depend upon my *handy* pen whenever I need to write something.

helpful Able to give aid: Mrs. Reynolds offered a *helpful* suggestion for those having trouble understanding the book.

practical Sensible and useful: The cook made *practical* meals with simple, healthful foods.

suitable Appropriate: A wrench is the most *suitable* tool for this job.
ANTONYMS: inconvenient, unhelpful, useless

very *adv.* To a high degree: I like to eat out with my family *very* much.

exceedingly Far from the ordinary: Yesterday was an *exceedingly* cold morning.

excessively Beyond the usual or proper limit: Mrs. Offerman became *excessively* angry when the mail carrier stepped on her flowers.

extremely To the utmost; to a great extent: Our neighbors are *extremely* pleased with their new front porch.

inordinately Beyond limits; excessive: Troy is *inordinately* given to telling unbelievable stories.

ANTONYMS: minimally, moderately, temperately

walk *v.* To move using the legs: Do most of these children *walk* to school?

file To walk with one person following behind another: We will have to *file* through this narrow passageway.

hike To walk a long distance, especially in the country: Sharon likes to *hike* in the hills.

march To walk together in formation; to walk in a determined way: All soldiers must learn to *march*.

shuffle To drag the feet while walking: You'll wear out your shoes if you *shuffle* like that.

stroll To walk slowly and casually: Visitors often *stroll* through the beautiful garden.

trudge To walk slowly and with difficulty: Hikers *trudge* up the steep trail to the top of the mountain.

wander To move about without an obvious purpose: I love to *wander* in the park when the autumn leaves are falling.

whole *adj.* Containing all parts; complete: Last night I read the *whole* chapter.

complete Full or entire; absolute: Coach Fernandez has *complete* confidence in my success at the track meet.

entire Total; complete; whole: I finished the *entire* test in less than half an hour.

full Containing as much as possible; occupying all the space: We will need a *full* supply of food before the trip.

unbroken In one piece; not shattered: It is important to find a bottle with an *unbroken* seal.

ANTONYMS: broken, empty, incomplete, partial

Thesaurus Index

A

abandon guard *v.*
abandon leave *v.*
abhor love *v.*
absorbing interesting *adj.*
accept believe *v.*
accept receive *v.*
accord argue *v.*
adjacent close *adj.*
admire love *v.*
adopt receive *v.*
adore love *v.*
adult child *n.*
afraid adj.
aged old *adj.*
agree argue *v.*
alarmed afraid *adj.*
allied combined *adj.*
allow let *v.*
alter change *v.*
amount number *n.*
amusing funny *adj.*
ancient new *adj.*
ancient old *adj.*
angry adj.
announce say *v.*
annoyed angry *adj.*
answer say *v.*
antique old *adj.*
anxious excited *adj.*
apparel clothes *n.*
appropriate bad *adj.*
appropriate good *adj.*
arctic cold *adj.*
argue v.
arrive leave *v.*
assembly audience *n.*
assume receive *v.*
attack honor *v.*
authentic fake *adj.*
authorize let *v.*
awful bad *adj.*
awful good *adj.*

B

bad adj.
bad good *adj.*
barely quite *adv.*
beautiful adj.
befall happen *v.*

behold see *v.*
believe v.
benevolent bad *adj.*
big small *adj.*
bizarre strange *adj.*
boiling hot *adj.*
boisterous silent *adj.*
bold afraid *adj.*
bolt eat *v.*
bordering close *adj.*
bored excited *adj.*
boring interesting *adj.*
brave afraid *adj.*
bravery courage *n.*
breathtaking beautiful *adj.*
brilliant smart *adj.*
broken whole *adj.*
burning cold *adj.*
burning hot *adj.*
bygone old *adj.*

C

calm afraid *adj.*
calm angry *adj.*
calm excited *adj.*
celebrated famous *adj.*
change v.
cheerful happy *adj.*
cherish love *v.*
chief major *adj.*
child n.
chilly cold *adj.*
chunk piece *n.*
circle turn *v.*
clamorous silent *adj.*
clever smart *adj.*
close adj.
clothes n.
cluttered neat *adj.*
cold adj.
cold hot *adj.*
colossal large *adj.*
combined adj.
come leave *v.*
common normal *adj.*
common special *adj.*
common strange *adj.*
complete whole *adj.*
completely quite *adv.*
conceal discover *v.*
conclude believe *v.*

concur argue *v.*
confident afraid *adj.*
consent argue *v.*
consent let *v.*
consume eat *v.*
contemporary old *adj.*
content angry *adj.*
contented happy *adj.*
continue change *v.*
conversely however *adv.*
cool hot *adj.*
courage n.
courageous afraid *adj.*
cover discover *v.*
cover outside *n.*
cowardice courage *n.*
crafty smart *adj.*
cravenness courage *n.*
credit honor *v.*
criticize honor *v.*
crowd audience *n.*
curious strange *adj.*
current new *adj.*
current old *adj.*

D

daring courage *n.*
debate argue *v.*
decline let *v.*
defend guard *v.*
delighted happy *adj.*
deny believe *v.*
deny let *v.*
depart leave *v.*
describe report *v.*
detect discover *v.*
detest love *v.*
diminutive small *adj.*
dine eat *v.*
dirty neat *adj.*
disappointed excited *adj.*
disappointing good *adj.*
disbelieve believe *v.*
disconnected combined *adj.*
discover v.
dishonest good *adj.*
dislike love *v.*
disorganized neat *adj.*
dispute argue *v.*
distant close *adj.*
distinctive special *adj.*
distinguished famous *adj.*

distressed sad *adj.*
doubt believe *v.*
doubtfully probably *adv.*
dreadful bad *adj.*
dress clothes *n.*
dubiously probably *adv.*
dull interesting *adj.*

E

eager excited *adj.*
earn receive *v.*
eat *v.*
elaborate fancy *adj.*
elegant fancy *adj.*
empty whole *adj.*
endanger guard *v.*
endure change *v.*
energetic tired *adj.*
enervated tired *adj.*
enormous large *adj.*
enormous small *adj.*
enthusiastic excited *adj.*
entire whole *adj.*
entirely quite *adv.*
entirety piece *n.*
essential major *adj.*
everyday strange *adj.*
examine see *v.*
exceedingly very *adv.*
excellent good *adj.*
excessively very *adv.*
excited *adj.*
exhausted tired *adj.*
exit leave *v.*
experienced new *adj.*
express say *v.*
exterior outside *n.*
extraordinary normal *adj.*
extraordinary special *adj.*
extremely very *adv.*

F

faintheartedness courage *n.*
fake *adj.*
false fake *adj.*
familiar old *adj.*
familiar strange *adj.*
famous adj.
fancy *adj.*
fans audience *n.*
far close *adj.*
fascinating interesting *adj.*
fast *adj.*
fast eat *v.*

fatigued tired *adj.*
faulty bad *adj.*
fearful afraid *adj.*
fictitious fake *adj.*
file walk *v.*
find discover *v.*
foolish smart *adj.*
fraction piece *n.*
freezing hot *adj.*
fresh new *adj.*
fresh old *adj.*
frightened afraid *adj.*
frigid cold *adj.*
frosty cold *adj.*
frosty hot *adj.*
frozen hot *adj.*
full whole *adj.*
funny adj.
furious angry *adj.*

G

garments clothes *n.*
gaudy fancy *adj.*
gaze see *v.*
gentle adj.
genuine fake *adj.*
gigantic large *adj.*
gigantic small *adj.*
give receive *v.*
glad sad *adj.*
gloomy happy *adj.*
glum happy *adj.*
glum sad *adj.*
gobble eat *v.*
good *adj.*
good bad *adj.*
gorgeous beautiful *adj.*
grand large *adj.*
great large *adj.*
grim happy *adj.*
grown-up child *n.*
guard *v.*
gulp eat *v.*

H

handy useful *adj.*
happen *v.*
happy *adj.*
happy sad *adj.*
hardly quite *adv.*
harsh gentle *adj.*
hasty fast *adj.*
hate love *v.*
heart courage *n.*

heartbroken sad *adj.*
heartsick happy *adj.*
helpful useful *adj.*
hide discover *v.*
hideous beautiful *adj.*
hike walk *v.*
hilarious funny *adj.*
homely beautiful *adj.*
honest good *adj.*
honor *v.*
horrible bad *adj.*
hot *adj.*
hot cold *adj.*
however *adv.*
huge large *adj.*
huge small *adj.*
hunger eat *v.*
hushed silent *adj.*

I

icy cold *adj.*
icy hot *adj.*
imitation fake *adj.*
immense large *adj.*
immense small *adj.*
important *adj.*
important major *adj.*
incomplete whole *adj.*
inconsiderate gentle *adj.*
inconvenient useful *adj.*
inform report *v.*
inherit receive *v.*
inordinately very *adv.*
inside outside *n.*
insignificant major *adj.*
interesting *adj.*
interior outside *n.*
intriguing interesting *adj.*
invent discover *v.*
isolated combined *adj.*

J

jeopardize guard *v.*
joint combined *adj.*
jolly happy *adj.*
joyful happy *adj.*
joyful sad *adj.*
joyous sad *adj.*

K

kid child *n.*

L

large *adj.*
large small *adj.*

latest new *adj.*
leading major *adj.*
least major *adj.*
leave *v.*
leisurely fast *adj.*
lengthy fast *adj.*
let *v.*
likely probably *adv.*
lilliputian small *adj.*
linked combined *adj.*
listeners audience *n.*
little large *adj.*
lively tired *adj.*
loathe love *v.*
love *v.*
lovely beautiful *adj.*
luxurious fancy *adj.*

M
major *adj.*
manageable neat *adj.*
march walk *v.*
marvelous good *adj.*
mature old *adj.*
mean gentle *adj.*
mention say *v.*
merry happy *adj.*
messy neat *adj.*
mild gentle *adj.*
miniature small *adj.*
minimally very *adv.*
minor major *adj.*
moderately very *adv.*
modern new *adj.*
modern old *adj.*
modify change *v.*
munch eat *v.*
muted silent *adj.*
mysterious strange *adj.*

N
narrate report *v.*
nasty good *adj.*
neat *adj.*
necessary important *adj.*
needless important *adj.*
neighboring close *adj.*
nevertheless however *adv.*
new *adj.*
new old *adj.*
nibble eat *v.*
noiseless silent *adj.*
normal *adj.*

noted famous *adj.*
noteworthy important *adj.*
notice see *v.*
notify report *v.*
novel strange *adj.*
number *n.*

O
obscure famous *adj.*
observe see *v.*
occur happen *v.*
old *adj.*
old new *adj.*
onlookers audience *n.*
oppose argue *v.*
orderly neat *adj.*
ordinary normal *adj.*
ordinary special *adj.*
ordinary strange *adj.*
organized neat *adj.*
original new *adj.*
ornate fancy *adj.*
outlying close *adj.*
outside *n.*
overjoyed happy *adj.*
overjoyed sad *adj.*

P
partial whole *adj.*
partially quite *adv.*
peaceful gentle *adj.*
peculiar strange *adj.*
permit let *v.*
petite small *adj.*
picturesque beautiful *adj.*
piece *n.*
plain fancy *adj.*
pleased angry *adj.*
pleased happy *adj.*
pleased sad *adj.*
portion piece *n.*
practical useful *adj.*
praise honor *v.*
pressing important *adj.*
primary major *adj.*
probably *adv.*
progress leave *v.*
prominent important *adj.*
protect guard *v.*

Q
quantity number *n.*
quarrel argue *v.*

question believe *v.*
questionably probably *adv.*
quite *adv.*
quotidian normal *adj.*

R
rapid fast *adj.*
rare normal *adj.*
rare special *adj.*
really quite *adv.*
reasonably probably *adv.*
receive *v.*
reconcile argue *v.*
refuse let *v.*
reject believe *v.*
reject receive *v.*
remain change *v.*
remark say *v.*
remote close *adj.*
renowned famous *adj.*
replace change *v.*
report *v.*
resourceful smart *adj.*
respect honor *v.*
retreat leave *v.*
reveal discover *v.*
revere love *v.*
revolve turn *v.*
ridicule honor *v.*
ridiculous funny *adj.*
riveting interesting *adj.*
roasting cold *adj.*
rotate turn *v.*
rough gentle *adj.*
routine normal *adj.*

S
sad *adj.*
sad happy *adj.*
say *v.*
scorching cold *adj.*
scorching hot *adj.*
scorn honor *v.*
scrap piece *n.*
section piece *n.*
see *v.*
sensitive gentle *adj.*
separate combined *adj.*
serene angry *adj.*
serious funny *adj.*
sharp smart *adj.*
shelter guard *v.*
shield guard *v.*
shuffle walk *v.*

silent *adj.*
silly funny *adj.*
silly smart *adj.*
simple fancy *adj.*
sizzling hot *adj.*
skin outside *n.*
slice piece *n.*
sloppy neat *adj.*
slow fast *adj.*
sluggish fast *adj.*
small *adj.*
small large *adj.*
smart *adj.*
solemn funny *adj.*
sorrowful happy *adj.*
sorrowful sad *adj.*
sorry sad *adj.*
soundless silent *adj.*
speak say *v.*
special *adj.*
spectators audience *n.*
spin turn *v.*
starve eat *v.*
state say *v.*
steaming hot *adj.*
strange *adj.*
stroll walk *v.*
stupid smart *adj.*
suitable useful *adj.*
sum number *n.*
summarize report *v.*
superb bad *adj.*
superb good *adj.*
suppose believe *v.*
surface outside *n.*
sustain change *v.*
swift fast *adj.*
sympathetic gentle *adj.*

T

temperately very *adv.*
tender gentle *adj.*
think believe *v.*
though however *adv.*
thrilled excited *adj.*
tidy neat *adj.*
timid afraid *adj.*
timidity courage *n.*
tiny large *adj.*
tired *adj.*
total number *n.*
total piece *n.*

treasure love *v.*
trivial important *adj.*
trivial major *adj.*
trudge walk *v.*
true fake *adj.*
truthful good *adj.*
tumultuous silent *adj.*
turn *v.*
turn away receive *v.*
twist turn *v.*
typical normal *adj.*

U

ugly beautiful *adj.*
unadorned fancy *adj.*
unattractive beautiful *adj.*
unbroken whole *adj.*
uncaring gentle *adj.*
uncommon normal *adj.*
uncommon special *adj.*
uncover discover *v.*
undersized large *adj.*
undersized small *adj.*
understand believe *v.*
unenthusiastic excited *adj.*
unfamiliar new *adj.*
unhappy happy *adj.*
unhappy sad *adj.*
unheard of famous *adj.*
unhelpful useful *adj.*
unimportant important *adj.*
unimportant large *adj.*
unimportant major *adj.*
uninterested excited *adj.*
uninteresting interesting *adj.*
unique special *adj.*
unknown famous *adj.*
unnecessary important *adj.*
unpleasant bad *adj.*
unpleasant good *adj.*
unrelated combined *adj.*
unruffled angry *adj.*
unsightly beautiful *adj.*
untrimmed fancy *adj.*
unusual normal *adj.*
unwise smart *adj.*
uproarious silent *adj.*
upset angry *adj.*
used new *adj.*
used old *adj.*
useful *adj.*
useless important *adj.*
useless useful *adj.*
usual normal *adj.*

usual special *adj.*
usual strange *adj.*
utter say *v.*

V

valor courage *n.*
very *adv.*
view see *v.*
violent gentle *adj.*
virtuous bad *adj.*
virtuous good *adj.*
vital important *adj.*

W

walk *v.*
wander walk *v.*
wardrobe clothes *n.*
weary tired *adj.*
weighty important *adj.*
well-behaved good *adj.*
well-known famous *adj.*
whole *adj.*
whole piece *n.*
wholly quite *adv.*
wise smart *adj.*
wistful sad *adj.*
witty funny *adj.*
worn new *adj.*
worn old *adj.*
worthless important *adj.*
worthy good *adj.*
wretched happy *adj.*

Y

young old *adj.*
youngster child *n.*
youth child *n.*

Using the Glossary

Like a dictionary, this glossary lists words in alphabetical order. It contains the Vocabulary Power words, the grammatical terms, the writing forms, and other important terms covered in this book. To find a word, look it up by its first letters.

To save time, use the **guide words** at the top of each page. These show you the first and last words on the page. Look at the guide words to see if your word falls between them alphabetically.

Here is an example of a glossary entry:

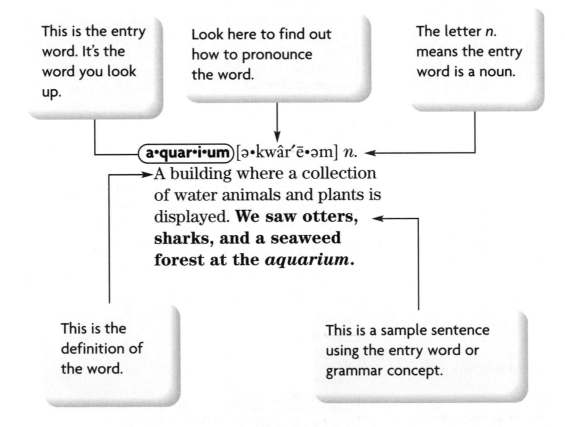

This is the entry word. It's the word you look up.

Look here to find out how to pronounce the word.

The letter *n.* means the entry word is a noun.

a•quar•i•um [ə•kwâr′ē•əm] *n.* A building where a collection of water animals and plants is displayed. **We saw otters, sharks, and a seaweed forest at the *aquarium*.**

This is the definition of the word.

This is a sample sentence using the entry word or grammar concept.

Pronunciation

The pronunciation in brackets is a respelling that shows how the word is pronounced.

The **pronunciation key** explains what the symbols in a respelling mean. A shortened pronunciation key appears on every other page of the glossary.

Pronunciation Key*

a	add, map	m	move, seem	u	up, done
ā	ace, rate	n	nice, tin	û(r)	burn, turn
â(r)	care, air	ng	ring, song	y$\overline{oo}$	fuse, few
ä	palm, father	o	odd, hot	v	vain, eve
b	bat, rub	ō	open, so	w	win, away
ch	check, catch	ô	order, jaw	y	yet, yearn
d	dog, rod	oi	oil, boy	z	zest, muse
e	end, pet	ou	pout, now	zh	vision, pleasure
ē	equal, tree	o͝o	took, full	ə	the schwa, an
f	fit, half	o͞o	pool, food		unstressed vowel
g	go, log	p	pit, step		representing the
h	hope, hate	r	run, poor		sound spelled
i	it, give	s	see, pass		*a* in *above*
ī	ice, write	sh	sure, rush		*e* in *sicken*
j	joy, ledge	t	talk, sit		*i* in *possible*
k	cool, take	th	thin, both		*o* in *melon*
l	look, rule	t͟h	this, bathe		*u* in *citrus*

Other symbols
- separates words into syllables
′ indicates heavier stress on a syllable
′ indicates light stress on a syllable

Abbreviations: *adj.* adjective, *adv.* adverb, *conj.* conjunction, *interj.* interjection, *n.* noun, *prep.* preposition, *pron.* pronoun, *syn.* synonym, *v.* verb

A

ab·bre·vi·a·tion [ə·brē′vē·ā′shən] *n.* A shortened form of a word. A period is used after most abbreviations: *Dr. Dulaney, 123 Front Ave., Mar.* **5**

ac·tion verb [ak′shən vûrb] *n.* A word that tells what the subject of a sentence does, did, or will do: **Hideo** *ran* **down the street.**

ad·jec·tive [aj′ik·tiv] *n.* A word that describes a noun or a pronoun. Adjectives tell *what kind, how many,* or *which one*: **The** *playful brown* **puppy licked Anwar's face. They were both** *tired*.

ad·verb [ad′vûrb] *n.* A word that describes a verb, an adjective, or another adverb: **Eva skated** *very quickly* **across the** *extremely* **thick ice.**

aer·o·bics [âr·ō′biks] *n.* Vigorous physical exercises designed to increase the body's capacity to take in and use oxygen: **Kim started doing** *aerobics* **three times a week to keep fit.**

an·thol·o·gy [an·thol′ə·jē] *n.* A collection of short works, such as poems, essays, or short stories: **Ben read an** *anthology* **of short stories by Poe.**

an·thro·pol·o·gist [an′thrə·pol′ə·jist] *n.* A scientist who studies how people have lived together, from ancient times to the present: **My aunt, an** *anthropologist*, **is an expert on ancient Egyptian culture.**

a·pos·tro·phe [ə·pos′trə·fē] *n.* A punctuation mark (') that shows possession or takes the place of one or more letters that are left out in a contraction: *Haven't* **you seen** *Joseph's* **new bicycle?**

ap·pos·i·tive [ə·poz′ə·tiv] *n.* A noun or noun phrase that renames another noun or noun phrase: **My favorite book,** *a mystery*, **is called** <u>**The Hidden Door**</u>**.**

ap·pren·tice [ə·pren′tis] *n.* A person who works for another person in order to learn a trade or business: **In colonial times, a boy or girl could learn a craft by being an** *apprentice* **to a master craftsperson.**

a·quar·i·um [ə·kwâr′ē·əm] *n.* A building where a collection of water animals and plants is displayed: **During our field trip to the** *aquarium*, **we saw otters and sharks.**

ar·chi·tec·ture [är′kə·tek′chər] *n.* The science or profession of designing and putting up buildings and other structures: **The study of** *architecture* **includes how buildings were designed in ancient Greece.**

ar·ti·cle [är′ti·kəl] *n.* The adjectives *a, an,* and *the* are called articles: **The school library has** *a* **copy of** *an* **old almanac.**

as·tro·nom·i·cal [as′trə·nom′i·kəl] *adj.* Having to do with astronomy: **The professor spoke to us about the stars, the planets, and other** *astronomical* **topics.**

B

busi·ness let·ter [biz′nis let′ər] *n.* A letter in a polite, formal tone, written to a person the letter writer does not know.

Its purpose can be to request information, to order something, to apply for a job, or to express an opinion: **Lisa wrote a *business letter* to the fire department to request fire safety information.**

car·di·ol·o·gy [kär′dē·ol′ə·jē] *n.* The study of the heart and its diseases and their treatment: **Dr. Nadal, who specializes in *cardiology*, treats people with heart problems.**

char·ac·ter stud·y [kar′ik·tər stud′ē] *n.* The form of expressive writing in which a writer describes a person or character: **Manuel wrote a *character study* that described an action hero he wanted to include in a story.**

clause [klôz] *n.* A group of words that has both a subject and a predicate: ***When we arrived at the movie theater*, we bought our tickets.**

co·lon [kō′lən] *n.* A punctuation mark (:) that is used in the following ways: to introduce a list of items, to separate the hours and minutes when writing time, and after the last word in the greeting of a business letter: **We raised the following *vegetables*: tomatoes, peppers, and carrots. *4:30* Dear Mr. *Martinez*:**

com·bin·ing sen·ten·ces [kəm·bīn′ing sen′tən·səz] *v.* Putting related ideas and information together in one sentence

instead in two or three sentences: **(separated) Bill gathered his library books. Then he went to the library. He returned them. (combined) After Bill gathered his library books, he went to the library and returned them.**

com·ma [kom′ə] *n.* A punctuation mark (,) that is used to separate words, phrases, or clauses in a sentence: ***Well*, my favorite foods are peanut *butter*, mashed *potatoes*, and watermelon. *Samantha*, my *cousin*, did her *homework*, played with her *dog*, and rode her bike. A newborn kitten cannot *see*, but it knows its mother.**

com·ma splice [kom′ə splīs] *n.* A comma splice occurs when only a comma is used to join two sentences: **(incorrect) We went to the theater, the movie had already started. (corrected) We went to the theater, but the movie had already started.**

com·mon noun [kom′ən noun] *n.* A word that names any person, place, thing, or idea: **This *week* our basketball *team* plays in the championship *game*.**

com·par·ing with ad·jec·tives [kəm·pâr′ing with aj′ik·tivz] *v.* An adjective can be used to compare people, places, things, or ideas: **My brother is *older* than you. Ronald Reagan was the *oldest* person to be elected President. A governor is *more powerful* than a mayor.**

a add	e end	o odd	o͞o pool	oi oil	th this	ə = { a in *above*
ā ace	ē equal	ō open	u up	ou pout	zh vision	e in *sicken*
â care	i it	ô order	û burn	ng ring		i in *possible*
ä palm	ī ice	o͝o took	yo͞o fuse	th thin		o in *melon*
						u in *circus*

com·par·ing with ad·verbs [kəm·pâr′ing with ad′vûrbz] *n.* An adverb can be used to compare actions: **This artist works *harder* in the mornings. Some painters work *more steadily* than others do. Of all subjects, she paints portraits *most frequently*.**

com·par·i·son/con·trast es·say [kəm·par′ə·sən kən′trast es′ā] *n.* An essay that tells how two or more things are alike (comparison) and how they are different (contrast): **In her *comparison/contrast essay*, Lynn showed how lizards and frogs are alike and how they are different.**

com·plete pred·i·cate [kəm·plēt′ pred′i·kit] *n.* All the words that tell what the subject of the sentence is or does: **Abigail Adams *wrote long letters to her husband*.**

com·plete sub·ject [kəm·plēt′ sub′jekt] *n.* All the words that name the person or thing the sentence is about: ***Only one President in history* was elected to four terms.**

com·plex sen·tence [kom′pleks sen′təns] *n.* A sentence made up of an independent clause and at least one dependent clause: ***After we saw the Washington Monument, we visited the White House. I wrote a report about the trip when I returned home.***

com·pound pred·i·cate [kom′pound′ pred′i·kit] *n.* Two or more predicates that have the same subject: **Benjamin Franklin *lived in Philadelphia* and *wrote an almanac*.**

com·pound sen·tence [kom′pound′ sen′təns] *n.* A sentence made up of two or more simple sentences joined by a coordinating conjunction such as *and, or,* or *but*: ***Benjamin Franklin began his career as a printer, but he later became an inventor*.**

com·pound sub·ject [kom′pound′ sub′jekt] *n.* Two or more subjects joined by a conjunction, usually *and* or *or*. Compound subjects have the same predicate: ***Marta* and *Atsuko* are on the swim team. *Friday* or *Saturday* will be the day of the swim meet.**

con·junc·tion [kən·jungk′shən] *n.* A word that joins two or more words, phrases, or clauses: **Leah *and* Anita take dancing lessons. We visited the aquarium *and* the zoo. They wanted to play ball outside, *but* it was raining.**

con·sti·tu·tion [kon′stə·t(y)ōō′shən] *n.* A written plan of government that states the basic laws or rules: **The *Constitution* of the United States established three branches of government.**

con·trac·tion [kən·trak′shən] *n.* The shortened form of two words written as one word. An apostrophe (') takes the place of one or more letters: ***We're* in the cafeteria. She *isn't* home right now.**

de·clar·a·tive sen·tence [di·klar′ə·tiv sen′təns] *n.* A sentence that makes a statement. It ends with a period: ***She lives in California*.**

de·pen·dent clause [di·pen′dənt klôz] *n.* A group of words that has a subject and a predicate but cannot stand alone as a sentence. A dependent clause does not express a complete thought: ***When we went to the beach,* we had fun.**

de·scrip·tive word [di·skrip′tiv wûrd] *n.* A word that is colorful and describes something clearly: **The *silvery* waves *spiraled* among the *jagged* rocks.**

de·scrip·tive writ·ing [di·skrip′tiv rī′ting] *n.* Writing that describes a place, a person, a thing, or an event by using a variety of sensory details: **After the rain, emerald leaves dripped in a steady rhythm, and the smell of wet earth rose like an invisible fog.**

de·tail [dē′tāl] *n.* A fact or an example that helps explain a topic in informative writing or supports a reason in persuasive writing: **(topic) There are many historic sites in Washington, D.C. (detail) The Lincoln Memorial honors Abraham Lincoln.**

di·a·logue [dī′ə·lôg′] *n.* A conversation in which two or more speakers take part. Quotation marks are used to show what each says: **"What are you doing this weekend?" asked Rachel. Tammi answered, "I'm going swimming."**

di·rect ob·ject [di·rekt′ ob′jekt] *n.* The word that receives the action of a verb. The direct object answers the question *whom* or *what* after the verb: **We splashed *Ben* with water. I caught the *ball.***

di·rect quo·ta·tion [di·rekt′ kwō·tā′shən] *n.* The exact words that someone has said. Quotation marks are used

before and after a direct quotation: **The gardener said, "My vegetables are growing well this year."**

ef·fec·tive sen·ten·ces [i·fek′tiv sen′tən·səz] *n.* Sentences that give information in a clear and interesting way that holds the reader's interest: **In some parts of Africa, travelers can see giraffes, gazelles, zebras, and other fascinating animals.**

e·lab·o·ra·tion [i·lab′ə·rā′shən] *n.* Developing and expanding a topic by adding details and reasons: **(topic) Fruit is a convenient snack. (elaboration) Apples, bananas, and oranges can be easily carried in a pocket or a book bag.**

en·tre·pre·neur [än′trə·prə·nûr′] *n.* A person who organizes and runs a business venture: **Luis is an *entrepreneur* who owns three video stores.**

en·vi·ron·ment [in·vī′rən·mənt] *n.* The conditions and surroundings that have an effect on the development of a person, an animal, or a plant: **Plants and animals in a desert *environment* have adapted to life with little water.**

e·val·u·ate [i·val′yo͞o·āt′] *v.* To judge the value of; appraise: **A writer can *evaluate* the effectiveness of a story by looking for words and**

a	add	e	end	o	odd	o͞o	pool	oi	oil	th	this		*a* in *above*
ā	ace	ē	equal	ō	open	u	up	ou	pout	zh	vision	ə =	*e* in *sicken*
â	care	i	it	ô	order	û	burn	ng	ring				*i* in *possible*
ä	palm	ī	ice	o͝o	took	yo͞o	fuse	th	thin				*o* in *melon*
													u in *circus*

sentences that might be
strengthened.

ex·cla·ma·tion point [eks′klə·mā′shən
point] *n.* End punctuation (!) for an
exclamatory sentence: **What a
beautiful painting!**

ex·clam·a·to·ry sen·tence
[eks·klam′ə·tôr′ē sen′təns] *n.* A
sentence that expresses strong feeling.
An exclamatory sentence ends with an
exclamation point: ***That was a
fantastic game!***

ex·ert [ig·zûrt′] *v.* To put forth or use
something such as one's influence; to
put forth effort or try hard: **Soccer
players *exert* a lot of energy
running down the field. They *exert*
themselves at every game.**

fas·ci·na·ting [fas′ə·nā′ting] *adj.* Strongly
attracting and holding the attention of
others; extremely interesting: **The
story was so *fascinating* that Reka
read it in one evening.**

fig·ur·a·tive lan·guage [fig′yər·ə·tiv
lang′gwij] *n.* Language that compares
an object to something that is quite
different. Common types include
similes, which use *like* or *as*, and
metaphors, which say that one thing is
the other: **The moon *was like a
shining pearl* in the starry sky. The
moon *was a shining pearl* in the
starry sky.**

form [fôrm] *n.* A document that requires
a person to write information in blank
spaces. Forms generally ask for
information such as name, address,
age, and telephone number: **Anyone

who applies for a job usually must
complete an application *form*.**

friend·ly let·ter [frend′lē let′ər] *n.* A
letter written in an informal, casual
tone to someone the letter writer
knows well. Its purpose is to exchange
news or send greetings: **Juan wrote a
friendly letter to his cousin, telling
him about the championship soccer
game.**

fron·tier [frun·tir′] *n.* An unexplored or
undeveloped area that lies beyond a
settled region: **Settlers on the
frontier were far from cities and
other people.**

future perfect tense verb [fyo͞o′chər
pûr′fekt tens vûrb] *n.* A verb that shows
action that will finish by a specific time
in the future: **After we finish this
unit, we *will have learned* a lot.**

fu·ture tense verb [fyo͞o′chər tens vûrb]
n. A verb that tells what the subject
will do or be at a time yet to come. The
future tense is formed by using the
helping verb *will*: **The people *will
vote* in November.**

graph·ic [graf′ik] *adj.* Having to do with
drawing, painting, photography, or
engraving: **A *graphic* artist can
make images with pens, paints,
or computer software.**

gro·tesque [grō·tesk′] *adj.* Distorted or
very strange or ugly in appearance or
style: ***Grotesque*, animal-like figures
called gargoyles used to be placed
on buildings as protection.**

568

hand·i·craft [han′dē·kraft′] *n.* Skill in working with the hands; also, a trade, occupation, or art requiring such skill: **His grandmother's *handicraft* is making beautiful quilts.**

help·ing verb [help′ing vûrb] *n.* A verb that works with a main verb to tell about an action or state of being: **I *am* reading an interesting book. *Will* you visit the observatory? The trip *should* be fun.**

how-to es·say [hou tōō es′ā] *n.* An essay that gives step-by-step directions that explain how to do something or make something: **Chin-Lin wrote a *how-to essay* about building a birdhouse.**

hy·phen [hī′fən] *n.* A punctuation mark (-) that connects two words to form a compound word. A hyphen is also used after a syllable of a word that has been divided at the end of a line: **Her *sister-in-law* is *thirty-two* years old. My sister wants to be an *astronaut* when she grows up.**

im·age·ry [im′ij·rē] *n.* Vivid language that helps the reader form a mental picture: **The *fragrant* breeze *tickled* my face and *made the daisies dance*.**

im·mi·grant [im′ə·grənt] *n.* A person who moves to a new land in order to live there: ***Immigrants* have come** from many countries to live in the United States.

im·per·a·tive sen·tence [im·per′ə·tiv sen′təns] *n.* A sentence that gives a command or makes a request. The subject *you* is understood. An imperative sentence ends with a period: ***Look in the dictionary for the definition.***

im·pro·vise [im′prə·vīz′] *v.* To make up (music, verse, or a speech) at the time of performance and without preparation: **The club president had to *improvise* a speech at the last minute.**

in·au·gu·ra·tion [in·ô′gyə·rā′shən] *n.* A ceremony installing a person in an office: **The President takes the oath of office at the *inauguration* in January.**

in·de·pen·dent clause [in′di·pen′dənt klôz] *n.* A clause that can stand alone as a sentence because it expresses a complete thought: **Benjamin Franklin invented many things.**

in·dus·try [in′dəs·trē] *n.* Businesses or manufacturing; also, a type of business, such as the clothing industry: **Singers and songwriters work in the music *industry*.**

in·form·a·tive writ·ing [in·fôr′mə·tiv rī′ting] *n.* Writing that gives information about a topic: **Martin Luther King, Jr., was awarded the Nobel Prize for Peace in 1964.**

in·ter·rog·a·tive sen·tence [in′tə·rog′ə·tiv sen′təns] *n.* A sentence that asks a

a	add	e	end	o	odd	ōō	pool	oi	oil	th	this
ā	ace	ē	equal	ō	open	u	up	ou	pout	zh	vision
â	care	i	it	ô	order	û	burn	ng	ring	
ä	palm	ī	ice	ŏŏ	took	yōō	fuse	th	thin	

ə = { *a* in *above*
e in *sicken*
i in *possible*
o in *melon*
u in *circus*

569

question. An interrogative sentence ends with a question mark: *What was the final score?*

in·vi·ta·tion [in′və·tā′shən] *n.* A form of writing used to invite someone to a party or other event: **Sara sent an *invitation* for her birthday party to each of her friends.**

ir·reg·u·lar verb [i·reg′yə·lər vûrb] *n.* A verb that does not end in *ed* in the past and past-participle forms: **Amber *saw* the birds before they *flew* away. The campers have *ridden* horses and *slept* under the stars.**

L

let·ter to the ed·i·tor [let′ər too the ed′i·tər] *n.* A business letter written to the editor of a newspaper or magazine. Its purpose is to express an opinion and to persuade others to agree: **Alex wrote a *letter to the editor* of the Daily News, explaining why he thought the new city park was a good idea.**

link·ing verb [lingk′ing vûrb] *n.* A verb that links the subject of a sentence to a word or words (in the predicate) that rename or describe the subject: **Texas and California *are* large states. The wind *feels* cold. The weather *became* colder overnight.**

M

main verb [mān vûrb] *n.* The most important verb in a verb phrase: **Teresa is *going* on the field**

trip. Her parents must *sign* a permission form.

met·a·phor [met′ə·fôr′] *n.* Figurative language that suggests, without saying *like* or *as*, that one thing is like another: **The river was a silver ribbon.**

me·te·or·ol·o·gist [mē′tē·ə·rol′ə·jist] *n.* A scientist who studies weather, winds, and the air around the Earth: **The *meteorologist* gives weather information during the evening news on television.**

N

neg·a·tive [neg′ə·tiv] *n.* A word that has "no" or "not" in its meaning: **He has *never* played chess before. He says *nothing* will stop him from learning how.**

news sto·ry [n(y)ooz stôr′ē] *n.* A form of writing that gives facts about an important or unusual event that happened recently: **I read the *news story* about the election in This Week magazine.**

notes [nōts] *n.* Brief facts or statements written on note cards, often for gathering information: **When you do research, it's important to take *notes* on the facts you want to remember or use in a report.**

noun [noun] *n.* A word that names a person, a place, a thing, or an idea: **The *mayor* works in this *office*. This *book* is about *freedom*.**

nu·tri·tion [n(y)oo·trish′ən] *n.* Food, nourishment; also, the process used by a body to take in and use food as

energy: **The Food Guide Pyramid
helps us choose foods for good
nutrition.**

ob·ject of the prep·o·si·tion [ob′jekt uv
th̶ə prep′ə·zish′ən] *n.* The noun or
pronoun that follows a preposition:
**Marta put the flowers on the *table*
beside the *candles*.**

ob·ject pro·noun [ob′jekt prō′noun] *n.* A
pronoun that takes the place of a noun
or nouns after an action verb or after a
preposition: **Rachel applied for the
job, and Mr. Nagata hired *her*. She
enjoys working for *him*.**

om·niv·o·rous [om·niv′ər·əs] *adj.* Eating
both animal and vegetable food; also,
eagerly taking in everything: **People
who eat both meat and vegetables
are *omnivorous*. An *omnivorous*
reader enjoys reading many kinds
of books and stories.**

o·pen·ing sen·tence [ō′pən·ing sen′təns]
n. The first sentence of a composition,
often written to lead into the main idea
and spark the reader's interest: **Some
writers use a question as an
opening sentence to get their
readers' attention.**

out·line [out′līn′] *n.* A form for
organizing information and putting
facts in order before writing. The main
idea of each paragraph is next to a
Roman numeral. The details that
support each main idea are listed next

to capital letters under each Roman
numeral: **Nina's *outline* helped her
organize the information for her
report and put it in the most
effective order.**

par·a·graph·ing [par′ə·graf·ing] *n.*
Arrangement of information or ideas in
paragraphs. Most paragraphs are
formed with a topic sentence and
supporting details and examples.
Paragraphs should be written in
correct order, or sequence, and
connected to each other by transitions:
**Luis used *paragraphing* to explain
each main idea and to make his
essay easy for the reader to follow.**

past par·ti·ci·ple [past pär′tə·sip′əl] *n.*
One of the four principal, or main,
parts of a verb. A past participle is
used with a helping verb in a verb
phrase: **Alan has *washed* the car.
His brother had *driven* it through
some mud.**

past per·fect tense verb [past pûr′fekt
tens vûrb] *n.* A verb that shows action
that happened before a specific time in
the past and that has stopped: **Lisa
had left by the time I arrived.**

past tense verb [past tens vûrb] *n.* A verb
that tells what the subject did or was
some time ago: **Our family *enjoyed*
our summer vacation. We *rode* a
train.**

a add	e end	o odd	o͞o pool	oi oil	t̶h̶ this		a in *above*
ā ace	ē equal	ō open	u up	ou pout	zh vision	ə =	e in *sicken*
â care	i it	ô order	û burn	ng ring			i in *possible*
ä palm	ī ice	o͝o took	yo͞o fuse	th thin			o in *melon*
							u in *circus*

571

per·fect ten·ses [pûr′fekt ten′səz] *n.* Verb tenses formed with the past participle and a form of the helping verb *have*. There are three perfect tenses: present perfect, past perfect, and future perfect: **He *has played* basketball all afternoon. He *had played* soccer earlier in the day. He *will have practiced* for several hours.**

pe·ri·od [pir′ē·əd] *n.* A punctuation mark (.) used as an end mark for declarative and imperative sentences and at the end of abbreviations: **We walked to *school*. Pick up your *book*. *Mr.* Harris teaches fifth *grade*.**

per·son·al nar·ra·tive [pûr′sən·əl nar′ə·tiv] *n.* A true story that a writer writes about himself or herself: **I enjoyed reading your *personal narrative* about going fishing with your grandfather.**

per·son·al voice [pûr′sən·əl vois] *n.* Each writer's individual way of expression; a writer's style: **This writer expresses her *personal voice* by describing the setting in great detail and by using lively dialogue for her characters.**

per·spec·tive [pər·spek′tiv] *n.* A way of seeing and judging things in relation to one another; viewpoint; outlook: **From Alan's *perspective*, the two friends had enough in common to resolve their differences.**

per·sua·sion [pər·swā′zhən] *n.* The act of persuading, or getting someone to believe, to do, or not to do something, by argument, urging, or advice: **One way to learn the art of *persuasion* is to participate in a debate.**

per·sua·sive writ·ing [pər·swā′siv rī′ting] *n.* Writing that is used to persuade others to do something or to agree with a point of view: **Advertisers use *persuasive writing* to try to convince people that they need their products.**

phrase [frāz] *n.* A group of closely related words that work together. A phrase does not contain a subject and a predicate: ***in the house, will be going, the first week***

play [plā] *n.* A story that is written in dialogue, which is the words that characters say to one another. The purpose of a play is to entertain an audience. Actors play the parts of the characters: **The *play* had seven characters and was about pioneers settling the western frontier.**

play·wright [plā′rīt′] *n.* A person who writes plays: **The *playwright* made some changes to the script after the first performance.**

plu·ral noun [ploͭor′əl noun] *n.* A noun that names more than one person, place, thing, or idea: ***sisters, lakes, dishes, mysteries***

plu·ral pos·ses·sive noun [ploͭor′əl pə·zes′iv noun] *n.* A noun that shows ownership by more than one person or thing: **The *students'* teacher spoke clearly. The *children's* mother was tall.**

po·em [pō′əm] *n.* A form of writing in which a writer uses vivid or unusual words to describe something or express feelings about a subject. Poems often have rhyme and rhythm: **Ram wrote a *poem* describing the**

beauty of autumn, and every other line rhymed.

por·trait [pôr′trit] *n.* A drawing, painting, or photograph of a person, showing especially the face: **Before photography, having a *portrait* drawn or painted was the only way to have a picture of someone.**

pos·ses·sive noun [pə·zes′iv noun] *n.* A noun that shows ownership. A singular possessive noun shows ownership by one person or thing. A plural possessive noun shows ownership by more than one person or thing: **The *student's* book is on the desk. The *students'* classroom is large.**

pos·ses·sive pro·noun [pə·zes′iv prō′noun] *n.* A pronoun that shows ownership and takes the place of a possessive noun. One kind of possessive pronoun is used before a noun. The other kind of possessive pronoun stands alone: ***My* team is going to the play-off. This ball is *mine.***

pow·er·ful [pou′ər·fəl] *adj.* Having great power or the ability or capacity to do something or to produce a certain effect: ***Powerful* words make a strong impression on readers.**

pred·i·cate [pred′i·kit] *n.* The part of a sentence that tells what the subject is or does: **Maribel *practices the piano every day.***

prep·o·si·tion [prep′ə·zish′ən] *n.* A word that tells the relationship of a noun or a pronoun to another word in the sentence: **The lamp is *on* the table.**

You can borrow books *from* the library.

prep·o·si·tion·al phrase [prep′ə·zish′ən·əl frāz] *n.* A phrase made up of a preposition, the object of the preposition, and any words between them. A prepositional phrase can answer questions such as *where, what kind, which one, when,* or *how*: **Gold was discovered *at Sutter's Mill.* People *with dreams of riches* went *to California.***

pres·ent par·ti·ci·ple [prez′ənt pär′tə·sip′əl] *n.* One of the four principal, or main, parts of a verb. A present participle is used with a helping verb in a verb phrase: **I *am reading* the movie listings in the newspaper. The movie *is playing* until Saturday.**

pres·ent per·fect tense verb [prez′ənt pûr′fekt tens vûrb] *n.* A verb that shows action that started in the past and that is still continuing: **We *have learned* a lot since we started this unit.**

pres·ent tense verb [prez′ənt tens vûrb] *n.* A verb that tells what the subject does or is now or that tells what happens over and over: **Our photography club *meets* today. We *meet* every Wednesday after school.**

prin·ci·pal parts of verbs [prin′sə·pəl pärts uv vûrbz] *n.* The forms of a verb that help it express time and action. The four principal, or main, parts are called the present, the present participle, the past, and the past participle: **(present)** *play;*

a add	e end	o odd	ōō pool	oi oil	th this	ə =	a in *above*
ā ace	ē equal	ō open	u up	ou pout	zh vision		e in *sicken*
â care	i it	ô order	û burn	ng ring			i in *possible*
ä palm	ī ice	ŏŏ took	yōō fuse	th thin			o in *melon*
							u in *circus*

(present participle) [is] *playing*;
(past) *played*; (past participle)
[have, has, had] *played*.

pro·noun [prō′noun] *n.* A word that
takes the place of one or more nouns:
She will ask *them* to join *her*. Did
you see *it*?

pro·noun an·te·ce·dent [prō′noun
an′tə·sēd′(ə)nt] *n.* The noun or nouns to
which a pronoun refers. A pronoun
must agree with its antecedent in
number and gender: *Gary and Jerry*
ran because *they* **were in a hurry.**
Nina **likes animals, and** *she* **wants
to be a veterinarian.**

prop·er ad·jec·tive [prop′ər aj′ik·tiv] *n.*
An adjective that is formed from a
proper noun. Proper adjectives are
capitalized: **Erica's dog is a** *French*
poodle. My aunt likes *Chinese* **food.**

prop·er noun [prop′ər noun] *n.* The
name or title of a particular person,
place, or thing: **The** *Camera Club*
will meet every *Tuesday* **in** *March*.
Ed **borrows books from the** *Clay
County Library* **in** *Jamestown*.

ques·tion mark [kwes′chən märk] *n.*
The end mark (?) of an interrogative
sentence: **Where is the game?**

quo·ta·tion marks [kwō·tā′shən märks] *n.*
Punctuation marks (" ") that are used
before and after a direct quotation and
in some titles: **Kim said, "I saw
leopards at the zoo." The name of
the song is "This Land Is Your
Land."**

rea·son [rē′zən] *n.* An explanation or
cause for an action or belief. In
persuasive writing, reasons are given
to convince others to agree with an
opinion: **The letter to the editor
listed three** *reasons* **why the new
sports field was needed.**

re·flex·ive pro·noun [ri·flek′siv prō′noun]
n. A pronoun that refers back to a
noun or pronoun. A reflexive pronoun
agrees with its antecedent in number
and gender: **Carmen sang softly to**
herself. **Jack and Luis set goals for**
themselves.

reg·u·lar verb [reg′yə·lər vûrb] *n.* A verb
that ends with *ed* in the past and past-
participle forms: **She** *danced* **in
the recital. She has** *painted* **for
several years.**

re·search re·port [rē′sûrch ri·pôrt′] *n.* A
form of writing that gives facts about a
topic that the writer has researched:
**Tak chose the Alamo as the topic
of his** *research report*.

run-on sen·tence [run′ôn′ sen′təns] *n.*
Two sentences with no punctuation
between them: **(run-on) Joel reads
a lot he also likes to write stories.
(corrected) Joel reads a lot. He
also likes to write stories.** *or* **Joel
reads a lot, and he likes to write
stories.**

sem·i·co·lon [sem′ē·kō′lən] *n.* A
punctuation mark (;) that may be used
to join two closely related simple
sentences into a compound sentence:

Lisa makes *kites;* she enjoys flying them.

sen·so·ry de·tails [sen′sər·ē dē′tālz] *n.* Details that appeal to the five senses by telling how something looks, sounds, feels, smells, or tastes: **In her *warm* kitchen, my *silver-haired* grandmother stirs the *bubbling* pot of chili that *smells deliciously spicy*.**

sen·tence [sen′təns] *n.* A group of words that expresses a complete thought: **Kim painted the fence.**

sen·tence frag·ment [sen′təns frag′mənt] *n.* A group of words that does not express a complete thought. In some fragments, the subject or the predicate is missing. Others may be dependent clauses without an independent clause: **(fragments) The soccer team. Played a great game. Because they had practiced regularly. (corrected) The soccer team played a great game because they had practiced regularly.**

sen·tence va·ri·e·ty [sen′təns və·rī′ə·tē] *n.* Different types of sentences in a passage: **A good writer uses *sentence variety* to keep readers interested.**

se·quence [sē′kwəns] *n.* The order in which a writer puts information to make it understandable. Two kinds of sequence are chronological, or time, order and order of importance: **First, I got the rake. Then, I raked the leaves into piles. Finally, I put** the leaves into bags and put the rake away.

se·quence of ten·ses [sē′kwəns uv ten′səz] *n.* Within a sentence or paragraph, the order of verb tenses that makes the order of events clear: **He *is sitting* where he *sat* yesterday. They *sang* well because they *had practiced* often.**

sim·i·le [sim′ə·lē] *n.* Figurative language that expresses how one thing is similar to another by using the words *like* or *as*: **The lake is *like a mirror*. The lake is *as shiny as a mirror*.**

sim·ple pred·i·cate [sim′pəl pred′i·kit] *n.* The main word or words in a complete predicate. The simple predicate is always a verb or verb phrase: **Amy *swam* across the pool. Mike *has played* all evening.**

sim·ple sen·tence [sim′pəl sen′təns] *n.* A sentence that expresses only one complete thought: **We live in Clarksville. My sister and I go to middle school. We do homework and study every weeknight.**

sim·ple sub·ject [sim′pəl sub′jekt] *n.* The main word or words in the complete subject: **The big *dog* barks loudly. My *mother* is a teacher.**

sin·gu·lar noun [sing′gyə·lər noun] *n.* A noun that names only one person, place, thing, or idea: ***Patricia* lives in *Texas*. Our *country* is a *democracy*.**

sin·gu·lar pos·ses·sive noun [sing′gyə·lər pə·zes′iv noun] *n.* A noun that shows ownership by one person or thing:

a add	e end	o odd	o͞o pool	oi oil	t͟h this		a in *above*
ā ace	ē equal	ō open	u up	ou pout	zh vision	ə =	e in *sicken*
â care	i it	ô order	û burn	ng ring			i in *possible*
ä palm	ī ice	o͝o took	yo͞o fuse	th thin			o in *melon*
							u in *circus*

Her *brother's* bicycle is blue. The *rake's* handle is plastic.

spe·cif·ic noun [spi·sif′ik noun] *n.* A noun that says exactly what the writer means: **(general) We played games at the playground. (specific) Alex and I played *basketball* and *volleyball* at the playground.**

stam·i·na [stam′ə·nə] *n.* Vitality; vigor; strength; endurance: **A runner must have *stamina* to complete a long race.**

stim·u·lus [stim′yə·ləs] *n.* Anything that stirs to action or greater effort. The plural of *stimulus* is *stimuli* [stim′yə·lī]: **The *stimulus* of the fans' applause helped the team make the winning touchdown. The smell of my favorite food is a *stimulus* that makes my mouth water.**

sto·ry [stôr′ē] *n.* A form of writing in which a writer tells about characters who solve a problem in a setting. A story has a beginning, a middle, and an ending: **The *story* was about three friends who solved the mystery of the disappearing cookies.**

sub·ject [sub′jekt] *n.* Names the person, place, thing, or idea that a sentence is about: ***Juan* often goes to the park. *Team members* sometimes practice there.**

sub·ject pro·noun [sub′jekt prō′noun] *n.* A pronoun that takes the place of one or more nouns in the subject of a sentence: ***I* will go tomorrow. *They* sing well together.**

sub·ject-verb a·gree·ment [sub′jekt vûrb ə·grē′mənt] *n.* Matching the form of a verb with the subject of the sentence. If the subject is singular, the verb must be singular. If the subject is plural, the verb must be plural: **This *book is* about volcanoes. Many *books are* about volcanoes.**

tap·es·try [tap′is·trē] *n.* A heavy ornamental cloth with designs or pictures woven into it, usually hung on a wall or used to cover furniture: **The *tapestry* on the wall had a picture of knights on horses.**

tel·e·phone mes·sage [tel′ə·fōn′ mes′ij] *n.* A written summary of information received in a telephone call for someone who cannot take the call: **She saw a *telephone message* from her cousin inviting her to go to the new movie.**

tense [tens] *n.* The tense of a verb tells the time of its action or state of being: **I *will go* to the school that my parents *attended*. Marcie *knows* the way because she *has been* there before.**

thank-you note [thangk yo͞o nōt] *n.* A form of writing used to thank someone for a gift or for doing something: **Sita sent her aunt a *thank-you note* for the birthday gift.**

tone [tōn] *n.* The feeling or emotion expressed by a writer through word choice. The tone may be humorous, sad, or suspenseful, or it may express other kinds of emotions: **Elena felt the muscles in her shoulders tighten as she stopped in the shadowy hallway. She held her**

breath, listening nervously. The scratching noise startled her.

top·ic sen·tence [top′ik sen′təns] *n.* A sentence that states the main idea of a paragraph: **A bicycle ride is a great way to enjoy a spring day.**

tran·si·tion [tran·zish′ən] *n.* A signal word that shows how the information or ideas expressed in different sentences or different paragraphs connect with one another. Signal words include *then, first, after, also,* and *because*: **On a bicycle ride, you can smell the fragrant spring flowers. *Also,* you can see the many colors of spring.**

val·iant [val′yənt] *adj.* Having or showing courage; brave: **The students made a *valiant* effort to complete the walkathon in the rain.**

verb [vûrb] *n.* A word or words that express action or being: **We *are* happy about the party. Lucia *invited* all of us. My cousin *will go*, too.**

verb phrase [vûrb frāz] *n.* A verb that includes two or more words: **They *are running* the marathon for charity.**

He *has finished* the job. He *should have done* it more carefully.

viv·id verb [viv′id vûrb] *n.* A strong verb that describes action in an interesting way: **Instead of the verb *run*, use a *vivid verb* like *sprint*, *dash*, or *scurry*.**

word choice [wûrd chois] *n.* Choice of words and phrases that have the effect that the writer intends: **Effective *word choice* involves using the specific nouns, vivid verbs, and figurative language that express the tone the writer wants.**

writ·er's view·point [rī′tərz vyoo′point′] *n.* The feelings and opinions expressed by an individual writer: **A reader can identify a *writer's viewpoint* by noticing his or her expression of likes, dislikes, fears, or fascinations.**

zo·ol·o·gist [zō·ol′ə·jist] *n.* A scientist who studies animal life: **A *zoologist* may take care of zoo animals or study animals in the wild.**

a add	e end	o odd	o͞o pool	oi oil	th this		a in *above*
ā ace	ē equal	ō open	u up	ou pout	zh vision	ə =	e in *sicken*
â care	i it	ô order	û burn	ng ring			i in *possible*
ä palm	ī ice	o͝o took	yo͞o fuse	th thin			o in *melon*
							u in *circus*

Vocabulary Power

aerobics One way to keep fit is to attend a weekly **aerobics** class.

anthology "The Raven" is one poem included in this poetry **anthology**.

anthropologist An **anthropologist** learns how people live by spending time with them and by asking questions.

apprentice A carpenter's **apprentice** learns carpentry by observing and helping the carpenter.

aquarium While touring the **aquarium**, we saw several dolphins in large tanks.

architecture My aunt studied **architecture**, and now she designs homes and buildings.

astronomical We carried in the telescope, the charts, and the other **astronomical** equipment.

cardiology People who need surgery for heart problems are treated in the hospital's **cardiology** unit.

constitution In many countries, a written **constitution** establishes rules for the government.

entrepreneur My uncle is an **entrepreneur** who has owned his own business for fifteen years.

environment Parrots are birds that live in a tropical **environment**.

evaluate You can **evaluate** the success of an exercise program by checking for increased strength and stamina.

exert People **exert** energy when working hard or doing exercises.

fascinating Tina could not stop watching the **fascinating** acrobats.

frontier Books about the western **frontier** tell of wide-open spaces and few settlements.

graphic A **graphic** artist may use computer software to draw, paint, or cut and paste.

grotesque The crooked and twisted gourd looked **grotesque**.

handicraft Woodworking is a **handicraft** I would like to learn.

immigrant This is a story about an **immigrant** who came to live in the United States in 1900.

improvise That comedian will **improvise** a skit from ideas he gets while on stage.

inauguration Will you watch the **inauguration** of the President on television?

industry The toy **industry** is always creating new playthings for children.

meteorologist Before we left, we listened to the **meteorologist** tell about the weather.

nutrition The body needs healthful foods for good **nutrition** so it can grow and repair itself.

omnivorous An animal that eats both meat and plants is **omnivorous**.

perspective The mystery story is told from the **perspective** of a detective.

persuasion Successful salespeople use **persuasion** to convince people to make a purchase.

playwright She is a **playwright** whose plays have been performed in theaters across the country.

portrait A **portrait** photographer specializes in taking pictures of people.

powerful He gave a **powerful** speech, and many people in the audience decided to vote for him.

stamina She had enough **stamina** to run the entire marathon.

stimulus The smell of onions cooking is a **stimulus** that can cause a feeling of hunger.

tapestry The hanging **tapestry** of a castle scene took a long time to weave.

transition Marta was careful to include a **transition** in each paragraph to connect it to the next one.

valiant The article is about the firefighters' **valiant** rescue of the family of five.

zoologist The **zoologist** tells the class that she specializes in the study of dolphins.

Index

N

O

P

W

Acknowledgments

For permission to reprint copyrighted material, grateful acknowledgment is made to the following sources:

Chronicle Books: Cover photograph from *Cities in the Sand* by Scott Warren. Copyright © 1992 by Scott S. Warren.

Delacorte Press, a division of Random House, Inc.: From *Ola Shakes It Up* by Joanne Hyppolite, cover illustration by Warren Chang. Text copyright © 1998 by Joanne Hyppolite; illustration copyright © 1998 by Warren Chang.

DK Publishing, Inc.: Cover photographs by Andy Crawford from *The Young Baseball Player* by Ian Smyth. Copyright © 1998 by Dorling Kindersley Limited.

Sheldon Fogelman Agency, Inc., on behalf of Diane Stanley: From *Leonardo da Vinci* by Diane Stanley. Text copyright © 1996 by Diane Stanley. Published by William Morrow and Company, Inc.

Harcourt, Inc.: From *Baseball in the Barrios* by Henry Horenstein. Copyright © 1997 by Henry Horenstein. Cover illustration by Diane deGroat from *The Gray Whales Are Missing* by Robin A. Thrush. Illustration copyright © 1987 by Diane deGroat.

HarperCollins Publishers: Cover illustration from *Live Writing: Breathing Life into Your Words* by Ralph Fletcher. Copyright © 1999 by Ralph Fletcher. From *Julie* by Jean Craighead George, cover illustration by Wendell Minor. Text copyright © 1994 by Jean Craighead George; illustration © 1994 by Wendell Minor. From *Mountains* by Seymour Simon. Copyright © 1994 by Seymour Simon. From *Have a Happy...* by Mildred Pitts Walter, cover illustration by Carole Byard. Text copyright © 1989 by Mildred Pitts Walter; illustration copyright © 1989 by Carole Byard. Cover illustration by Gabriela Dellosso from *The Indian School* by Gloria Whelan. Illustration copyright © 1996 by Gabriela Dellosso. From *Little Town on the Prairie* by Laura Ingalls Wilder, illustrated by Garth Williams. Text copyright 1941 by Laura Ingalls Wilder; text copyright © renewed 1969 by Charles F. Lamkin, Jr.; illustrations copyright 1953 by Garth Williams; illustrations copyright © renewed 1981 by Garth Williams.

Highlights for Children, Inc., Columbus, Ohio: "The Long Ride" by R. E. Richards from *Jack's Best Boots and Other Stories of Long Ago*, compiled by the Editors of Highlights for Children. Text copyright © 1988 by Highlights for Children, Inc.

Hyperion Books for Children, an imprint of Buena Vista Books, Inc.: From *Guests* by Michael Dorris, cover illustration by Ellen Thompson. Text copyright © 1994 by the Estate of Michael Dorris; illustration © 1994 by Ellen Thompson. Cover illustration by Brian Pinkney from *Alvin Ailey* by Andrea Davis Pinkney. Illustration copyright © 1993 by Brian Pinkney. Cover photograph by Jeffrey Jay Foxx from *Angela Weaves A Dream* by Michéle Solá. Photograph copyright © 1997 by Jeffrey Jay Foxx.

Lerner Publications Company, Minneapolis, MN: Cover photograph by John Madama from *Clambake: A Wampanoag Tradition* by Russell M. Peters. Copyright © 1992 by Lerner Publications Company. Cover photograph from *Songs from the Loom: A Navajo Girl Learns to Weave* by Monty Roessel. Copyright © 1995 by Lerner Publications Company.

Little, Brown and Company (Inc.): Cover illustration from *Ben and Me* by Robert Lawson. Copyright 1939 by Robert Lawson.

G. P. Putnam's Sons, a division of Penguin Putnam Inc.: Cover illustration by Tomie dePaola from *Shh! We're Writing the Constitution* by Jean Fritz. Illustration copyright © 1987 by Tomie dePaola.

Scholastic Inc.: Cover illustration by Christa Keiffer from *Treasured Horses Collection: Ride of Courage* by Deborah Felder. Illustration copyright © 1997 by Scholastic Inc. From *Fur, Feathers, and Flippers* by Patricia Lauber. Text copyright © 1994 by Patricia Lauber.

Sierra Club Books for Children: Cover photographs by Sidnee Wheelwright from *Come Back, Salmon* by Molly Cone. Photographs copyright © by Sidnee Wheelwright.

Steck-Vaughn Company: From *The World's Top Ten Deserts* by Neil Morris, illustrated by Vanessa Card. Text copyright © 1997 by Neil Morris; illustrations copyright © 1997 by Vanessa Card; text and illustrations © copyright 1997 by Steck-Vaughn Company. Cover photographs by Zul Mukhida from *Weaving* by Susie O'Reilly. Copyright © 1993 by Wayland (Publishers) Ltd.; U.S. version copyright © 1993 by Thomson Learning.

Franklin Watts, Inc.: From *Exercise and Fitness* (Retitled: "Looking and Feeling Your Best") by Brian R. Ward. Text © 1988 by Franklin Watts.

Photo Credits

Page Placement Key: (t)-top (c)-center (b)-bottom (l)-left (r)-right (fg)-foreground (bg)-background.

Harcourt Photos by David Waitz: Pages 83, 85, 146, 148, 151, 153, 219, 223, 225, 291, 293, 294, 366, 369, 371, 411, 434, 436, 439.

Abbreviations for frequently used stock photo agencies: PR–Photo Researchers, NY; SM -The Stock Market NY; TSI -Stone.

Unit One: 22–23 Terry Donnelly/TSI; 24 Lawrence Migdale/PR; 26 Adam Woolfitt/Corbis; 27 Paul Chesley/TSI; 28 Will & Deni McIntyre/TSI; 31 Art Resource, NY; 34 Art Resource,NY; 35 Christie's Images; 38 Andy Sacks/TSI; 39 Thomas Brase/TSI; 41 Historical Picture Archive/Corbis; 51 The Image Bank; 52 Gregory K. Scott/PR; 53 Steve Vidler/TSI; 55 The Newark Museum/Art Resource, NY; 57 Sucession H. Matisse, Paris/ARS, NY/Art Resource NY; 66 Harcourt; 67 Sean Ellis/TSI; 90–91 Index Stock Photography.

Unit Two: 92–93 Moshe Zur/Envision; 94 The Granger Collection, New York; 95 Jose Fuste Raga/SM; 97 The Granger Collection, New York; 104 Brownie Harris/SM; 105 M.E. Warren, PR; 106 The Granger Collection; 107 ARCHIV/PR; 109 Index Stock Photography; 122 Frank Siteman/TSI; 125 The Granger Collection, New York; 126 Roy Morsch/SM; 129 Nick Gunderson/TSI; 132 Corbis/Bettmann-UPI; 133 Randy Wells/TSI; 135 Ross Ressmeyer/Corbis; 137 The Granger Collection; 139 The Granger Collection, New York; 154 Harcourt; 158–159 The Granger Collection, New York.

Unit Three: 164–165 John Skowronski/Folio; 166 Corel; 167 Tim Davis/SM; 168 Mark A. Johnson/SM; 169 (l) Tom Stewart/SM; 170 Francois Gohier/PR; 172 Sharon Green/SM; 176 Johan Elzenga/TSI; 177 Paul Steel/SM; 178 Roy P. Fontaine/PR; 181 Zielinski Photography/PR; 194 Dr. Jean Lorre/Science Photo Library/PR; 195 Space Exploration CD, Digital Stock; 197 World Perspectives/TSI; 199 NASA; 201 NASA; 207 Myke Gerrish/SM; 208 Stormchasers CD; 210 Tom McHugh/PR; 211 Stormchasers CD; 214–215 Dennis O'Clair/TSIUnit 6: 216 Howard Kingsnorth/TSI; 230–231 Thomas H. Brakefield/SM.

Unit Four: 232–233 David Epperson/TSI; 234 Lance Nelson/SM; 235 Mark Gamba/SM; 236 Erica Lansner/TSI; 237 Chris Rogers/SM; 239 Andy Sacks/TSI; 241 Roy Morsch/SM; 244 Robert E. Daemmrich/TSI; 245 Ralph Cowan/TSI; 247 Chuck Savage/SM; 249 Mark Gamba/SM; 263 John Eastcott/Yva Momatiuk/Stock, Boston; 265 John W. Karapelou, CMI/Phototake; 267 David Barnes/TSI; 272 Don Mason/SM; 273 Index Stock Photography; 277 Patrick Piel/Gamma Liaison; 300–301 Amy C. Etra/PhotoEdit.

Unit Five: 308–309 Hiroyuki Matsumoto/TSI; 310 John Reader/Science Photo Library/PR; 311 S.J. Krasemann/Peter Arnold, Inc.; 312 M.B. Duda/PR; 313 Harvey Lloyd/SM; 316–317 David Stoecklein/SM; 317 Jacques Jangoux/TSI; 320 Peggy and Ronald Barnett/SM; 323 The Granger Collection, New York; 325 David Lawrence/SM; 327 Courtesy, United States Mint; 338 National Cowboy Hall of Tom/McHugh/PR; 339 G. Brad Lewis/TSI; 341 David Stoecklein/SM; 345 Mark Rollo/PR; 348 John Madere/SM; 349 Wayne Eastep/TSI; 350 Larry Ulrich/TSI; 351 Culver Pictures; 352 David Travers/SM; 358–359 Kim Westerskov/TSI; 358 Toshihiko Chinami/The Image Bank/PictureQuest; 360–361 Tom Campbell/Photo Network/Picture Quest; 363 R. Thompson/Archive Photos/PictureQuest; 376–377 Art Wolfe/TSI.

Unit Six: 378–379 Terry Sinclair/Harcourt, Courtesy of Civic Theatres of Central Florida; 381 Elisabeth Murray/ChromaZone Images/Index Stock Imagery; 383 Ansel Adams Publishing Rights Trust/Corbis; 385 Anthony Redpath/SM; 391 Carol Rosegg/NETworks Productions; 392 Van Bucher/PR; 393 Capital Pictures/Gamma; 398 Jack Vartoogian; 412 The Granger Collection, New York; 413 John Lamb/TSI; 415 The Granger Collection, New York; 418 Lynn Goldsmith/Corbis; 419 David Ball/TSI; 421 Ken Karp/Harcourt; 423 Herman Leonard/Stage Image; 444–445 Civic Theatres of Central Florida.

Extra Practice: 457 Historical Picture Archives/Corbis; 458 Anthony Redpath/SM; 459 Adam Woolfitt/Corbis; 460 Dr. Jean Lorre/Science Photo Library/PR; 461 Chuck Savage/SM; 463 M. B. Duda/PR; 464 Patrick Piel/Gamma Liaison; 465 Paul Steel/SM; 467 Carol Rosegg/Networks Productions; 469 Andy Sacks/TSI; 470 Mark Gamba/SM; 471 M. E. Warren, PR; 473 Johan Elzenga/TSI; 475 Mark Gamba/SM; 476 Jose Azel/Aurora/PictureQuest.

Royalty Free Sources:

Photodisc: 62, 89, 101, 111, 117, 124, 156, 175(l), 299, 321, 340, 343, 387.

Corel: 46, 69, 86, 87,88, 114, 115, 116, 154, 155, 157, 166, 204, 175(r), 226, 227, 228, 229, 297, 298, 353, 380, 389, 408, 410, 425, 440, 442.

flowers; stem
peple